THE BEST TRANSPORTATION
SYSTEM IN THE WORLD

THE BEST TRANSPORTATION SYSTEM IN THE WORLD

Railroads, Trucks, Airlines, and American Public Policy in the Twentieth Century

MARK H. ROSE, BRUCE E. SEELY, AND PAUL F. BARRETT

PENN

University of Pennsylvania Press

Philadelphia · Oxford

First published 2006 by The Ohio State University

Copyright © 2006 The Ohio State University. All rights reserved.
No part of this book may be reproduced or transmitted in any form
or by any means, electronic or mechanical, including photocopying,
recording, or by any information storage and retrieval system, without
permission in writing from the Publisher.

Paperback reprint published 2010 by
University of Pennsylvania Press
Philadelphia, Pennsylvania 19104-4112

Printed in the United States of America on acid-free paper

10 9 8 7 6 5 4 3 2 1

Library of Congress Cataloging-in-Publication Data
ISBN 978-0-8122-2116-9

In memory of Paul Barrett,
friend, scholar, coauthor, 1943–2004

CONTENTS

LIST OF ILLUSTRATIONS

PREPARATION OF THIS book by Paul Barrett, Mark Rose, and Bruce Seely rested on congenial and productive relationships developed over the course of more than a quarter century. In 1979, Bruce was starting his dissertation at the University of Delaware, and Mark was working as a research associate at the Franklin Institute in Philadelphia. Because of their interest in American highway politics, one morning they met at the Temple University Library. In 1981, Paul and Mark met in Milwaukee at the Annual Meeting of the Society for the History of Technology. Paul had recently completed his dissertation focused on automobile and transit politics in Chicago between 1890 and 1930; and Mark had become general editor of a monographic series published by Temple University Press titled "Technology and Urban Growth." Mark persuaded Paul to submit his manuscript to the series at Temple, where it was subsequently published in 1983. Bruce also published his book, *Building the American Highway System* (1987), in the "Technology and Urban Growth Series."

Since that time, the three of us worked together on a number of scholarly projects. As part of Paul's interest in aviation and airports, he and Mark coauthored an essay for the *Journal of Urban History* focused on the politics of transportation statistics. From 1986 until 1990, Bruce and Mark were colleagues at Michigan Technological University (located on Michigan's Upper Peninsula, where snow fell almost daily from November to May). In our frequent conversations about social, political, and urban history and about the history of transportation and technology, we often focused on the gloomy economic times of the 1970s and 1980s. We also talked about the politics of industrial and population decline in the Upper Middle West; and in less doleful moments, we discussed the "politics" of collegiate hockey.

In the late 1980s, Bruce and Mark also conducted research for the Public Works Historical Society on the politics of getting the Interstate Highway System constructed, a portion of which was published in the *Journal of Policy History*. In the course of research for that article, no event or document impressed us more than an unforgettable conversation with several demoralized Ohio state highway engineers who had suffered years of organization downsizing, a loss of professional autonomy, diminished budgets, and public castigations at the hands of politicians, environmentalists, and local citizens' groups. Later, we recognized that those senior highway builders were experiencing a process we described as the devolution of authority from engineering experts to local politicians and ordinary citizens.[1] During that same period and extending almost to the present day, Bruce and Paul opened their own conversation about engineering education. All in all, Paul, Bruce, and Mark had spent years writing and talking about politics, whether that politics was connected to roads, cities, social networks, or engineers and technologists.

By the mid-1990s, as the three of us commenced research on this book, we took for granted several ideas about government and transportation. We began by studying technological questions, but soon found that stories of invention and innovation were in fact subordinate to another narrative concerning how each new technology required changes in public policy in order to be widely adopted. The situation is somewhat analogous to historian David A. Kirsch's explanation of the fate of the short-lived electric automobile of the early twentieth century, for in both situations a range of factors shaped the development of new technologies.[2] In the cases of the truck, rail, and airline industries that we have studied, government rather than technology framed the range of choices available to transportation executives and their counterparts in labor unions. In other words, the introduction and operation after 1920 of technical means of delivering transportation services—railroads, trucks, and airlines alike—rested on distinctly political decisions made in political arenas. In virtually every discussion of transportation innovation, regulation, and deregulation, we find that politics was in the driver's seat.

That government was and remained important in the American economy and in the organization and operation of American transportation during the past century is a concept that historians do not doubt. Antitrust and subsidies, for example, comprise two often-contentious areas in which government has played a central and well-recognized role in the transportation field. During both the nineteenth and twentieth centuries, government subsidies such as land grants, highway construction funds, and appropriations in support of airway improvements were important in development of railroads, auto and truck transport, and then airlines. Even in the mid-1990s, more than a decade after the disappearance of extensive federal regulation of railroad, airline, and truck rates and service, government officials at every level still subsidized construction and maintenance of roadways and airways, sometimes in lavish fashion. Similarly, antitrust policy always loomed large in the development and organization of American transportation. Before and after the period of federal regulation of price and service, which ended for airlines in 1978 and for trucking and railroads in 1980, government officials continued to determine whether executives of an airline, truck, or railroad corporation could purchase a competitor, thereby perhaps achieving a commanding position in local or regional markets. Again, the centrality of government subsidies and antitrust have been long studied among historians. Whether in the form of subsidies or antitrust policies, moreover, all or most historians recognize the value of studying in some detail the precise consequences of implementing those policies for the workings of corporations, industries, and institutions over extended periods of time.

Curiously, the important role played by direct government action in structuring industries and markets has sometimes been neglected. One reason perhaps for this oversight in the realm of transportation is the paradox of American individualism in a nation built around large-scale organizations. As one example, truck operators perceived themselves as self-made men (and during most of the twentieth century, trucking was virtually an all-male domain). Right through the 1970s, writers for trucking organization publications reminded readers of their storied beginnings as lonely drivers battling poor roads with rickety equipment. Often, these writers for trucking publications reported on equally tough battles fought and won against the dreaded, fly-by-night "gypsy" truckers of the 1920s and 1930s. Still other reports in truckers' publications narrated the legal and legislative fights of the past and others to come against the lurking executives of railroad corporations, who were always described as possessing formidable resources. Whether in their own publications or in testimony before committees of the U.S. Congress, between the 1930s and 1980, trucking executives and publicists never grew tired of representing themselves as isolated operators fighting only for reasonable treatment at the hands of gypsy truckers, insular government officials, and haughty railroad executives. This attitude persisted even after executives of a large segment of the trucking industry had organized state and national associations during the 1930s to fight legal and legislative battles against "gypsy" truckers and railroad executives still regularly described as dangerous or "lurking."

Railroad and aviation executives recounted similar stories of heroic leaders who had developed their firms and industries against great odds. In these retellings, rail and airline officials represented themselves as persons committed to preservation of individual choice and initiative no matter how large the organizations they came to direct. Ironies abounded. For example, like their counterparts in trucking, during the 1930s, railroad and airline executives organized to fight in courts and Congress against truckers and one another with a view toward protecting their share of freight and passenger traffic. Those would-be individualists working at railroad and airline firms (again, virtually an all-male group and virtually all preferring to think of themselves as self-made) never grew fatigued of repeating historical narratives that highlighted the problems of unfair competition. Most importantly, by the mid-1930s, leaders of airline firms had joined their counterparts in the trucking field to conclude that government regulation represented the best and only answer to competitive pressure and especially to the real threat that railroad leaders would enter or "invade" trucking and airline operations with their own trucks and aircraft. In reality, government at every level had subsidized the railroad, trucking, and airline businesses; and in fact, those businesses and most of the actions of the men who operated them were and remained creatures of federal law and regulatory pronouncement. Even so, right up to the late 1970s and the final days of the regulatory regime, transportation leaders routinely affirmed their individualism and regularly recounted to one another their monumental struggles to survive and grow.

This book is not focused exclusively or even directly on the paradox of individualism in a political economy built around regional and national institutions. Nor is our specific focus on government subsidies of roadways or airways; and antitrust enters our work only insofar as transportation executives and federal officials occasionally brought it to bear as part of an effort to shape the competitive environment. Instead, these three sets of ideas about subsidies, antitrust, and the paradox of individualism in a collective age weave their way through portions of this book at a background level. In briefest form, however, our book focuses directly on the centrality of government in organizing the nation's transportation industries, including the organization of transportation markets. (Often, we describe government with terms such as the "state," or "state actors," but always we mean federal officials working as judges, as senators and representatives, as regulators at the Interstate Commerce Commission and the Civil Aeronautics Board, or as president of the United States.)

We conceive each portion of this book around the idea that government officials organized rail, truck, and airline firms into three separate and distinct industries and three separate and distinct markets. At the outset of our research, we had no reason to doubt the idea that the historical and contemporary presence of railroad, trucking, and airline industries rested on the natural distinctions of technological systems. Railroads such as the Pennsylvania and New York Central used great coal and diesel locomotives to pull lengthy, steel-wheeled trains on steel rails owned by those companies. Gasoline and diesel-fueled tractors owned by the largest and smallest truckers still pulled only one or two trailers. Those trailers and tractors, it was obvious, used rubber tires on publicly constructed roads made of concrete and asphalt. Although air carriers such as United Airlines made use of public space, they, too, were privately owned. Even after World War II, when airline travel on United and the other "trunk" carriers acquired a routine quality, surely, we assumed, those high-tech airplanes piloted by once-daring aviators had made the airline business different than that of slower-moving trucks and that of old-fashioned, smoky, money-losing railroads. Prior to starting this project, then, we accepted the language of transportation officials, academic experts, and government officials who defined railroad, truck, and airline firms as members of distinct and impermeable transportation modes. Indeed, as early as the 1910s, members of Congress and officials at the Interstate Commerce Commission (ICC) had already determined that railroad firms could not simultaneously own and operate steamships. We soon came to understand that whether in 1920 or in the mid-1990s, railroads, airlines, and trucking firms were and remained creatures of public policy. Put another way, distinct transportation industries emerged from a political setting rather than from some "fact" embedded in rail, air, or truck technology.

This conception of each form of transportation as an independent and separate mode of service also affected the way federal officials set up regulatory agencies. Once having identified rail, truck, and air as distinct and impermeable forms of transportation, members of Congress chose to regulate each of them through separate agencies whose officials bore no responsibility to foster connections between, say, truck and train. Again, there was nothing natural about this structure of regulation. Starting in the 1920s, we learned, many in and out of government began to envision an alternative transportation regime, one that would permit railroads to own truck and airline firms, leading to formation of transportation companies. ICC commissioner Joseph B. Eastman and other advocates of creating transportation firms (rather than railroad, airline, and trucking companies) urged that operators of those intermodal transportation firms would fall under the purview of a single federal regulatory agency, not several of them. In short, during the 1920s and 1930s, when fundamental definitions of transportation remained fluid, we learned the importance of politics and public policy rather than technology in setting air and ground transportation on a course of multiple regulators, multiple industries, and multiple markets.

With government officials as the principal authors of the transportation industries, we discovered by contrast that academic experts played only marginal roles in creating these industries and later in dismantling the regulatory regime. In earlier publications, each of the three of us had devoted substantial attention to the role of experts in the development of policy, and we had expected to find engineers and later academic economists deeply involved and at least partially determinative in framing transportation policies.[3] In the often disjointed fields of transportation, however, experts rarely dominated policy debates. Instead, despite their high visibility and their ability to assert a professional disinterest in any particular outcome, economists such as William Z. Ripley, Emory R. Johnson, and Harold G. Moulton in the 1920s and Paul W. MacAvoy and Alfred E. Kahn in the 1970s often played only limited roles in the outcome of legislative debates about transportation policy.

The main reason that appeals to apolitical experts gained even limited authority in setting transportation policy was the deep and inherently political nature of that process. That insight soon led us to reconsider the role of presidents in the policy process. Only at a few key moments, we originally thought, had presidents exercised their growing clout to articulate transportation policy for air, road, and rail. For example, Woodrow Wilson played no role in preparation of the Transportation Act of 1920, which framed railroad policy for decades to come. After 1922, Presidents Warren G. Harding and Calvin Coolidge met only reluctantly with railroad officials to discuss whether freight rates on agricultural commodities might be reduced in order to help economically struggling farmers. Early in the Great Depression, President Herbert Hoover proposed creation of the Reconstruction Finance Corporation in large part to bolster the railroads. In 1933, President Franklin D. Roosevelt launched major studies of transportation designed to shape policies to assist truckers, railroaders, and aviators coping with the effects of hard-depression days. Then in 1935, Roosevelt signed the Motor Carrier Act, permitting truckers to organize with an eye toward fixing rates and routes. And in 1938, President Roosevelt approved the Civil Aeronautics Act, directing members of the Civil Aeronautics Administration (later, the Civil Aeronautics Board) to regulate and promote the aviation industry in concert with executives of major airlines such as Delta and American. We also knew that decades later, in 1962, President John F. Kennedy sought to bring about a partial deregulation of transportation firms. We realized as well that between 1978 and 1980, President Jimmy Carter presided over deregulation of the airline, railroad, and trucking industries. Other than these and a few other initiatives in the transportation field, we assumed that between 1920 and the mid-1990s, presidential interest in transportation legislation had been intermittent in nature.

Rather than confirming these important but sporadic presidential initiatives in transportation, our research led us to identify the presence of a long-term and persistent presidential hand in efforts to structure transportation industries and transportation markets. In brief, presidents of the United States and their senior advisers emerged over time as the primary architects of transportation policy. We learned, for example, that President Roosevelt had considered legislation to permit rail and truck firms to merge into transportation companies. We also discovered that each president of the United States starting with Dwight D. Eisenhower and ending with William J. "Bill" Clinton attempted to diminish or eliminate federal transportation regulations. Indeed, proclaiming his interest in protecting the consumer, as early as 1955, President Eisenhower and his Secretary of Commerce Sinclair Weeks made a short-lived effort to change ICC rules and permit rail and truck executives to set rates within a predetermined "zone of reasonableness." (During the 1950s, at the height of the cold war, only the scheduled airlines were to remain the protected wards of government.)

Presidents also took a great interest in the agencies that directly regulated transportation rates and service. We had assumed, inaccurately it turned out, that each president starting with Woodrow Wilson and concluding with Bill Clinton had simply appointed members of the Interstate Commerce Commission (ICC) and the Civil Aeronautics Board (CAB). In turn, we believed, those appointees at the ICC and CAB along with transportation experts and attorneys for shippers and receivers had determined shipping rates and shipping rules outside the purview of presidents. Nothing in our prior research had induced us to consider the prospect that presidents of the United States would take an active interest in such presumably boring details as the exact rates that rail, air, and truck executives charged for shipping automobiles, corn, rocking chairs, steel, passengers, roasted peanuts, coal, and frozen or fresh chicken.

Starting with Calvin Coolidge and extending into Bill Clinton's first term, however, American presidents judged ICC and CAB rulings on transportation rates and routes not only in terms of the immediate significance of a proposed freight rate hike for farmers or urban consumers, but as part of their overall stewardship of the American political economy. Again, President Roosevelt considered the impact of regulation on the railroads and for a time entertained the possibility of a different approach to transportation regulation, even the possibility of an entirely new regulatory regime focused on transportation companies rather than on railroad, truck, and airline firms. Eisenhower and Weeks talked about deregulation as a device for protecting consumers from rising prices. The more immediate problem, as Eisenhower and Weeks judged it, was to rescue economically declining railroads by forcing ICC officials to permit "zone of reasonableness" pricing. During the 1960s, moreover, President Lyndon B. Johnson fostered creation of the U.S. Department of Transportation whose officials, he expected, would soon turn their attention to securing deregulation of freight rates. In the prosperous 1960s, deregulation comprised another element of presidential "fine-tuning" of the American economy. During the 1970s and the period of economic "stagflation," however, Presidents Richard M. Nixon, Gerald R. Ford, and Jimmy Carter sought deregulation both to rescue the many, now bankrupt railroads and to foster an overall reduction in fast-rising inflationary pressures. Although the goals of presidential deregulation varied from one decade to the next, the effort to bring about deregulation started in the 1950s as a presidential initiative and ended in 1980 as a presidential initiative. Nonetheless, deregulation lacked a constituency until Presidents Ford and Carter's staffs organized one. Once implemented at the ICC and CAB by Carter's appointees such as Alfred Kahn and later approved by members of Congress, deregulation represented not a return to some primordial market, but an effort, again principally directed by American presidents, to restructure transportation industries and to alter and presumably reduce prices charged in transportation markets. In the realm of transportation, American presidents during the twentieth century served as the nation's Chief Economic Officers. Under presidential direction, the idea that markets rather than regulators would guide the formation of transportation industries and the determination of transportation prices emerged as the essence of federal policy.

Nor did we appreciate at the beginning of work on this book what had taken place in the transportation industries following deregulation in 1978 and 1980. Originally, we intended to begin our story with the Transportation Act of 1920 (the Esch-Cummins Act) and conclude it with the package of legislation that accompanied deregulation of air, truck, and rail in 1978 and 1980. We found it essential, however, to extend our analysis to consider not only the creation of policy, but also its implementation. At first we had in hand only a few pages by historians regarding the postderegulation era, leading us simply and even naively to assume that after 1980, market factors began to determine the price and service levels of transportation firms. Indeed, before starting research, the concept of deregulation followed by a restoration of markets, as the favored expression went, seemed to describe the inevitable and perhaps the natural order of persons and organizations in the transportation industries once freed of government. Actually, starting in 1978 with airlines and in 1980 with railroads and trucking, transportation firms entered a period in which authority for rates, routes, and service devolved from the hands of government regulators at the CAB and ICC to the hands of transportation executives. In turn, leaders in the transportation industries and especially the trucking industry quit organizations such as the Regular Common Carrier Conference and reshaped other organizations such as their rate bureaus. In the period between 1980 and the mid-1990s, executives at railroads, trucking firms, and airlines modified ways of conducting business constructed over the course of the previous half century and longer. We characterize these processes of change as those of devolution and deinstitutionalization. These processes involved much more than a return to "free" markets.

After 1980 as before, government remained central to the organization of transportation industries and firms. For instance, government officials permitted airline executives such as Robert L. Crandall of American Airlines to construct "fortress hubs" at key airports; and government leaders permitted railroad executives such as John W. Snow at CSX, originally a railroad company, to create intermodal companies owning barges and ocean-going container ships. During the 1990s, federal officials even abolished the Interstate Commerce Commission as well as remaining state laws regulating truckers' rates and service. In the 1990s, federal abolition of state law was called preemption. After the 1980s, then, government still framed the transportation industries, and government was and also remained the principal author of transportation markets. Stated once again, in the realm of framing these three main transportation industries, their firms, and their markets, leaders of the American state always sat squarely in the driver's seat.

Consequently, we structure this study around long-term periods of transportation governance and long-term periods of government-constructed markets during the twentieth century. For all the litigating and lobbying that surrounded the business of transporting freight and passengers over that lengthy period of time, we identify three main periods in the political economy of American transportation. In the first period, between 1920 and 1940, leaders in the federal government, who had before considered the railroads as the nation's primary form of transportation, struggled to deal with new means of moving people and goods. In the 1920s, however, members of Congress as well as leaders at the ICC advocated consolidation of the railroads as the answer to the nation's transportation problems. Only during the Great Depression did members of a new group of federal officials begin to shape specialized policies for trucks and airlines, including for a moment the option of allowing coordination of services among different forms of transportation. Yet after nearly two decades of hearings, studies, and speeches, and after a decade of depression, neither policy proved sufficiently attractive to reshape the now ingrained patterns of competition between rail, air, and truck. Instead, by 1940, leaders of the American state and especially key members of Congress such as Senator Patrick A. McCarran had joined with truckers and airline executives to construct three transportation industries and three nearly impermeable transportation markets, one for railroads, yet a second for truckers, and then a third for airlines.

We describe the years between 1946 and 1980 as the period of the regulatory regime. Now, three sets of regulators oversaw prices and service levels in three now distinct industries, including the airline industry. After World War II, moreover, airlines emerged as vital components of the cold war. Equally, officials at the CAB took seriously their responsibility to nurture and protect the main trunk carriers. Even so, CAB officials starting with James M. Landis in 1946–1947 helped launch a process of converting air travel from service for a privileged few to a mass service. In broad principle and in precise detail, officials at the CAB framed airline markets.

The regulatory regime worked differently in the realms of trucking and railroading. Much of the lobbying and litigating of this period revolved around efforts by rail or truck executives to create new operating authority for themselves, always at the expense of a competitor who already possessed that authority. At the same time, regulators at the ICC issued precise and exacting rules regarding rates and service, in many cases opening new opportunities to litigate and lobby before those regulators, before Congress, and even with presidents. Not even presidents of the United States starting with Eisenhower and extending through Nixon were able to dislodge this regime; and given the perceived savvy and clout of truckers, presidents were often loath to make the attempt.

We characterize the period after 1980 as one of devolution and deinstitutionalization. With the devolution of price and service authority to transportation executives, prices fluctuated and bankruptcies and layoffs followed, especially among truckers. At the same time, railroad executives such as John W. Snow at CSX purchased barge and steamship lines, at last creating intermodal firms. As well, many of Snow's contemporaries in trucking quit trade associations and rate bureaus that during the earlier period of the regulatory regime had protected trucking firms in particular against railroad ownership. In the course of leaving their trade associations and rate bureaus, members of this generation of truckers diminished institutions and dissolved relationships constructed over the course of the last century. During the period between 1980 and 1995 or so, however, we do not identify a "restoration" of markets. Instead, deregulation, we find, represented only a new strategy by which leaders of the American state organized transportation industries and markets.

Finally, as we wrote this book, we came to see yet another way in which ideas about historical events were put to use in shaping those transportation industries and markets. Between 1880 and 1920, reports historian K. Austin Kerr, the vehemence of public resentment at the abuses of power exercised by railroad executives before 1900 rested on the image of rail carriers as predatory monopolists whose power threatened both economic and political liberty.[4] Survival of this outlook into the decades after World War II, long after railroads had ceased to dominate transportation, is intriguing and important. Even in the 1970s, inflammatory rhetoric gave railroad opponents, especially truckers and politicians speaking for "isolated industries," a powerful voice in transportation policy debates. In all, references to history comprised another part of the institutional fabric of the regulatory regime.

Ultimately, in writing this book we had in mind a different kind of historical account of the development of transportation policy in the United States. We did not envision a formal history of transportation in the United States, nor did we envision a history that emphasized individual transportation systems and related policy developments. Instead, we set out to identify and examine several overarching factors that formed common elements in the development of public policy governing transportation. Ultimately, we identify six themes in the development of American transportation industries and their markets. The first and most obvious theme was the fact that leaders of the nation's legislative and executive institutions never succeeded in developing a single or overarching transportation policy. In place of an often-discussed vision of American transport built around transportation companies, members of Congress and President Roosevelt produced a fractured system that included a rail network as well as systems of roads, cars, and trucks, barges and waterways, and airways and airlines that were and remained unconnected to one another. A second basic theme of this study follows closely from the first. The inability of the numerous actors in the public policy process to adopt overarching formulations for transportation never diminished the preeminence of federal officials and public policy in structuring those transportation systems. Indeed, even after deregulation of airlines in 1978 and deregulation of rail and trucking in 1980, we determine that federal officials continued to frame transportation industries and markets. Yet another theme, our third, is that of the centrality of politics in the determination of transportation policy, for in virtually every discussion of transportation innovation, regulation, and deregulation, we find that politics was preeminent. In the more arcane language of political science, we find that the entire transportation field, whether at the level of great industries or down at the level of calculating delivery charges, rested on political constructions. As a fourth and more surprising theme, we also discovered that the history of dislike for the railroads—fairly or not—comprised an important element around which politicians and especially truck operators constructed American transportation policies. Still a fifth theme running through this book is that of experts and their apparent lack of influence in shaping fundamental transportation outcomes. Our sixth and final theme is that of the ascendance of presidents of the United States in the prosaic business of shaping transportation industries and markets. By the late 1970s, experts such as Paul MacAvoy and Alfred Kahn and members of Congress alike took most of their cues about transportation policy from Presidents Ford and Carter. All in all, we seek to explain long-term, durable changes in the locus of authority and in the political construction of rail, truck, and airline industries and their markets

Participants in American transportation never viewed their political and business dealings in the semiorderly fashion suggested here. Instead, railroaders, truckers, and airline executives relied on exhaustive litigation and tireless lobbying to preserve or extend the legal scope of their industry and the right to sole possession of a particular market. Truckers and railroaders scrapped endlessly about who "owned" the over-the-road market. For all the uncertainty and expense of this lobbying and litigating, still regulators and truckers and nearly everyone else between about 1946 and 1980 routinely affirmed the contention (demonstrated, it was said, by history) that through regulation the United States had produced "the best transportation system in the world."

In developing our main themes and in periodizing them, we rely in part on the work of distinguished colleagues. Professional historians will recognize the degree to which books and articles by Christopher Armstrong, Mansel G. Blackford, John C. Burnham, Alfred D. Chandler Jr., William R. Childs, Louis Galambos, Ellis W. Hawley, Samuel P. Hays, Joan Hoff, Thomas P. Hughes, K. Austin Kerr, Pamela W. Laird, Thomas K. McCraw, Albro Martin, Martin V. Melosi, H. Viv Nelles, Philip Scranton, Joel A. Tarr, and Richard H. K. Vietor informed our preliminary approach to the study of transportation history and to the history of the American state and surrounding society as a whole. Although our research encouraged us to challenge a number of findings and assumptions developed by these distinguished historians, the vast body of scholarship they produced and the cogency of their ideas nonetheless informs this book in ways no longer identifiable. Our research led us nonetheless to place state actors and political institutions at the center of our narrative. Again, historians will recognize the historical institutionalism of Brian Balogh, Richard F. Bensel, Colleen A. Dunlavy, Richard R. John, William J. Novak, Gail Radford, Theda Skocpol, Stephen Skowronek, and Olivier Zunz.

Every academic person realizes the degree to which scholarly publication rests on the support of deans, chairs, colleagues, and funding agencies. At Florida Atlantic University, we are pleased to recognize a sabbatical as well as travel and duplication funds provided by former dean Manley Boss and by history department chair Stephen D. Engle. No one could have a better chair than Stephen. A grant provided by the Woodrow Wilson International Center for Scholars permitted Mark to conduct research at the George H. W. Bush Presidential Library. Support at Michigan Tech came from the Social Sciences Department and from a sabbatical leave. Bruce is also grateful to have enjoyed a fellowship at the Dibner Institute for the History of Science and Technology at MIT, which permitted him to spend weeks in Baker Library of the Harvard Business School and in the various libraries at MIT immersed in transportation journals and books. Many of the items in those magnificent collections had not been checked out since Alfred D. Chandler Jr. signed them out in the 1950s!

Professional historians also recognize the degree to which each book and article rests on the careful and underremunerated work of librarians and archivists. At the Florida Atlantic University Libraries, we benefited from the wonderful services of Bruce Barron, Ken Frankel, Magdalynne Ghannoum, Holly Hargette, Rita Hollingsworth, Stacey Mihm, Darlene Ann Parrish, Dawn Smith, and Teresa VanDyke. Their helpful and talented counterparts at Michigan Technological University include Cathy Greer, Barbara Kosky, and Stephanie Reed. During Bruce's sojourn at the National Science Foundation, reference librarians offered equally invaluable aide as they cheerfully located obscure items. At the presidential libraries, we enjoyed the useful advice of hardworking archivists including Debbie Griggs Carter, Barbara Constable, Gary Foulk, David Haight, Karen B. Holzhausen, David Horrocks, Mary Knill, Nancy Mirshah, Herbert Pankratz, E. Philip Scott, Keith J. Shuler, Jennifer A. Sternaman, Dwight Strandberg, and members of the team at the Franklin D. Roosevelt Library. At the University of Washington Archives, Nicolette A. Bromberg, Gary Lundell, Shannon Lynch, and Carla T. Rickerson helped us identify valuable items in their first-rate photo and print collections. At the Harvard Law School Library Special Collections, Lesley Schoenfeld was kind enough to locate terrific photos for our review. Similar assistance came from the staff of the Harvard University Archives, from the Special Collections staff at Baker Library in the Harvard Business School, and from Daria D'Arenzio, Archivist of the College, Robert Frost Library, Amherst College.

During the course of more than a decade in writing this book, we enjoyed conversations with scholars whose comments and concerns pointed us in important directions. At the outset, Kenneth J. Lipartito suggested that we write a book on the history of American transportation. Thereafter, our research and writing benefited in countless ways following conversations and e-mail correspondence with Michael A. Bernstein, W. Roger Biles, Christopher J. Castaneda, William R. Childs, Amy Louise Nelson Dyble, Michael R. Fein, Mark V. Frezzo, Joseph Heathcott, George W. Hilton, Clifton Hood, Richard R. John, Richard R. John Sr., Pamela W. Laird, Raymond A. Mohl, David A. Moss, Gail Radford, Richard Saunders, Joel A. Tarr, Helmut Trischler, Rudi Volti, James A. Wooten, and with many participants at the biennial meetings of the Policy History Conference.

Others were kind enough to provide us with valuable comments on early versions of this book presented in papers at professional meetings. We appreciate having the thoughtful and useful comments of Deborah G. Douglas, Colleen A. Dunlavy, and David M. Welborn. At a later stage in the book's development, we appreciated the valuable ideas provided by Janet R. Daly-Bednarek, Michael A. Bernstein, Bill Childs, Eric Prier, and Judith Stein. Each corrected errors of fact and commented in detail on interpretive themes. When Paul Barrett became ill, Mary Carroll, a friend of Paul's, very kindly and carefully rewrote the airline chapter several times, and Mark took responsibility for bringing most (but not all) of Paul's footnotes into standard form. Still others provided equally thoughtful and careful readings of the entire manuscript. We are in the debt of our editors, Mansel G. Blackford and K. Austin Kerr, for several timely and perceptive markups, wise advice, and remarkable patience. As an anonymous reader for The Ohio State University Press, William H. Becker prepared a useful set of comments that guided portions of our revisions. Our great thanks also to Albert J. Churella, Richard R. John, and Maggie Walsh for thorough and penetrating comments on the next-to-the-last draft. Professor Churella also responded to many inquiries regarding the important details of railroad operations. In the course of dealing with three industries across nearly a century of time, we had committed mistakes of fact and failed to conceptualize fully and precisely. Altogether, the manuscript is immeasurably stronger for the counsel of the many persons with whom we spoke and the efforts of these and other scholars who took valuable time to reply to our many questions and to mark up draft after draft. We alone are responsible for remaining errors (few, we fervently hope) and for interpretive stances found wanting.

Almost by virtue of preparing a book over such a lengthy period of time, each of the three of us accepted new responsibilities. Originally, we divided research and writing for this book into three parts based on periods of time. Bruce concentrated on developments up to 1940; Paul undertook work on the period after World War II up to about 1960; and Mark, we assumed, could focus on the period of the 1960s and 1970s. Not long after we began this project, however, Paul accepted an appointment as chair of his department; and Bruce accepted an appointment first as a program officer at the National Science Foundation and then as chair of his department. In the course of reshuffling our research and writing assignments, Bruce prepared the first two chapters, ending, as planned, in 1940. Paul produced the next chapter on the postwar airline industry. Mark pushed his research back into the mid-1950s and extended it up to the mid-1990s. Mark wrote an early draft of the preface and all of chapters 4 through 9. Following Mary Carroll, Mark also provided several rewritings of Paul's airline chapter. Given Paul's and Bruce's greater administrative responsibilities, Mark served de facto as the book's senior author. Yet this book remains a distinctly collaborative undertaking, thanks in some measure to the emergence of electronic communications and thanks in greater measure to a desire among the three of us starting a quarter century ago to share ideas about transportation and public policy.

Because research and writing this book stretched over such a lengthy period of time, we also entered new stages in the life cycle. On October 15, 2004, our friend, colleague, and coauthor Paul Barrett died following a lengthy battle with metastasized prostate cancer. Paul was sixty years of age and a longtime member of the Department of Humanities at Illinois Institute of Technology (IIT) in Chicago. With a personal style that was usually diffident and always playful, Paul was an original thinker, a committed scholar, and a delightful force for the scholarly life. Paul had hoped to live long enough to vote for John Kerry and John Edwards; and he had also hoped to live long enough to witness publication of this book. Paul's quick wit and intellectual power will be missed by students and colleagues at IIT; and we will always miss Paul's warmth, intelligence, and our many collaborations. We are especially sorry that Paul did not live to see the publication of this book, to which he contributed so much in its final form.

Yet a final debt is owed to members of our families. Bruce's wife, Nancy, son Michael, and daughter Karen endured vacation stops at archives and libraries as well as the protracted absence of a sabbatical. Mark's wife, Marsha Lynn, endured as well absences to distant archives. During the preparation of this book, Marsha Lynn and Mark welcomed Liana's husband, Josh, Amy's husband, Wally, and grandchildren Andrew and Sierra into their extended family. Hopefully, members of this next generation will share the authors' enthusiasm for the study of history. Together, Bruce and Mark are grateful for the love and support of family members on still another project about roads and transportation.

Mark H. Rose,   Bruce E. Seely,
Coral Springs, Florida   Houghton, Michigan

SEEKING A NEW REGULATORY REGIME IN TRANSPORTATION: RAILROAD CONSOLIDATION IN THE 1920S

THERE HAS ALWAYS BEEN A RAILROAD PROBLEM.
—HAROLD G. MOULTON, 1933[1]

UNTIL 1920, railroads were the unrivaled backbone of the American transportation system. As historian Albro Martin explained, "In its day, which lasted almost a century, the train was as totally in command of national mobility as the car has been since."[2] That transition to the automobile came quickly between 1920 and 1940, and railroad leaders and workers soon found themselves part of a mixed transportation system that included cars and trucks, as well as airlines and pipelines. The technological symbols of this more complex transportation landscape, such as Model Ts, parkways and multilane express highways, Greyhound buses, tow boats and dams on the Mississippi River system, and Ford Trimotors or DC-3s, attracted both public and scholarly attention. Yet the adoption of new transportation technologies was far more a political than a technical accomplishment, because the widespread use of trucks, buses, and airplanes depended on politics and public policy choices.

State actors, particularly at the federal level, shaped the basic parameters within which these transportation systems operated. This connection between federal policy and rapid transportation change exemplifies why historians and scholars interested in political economy recently have called for bringing the state back into American historical accounts of the various transformations that marked the turn of the twentieth century.[3] Federal authorities, most notably commissioners of the Interstate Commerce Commission (ICC), assumed responsibility for establishing both an overarching framework and many of the day-to-day decisions governing the parameters within which railroad executives and shippers operated. In addition, members of both houses of Congress and, on occasion, the justices of the Supreme Court and even presidents of the United States also had voices in working out the details of the regulatory regime for transportation with shippers and railroad executives. In other words, the nature and shape of transportation in this country was constituted by leaders of the state as much as by corporate managers, private investors, or technical possibilities.

At the same time, American political leaders never developed an overarching transportation policy, despite occasional claims to the contrary. Instead, the best that the political system could accomplish during the 1920s and 1930s were policy initiatives governing individual forms of transport, worked out in isolation from other transport technologies.[4] Ironically, this situation reflected the inherently political (as opposed to economic or technocratic) nature of American decision making regarding transport.[5] Thus the 1920s witnessed a contest among transportation providers in which railroad executives, truckers, waterway users, shippers, aviation executives, and public officials worked to adjust both policy and the rail-based transportation system it was intended to regulate to a world of multiple technical possibilities. After 1920, activities as diverse as determining the valuation of railroad investment, setting freight rates, appointing ICC commissioners, and planning to consolidate the nation's rail lines into regional systems demonstrated the preeminence of politics in setting railroad policy. The net result of these many activities was a significant federal structuring of transportation industries. These efforts to shape transportation policy are comprehensible only in light of several decades of history related to railroad-government relations.

BACKGROUND: THE IMPACT OF HISTORY

Even as Americans after 1920 began to explore the use of automobiles, trucks, and airplanes for transportation, anger and frustration at railroad executives still informed the making and implementation of federal railroad policy. After 1870, ordinary Americans and political leaders, responding to the history and politics of the development of large railroad corporations, had grown to resent the enormous economic and political influence wielded by railroad executives. One result was a popular view of rail carriers as dangerous monopolies threatening American democracy. Numerous scholarly studies suggest the danger of accepting this formulation at face value, for the economic grievances of shippers and of commercial and business interests may have been more powerful factors in promoting antirailroad attitudes.[6] But we should not dismiss the popular outlook on monopoly as a factor in congressional actions that made railroad corporations the first regulated industry in the country. Such rhetoric was much in evidence in 1887 when Congress created the Interstate Commerce Commission (ICC) with five commissioners appointed by the president, and directed the commissioners to review railroad rates and protect shippers.[7]

The first commissioners struggled for more than a decade against both the courts and rail executives to carry out their charge to monitor railroads. Then in 1906 and 1910, Congress extended the ICC's authority over rates and operations in the Hepburn Act and Mann-Elkins Act. Again in 1912, authors of the Panama Canal Act prohibited railroads from owning any shipping lines that might compete with railroads and outlawed any railroad-owned vessel from using the Panama Canal.[8] This legislation rested on the continued public perception of rail carriers as monopolists, which steamship lines deftly used to forestall potential competitors. More importantly, by separating different transportation technologies into industries walled off from each other, this legislation was a crucial step in the federal constitution of transportation markets. Similar attitudes could be discerned in the body of state legislation that also controlled and defined the activities of the nation's rail carriers.[9] Judged a political and economic danger, the net result was that railroads were both regulated and isolated from other types of transportation.

During the 1910s, however, the nation's "Railroad Problem" began to change. Although strong and profitable railroads such as the Pennsylvania, New York Central, Union Pacific, and the Burlington dominated the industry, other rail carriers were in financial straits. In 1910–11 and again in 1913–14, attorneys for the railroad industry unsuccessfully petitioned the ICC for permission to increase rates to offset steadily rising costs. ICC commissioners refused, however, stymied in part by the "weak line/strong line problem." Any effort to provide smaller and weaker lines with the increased revenues that might attract much-needed additional capital, critics argued, would translate into windfall profits for well-off carriers. The financial bind of rising costs and fixed rates forced executives of several weak rail lines, including the Rock Island and Missouri Pacific, to declare bankruptcy. The outbreak of World War I in Europe in August 1914 brought better times (i.e., more traffic), but troubled rail carriers with limited financial resources were ill-equipped to respond to the new conditions. By the winter of 1917, the flood of freight bound for Europe swamped eastern carriers, as inefficiencies at East Coast ports—especially New York—stalled trains carrying war supplies and coal for home heating. Freight cars clogged railyards nearly one hundred miles from New York City. When rail executives failed to eliminate the congestion, in late December 1917 Congress passed emergency legislation turning the nation's rail system over to a new government agency, the U.S. Railroad Administration (USRA).[10] Run by railroad officials and managers, the USRA solved the traffic problems but convinced almost no one of the desirability of government operation of the railroads. By 1919, observers within and without the industry agreed that rail carriers needed to be returned to private control. In April 1920, the Transportation Act of 1920 (Esch-Cummins Act) accomplished this task, and much more besides.[11]

The legislation was guided through Congress by two Republicans, Iowa senator Albert B. Cummins and Wisconsin representative John J. Esch. Trained as an engineer, Cummins was widely respected as the Senate's expert on railroad policy. He had worked for the Cincinnati, Richmond, and Fort Wayne Railroad before studying law and moving to Des Moines, Iowa, to practice law as a railroad attorney. In 1908, he entered Republican Party politics and won election to Congress, and later to the Senate. Representative John Esch entered Congress in 1899 after practicing law in La Crosse, and the legislation that bore his name was his crowning achievement.[12] The 1920 bill emerged from highly contentious debates about the future of American railroads between railroad supporters and those who feared the economic and political influence of railroad corporations. The discussions began as soon as World War I ended in November 1918 and after many compromises led to the decision in Congress to award unprecedented regulatory authority over the operation of the nation's private railroads to the ICC commissioners. Esch and Cummins's bill directed the commissioners to set minimum as well as maximum railroad rates, approve the issuance of railroad securities, and review and approve both new construction and line abandonments. These and other elements reflected the depth of political animosity toward the railroads in some quarters, a powerful and continuing motive behind regulation. At the same time, authors of the Transportation Act of 1920 also enforced constructive steps designed to remove obstacles to better railroad transportation, especially the structural difficulties posed by the unequal profitability of rail carriers. Congress ordered ICC commissioners to set rates that allowed rail corporations to earn at least 6 percent on investment, but also directed the ICC to "recapture" half of profits above this figure to support "weak lines." Most significantly, the Congress required ICC commissioners to develop a plan to consolidate the nation's railroads into profitable, parallel, regional systems and eliminate the weak/strong dichotomy.[13]

While the 1920 legislation retained substantial antirailroad language, it sought to accomplish quite different purposes. Some transportation economists had argued that the industry's problem was wasteful and inefficient competition, and while not everyone accepted this prognosis, one historian noted that the intent of the new legislation was "a more rationally conceived, stable, and profitable railroad industry."[14] This new version of railroad regulation mandated that ICC commissioners take account not only of the concerns of shippers and the public, but also of the financial health of the nation's rail carriers. This change engendered hopes among some railroad leaders about less stringent regulatory control, but the ICC, considered by most observers the preeminent independent regulatory agency, rarely failed to exercise the increased authority it enjoyed after 1920.[15] The ICC commissioners and an array of government agencies and actors, in concert with railroad executives, sought to accomplish the lofty ideal of insuring "adequate transportation service" as mandated by the 1920 legislation. Whether they succeeded is problematic.

THE POLITICS OF RAILROAD REGULATION IN THE 1920S

The Transportation Act of 1920 led almost everyone connected with railroads to anticipate that the era of restrictive, negative railroad regulation had ended. ICC commissioners asserted "that adequate transportation should be a guiding feature, and that Government should take the responsibility of seeing that adequate transportation was supplied."[16] Because the legislation identified the financial health of the railroads as a significant factor guiding railroad regulatory policy, Alfred P. Thom, vice chairman and general counsel of the Association of Railroad Executives, concluded the law abandoned "the old and mistaken view that the responsibility of government is fully performed when it punishes misdeeds."[17] The question of the hour was whether this vision would become reality, for such an outcome required overcoming the burden of past regulatory history and significant political opposition. As it turned out, political considerations triumphed in the process of shaping railroad regulation at the ICC, in the halls of Congress, and inside the office of the president.

Almost immediately, ICC commissioners had an opportunity to act upon the new regulatory changes. Before the war, commissioners had hesitated to raise rates and acted only after holding lengthy deliberative proceedings, thanks to heavy pressures from shippers and Congress. In 1920, however, postwar inflation put railroads under enormous financial pressure, and rail executives sought increased freight rates ranging from 24 percent to 31 percent in order for companies to earn the "reasonable" rate of 6 percent allowed by the 1920 legislation. Commissioners not only agreed with these corporate officials, but also allowed another increase when the new Railway

Labor Board ordered wage increases for unionized railway employees in 1920. This time ICC commissioners had acted in only nine days![18] Shippers complained and state regulators who controlled intrastate rail rates expressed outrage at being undercut by their counterparts at the ICC. Several state officials took the commission to court, one example of the continuing skirmishes over the centralization of authority by federal officials.[19] ICC commissioners eventually prevailed in a court battle in which the justices affirmed their authority over interstate commerce, and thus their centrality in railroad policy matters.[20] Railroad executives grumbled about rate cuts later ordered during the depression of 1921 and 1922, but a significant change in the regulatory regime apparently had occurred.[21] Now ICC officials framed the discussions about transportation rates.

Other actions taken by ICC commissioners reinforced the signs of regulatory change during the early 1920s. The shortages of freight cars and delivery delays that had prompted government's operation of the railroads in 1917 continued to plague railroad managers, despite the availability of one hundred thousand new freight cars built by the USRA. In 1920, neither eastern coal mines nor western grain farmers could secure a sufficient number of cars. When labor unrest left many cars undelivered or sitting idle, ICC officials invoked emergency powers to shift cars to areas of need. Similarly in 1922, ICC staffers resolved freight car shortages occasioned by striking eastern coal miners and railway shop workers.[22] Yet full implementation of the goal of prosperous railroad systems proved elusive, for many ICC officials did not abandon the traditional image of railroads as economic predators. In this way, politics remained central to rail regulation, for concerns about the growth and stability of rail carriers comprised only a small part of regulatory politics.

THE VALUATION PROJECT

More important than concern for railroad finances in the deliberations of ICC officials was a massive and costly project that embodied continuity with older ways of thinking, namely, the effort launched before World War I to establish a valuation of the physical properties of the nation's railroads. The idea for this study could be traced to the ICC's chief statistician in the late 1880s, who envisioned using a precise determination of the "fair value" of the physical property of the railroads as the first step in developing an objective method of setting rates. The intent was to insure a just rate of return for the rail carriers without gouging shippers and consumers. To find this balance, some reformers argued, accountants and regulators needed to know the value of railroad property. In an era of speculation and financial manipulation personified by Jay Gould and other rail executives, few observers assumed that the stated capitalization or debt of railroad corporations provided a useful measure from which to compute a rate of return. The ICC statistician's calls for a valuation study made little headway for two decades, but reformers and railroad critics eventually embraced the idea that a detailed statistical analysis of railroad property could prove once and for all that overvalued or "watered" stock had produced inflated rates that hurt shippers, especially farmers. Not until 1913, however, could Wisconsin senator Robert LaFollette persuade Congress to direct the ICC to determine the "real" value of the railroads. Such a "scientific" study typified turn-of-the-century faith in reforms that sought to remove politics from government administration by utilizing objective data and nonpolitical experts.[23]

Whatever railroad critics such as LaFollette said about scientific study, railroad officials distrusted former ICC commissioner Charles Prouty, who led the valuation project. Railroad executives therefore launched a parallel study of their own. Starting in 1914, two teams of engineers, accountants, and lawyers counted every rail, spike, building, acre of land, and machine, a task that remained incomplete in 1920. ICC officials struggled to make sense of the mountain of statistical data for each railroad, and final valuations were not ready in many cases until 1927, as the process limped through lengthy hearings and appeals.[24] ICC commissioners also faced two court challenges to the project. Although each case involved esoteric legal issues, the outcomes highlighted the dominant position of the commissioners in railroad policy, even when the Supreme Court rebuked the commissioners for arrogantly ignoring earlier rulings on the definition of valuation.[25]

The final complication in finishing the valuation project in a timely fashion came from a change in the purpose of valuation. After passage of the Transportation Act of 1920, the project's valuation findings were to guide the ICC's enforcement of the "reasonable" rate of return set by Congress (6 percent the first year), and the so-called "recapture clause," by which the government would recover half of any profits above that level. To do so, commissioners needed to update the data continuously to meet a new and different assignment from that originally envisioned in 1913. The initial purpose of this data collection effort had been to assess the static question of past railroad financial behavior in terms of securities., Representative Esch, Senator Cummins, and others, however, expected the valuation findings to guide rate setting. The original assignment called for taking a snapshot of railroad property holdings in 1913, while the rate-setting process inaugurated in 1920 demanded continuously current valuation data—a huge and expensive task. Commissioners resisted, for Congress provided no new funds, but Congress also ignored the ICC commissioners' requests to drop the entire exercise.[26]

The valuation project began to wind down when the Supreme Court rebuked the commissioners in 1928 for a unilateral attempt to redefine valuation, even though Congress kept the project alive until 1933.[27] The final product produced forty-seven massive volumes listing every item of railroad property, prepared at a cost of about $45 million—perhaps half of the ICC budget since 1913. Rail carriers spent approximately $138 million more on their parallel study.[28] Even as the commissioners attempted to harness valuation data to the demands of the 1920 legislation, the project could not transcend the original intentions of its supporters, namely, to demonstrate the allegedly illegal financial manipulations of railroad executives. The ICC reports concluded that watered stock and other manipulations were not evident, seeming to confirm the claims of railroad management that they had abandoned the abusive financial practices of the 1880s. The hope of reformers such as LaFollette that objective statistics would resolve the political and economic questions about rates ultimately was misplaced.[29] Even so, the valuation exercise—especially the court battles over the definition of valuation—not only demonstrated that the older, punitive regulatory mind-set remained firmly in place in many quarters of the government, but also indicated how agencies beyond the ICC helped shape the efforts to establish new approaches to transportation regulation during the 1920s.

RATE SETTING AND RAILROAD ACCOUNTING

The inability of would-be reformers and ICC officials to use objective data to resolve the valuation problem was matched by similar difficulties in harnessing accounting standards as a nonpolitical guide to the setting of railroad rates.[30] As far back as the 1880s, ICC officials had advocated the application of uniform accounting principles to railroads as a device for gauging railroad rates and profits in an objective fashion. The ICC's statistician argued that shippers, consumers, and the railroads themselves would benefit from lower rates while the companies earned a fair profit.[31] After the Hepburn Act granted the ICC authority to prescribe a uniform accounting structure for all carriers in 1906, officers of the Association of American Railway Accounting Officers worked cooperatively with ICC officials on this task. In 1907, the ICC issued guidelines for calculating railroad operating expenses, revenues, and expenditures; the complete rules became effective July 1, 1909.[32] Here was yet another way in which the ICC commissioners helped shape the railroad industry.

Yet turning railroad accounting practices and data into regulatory tools proved more complicated than ICC statisticians expected, primarily because of the nature of railroad operations. Railroad tracks, right-of-way, bridges, stations, and shops were utilized both for the carriage of passengers *and* the movement of freight. Following the logic proposed by Harvard economics professor F. W. Taussig in the 1880s, accountants generally agreed that it was not possible to separate the "joint costs" of these two different services. These same accountants assumed that the fixed costs of railroad operation were so high that it made little sense to worry about the specific costs of individual freight or passenger services.[33] Moreover, another economic reality conspired to force the attention of railroad executives away from detailed cost evaluations: freight rates largely determined how far mine operators and farmers could ship their low-value bulk commodities such as coal and grain. Therefore, the railways, if they wished to move these commodities (and the assumptions both about railway economics and national prosperity led them to believe they should), could not charge the same price for moving grain as for moving industrial machinery.[34]

The railroads had learned this lesson about freight rates decades earlier. As historian Albro Martin explains, as soon as American railroads provided long-distance service in the 1830s, they discovered they could not set rates just by multiplying local rates to cover distance. The rates that the B&O charged for service in Baltimore "might well produce an exorbitant rate if applied to Harpers Ferry, a confiscatory rate to Cumberland, and a bad joke to Wheeling."[35] This economic logic led the railroads, and later the ICC, to the political decision to set rates on the basis of "value-of-service."[36] Bulk commodities that had the least value per ton enjoyed the lowest rates, while higher-valued manufactured goods commanded higher freight rates. The actual cost of shipping the goods, whether grain or machinery, was not central to the determination of each particular freight rate. In practice, this rate system discriminated against manufactured goods and subsidized shipment of bulk products, especially grain. This was especially true of western carriers that served as economic development agencies, opening unsettled territory rather than serving existing traffic. Once the rate pattern was established, it became difficult to alter. The viability of communities, firms, and basic patterns of the American economy were inextricably linked to these early decisions about railroad rates.[37]

Once established, no one benefited more from this system of rate making than farmers and mining companies whose grain and other bulk commodities were shipped to distant markets. Yet those same customers of the railroads were the most vocal opponents of another form of discriminatory rates, the so-called long-haul/short-haul controversy, an issue that had created more enemies for railroads than any other topic. Railroads argued that long hauls often cost less than moving goods a shorter distance. Yet it seemed unfair to a merchant in Harrisburg to pay more for goods shipped from Philadelphia than his counterpart in Pittsburgh did, despite a shorter haul. Railroad critics viewed such rate discrimination as additional evidence of the monopolistic tendencies of railroad management. Moreover, the ICC was charged by law with determining if railroad rates were "just and reasonable." Yet the "value-of-service" principle of rate setting left both ICC officials and railroad executives poorly equipped to refute claims that specific discriminations were unjust and unreasonable. Generally, railroad leaders' cost data were not detailed enough to show the cost of moving a single car of a given commodity. Clearly, the railroads were on the horns of a dilemma, as became apparent in the highly publicized rate hearings of the 1910s, when lawyer Louis D. Brandeis used this lack of statistical information to portray the carriers as inefficient. Unable to counter Brandeis's arguments with definitive data, the carriers twice failed to win requested increases.[38]

Political scientist Gerald Berk argues that "the regulatory predicament" facing both the ICC commissioners and the rail carriers stemmed from the flawed assumption that cost accounting, rigorously applied, was "a measure beyond politics" that could yield unambiguous, objective answers regarding exact railroad rates.[39] Berk's point is that objective accounting data, even in the hands of presumably fair-minded regulators, could not by itself guide such complex and contentious matters as rate setting. Yet neither the ICC nor rail executives could simply replace the underlying value-of-service basis for determining freight rates. Industries and communities had institutionalized value-of-service rates into every economic relationship. Given the limits before them, ICC officials slowly increased their reliance upon cost data in their decisions about railroad rates, especially after 1920, when by law the commission had to consider the impact of its decisions upon the railroads. Writing in the 1930s, economist I. L. Sharfman argued that the commission came to view costs as establishing the floor for rates, while value of service calculation provided a ceiling.[40] Somehow, railroad managers had to navigate between the ICC's value-of-service accounting philosophy focused on overall rates of return while shippers, farmers, and the public embraced an alternative philosophy that considered only the specific costs linked to specific shipments. This situation guaranteed conflict. The federal government had helped constitute the railroad industry and its markets, but in moments of economic distress, no one, including members of Congress or presidents, liked the outcome.

As if this uncertainty about the determination of equitable freight rates was not difficult enough for both regulators and the regulated railroads, during the 1920s members of Congress sought to influence railroad rates directly. Even though they had authorized the ICC commissioners to govern such matters, during the 1920s Senator LaFollette and many colleagues frequently talked about railroad rates. To the arcane debate about costs versus value of service, midwestern senators added the question of the effect of railroad rates on farmers then experiencing an agricultural depression. These senators' stances suggested that many in Congress retained the older view of the railroad executives as dangerous monopolists who connived to increase the costs of transportation essential for farmers and small business owners. This outlook justified continued political intervention by Congress into the ICC's regulatory sphere of transportation policy even after 1920, especially in the form of legislation ordering the ICC to adjust freight rates to promote economic recovery. An editorial writer in *Railway Age* caustically observed in 1922, "It having become the custom to regulate freight rates more in accordance with the needs or wishes of shippers than of the railroads . . . Congress and the commission began to be flooded with demands for action to reduce rates in order to revive business."[41] Even the editors of *Railway Age* agreed that "farmers as a class have suffered the greatest reductions in the prices of their products within the last year and a half."[42] Although several members of the Senate introduced bills to that purpose, railroad managers resisted cutting freight rates.[43]

Beginning in the early 1920s, presidents of the United States and their top appointees could no longer deny themselves a voice in the politics of railroads, until then a province of Congress and the ICC.[44] During the postwar debates about railroads in 1919–20, President Woodrow Wilson deliberately rejected requests to propose legislation. In April 1921, however, new president Warren G. Harding and members of his cabinet talked at length about economic recovery in agriculture, industry, and transportation. As the editors of *Railway Age* put it, "The President and his advisers appear to have been persuaded that the railroad question is the key to the whole problem, but they have as yet found no 'plan' or 'solution.'"[45] At a time when the executive branch possessed only a limited capacity to foster an economic recovery, the adjustment of railroad freight rates was one of the few weapons in their arsenal.

Secretary of Commerce Herbert C. Hoover became deeply involved in discussions about the broader economic significance of railroad rates. The most famous engineer of the era, Hoover enjoyed an aura of objective expertise so dear to the hearts of earlier reformers. In nearly every major economic issue of the day, from coal strikes and radio regulation to the 1927 floods on the Mississippi and transportation, one could find Hoover's ideas as he became known as the leading problem solver in Washington.[46] The commerce secretary sympathized with farmers, but realized that under the new rules of the Transportation Act of 1920, ICC commissioners needed to consider the economic impact of rate decisions on rail corporations. Hoover concluded that rate cuts on agricultural commodities would damage rail carriers and proposed instead that ICC commissioners undertake a "systematic overhaul" of railroad rates, with the aim of lowering rates generally without sacrificing railroad income. "I am convinced that lower rates would recover lost traffic," Hoover argued. In May 1922, President Harding joined the conversation, prompted by Secretary of Agriculture Henry Wallace's vocal concerns about the negative effects of high freight rates on farmers. Harding invited railroad executives to dinner at the White House and asked them to consider voluntary rate reductions on basic commodities, after business conditions improved. A committee of railroad presidents met the next day with ICC staffers, but nothing came from this initiative.[47]

Such direct involvement by the president in railroad issues marked a new departure for members of the executive branch. Adopting Hoover's perspective, Harding met with railroad presidents and remained "in close touch" with ICC commissioners, especially chairman Charles McChord.[48] Harding also recognized the novelty of his efforts, and his staff issued a clarifying statement to the effect that " . . . he was attempting none of the duties of rate-making nor recommendations," and that Harding only sought to encourage the cooperation of the railroad leaders with the ICC.[49] Harding's successor, Calvin Coolidge, a man normally inclined to leave well enough alone, continued this approach and remained involved in discussions of agricultural freight rates. In mid-1923, Coolidge asked the president of the Pennsylvania Railroad to offset lower freight rates on exported wheat with increased rates on coal for export. Editorial reactions were mixed, but Coolidge had recognized that any cuts in agricultural freight rates required trade-offs elsewhere. By 1923, Presidents Harding and Coolidge and Commerce Secretary Hoover had become involved in efforts to maintain adequate railroad service, foster railroad profits, and boost overall levels of economic activity. The politics of transportation were becoming more complex.[50]

At first, ICC officials refused to respond either to executive pressures or to economic conditions they judged to be temporary in nature. After reducing all freight rates in 1921, the commissioners ignored equally calls from farm-states residents for further reductions in agricultural commodity rates and Hoover's suggestion of a general review of rates.[51] Former representative John Esch, who had coauthored the Transportation Act of 1920, was appointed to the ICC in 1921 after losing his seat in Congress. He spoke for the commission in the mid-1920s, recommending that the ICC review rate structures only if Congress funded a major investigation. But the deepening agricultural depression brought insistent demands for changes in freight rates.[52] By May 1924, both houses of Congress conducted hearings on bills to repeal the two linked clauses in the Transportation Act of 1920 that specified a reasonable rate of return for railroad corporations and the "recapture" by the ICC of "excess" rail carrier profits. Leaders of farm groups apparently had concluded they could more easily secure rate reductions if the ICC commissioners could, as before 1920, ignore railroad finances.[53]

Farm groups initially won little support for such an approach to reducing freight rates. The issue gained momentum only after Senator E. D. Smith of South Carolina introduced a nonbinding resolution calling "agriculture a basic industry of the country." Smith's resolution ordered ICC commissioners to "'promote the freedom of movement of the products of agriculture at the lowest possible rates.'" Representative Homer Hoch had proposed a similar nonbinding resolution directing ICC commissioners to consider the market values of commodities in setting freight rates and to begin a large-scale investigation of railroad rates. In early 1925, the Hoch-Smith resolution emerged from Congress, declaring that "the true policy in rate making" was to adjust freight rates to fit the economic circumstances.[54] Only five years after giving the ICC authority to set railroad rates that would lead to healthy rail corporations, a majority of Congress now urged that rates be regulated to serve organized constituents, in this case farmers.

Railroad executives complained that the Hoch-Smith resolution violated key elements of the Transportation Act of 1920. ICC officials had a legal responsibility not to cut freight rates on agricultural commodities without first considering the financial consequences such a move would have on rail corporations; they also lacked enthusiasm—and the necessary budget—for a major review of rates. Railroad rates had become an incredibly convoluted subject, thanks to long-established patterns which included charging the highest rates for the most valuable commodities. But ICC commissioners more than most realized that the traditional policy of encouraging the long-distance shipment of bulky, low-value materials such as coal and grain at low rates had shaped the geography of the American economy. Altering this practice, which some economists even then were arguing promoted enormous inefficiency within the nation's economy, would have had far-reaching consequences for established industries and commercial relationships. The ICC commissioners had no stomach for such a Sisyphean task.[55] Yet they were not eager to defy Congress, even though the Hoch-Smith resolution did not have the force of law. Instead, the commissioners launched a study labeled docket No. 17000, Rate Structure Investigation. This examination of agricultural commodity rates continued through 1926, at which time the commissioners issued yet another report that satisfied no one. They denied rail carriers a rate increase, a move that rail executives denounced as proof the ICC was ignoring the legal requirement that railroads be allowed to earn a reasonable rate of return. Commissioners also refused to reduce freight rates for agricultural commodities, complaining that "None of the parties [favoring rate reductions] presented any definite plan for compensating increases in rates on other traffic."[56] Caught between growing political demands to help farmers and the legal requirements of the new regulatory structure that required consideration of the health of the transportation system, the commissioners decided to take no action.

The problem facing the ICC commissioners was more political than economic. They were opposed, Commissioner Balthasar H. Meyer explained later, to using railroad rates as a "shock absorber and balance wheel for the entire economic life of industry." Doing so, he said, required "the wisdom of a hundred Solomons."[57] As they launched the rate study in 1926, ICC officials sought to reaffirm the special legitimacy of scientifically based, apolitical decision making. Some saw this approach as the basic reason the commission existed, as the president of the National Industrial Traffic League (NITL), R. C. Fulbright of Houston, Texas, told the Senate in 1924. The ICC, he argued, was supposed to be "a non-partisan and non-political body and provided with a corps of experts who are spending their lives working out the complex problems of the rates, fares, and practices of the railroads, and that it should be left free and untrammeled to pursue its duties under such rules and regulations as it should find to be in the public interest." He added that the NITL "would like to see the railroads out of politics."[58] To that end, ICC examiners asked the railroads for huge volumes of information on the origin, destination, and trends of movement of cattle, gasoline, automobiles, bar iron, wheat, potatoes, hay, and lumber (hardwood and others)—the controlling commodities in terms of rates. (Wheat controlled all other grains, for example.) Just to study grain rates, ICC staffers convened meetings in Dallas, Wichita, Minneapolis, Chicago, Seattle, Portland, and Los Angeles, generating fifty-five thousand pages of transcript and 2,106 exhibits by 1928. The investigation of cottonseed rates involved hearings at a similar range of sites, producing another 13,133 pages of transcript and 1,588 additional exhibits.[59]

The ICC commissioners failed, however, to silence political concerns over the reams of statistical data developed by experts and economists. Bowing to political pressure, in 1927 commissioners finally adopted the principles of the Hoch-Smith resolution, which called for rates to be adjusted to fit the economic circumstances of particular industries. In three cases, the commissioners lowered rates on a limited range of agricultural commodities.[60] Railroad executives protested bitterly. "This may have been good politics, but it is bad economics," claimed a *Railway Age* editorial writer, who asked whether it would be fair to discriminate in favor of automobiles against farmers.[61] In the end, the Supreme Court agreed with the carriers, who took the issue to court. The justices ruled that a nonbinding resolution like Hoch-Smith had not changed "the basic law. . . . We are of the opinion that the commission's construction cannot be supported."[62] For the moment, one branch of the federal government had overridden another, but the case hardly validated the ICC's preference for expert-based, as opposed to politically motivated, decisions. As editorial writers at *Railway Age* complained, millions of dollars had been wasted in challenging a politically driven congressional dictate.

Nor was this the only instance of attempted congressional intervention in transportation regulation. Politicians seized several opportunities in attempts to legislate specific ICC actions. In 1923, Senator Smith W. Brookhart of Iowa authored a bill that proposed a dramatic reduction in the stated value of the railroads. Brookhart wanted Congress to repeal the reasonable rate of return clause in the Transportation Act of 1920. *Railway Age* editors claimed that proposal was "designed to let the Interstate Commerce Commission reduce rates to any desired level without consideration of the effect on railroad finances."[63]

Brookhart's proposal was not the only effort to inject Congress directly into the details of transportation policymaking. In 1924, congressional representatives introduced more than 170 bills dealing with the railroads, 59 concerned with rates and 27 with labor issues. Nine others would have strengthened the legal authority of state regulatory commissions in contests with the ICC.[64] A bill by Senator Frank R. Gooding of Idaho directed the ICC to gather information about railroad support for speakers, advertising, public opinion surveys, and information distribution "for the purpose of creating public sentiment favorable to the railroad interests."[65]

Gooding also hoped to prohibit ICC-granted exceptions to the rule requiring that railroads charge more for long hauls than short hauls. This old issue had been a primary cause of the anger shippers and business interests directed at railroads during the nineteenth century and it continued to haunt railroad officials even though the Transportation Act of 1920 allowed for exceptions. Basically, the ICC could approve such a rate for railroads hauling goods in competition with water-born shipments between the coasts. The traditional rhetoric of predatory railroad behavior had not disappeared, as Gooding claimed "the majority of [ICC commissioners] are just tools for the railroad corporations."[66] Despite strenuous objections from

FIGURE 1. "Mischief Still to Do"
This political cartoon originally from the *New York Evening Post* appeared in
Railway Age in 1924. It conveys a widely held perception among railway man-
agers concerning the nature of congressional efforts in regard to railroads. Source:
Railway Age 76 (April 26, 1924): 1044. Used with permission.

the commissioners that Gooding's bill "disregards the commercial and
industrial conditions which have led to the establishment of [specialized
industrial centers]" and was "absolutely unworkable," the proposal passed
the Senate in 1924. Predictably, a writer for *Railway Age* labeled it "one of
the most dangerous bills for the regulation of rates ever introduced in Congress," and it never came to a vote in the House.[67] The Gooding Bill resur-
faced in the Senate in 1925 and 1926, but not even the defeat of this measure ended the enthusiasm of politicians for lowering their constituents'
transportation costs.[68]

The economic downturn in agriculture and the continuing hostility
toward the railroads animated these efforts to reduce freight rates. The animosity had not diminished much since Pennsylvania Railroad vice president

A. M. Schoyer had reported in 1914 that "the railways are not yet popular" with the citizens, politicians, or regulators.[69] Herbert Hoover judged this deep-rooted animus a "veritable witches cauldron being fed constantly with hates distilled from the misdeeds of railway promoters in the past." Hoover believed it was time to "call off the witches."[70] Few embroiled in the politics of transportation were inclined to act on Hoover's recommendation.

ICC APPOINTMENTS

Hostility toward the railroads and conflicts over freight rates spilled over into Senate confirmation hearings for ICC commissioners. Railroad executives had long complained that presidents and Congress considered few persons with railroad experience for appointment to the ICC. Indeed, most commissioners were lawyers who had served on state regulatory commissions. Moreover, rail leaders perceived most appointees to be hostile to railroad interests.[71] In 1925, for example, two appointees of President Coolidge, railway economist Thomas F. Woodlock and former railroad vice president Richard V. Taylor, encountered significant opposition at Senate hearings. Senators grilled Woodlock and Taylor, according to *Railway Age*, because of their corporate backgrounds. Both men, but especially Taylor, had to explain their views on key issues such as rates and management prerogatives, while the editor of *Railway Age* alleged that appointees perceived as railroad opponents never were called to appear before the committee. "The obvious purpose was to try to make sure that no man would get on the Commission who would begin his work without some bias against the railways."[72] For all the debate about appointments, apparently no one in or out of government doubted that the locus of authority regarding the railroad industry rested with the commissioners of the ICC.

In 1928, the reconfirmation hearings of ICC commissioner John Esch provided another opportunity for senators to influence freight rates and ICC actions. Only seven years earlier Representative Esch had helped craft the Transportation Act of 1920. After losing his seat, President Harding appointed him to the ICC in 1921, and hearings on his reappointment took place in 1928. Several senators used the occasion to attack an ICC ruling on a relatively minor case regarding rates for coal shipped from Appalachian mines to the Great Lakes. They accused Esch of changing his position during deliberations on that case to curry favor with Pennsylvania's senior senator and secure reappointment, a charge Esch vehemently denied.[73] In fact, few doubted Esch's personal integrity, but as Senator Matthew M. Neely of West Virginia explained, "We are not fighting his confirmation as a man, but because the decision he and the commission have rendered has crucified the coal industry of the State I represent."[74] Despite strong support for Esch from leaders of the Coolidge administration and warnings that members of Congress were placing the supposed independence of commissioners at risk for holding views that angered Congress, the committee and the Senate as a body rejected Esch's reappointment.[75]

So central were the railroads to American politics that freight rates and policy questions emerged as part of presidential campaigns. In 1924, Progressive Party candidate Robert LaFollette made freight rates the central issue in his presidential campaign. That decision prompted the editors of *Railway Age* to comment that "Never has the railroad question been so fully discussed in any national campaign." Four years later, in 1928, candidates paid less attention to railroads. Nonetheless, a group of securities holders asked both presidential contenders about their plans for increasing the profitability of railroads in the western states. *Railway Age* editorial writers expressed frustration when both Herbert Hoover and Alfred E. Smith supported the development of inland waterways. Following Hoover's election, another editorial writer concluded that his overwhelming victory "cannot be construed otherwise than as an endorsement by the public of his general views regarding the proper relations between government and business." The election mattered, argued *Railway Age*, because Congress passed regulations and the Senate confirmed ICC commissioners, but "the president usually has a strong influence on legislation, and he has the initiative in determining the membership of the commission. . . . It seems reasonable to assume, therefore, that under his administration, the influence of the presidential office will be exerted in favor of fair and constructive regulation."[76] Perhaps without realizing the full significance of this comment, the editorial writer highlighted the slow appearance of a fundamental change during the 1920s, namely, the emergence of the president and his staff as active participants in the development of transportation policy.

This renewed political interest in railroads suggested that the authors of the Transportation Act of 1920 had not succeeded in convincing regulators and members of Congress alike to accept rate regulation that considered the financial health of rail carriers and the new policy goal of securing a strong transportation system. Congressmen, senators, and presidents were regular participants in the politics of railroad regulation, in part because public distrust of the railroads remained so strong that no one was willing to leave to the ICC commissioners the task of interpreting the mandate to oversee creation of an adequate transportation system. The resulting atmosphere of uncertainty was only strengthened by disagreements among the commissioners themselves, especially visible during the lengthy debate and discussions about implementing the one really radical element of the Transportation Act of 1920—the requirement that the ICC develop a plan to consolidate the nation's railroad system.

RAILROAD CONSOLIDATION IN THE 1920S

Railroad consolidation—combining the nation's private rail corporations into a smaller number of larger regional rail carriers—was in some ways the new and essential element around which Congress sought to create a national transportation policy in 1920. In line with many reform programs of the early twentieth century, several framers of the 1920 bill presented consolidation as a mechanism for allowing scientific expertise, supposedly removed from politics, to shape public policy. In this case, the goal was to eliminate what those experts considered wasteful and inefficient competition by the removal of inappropriate political interference. In fact, politics always was part of the creation of the new regulatory regime.

The concept of government-directed consolidation at first appears out of place in a nation that espoused the centrality of private enterprise and competition.[77] Yet the general application of the principle of consolidation to railroads had a long history. During the 1910s, economists such as Emory R. Johnson, dean of the University of Pennsylvania's Wharton School of Business, and Harvard economics professor William Z. Ripley had advocated restructuring the nation's railroads, in part to achieve operating efficiencies.[78] As early as 1918, others close to the railroads asserted the public would soon recognize that "the five competitive trains leaving Chicago for the Twin Cities or Omaha at about the same hour is just as expensive . . . as two sets of gas pipes in the same streets."[79] By 1920, Johnson, Ripley, and other professors had gained a legitimate place for themselves in national transportation policy debates.

Executives of a handful of railroad corporations, such as the Pennsylvania, the Southern, and several western rail lines had pursued their own strategy of railroad consolidation for a couple of decades. As early as 1891, Collis P. Huntington of the Southern Pacific argued, "I am satisfied that the best results will not be reached until all the transportation business in the country is done by one company. . . . What is wanted is not more than two or three—and one would be better—great carrying companies." In 1915, a study by Wharton School's Johnson concluded that railroad leaders had been pursuing this vision, as ten investment groups controlled 70 percent of the country's rail mileage (174,000 miles); and five corporate/banking empires controlled half the total.[80]

FIGURE 2. Emory R. Johnson, transportation economist and dean of the Wharton School of Business. Johnson was a frequent participant in discussions concerning transportation policy during the period 1910–1940. Source: The Collections of the University of Pennsylvania Archives. Used with permission.

During the debates leading up to the Transportation Act of 1920, Ripley, Johnson, and other railroad economists took pains to answer the complaints of critics who saw consolidation plans as new evidence of the monopolistic and predatory instincts of railroad executives. Under the direction of the ICC, Johnson and Ripley asserted, consolidation could provide a potential remedy for regulatory difficulties, notably the weak line/strong line problem that had hamstrung railroad rate setting. By properly arranging

FIGURE 3. William Z. Ripley, transportation economist, Harvard University. After 1921, Ripley served as consultant to the Interstate Commerce Commission and prepared the original ICC consolidation plan for the nation's railroads, pursuant to the Transportation Act of 1920. Source: The Collection of the University Archives, Harvard University. Used with permission.

companies into parallel regional systems, consolidation might produce uniformly strong carriers and eliminate wasteful duplications, all while preserving competition. Such logic explained the inclusion of the consolidation concept in the Transportation Act of 1920, especially after ICC commissioners endorsed the idea.[81] ICC officials assumed they could more easily regulate a few large companies than 170 Class I railroads and almost 750 smaller carriers. Thus ICC commissioners supported the legislative clause directing them to prepare plans to consolidate the nation's railroads into twenty to thirty competing regional systems.[82]

Only months after Congress passed the Transportation Act of 1920, the Interstate Commerce Commission hired William Ripley as a special expert to craft this consolidation plan. Ripley, who earned his doctorate in economics at Columbia after finishing a bachelor's degree in civil engineering from MIT in 1890, had won a reputation at Harvard as an expert on trusts, railway finances, and railroad regulation.[83] In keeping with the ideals of expert service pioneered by such university economists as Richard T. Ely of Johns Hopkins and Frank W. Taussig of Harvard, Ripley offered practical solutions to the complex utility and transportation problems of their day.[84] As early as 1915, Ripley had argued that "some affirmative action be taken . . . to encourage co-operation among carriers as shall tend to eliminate the economic wastes of competition, without endangering its manifest advantages to the public at large."[85] Ripley had an opportunity rarely afforded academic experts—to bring expertise and theory to the center of the policy arena.

Ripley and the ICC commissioners faced one important limitation as they began work on a consolidation plan in 1920: they could not compel carriers to accept it. After much debate, the authors of the Transportation Act of 1920 had limited the ICC's authority so that commissioners could only withhold approval of nonconforming consolidation proposals. This requirement meant that Ripley had to consider the preferences and gain the trust of railroad managers and stockholders. After eighteen months of data gathering, he unveiled a plan with twenty-one regional systems; the commissioners reworked it to include nineteen systems and then adopted it as their tentative plan in late 1921.[86] ICC commissioner Mark W. Potter wrote Ripley, "The merit of your work in the consolidation matter grows upon me every time I pick up your report. I continue to wonder how it was possible for you to evolve such a product. . . . We could not have functioned without you."[87]

Such laudatory comments continued until April 24, 1922, when ICC commissioners opened hearings that extended up to December 4, 1923. Ripley and the commissioners had inserted their own regional perspective in assembling the plan. ICC commissioners often ignored existing corporate relationships or traditional connections, emphasizing instead formation of working, competitive, parallel systems. In effect, the ICC plan disassembled the nation's railroad map and put it back together with only nineteen companies. Ripley and ICC officials asked railroad executives and others to help fine-tune their map. Instead, most witnesses at the hearings strongly resisted that idea, determined to maintain existing identities and connections between carriers. From the first day rail executives refused to offer alternative schemes, apparently believing that debating the details would imply acceptance of the ICC's parameters for consolidation. Almost every rail executive looked at what the plan meant for his existing company.[88] As a writer in the *New Republic* noted after the testimony of the New York Central's president A. H. Smith, "Mr. Smith's ideas, boiled down, show a maximum of thought about the New York Central and a minimum, and a very small one at that, about the consolidation scheme—whether it is sound or unsound, right or wrong."[89] Even those leaders whose companies formed the cores of regional consolidations failed to support the ICC plan. At one point, a frustrated William Ripley asked Hale Holden of the Chicago, Burlington & Quincy why western lines would not help the commission develop a practicable plan. "We are breaking our hearts in the commission," Ripley observed, "trying to develop such a plan and not merely an academic one." Holden answered that he also had been thinking about it for eighteen months, "and although he did not want to get ahead of the other western railroad executives, he thought they should all get around a table and try to develop something that will help the commission." Asked by Ripley about specific routes that would link to his line or others, however, Holden refused to express an opinion.[90]

By the end of the hearings, Ripley's consolidation plan had many critics and few supporters. Some had attacked the premise that consolidation would produce substantial operating savings. For example, John Worley, professor of transportation at the University of Michigan, worried that efficiency benefits could not offset other, intangible losses. "No industry, railroad or other," he argued, "can expect success which has none or has lost its traditions."[91] Even the leading voice for large shippers, the National Industrial Traffic League, asked ICC commissioners to "recognize the impossibility of adopting a plan of the character prescribed by Congress at this time and under present conditions."[92] In this negative environment ICC commissioners pulled back from their initial enthusiasm for consolidation. Commissioner Mark Potter, once Ripley's admiring supporter, wrote in January 1924 that he doubted consensus could be reached, yet he opposed compulsory consolidations.[93] With the railroads increasingly identified as a key factor in the nation's economic health, however, first President Harding and then President Coolidge endorsed the importance of railroad consolidation.[94]

Early in 1924, Senator Albert Cummins sought to break the impasse by introducing a consolidation bill widely credited to Commerce Secretary Herbert Hoover. As a principal author of the Transportation Act of 1920, Cummins was highly regarded in Congress for his knowledge of railroad finance, rates, and operations. This time he sought to salvage the consolidation idea, a key element of the 1920 bill to which his name was attached. Cummins suggested amending the requirement that the ICC prepare a single master plan. Instead, Cummins proposed that railroad managers could pursue initiatives on their own for two years, after which time a commission-appointed committee would broker additional consolidations for five more years. After seven years, the ICC would round out regional systems

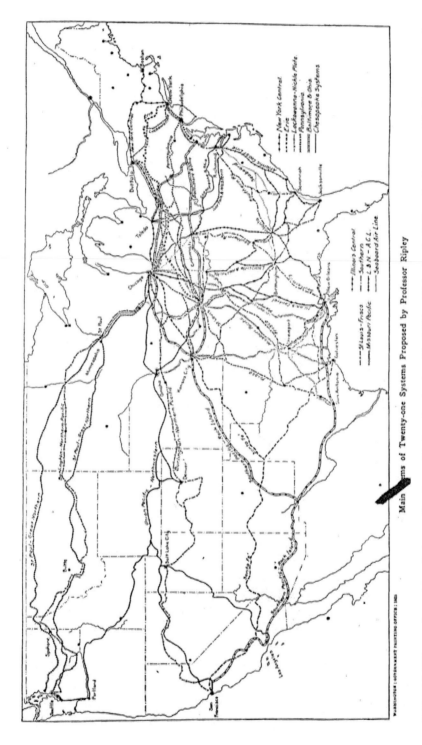

FIGURE 4. This map shows the preliminary railroad consolidation plan developed by William Ripley for the ICC, under the terms of the Transportation Act of 1920. Source: *Railway Age* 71 (October 1, 1921): 610. Used with permission.

using condemnation proceedings. As a final inducement to the railroads, Cummins's bill proposed federal incorporation of railroads, an older idea designed to limit the authority of state utility commissioners over many facets of rail operations.[95] But the bill stalled in committee and Cummins could not revive it in later sessions, despite the addition of a plan to use the recapture of excess profits to punish railroads that thwarted consolidation plans. In the mid-1920s, few members of Congress were prepared to revisit the consolidation issue, and Cummins's death in 1926 largely ended pressure for action.[96]

Yet if politicians such as Cummins, experts such as Ripley, and the ICC commissioners could not deliver a consolidation plan, leaders of several railroads pursued independent consolidation schemes in the tradition of Collis Huntington. The primary impetus after 1925 came from Oris P. and Mantis J. Van Sweringen, brothers developing a railroad empire from their corporate base in Cleveland. In 1916, their holding companies acquired control of the Nickel Plate Road and they added the Chesapeake & Ohio Railroad in 1923. The holding company mechanism afforded the brothers a means of avoiding ICC restrictions on stock issues and appointments of boards of directors, for ICC commissioners concluded they lacked legal authority to regulate state-chartered holding companies. The Van Sweringens' efforts prompted other rail executives, notably W. W. Atterbury of the Pennsylvania, to consider using holding companies to control the consolidation process. In late 1924, the leaders of the largest eastern railroads met to discuss creation of four large railroad systems in the eastern United States, where the ICC plan had called for seven systems. These railroad leaders built a plan around the New York Central, the Pennsylvania, the B&O railroads, and the Van Sweringen holdings. But these discussions fell apart because of jealousy and disagreements between the messengers about the specific lines each large carrier would control.[97]

Ignoring the ICC consolidation plan, the Van Sweringens continued building a railroad empire through leveraged stock purchases. They took control of the Erie, the Hocking Valley, and the Pere Marquette railroads, which the ICC commissioners and Ripley had tentatively assigned to three different systems. ICC commissioners, especially Joseph Eastman, were piqued by this end run using the legal loophole of holding companies and feared their consolidation program would collapse. Ripley forcefully denounced the Van Sweringens' financial manipulations, predicated upon a holding company structure and the issuance of nonvoting stock that allowed them to leverage very small investments into controlling corporate interests. In 1926, the ICC denied the brothers permission to consolidate their newest acquisitions with the original holdings of the Nickel Plate and

Chesapeake & Ohio railroads. The brothers responded by forming a second holding company to connect their railroad holdings, a pyramid structure typical of the speculative financial climate of the 1920s. By 1928 the Van Sweringens were buying the stock of western railroads, beginning with the Missouri Pacific.[98]

The Van Sweringens were relatively unique in their speculative approach to rail carriers, but were far from the only rail executives to pursue consolidations and larger systems during the 1920s. Executives at several eastern carriers continued to lease and purchase (albeit under ICC supervision) smaller lines that provided important connections, and by the end of the decade, W. W. Atterbury of the Pennsylvania had adopted a holding company strategy for certain acquisitions. In 1925, the B&O leased the Cincinnati, Indianapolis & Western; in 1928, the Pennsylvania bought a controlling interest in the Norfolk and Western and the New York Central acquired additional shares in the Lehigh Valley. The New York Central and B&O in concert expanded their joint holdings of the Reading. Similarly, in 1927 officials at the Northern Pacific and Great Northern proposed a combination, while the managers of the Kansas City Southern set out to acquire the stock of the Missouri, Kansas and Texas Railroad. ICC commissioners rejected the latter proposal strictly on financial grounds, claiming its structure copied the Van Sweringens' holding company strategy in order to bypass ICC regulatory oversight.[99]

Faced with emerging rail systems that did not conform to their tentative plan, ICC commissioners concluded they could no longer delay approving a formal consolidation scheme. In 1929, they reluctantly issued a final plan that differed only in minor details from the map Ripley had proposed in 1921. As before, industry leaders showed little enthusiasm.[100] In 1930, Congress launched another round of hearings on several consolidation bills first introduced in 1928. One impetus for renewed congressional action was the lack of railroad efforts to implement the ICC's program; another was anger at the way Van Sweringen holding companies circumvented ICC oversight of the appointments of boards of directors and requirements for financial reporting. The spectacular collapse of several utility holding companies early in the Depression also spotlighted the financial and speculative abuses underpinning some holding companies, and the obvious financial weakness of the Van Sweringen empire attracted sustained congressional scrutiny. In April 1930, Senator James C. Couzens of Michigan launched hearings on a resolution to halt all railroad consolidations until the ICC issued its final plan. Couzens's proposal attracted attention in the press, but failed to win congressional approval.[101]

Montana Senator Burton K. Wheeler joined Couzens in criticizing railroad management and ICC consolidation plans alike. Wheeler was furious that ICC commissioners had approved a tentative combination of the Northern Pacific and Great Northern, accusing them of undoing one of the most famous antitrust decisions of Theodore Roosevelt's administration. In the Northern Securities case of 1904, the Supreme Court had blocked railroad magnate E. H. Harriman's efforts to dominate the nation's railroads, ruling that his Northern Securities holding company acted to restrain trade by controlling the parallel lines of the Great Northern, the Chicago, Burlington & Quincy, and the Northern Pacific. Reflecting the decades-long distrust that railroads could still engender, Wheeler judged consolidation activities in the 1920s by the standards of 1904, and wanted the ICC to punish monopolistic railroads, not consolidate them.[102]

Perhaps the only person retaining enthusiasm for the ICC consolidation plan was William Ripley, its architect. Engaging in debates with academic economists and writing a number of articles for the popular press, Ripley kept the idea of railroad consolidation in front of politicians and ordinary Americans. Many observers credited Ripley for the ICC commissioners' rejection of the first Van Sweringen proposal in 1926.[103] In 1930, Ripley launched a final effort to bring his plan into reality. On his own, Ripley brought together the presidents of the B&O, the Pennsylvania, the New York Central, and the Chesapeake & Ohio. He cajoled, praised, and threatened; he invoked the authority of President Hoover; and Ripley even threatened to go to the ICC as a railroad stockholder. Eventually, he persuaded rail officials to accept a four-trunk line consolidation plan for the East Coast. In October 1931, rail officials sent their proposal to the ICC commissioners, who approved it in July 1932 after lengthy hearings.

Yet as had been true of other activities of the ICC, such as the valuation project, little came of this apparent breakthrough. At the low point of the decade-long economic depression, no rail corporation could afford to buy anything in 1932. Finally, in 1940 Congress repealed the section of the Transportation Act of 1920 that required the consolidation of rail corporations. Thereafter the concept of consolidation found no official support until the start of a period of renewed interest in mergers appeared during the mid-1950s.[104]

Contemporary observers of the ICC, such as academic economist and author of the classic history of the Interstate Commerce Commission I. L. Scharfman, as well as later analysts and historians, have judged the commissioners' handling of railroad consolidation one of the ICC's low points.[105] And it may be that this episode began the process of eroding the ICC's reputation as the nation's model regulatory agency because of the superior expertise in t... ublic service. Yet given the realities of the regulatory system over which the commissioners presided, few options were available to them. Whether it was the effort to determine rates, consolidate railroad firms, foster accounting standards, or judge the value of railroad investments, federal regulation was and remained an inherently political process that numerous economic and engineering experts influenced only at the margins. Despite the shift in focus supposedly mandated by the Transportation Act of 1920 to balancing the health of rail corporations and the needs of the shippers, in practice the guiding regulatory principle for many in Congress and elsewhere remained the continued distrust of railroad executives and their corporations. The valuation project perfectly reflected this situation, for it never separated the rate-setting goals of the 1920s from the program's origins as an investigation into railroad wrongdoing. Similarly, when none of the parties involved supported consolidation, political gridlock ensued because the commissioners lacked coercive authority (or the will) to order compliance with their unpopular (or perhaps unrealistic) plans.

Focusing on the ICC's inability to consolidate the railroads into a smaller number of regional systems obscures, however, a much more significant yet sometimes little remarked component of the transportation and regulatory environment during the 1920s—the emergence of serious competitors to the railroads. The framers of the new railroad policy in 1920 had assumed that railroads were natural monopolies and shaped their directions to the ICC commissioners accordingly. Yet even as commissioners pursued valuation, consolidation, and other programs designed to control or limit the actions of railroad executives, the emergence of real transporation alternatives to railroads "undermined," in the word of legal historian James W. Ely Jr., the very reason for those actions. In other words, a disconnect existed between the basic premise of the Transportation Act of 1920 and the everyday realities of American transportation. After 1920, truckers began to take freight away from rail carriers, and even more quickly bus services and personal automobiles had started to siphon off rail passengers. At the same time, inland water transport gained renewed strength, even as airplanes appeared on the scene. As Ely observes, "In this new and more competitive world, the restrictive feature of the Transportation Act badly hurt the very industry it was intended to assist." According to historian Ely, then, what took place during the railroad regulation of the 1920s was that "legislators and regulators were preoccupied with yesterday's issues, and displayed no clairvoyant grasp of the future."[106] Put another way, during the 1920s federal officials, including Esch and Cummins and their congressional colleagues as well as ICC commissioners, had structured the railroad industry and attempted to set the terms of the railroad marketplace down to the last detail.

No similar organization and oversight had been imposed on operators of emerging transportation firms such as trucking companies and airlines. Indeed, with presidents, members of Congress, ICC commissioners, and professors such as Ripley and Johnson focused on railroads, few officials took notice as new technical possibilities in transportation began to alter profoundly every aspect of the nation's transport system, including public policy. New technologies such as trucks and airplanes, however, did not simply appear. To thrive, owners and managers of each of them required the adjustment of the boundaries between themselves and competitors, and also between themselves, shippers, and government. Such adjustments took the form of new public policies created to govern such matters as highway construction, airmail subsidies and air navigation aids, waterways improvements, and still more legislation in 1935 and 1938 to regulate the organization and markets of the emerging truck and airline industries. Thus the new transportation options remained as inextricably tied to the state as the railroads. In other words, the technical possibilities in transportation expanded enormously after 1920, in large part because of the manner in which the state helped constitute those possibilities.

CHAPTER 2

THE NEW TRANSPORTATION PROBLEM: THE POLITICS OF TRANSPORTATION COORDINATION, 1925–1940

WE ARE NO LONGER RAILROADS ALONE; WE ARE TRANSPORTATION COMPANIES.
—W. W. ATTERBURY, PENNSYLVANIA RAILROAD, 1929

BETWEEN 1920 AND 1940, federal officials, managers of trucking and bus firms and airlines, and ordinary Americans carried out another transportation revolution that ended the railroad monopoly over transportation. In 1920, railroads still served as the backbone of the nation's transport system, carrying nearly all traffic—almost 2.5 billion tons of freight and 1.2 billion passengers. During the next twenty years, however, federal, state, and local engineers expended $1.7 billion on inland waterways and harbors and improved and surfaced almost a million miles of highways. Just between 1920 and 1929, the number of registered motor vehicles increased from 10.5 million to 26.7 million.[1] The federal government also financed the development of an air navigation system and paid early airlines to carry the mail as a means of encouraging creation of a private airline system.

These alternative forms of transportation such as trucks offered various combinations of greater efficiency, better service, and lower costs. With startling quickness, shippers and travelers began to abandon the railroads that had carried them and their freight for nearly a century. By 1929, automobiles already carried 81 percent of intercity passenger miles, compared to 15 percent by rail and 3.3 percent by motor bus, numbers that reflect an astonishingly rapid change in the nation's travel and shipping patterns.[2] During the 1930s with its harsh depression, the railroad's share of freight deliveries continued to decline, accounting for only 64.4 percent of the freight between cities (370 billion ton-miles), while inland waterways carried 16.7 percent (96 billion ton-miles), oil pipelines 9.7 percent (56 billion ton-miles), and trucks 9.2 percent (53 billion ton-miles).[3] These statistics found direct meaning in the experiences of American consumers, say, those living in Chicago. By the early 1930s, the milk they drank for breakfast, the tomatoes from Tennessee and Kentucky on their dinner table, and even the table itself and other furniture increasingly moved by truck rather than by train.[4]

It is tempting to consider this transportation revolution as a story of newer and better technologies developed through the hard work and promotion of truckers and airline executives, and the wise choices of private investors. Innovations such as the motor truck and paved highways brought lower transport costs, greater ease and convenience, and faster service to millions of consumers. Entrepreneurship and technological innovation comprised a part of the story, but certainly not all, or even most, of it. Instead, public policy choices made in Congress, the executive branch of the federal government, and sometimes in the states proved integral to the ability of operators of these newer transport systems to compete with the railroads after World War I. To be sure, the arrival of trucks and airplanes vastly complicated the development and implementation of public policy in the field of transportation. In some respects, federal officials approached transportation after 1920 just as municipal officials in Chicago approached the competing demands of transit companies and auto motorists during those same years. Chicago's elected officials made choices that in effect penalized street railway franchises, which they judged corrupt, old-fashioned, and undemocratic, while celebrating automobiles as individualistic, modern, and democratic.[5] On the national scene, politicians similarly encouraged truck, bus, and airline operators—or at least left them alone—while the generally distrusted railroads were tightly controlled by the ICC. Truckers, for example, enjoyed use of an emerging road network and generally favorable rulings in the courts; airlines and water transport operators received outright subsidies. That the regulation of railroad competitors differed in form and style represented a public policy choice that defined the boundaries of what came to be called the transportation industries or modes.

Railroad managers, such as the top executives at the Pennsylvania or the Chicago, Burlington & Quincy, bitterly complained about an inequitable double standard, especially in light of the changed attitude toward the health of rail carriers supposedly mandated by the Transportation Act of 1920. They occasionally invoked the specter of government ownership and claimed that state and federal regulators sought such a goal. This was a "straw man," for nationalization found no demonstrable public support. Rail executives also sought (without success) higher freight rates and the application of a similar regulatory structure to truck and bus operators. Eventually, rail carriers explored the use of buses and trucks as extensions of their rail networks. Only the crisis of the Depression forced ICC officials, members of

Congress, and transportation executives alike to consider new approaches to regulating and delivering American transportation.

The policy option that attracted the most attention emerged from transportation economists and outside experts who had for some time advocated coordinated control over the nation's increasingly complex transportation system. Coordination required adopting a different philosophy of transportation. Rather than a vision of walled-off and separated technologies, advocates of coordination evaluated transportation as a whole, urging cooperation and even collaboration between operators of different transport technologies, as for instance between truckers and railroads. In other words, supporters of coordination accepted reconfiguring an array of hitherto independent technological and business choices (trains, trucks, pipelines, canals, etc.) into an effective national transport system. As had been the case in 1920, when Congress approved the Transportation Act of 1920, independent analysts and academic experts played pivotal roles in formulating conceptions of coordinated transportation. Economists predominated in these deliberations, men whom economist and historian Michael A. Bernstein describes as being committed to service as architects of strong government programs. Reformers in the mold of William Z. Ripley gave way to institutional analysts such as Harold G. Moulton of the Brookings Institution. Nonetheless, these experts, including ICC commissioner and later Federal Transportation Coordinator Joseph B. Eastman, retained the Progressive-era rhetoric of rationality and interest-free, nonpolitical decision making.[6]

By the end of the 1930s, however, transportation experts such as Moulton and Eastman had not significantly altered the shape of American transportation policy. Opponents of transportation coordination, such as truck operators, continually called forth the specter of the supposedly predatory economic power of the railroads. More important was the undeniable preference of truck operators, airline executives, and politicians such as Senator Patrick A. "Pat" McCarran for maintaining transportation technologies as independent *modes.* Supporters of this concept not only held that each form of transport was different, but also that the public was better off if each *mode,* such as trucks or trains, remained a freestanding enterprise in competition with one another. Thus as noted in chapter 1, congressional authors had specifically prohibited railroads from owning shipping lines that competed with rail services, in effect mandating that each type of transportation should operate independently.

Executives of trucking firms, bus lines, barges on inland waterways, and later airlines adamantly favored walling off the railroads. In this way, leaders of the new types of transportation wanted to reduce competition, even while painting railroads as dangerous monopolies despite the emergence of competitors during the 1920s. In the end, proponents of distinct and separate transportation modes triumphed over those who had articulated a vision of transportation coordination. In particular, expert opinion such as the views of academic economists or the positions of the ICC's Joseph B. Eastman exercised limited influence in the milestone transportation legislation passed by Congress in 1935, 1938, and 1940. Although couched in the new language of coordination, these bills embraced the bedrock assumption that transportation was a series of modes. The result was a "national" system composed of separate transportation industries and separate transportation markets, each now defined variously as technology or mode and governed by several equally disconnected policies and regulatory agencies.

TRANSPORTATION ALTERNATIVES TO RAILROADS

The concept of transportation coordination only made sense to policymakers and transportation executives when motor vehicles, airplanes, and barges existed as viable competitors to the railroads after 1920. Freight carriage on inland waterways, for example, had largely disappeared after 1860 as rail carriers displaced traffic from canals and inland rivers. Yet efforts to improve waterways never ceased and occasional legislative initiatives to increase federal funding for projects directed by the Army Corps of Engineers grew more frequent during the late nineteenth century. The National Rivers and Harbors Congress of 1902 and formation of the Lakes-to-Gulf Deep Waterway Association in 1906 signaled the strengthening of efforts to win congressional support. In 1907, President Theodore Roosevelt appointed a Waterways Commission to study federal support for waterways, but the commissioner's report did not translate into new federal programs. Instead, the Army Corps of Engineers steadily worked on the Mississippi River and the Atlantic Intracoastal Waterway. All told, between 1890 and 1931 the federal government expended about $1.369 billion on waterways; by 1920, the states had spent another $300 million.[7]

Several factors explained this revival of interest in waterways, including hostility toward the railroads, classic booster sentiment, and the support of two powerful presidents. Public antagonism toward the railroads among midwestern farmers remained a powerful motivation, for even in 1935 Representative Charles J. Colden of California characterized railroads as dangerous monopolies. This "tame the railroads" logic held that waterways were by definition cheaper than railroads for bulk shipments; therefore, asserted proponents, transportation on waterways automatically forced reductions in monopolistic railway rates. In the 1920s, such attitudes partially undergirded

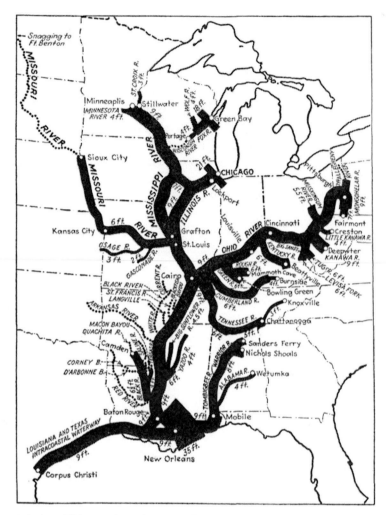

FIGURE 5. This map shows the status of improved inland waterways ca. 1930.
Source: Sidney L. Miller, *Inland Transportation Principles and Policies* (New York:
McGraw-Hill Book Company, 1933), 648.

President Herbert Hoover's promotion of a massive navigation and power
project for the St. Lawrence River in the 1920s. Most boosters of water
transportation, however, overlooked the costs of transshipping cargoes from
waterways to railroad cars (or motor trucks), expenses that eliminated most
economic advantages. Others argued that waterways were vital safety valves
for meeting occasional shortages of railcars for hauling grain at harvest time.
Additionally, members of self-interested chambers of commerce and civic
groups assumed that communities had little to lose and much to gain from
federally funded waterways projects.[8] Finally, according to transportation

expert Sidney L. Miller writing in the early 1930s, Presidents Theodore Roosevelt and Herbert Hoover played important roles in shaping public thinking and policy choices concerning inland waterways. Roosevelt's efficiency-based conservation program included many inland waterways and irrigation projects, while Hoover, both as secretary of commerce and president, "let pass no opportunity to lend the support of his personality and office to the formulation and approval of an inland waterway plan of broad scope."[9]

The clearest sign of the federal government's commitment to inland waterways was the federal operation of a barge line on the Mississippi River for more than forty years after World War I. Initially justified by the wartime freight backups on eastern railroads, Congress chartered the Inland Waterways Corporation in 1924 with the mandate to demonstrate the feasibility of commercial barge service. The secretary of war oversaw this project, which eventually spread from the Lower Mississippi and Warrior Rivers to the Upper Mississippi and later to the Illinois and Missouri Rivers. The operation grew to include a number of terminals and a fleet of equipment, but its profitability was always contested, especially if the fixed costs of equipments and improvements were included. Even so, the Inland Waterways Corporation survived numerous investigations until it ceased operation in 1963.[10]

Railway leaders, transportation economists, and a few congressional representatives criticized federal waterways activities, especially the barge corporation. The editor of *Engineering News-Record*, Charles Whiting Baker, pointed to uncertain reliability, high costs, and lack of demand, arguing that navigation improvements made sense only on the Great Lakes and perhaps on the Mississippi and Ohio River systems.[11] Harold G. Moulton, the first head of the Brookings Institution, was one of several transportation economists who criticized federal subsidies to inland waterways development, both in general and specifically in the case of Hoover's proposed St. Lawrence River project. Government policy, Moulton contended, was unfair to the railroads. Yet by 1963, the total investment on waterways since 1824 stood at about $5.5 billion, with 57 percent spent on inland waterways and 11 percent on the Great Lakes. In a system built by public policy, proponents of waterway development had reemerged as actors in American transportation politics after 1900.[12]

As with waterways, government officials played pivotal roles in guiding the formation of commercial airline service. Aviation was the glamorous newcomer to transportation. Fragile planes had proven themselves over the battlefields of France, and a generation of pilots trained at government expense (typified by the future hero Charles A. Lindbergh) came home

FIGURE 6. This cartoon from the *New York Herald Tribune* (1932), reproduced in *Railway Age*, shows the attitudes of railroad executives toward inland waterway projects. This and other political cartoons reproduced in this chapter illustrate the political tensions that existed between railroad managers and the operators of the newer transportation competitors that had emerged during the 1920s. These tensions also reflected the definition of transportation as separate industries and markets governed by separate rules. Source: *Railway Age* 93 (December 3, 1932): 817. Used with permission.

eager to develop commercial air transportation. Their progress was slow; even in 1940, airplanes presented no serious challenges to long-distance railroads or even buses. While Lindbergh and Amelia Earhart embodied popular enthusiasm for aviation and the image of men and women challenging both the business odds and the laws of gravity, airmail subsidies and other government assistance were more important.[13]

Historians of aviation have chronicled a number of pioneering attempts to launch air transport companies. After halting starts in the 1910s, a survey conducted in 1921 found 88 airline operators in existence, while a similar investigation in 1923 reported 129 companies. Only seventeen enterprises appeared on both lists.[14] This struggle for existence helps explain the scholarly and popular tendency to celebrate indomitable entrepreneurs such as Juan T. Trippe, the founder of Pan American Airways, who developed aviation connections between the United States, Mexico, and South America. More was involved than Trippe's indomitable spirit, however. Historian Nick Kommons observes that "The airplane's potential would not—in fact, could not—be realized by a community of businessmen acting alone. The Federal Government would stand at their side, becoming, in effect, civil aviation's indispensable partner."[15]

This partnership had two formal elements. The first involved assistance to airplane builders. During the 1920s, the National Advisory Committee on Aeronautics (NACA) undertook an extensive research and development effort that produced incremental technical improvements such as engine cowlings. Such innovations translated, in turn, into greater speed, altitude, and operating efficiency for new airplanes into the 1930s. At the same time, direct military purchases of aircraft largely determined the profitability of individual plane manufacturers. The second and perhaps more important aspect of government support of commercial aviation involved less direct encouragements. The most significant, without doubt, were subsidies for airmail service. Experiments in the 1910s eventually culminated in a post office airmail program in 1918 that allowed a generation of war-time pilots to continue flying in often risky service. Service across the continent, initially established in 1919 and 1920, was supported by the development of a system of navigational beacons and emergency landing fields with lights, completed in 1925.[16] Government support for airmail service proved essential to demonstrating the concept of mail deliveries by airplanes.

Government activities also set the parameters for the eventual operation of private aviation firms, especially in passenger service. The crucial uncertainties facing entrepreneurs and a few intrepid investors extended to finances, insurance, and operational rules. At first, state regulators tried to secure basic stability, with Connecticut requiring aviation licensing and registration in 1911. Massachusetts followed suit two years later, and by 1926, five other states had introduced regulations, all quite dissimilar. Many observers, such as Commerce Secretary Herbert Hoover, assumed that the direct subsidies from the federal government were needed. Aviation, Hoover reported, was "the only industry that favors having itself regulated by Government."[17] Hoover, in fact, again led efforts to develop a viable commercial

FIGURE 7. The railroad view of airline subsidies from the federal government can be seen in this cartoon from *Railway Age* (1932). Source: *Railway Age* 93 (December 3, 1932): 822. Used with permission.

aviation sector. He contended that, given government assistance to water transport, federal agencies had an equal responsibility to aviation. "We can no more expect the individual aviator or the individual shipping company to provide [basic services such as lights and channels] on the sea."[18]

At first even Hoover could not find a way to configure a federal policy for aviation. From 1918 through 1924, members of Congress endlessly debated the matter, at which point President Calvin Coolidge tipped the scales by forming a presidential investigative board. From that committee emerged the Air Mail (or Kelly) Act of 1925, which determined that the federal government would contract with private carriers to carry the mail. By 1926, steady payments for mail delivery had created a stable financial base for the twelve private air carriers that received mail contracts; indeed, up to the end of the twentieth century, the successors of these first carriers (American, Delta, Northwest, United, etc.) continued to form the core of American aviation.

Government officials also helped create an infrastructure that supported private carriers.[19] A central figure was William P. McCracken, who became the first head of the new Bureau of Aeronautics in the Commerce Department in 1925, where he tackled basic regulations, licenses for pilots, and certification of mechanics, planes, and engines. He also expanded the post office's system for marking air routes with rotating beacons and soon added radio as well. By 1933, one historian noted, "A typical 1,000 mile segment of airway had 30 intermediate fields, 60 electric light beacons, 230 gas beacons, 5 radio stations, 5 radio range beacons, and a number of strategically placed radio marker beacons." About all the bureau could not do was build airports, which remained a municipal activity.[20] Still, this government-built structure turned independent barnstormers into regular paid employees flying prescribed paths for private delivery services.

As president, Herbert Hoover and his administration continued to develop other forms of assistance to the young industry. For example, the leaders of the Commerce Department's Bureau of Aeronautics worked to replace inconsistent state regulations with uniform federal rules.[21] An even more important aspect of government efforts to structure aviation began when Postmaster General Walter Folger Brown attempted to use airmail contracts to stabilize private commercial aviation. The post office had played a consistently supportive role in developing airmail, but Brown, an Ohio lawyer prominent in Republican politics, carried that support to new heights. He concluded that open bidding for mail contracts would undermine efforts to expand and develop a rational commercial air network. He persuaded Congress to amend the existing airmail legislation (the McNary -Watres Act of 1930) to set payments to airmail carriers by the size of the plane, not the weight carried, a move that favored larger, more stable carriers. Brown then manipulated the renewal of contracts in May and June 1930 by ruling that many new routes were extensions of older contracts, a decision that allowed him to assign, rather than bid, contracts for these extensions. He achieved his goal of stability for contract holders, as only ten firms received contracts and four airlines (Eastern, TWA, United, and American) carried 89 percent of the mail.[22] In other words, Brown had moved beyond the use of federal resources to support mail delivery by air to a program of using mail contracts to subsidize private commercial carriers struggling to develop passenger and freight service. Because of Brown's activities, the structure of the early aviation industry was essentially a creature of the state.

Between 1930 and 1932, the air system doubled in mileage with the addition of 5,700 miles of transcontinental routes and 8,900 miles in extensions. Meanwhile, passenger miles flown increased from 84 million in 1930 to 127 million in 1932 despite the Depression, while the number of passengers carried rose from 160,000 in 1929 to 474,000. The introduction of new aircraft contributed to this rapid growth. The Boeing 247 and Douglas DC-2 adopted aluminum stressed skin construction, single cantilever wings, retractable landing gears, variable pitch propellers, and NACA cowlings that reduced wind resistance over engines.[23] While faster and more efficient, the greater cost of these planes posed financial demands on early aviation managers that explained Brown's desire for stable, controlled growth in the industry.

Members of Congress, however, expressed concern about the growing subsidy to air carriers—almost $14 million in 1932. Shortly after the inauguration of President Franklin D. Roosevelt, new postmaster general James A. Farley accused his predecessor of manipulating airmail contracts. The charge set off a protracted investigation by Senator Hugo L. Black. When Black's hearings in 1934 detailed Brown's activities, the public outcry caused Roosevelt to cancel the airmail contracts. Assured by his generals that army pilots could handle the job, in February 1934 Roosevelt ordered the army to deliver the mail until airline executives could submit new bids. War Department officials had vastly underestimated the magnitude of the task, however, and army pilots, who flew only 11,000 miles of the 27,000-mile system, suffered several highly publicized fatal crashes. In April, post office officials finally opened new bids and quickly returned airmail service to private carriers. Just as Brown had feared in 1930, most air carriers struggled to break even on the lower bids they had submitted in order to maintain control of contracts. More important, the president launched a review of aviation policy in 1934, from which eventually emerged new federal aviation legislation.[24] Thus while Postmaster General Brown was discredited, the efforts of the executive branch and the Congress to structure the commercial aviation industry had not ended. From their earliest days, private civil aviation firms were and remained inextricably linked to public policy decisions, if not actually dependent upon the government.

Federal and state officials also promoted development of a highway system for motorists and truckers. The resulting highway/motor vehicle system became the most serious challenge to the railroads during the interwar period as motor vehicles took more business from railroads faster than any other form of transportation. As early as 1911, a survey by the Union Pacific Railroad found declines in their short-haul freight and passenger business. By 1916, automobiles already accounted for 54 billion passenger miles, surpassing the railroads, which delivered only 35 billion.[25] Central to these developments was another government program, the federal-aid highway system.

As had been true with waterways, government funding of roads was not new, but during the nineteenth century federal support had disappeared as canals and then railroads provided long-distance transportation. Popular fascination with the bicycle in the 1880s convinced Congress to establish the Office of Road Inquiry in the Agriculture Department in 1893. This

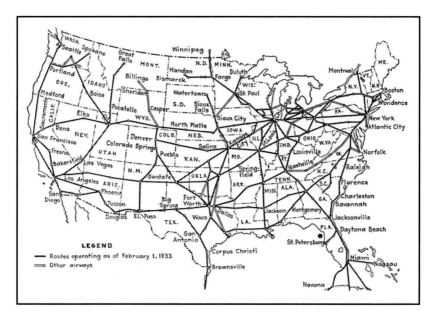

FIGURE 8. This map indicates the extent of commercial aviation routes used for airmail in 1933. Source: Sidney L. Miller, *Inland Transportation: Principles and Policies* (New York: McGraw-Hill Book Company, 1933), 703.

office, renamed the Bureau of Public Roads (BPR) in 1918, became the leading source of technical information and guidance on all matters related to highway policy and construction. In 1916, technical leaders of the BPR helped persuade Congress to inaugurate the federal-aid highway program, with federal and state officials sharing authority and funding responsibility. Engineers working in state highway departments planned, constructed, and then maintained roads used for mail delivery outside of cities and towns, while federal engineers certified the competence of all state highway departments and inspected and approved all plans. Costs initially were split 50/50, with the federal share capped at $10,000 per mile.[26] In practice, federal engineers dominated both policy and technical discussions with their state counterparts, thanks to superior expertise. Federal officials, however, carefully instilled a sense of "partnership" with state officials, employing a cooperative style that slowly built up not only a national road system but also produced competent state road-building agencies. Even so, the public's acceptance of the claim of federal highway engineers to be apolitical experts enabled them to act as arbiters of the nation's technical, administrative, financial, and legislative highway policies from the early 1900s into the 1960s. Nowhere in the realm of transportation was expertise so respected and such a powerful political tool.[27]

After 1921, the initial federal emphasis upon roads for rural mail delivery gave way to attention to a limited system comprising 7 percent of each state's total mileage. These most important roads generally connected cities and towns and constituted the first national highway system, which grew from 169,000 miles in 1921 to 194,000 miles in 1930. Both the railroad and aviation systems had grown in this way, initially focusing on local links before developing national systems. The most obvious outcome of the federal-aid highway program was the construction of more miles of surfaced roads for motorists, including the early pioneers of commercial trucking businesses. Once again, federal policy supported the development of a new form of transportation.[28]

The federal-aid highway program provided only the core funding for this work. During the 1920s, federal appropriations for highways accounted for only $839 million of total construction expenditures of $7.9 billion. Finding this vast sum challenged many local and state officials, who resorted to a variety of mechanisms (bonds, labor taxes, registration fees, property taxes) until financial salvation came from the gasoline tax. Oregon introduced the first gasoline levy in 1919, and by 1936, every state collected what historian John C. Burnham labeled the only popular tax in American history. In other words, during the first three decades of the twentieth century, road construction had become a central activity of government at every level. Indeed, roads had assumed such priority within the government that the Depression-era relief programs of Presidents Hoover and Roosevelt emphasized road construction. Harold Ickes, who directed work relief expenditures through the Public Works Administration, observed that "Dollar for dollar, more money was spent for direct labor in road building than in any other kind of work."[29] Whether at the federal or state levels, moreover, highway policy developed with a single-minded blindness to all but the users of roads.[30]

Why was the motor vehicle favored in this way? A crucial reason was the early ability of carmakers to persuade consumers that the cars they drove conveyed social status and personal identity. Equally important, government officials and many ordinary Americans perceived motor vehicles as inherently democratic. The ability of motorists to go where they wanted when they wanted has symbolized American freedom of choice—a very positive image compared to the public reputation of railroads. Like streetcars, railroads carried significant political and moral baggage of corruption and abuse, even as they appeared to be old, dirty, inconvenient, uncomfortable, and slow. Officials at every level of government found it easy and popular to justify public policy choices that fostered highways and enabled motor vehicle transportation. In this basic fashion, policy decisions effectively decoupled highways, waterways, and aviation from railroads, erasing the prospect of developing an integrated vision of transportation.[31]

Motor vehicle competition with the railroads rapidly unfolded against this backdrop of public and policy support. As noted above, railroad movement of passengers first felt the effect of cars, and earlier than many might suppose. Between 1921 and 1930, automobiles decimated railroad passenger traffic by delivering 80 to 90 percent of all intercity passenger miles. The decline in rail travel amounted to 20 billion passenger miles, with individual railroads reporting enormous changes. The Cotton Belt Railway delivered only 29 million passenger miles in 1929, compared to 137 million passenger miles in 1920, while executives at the Missouri Pacific watched passenger revenue decline from $21 million in 1920 to $10 million in 1930. During the interwar period, trains still carried most people on long trips, but even for this purpose, automobiles challenged train service.[32] Underwritten by governmental spending on highways, travel preferences were changing, launching railroad passenger service on a long, painful, and slow downward spiral. As passenger miles contracted, railroad executives began asking state and federal regulators for permission to abandon passenger service on many lines that had long sustained communities and businesses.[33]

Meanwhile, truck drivers and bus operators joined motorists as factors in this changing American transportation picture. In 1920, few transportation experts believed that trucks posed a competitive threat to the long-haul freight service of railroads; indeed from 1921–1930 the ton-miles of freight moved by rail increased 23 percent. As railroad historian Herbert H. Harwood commented, "Nobody thought much about intercity trucking."[34] If observers considered motor trucks at all, it was as an auxiliary to railroads, since they offered the crucial advantage of door-to-door delivery that could ease congestion at busy railroad terminals. Early truck operators, however, perceived a business opportunity in local delivery services, often using modified automobiles. In Louisville in 1914, for example, Henry C. Kelting removed the seats from a Ford so he could haul light freight. After going bankrupt in the postwar depression, Kelting's second business venture prospered during the 1920s as small manufacturers found trucks cut delivery times from four days to one. Similarly, John Ernsthausen of Norwalk, Ohio, modified a 1909 Overland to haul eggs. By 1921, his produce-hauling operation included a regular run to Cleveland; three years later, his Norwalk Truck Line used three vehicles for general freight hauling.[35] Years later, the retelling of these early narratives of individual initiative in the face of giant railroads and poor highways served as a staple element in trucker politics.

Farmers acted first when these early truckers provided the opportunity to move produce, milk, and livestock from farm to town; furniture

TABLE 1. American Bus Usage

Year	Electric Railways	Steam Railways	Motor Carriers	School Buses	Interstate Carriers
1922	355				
1923	1,200				
1924	2,915				
1925	5,150	375	24,634	27,000	659
1926	7,284	522	26,878	32,800	2,468
1927	8,492	994	27,106	35,900	3,012
1928	10,062	1,256	28,332	40,875	3,667
1929	11,256	1,454	29,940	45,067	4,269
1930	11,827	1,759	31,064	48,775	4,543
1931	12,050	1,500	31,850	51,500	5,558
1932	11,541	1,246	32,123	59,000	na
1933	11,000	720	33,280	60,300	na
1934	11,600	1,410	29,990	64,130	na
1935	12,600	1,750	30,650	71,850	na
1936	12,850	1,750	34,400	73,900	na
1937	13,700	1,800	36,000	78,100	na
1938	18,000	1,800	29,400	81,100	na
1939	18,000	1,700	29,249	85,700	na
1940	18,000	1,775	30,525	87,300	na

Source: "Salient Facts and Figures on the Transportation Industry," *Bus Transportation* 6 (February 1927): 62, 64; "Expansion Continues at Steady Rate," *Bus Transportation* 9 (February 1930): 84-87; "Basic Facts about the Bus Industry," *Bus Transportation* 11 (February 1932): 54, 60; "Ibid.," 14 (February 1935): 40; "Bus Output Spills Over the Top," *Bus Transportation* 11 (January 1938): 52-53; Carl W. Stocks, "How Big Is the Bus Industry?" *Bus Transportation* 18 (January 1939): 49-50; Carl W. Stocks, "The Size and Growth of the Bus Industry," *Bus Transportation* 20 (January 1941): 48-49.

manufacturers also adopted truck shipments early on. Truck owners next focused on the most valuable freight carried by the railroads, less-than-car-load lots (LCL). Railroads charged a premium to move freight that did not fill a boxcar, in part because of the cost of picking up, loading, carrying, transshipping, and then delivering such freight through often crowded urban freight terminals. Trucks bypassed much of the confusion by picking up and delivering directly to front doors, often with little transshipping. By 1931, their greater speed and convenience, and their lower prices, allowed truckers to move 90 percent of LCL freight shipped less than 50 miles, 75 percent of the LCL shipments of 50–100 miles, and about half of the shipments within a radius of 100–150 miles. Longer truck hauls emerged more slowly as the highway system improved, often spurred by truck owner-operators who took advantage of the low barriers to entry—all they needed was their truck. By the late 1920s, the resulting cutthroat competition from so-called gypsy truckers who did not post regular rates made trucking a disorderly enterprise. Yet truckers aggressively resisted any hint of regulation as they began to take business away from railroads.[36]

Motor bus transportation developed less chaotically, following two different business strategies, that of providing either local urban or intercity service.[37] Unlike some truckers, bus owners could not succeed with a single vehicle. And fleets of buses required maintenance garages and terminals with ticket booths, waiting rooms, and in many instances, restaurants. In turn, starting as early as the mid-1920s, these capital-intensive services encouraged the steady consolidation of the industry. Intercity bus operators, in particular, coalesced into regional enterprises. In 1923, only five firms had fleets with as many as one hundred buses, but in 1925 there were twenty-one fleets of this size. Only a year later twenty-nine fleets of one hundred buses were in service, while there were forty-one large fleets by 1928. (See table 1.)

Two factors shaped this rapid growth of larger enterprises. First, railroad executives played a part in the emerging regional configuration of intercity bus service. As early as 1922, operators of a few electric interurban railways experimented with motor vehicles, and by December 1923, 121 electric railways operated 1,000 buses; by 1924, 204 interurban lines owned 2,915 buses.[38] Executives of mainline steam railroads exhibited more caution, but a few large rail carriers (notably the Great Northern, Pennsylvania, Union Pacific, and Southern Pacific railroads) eventually launched motor bus subsidiaries. The number of railroad-operated bus lines rose from ten in 1925 to seventy-eight in 1929.[39] The second factor in bus consolidation was the introduction of improved vehicles that allowed buses to carry thirty persons at highway speeds. Soon, streamlined bodies, rear-mounted engines, and luggage storage under elevated seats offered quieter and more comfortable rides. In 1929, Pickwick Stages, a large California bus operator, even introduced a sleeper bus for overnight runs.[40]

By the late 1920s, executives at such large regional networks developed grander plans. The managers of Pickwick Stages, for example, contemplated a national bus system built off their Pacific coast backbone, but the large midwest carrier, Northlands Transportation Co., provided the base from which Greyhound Bus Lines emerged in 1929. Determined to offer national service, managers at Greyhound acquired West Coast bus lines Pickwick Stages and Pioneer Yelloway, as well as bus subsidiaries from the Southern Pacific, Great Northern, and Pennsylvania Railroads (more about this below). Structured as a holding company similar to the Van Sweringen railroad empire, Greyhound loosely controlled a web of regional subsidiaries, meaning that long-distance bus activities were firmly in the hands of large corporate enterprises. Many independent bus operators remained in business, but Greyhound dominated the long-haul industry as its managers continued to acquire rail-owned bus subsidiaries through the 1930s. Indeed,

Greyhound was so strong that in 1936 the ICC encouraged the formation of a competitor—National Trailways.[41] As one observer commented in 1928, "Long-distance travel by bus is the transportation demand of the hour." The favorable public response to buses showed in the 1934 Hollywood film *It Happened One Night*, where a long-distance bus figured prominently in the romance between Clark Gable and Claudette Colbert.

Bus operators differed noticeably from early truckers in their acceptance of government review of prices and operating conditions. Generally, executives of bus firms such as Pickwick Stages embraced state regulation of rates and safety requirements, which spread quickly. In 1922, nineteen states had enacted regulatory legislation; by 1929, every state but Delaware regulated commercial buses.[42] The safety issues associated with carrying people instead of freight help explain this outcome, although another pivotal factor was the desire of operators and the public for order and regularity in passenger fares. A final reason bus regulation found favor was the desire of early providers of transportation services for protection from latecomers. Most state regulators assumed that intercity bus companies were natural monopolies, so that regulatory programs rested on the possession of certificates of convenience and necessity to prevent development of duplicate services. Managers of both steam railroads and electric interurban railways urged state regulators to apply this rule to motor buses, and public utility commissions, including the first such body established in Pennsylvania in 1914, initially considered the impact of bus service on existing railroad lines in their decisions. By the mid-1920s, however, many state commissions proved less willing to preserve railroad monopolies and it became easier to win approval for bus routes that paralleled railroad lines. Under the guise of regulatory protection for buses, state agencies helped shape the motor bus industry.[43]

Actions *not* taken in the federal arena also structured motor vehicle transportation. Significantly, neither buses nor trucks faced federal oversight. One historian characterizes the Interstate Commerce Commission's response to the rapid growth of truck and bus operators after World War I as one of "indifference."[44] In 1926, the U.S. Supreme Court ruled that state regulation of bus companies in interstate commerce was unconstitutional, signaling the beginning of greater federal attention. Importantly, most interstate bus operators favored regulation as a way to limit "predatory" competitors who resorted to rate-cutting and low service standards. Even so, debate, not action, marked early efforts.[45] In 1926, Senator Albert Cummins of Iowa (coauthor of the Transportation Act of 1920) introduced the first bill to regulate commercial motor vehicles operating as common carriers, but a more important event that year was the decision of ICC to investigate motor transport. Based on hearings in thirteen cities, ICC commissioners

Courtesy of Chicago Tribune

There Seems to Be Something in What He Says

FIGURE 9. A continuing complaint of railroad managers was the unfair sub-
sidies received by commercial motor vehicles, as seen in this cartoon from the
Chicago Tribune (1932). Source: *Railway Age* 93 (December 3, 1932): 811.
Used with permission.

urged a limited extension of federal regulation to trucks and buses in service
on posted routes (common carriers), and called for the issuance of certificates of public convenience only after regulators considered the impact of
new service providers on existing transportation operators. The report also
endorsed an idea broached by Cummins's in his 1926 legislation, delegating
authority for regulating interstate motor commerce to the forty-eight state
public utility commissions, with rights of appeal to the ICC. Over the next
several years, members of Congress debated several bills incorporating these
principles, but consensus on federal policy failed to emerge. With truck and
bus operators fearful of a cumbersome regulatory process, during the late
1920s every bill stalled. A second round of ICC studies from 1930–32 did
not alter the situation, and regulation of motor vehicles waited until the
New Deal.[46] Buses and trucks therefore operated under entirely different

SAYS OLD MR. RAILROAD—

"If those little things don't stop running, I'll be ruined." (See Editorial: "DON'T WEEP, THINK.")

FIGURE 10. The competitors of the railroads also had a viewpoint about competition with the railroads, as seen in this cartoon from the *Chicago Herald and Examiner* (1931). Source: *Bus Transportation* 10 (January 1931): 14.

rules and expectations than the railroads. As had been true for water transport and aviation, public policy choices, including the choice not to regulate, facilitated the development of buses and trucking as alternatives unconnected to the railroads.

THE POLITICS OF TRANSPORTATION COORDINATION, 1925–1940

The rapid appearance of alternatives to railroads, especially trucks and buses, confounded the existing transportation policy spelled out in the Transportation Act of 1920. Framers of that legislation, including Senator Cummins and Representative Esch, had assumed that transportation in America meant railroads. Within five years, however, this basic assumption and the policy it supported—tight ICC regulation of all aspects of railroad operations without regulatory attention to operators of buses, trucks, and barges—was mismatched to a much more complex transport situation. After 1925, a handful of railroad officials and transportation experts began calling for a unified transportation policy. Often they advocated *transportation coordination,* a term with more than one meaning. Most proponents agreed on the desirability of allowing operators of railroads, buses, trucks, barges, and even airplanes to cooperate in providing passenger service and cargo deliveries. Some defined the concept of coordination to include uniform federal regulation for all commercial carriers (railroads, motor vehicles, and barges alike) and elimination of federal subsidies to nonrail transport systems. A few academic and transportation economists went further still and envisioned a coordinated transport system in which private carriers operated several types of transportation, such as allowing railroads to operate motor trucks and buses.

Certain federal officials, most notably Joseph Eastman (a long-serving ICC commissioner and later an important figure in New Deal efforts to define transportation policy), played central roles in the attempt to structure American transportation by using some form of these ideas. Ultimately, however, Eastman and other like-minded transportation leaders failed to establish coordination as the foundational concept for transportation policy. The net result was that transportation policy and the American transport system continued to be defined by individual modes—with executives of railroad, truck, bus, barge, and airline firms acting independently with little ability or desire to cooperate.

The concept of coordinated transportation did not come naturally to either American transportation executives or government officials. Then

FIGURE 11. "Coordinated Effort Means Efficient Transportation." This drawing portrays the ideals behind the promotion of the concept of transportation coordination by academic experts and others during the late 1920s and 1930s. Source: *Automotive Industries* 37 (August 2, 1933): 207. Used by permission of the publisher.

again, neither railroad executives nor anyone else anticipated the declining passenger volumes and the loss of short-haul and less-than-carload freight traffic that followed the appearance of automobiles, commercial trucks, and buses after 1920. At first, most railroad managers responded slowly to these profound changes. Many carriers answered with traditional measures such as improvements to facilities, locomotives, and rolling stock. Executives with the Pennsylvania, Great Northern, and Virginian railroads experimented with electric locomotives after 1920, while many carriers and locomotive builders explored diesel-powered switching locomotives.[47] A handful of railroad managers, however, launched experiments with motor vehicles, such as the bus subsidiaries noted above. Decades later, economists described such an approach as intermodal transportation.

Traffic snarls at East Coast rail freight yards during World War I were one factor behind the first attention by transportation managers to coordination. Specifically, the complex transport challenges at the port of New York prompted transportation officials to examine the articulation between ships and railroads, as well as port connections to inland waterways and highways. Such interest in transport efficiency also took the form of a short-lived postwar effort by a few reformers to establish a cabinet-level department of transportation, although few in government showed any enthusiasm for that proposal. Similarly, leaders of the Port of New York Authority determined to prepare a Comprehensive Plan for Transportation in New York Harbor in the early 1920s, but this plan also found few adherents among politicians or transport executives.[48] Another early instance of planning based on transport coordination was the Regional Plan for metropolitan New York, developed during the 1920s with a million-dollar grant from the Russell Sage Foundation. The Regional Plan's transportation section adopted civil engineer William Wilgus's proposal for a concentric network of rail lines, linked by underground narrow-gauge electric railroads discharging freight into combined truck and rail depots. Other elements of the plan included highway belt lines, and major transit and waterways improvements. The onset of the Depression largely ended planning for transportation around the port of New York.[49]

Legal coordination among transportation companies, if not complete integration of different transportation technologies, actually had a lengthy history. The desire to connect modes of transportation during the 1920s motivated such developments as the Cleveland Union Terminal, which the Van Sweringen brothers designed to connect mainline and interurban railroads with local transit. In Detroit and Los Angeles during the 1920s, elected officials developed transportation master plans that linked improved highways and streetcars on the same right-of-way.[50]

In similar fashion, railroad officials had long attempted to cooperate among themselves in areas where antitrust legislation did not apply.[51] Rate bureaus or traffic associations were perhaps the best examples of joint action. Using these voluntary organizations, railroad managers jointly set rates in given geographic areas for all member carriers. These bureaus later assumed much greater importance in the motor trucking industry after the mid-1930s, but the railroads first developed the concept, which required approval of ICC commissioners because of their antitrust implications. The rate-setting process at a bureau began when a carrier announced a proposed change; bureau officials then contacted all other railroads and affected shippers. Such a process worked slowly, but provided an important communication mechanism that forestalled the main concern of many shippers at the turn of the century—secret manipulation of rates. Rate bureaus achieved stable rates, since good information flows removed many of the incentives for rate cuts. Regulators and shippers deemed these benefits important enough to accept the trade-off of slightly higher rates, since the process was not subject to full public scrutiny.[52]

Against this backdrop of interfirm cooperation, several transportation leaders began to judge the prospect of achieving enhanced coordination among railroads, motor vehicles, and other transportation modes desirable rather than far-fetched, despite the predominant American ethos of competition.[53] In 1923, for example, leaders of the U.S. Chamber of Commerce examined the concept of coordination at the instigation of Commerce Secretary Herbert Hoover, who was involved in every aspect of transportation policy during the 1920s. G. D. Ogden, an executive of the Pennsylvania Railroad, later concluded that the concept of "coordinated transport" entered the conversation of transportation executives following publication of the Chamber's report, *The Relation of Highways and Motor Transport to Other Transportation Agencies.* Members of the blue-ribbon committee included vehicle manufacturers and users, general manufacturers, railroad executives, barge operators, and the press, while Emory Johnson, dean of the University of Pennsylvania's Wharton School and another fixture within the transportation policy community, served as technical adviser and likely author of the report. The committee acknowledged the rapid appearance of new transport technologies and advocated coordination instead of wasteful competition, consistent regulation of all forms of transportation, and acceptance of railroad use of motor vehicles to replace trains in certain situations.[54]

Even before the chamber's report, however, a few railroad executives had begun to experiment with motor vehicles.[55] These tests took place in urban areas facing special operating problems and terminal congestion. In 1922, for example, executives of the Erie Railway first tested motor trucks for moving freight containers into Manhattan from its New Jersey freight terminals. Several carriers tried motor buses, including the Spokane, Portland, and Seattle, which launched perhaps the first railroad-owned bus service during 1924 on a forty-eight-mile run between Portland and Rainier. The Great Northern followed suit in Minnesota, while the B&O bused passengers from its Jersey City terminal into Manhattan via the newly opened Holland Tunnel. In 1922, executives of the Pennsylvania Railroad designed extended tests to compare the costs and utility of rail and motor vehicle operations. In 1926, they reported that motor vehicles possessed superior flexibility for short hauls of light loads and announced plans to launch a trucking operation. After Governor Gifford Pinchot and members of the Pennsylvania Public Utility Commission challenged the legality of railroad operation of motor vehicles on routes paralleling its tracks, the railroad's executives could only create a motor vehicle subsidiary.[56]

During the mid-1920s, railroad executives moved beyond experimenting with trucks and buses. By December 1925, thirty-one mainline railroads had acquired 379 buses and fifteen operated trucks; by 1929, sixty-two Class I railroads owned more than 1,200 buses and fifty-five had trucks. Reflecting this growing interest, in 1926 rail executives from most of the large carriers formed a Motor Transport organization, the same year that editors of the *Railway Age,* the leading trade journal for the industry, began to publish a regular "Motor Transport Section." As a *Railway Age* editorial noted, "It is important that no obstacle stand in the way of railway operation of motor vehicles."[57] Moreover, other forms of coordination emerged, as the Pennsylvania launched a partnership with the Santa Fe Railroad and Transcontinental Air Transport (TAT) in 1929 to provide combined air-rail service that carried passengers from New York to Los Angeles in forty-eight hours. Intrepid travelers rode the night train from New York's Pennsylvania Station to Columbus, Ohio, where they boarded a plane that flew to Indianapolis, St. Louis, Kansas City, Wichita, and Waynoka, Oklahoma. Here passengers rode the Santa Fe overnight to Clovis, New Mexico, before catching a plane for the final leg into Los Angeles. In 1929, W. W. Atterbury, president of the Pennsylvania, announced, "We are no longer railroads alone; we are transportation companies."[58]

The primary question was whether regulators, legislators, and ordinary shippers and passengers would accept Atterbury's vision of coordination in which transportation firms replaced individual truck, bus, rail, and airline companies. Pinchot's resistance to the Pennsylvania Railroad's bus-and-truck plans in 1926 indicated that those holding traditional antirailroad views opposed such transport organizations. Similarly, congressional debates on railroad regulation, valuation, and rate setting during the 1920s demonstrated that many national political leaders had not altered their view of the railroads as dangerous monopolies. Consequently, efforts to change public policy to reflect that new reality of multiple forms of transportation encountered many obstacles. As early as 1922, editors of *Railway Age* had predicted that, "The professional railroad baiters will probably contest a provision [to allow railroads to operate steamships] just as they would any proposal to allow the railroads to engage in highway transportation on any considerable scale."[59] It mattered little that Emory Johnson and other experts reported that railroads no longer exercised monopoly power. As before, history mattered in the shaping of transportation policy.

Transportation economists, however, continued to promote transportation coordination. In 1930, G. Lloyd Wilson, another Wharton School professor, offered what became the standard definition of transportation coordination. His main point was that "each unit occupies its proper place," as determined by some measure of relative efficiency. Any contest between the use of motor vehicles or railroads, contended Wilson, should be decided by economic performance. Responding to continued concern about the supposedly predatory habits of railroad executives, Wilson claimed regulatory controls could address fears that railroads sought to drive independent bus and truck competitors out of business. Legal restrictions on railroad ownership of new, competing technologies, went the reasoning, would prevent predatory practices.[60]

In the early 1930s, Wilson's suggestion that each transportation technology, such as trucks or railroads, had its proper economic place in the overall transport system found increasing acceptance among transportation observers. Throughout the Depression years, many in and out of government sought improved coordination among business firms, hoping to achieve greater economies and boost employment. Efforts of transportation officials and politicians comprised another part of that interest in fostering coordination. Thus Samuel Dunn, editor of *Railway Age*, asked, "If we are to have a co-ordinated system of transportation . . . are the railways or other companies, or both, to operate carriers by highway and waterway?" Dunn argued that railroads needed to enjoy the same unrestricted choices available to companies engaged in water and highway transportation.[61] Silas H. Strawn, chairman of the large department store and mail-order chain Montgomery Ward, agreed, as did Sidney Miller, one of many academic experts who endorsed the concept of coordination. Miller added that cost calculations should include not just operating expenses, but social considerations as well. The challenge before regulatory bodies, he argued, was "to devise an appropriate system of transportation to which each agency contributes in an appropriate and prescribed manner."[62]

Others joined the growing chorus seeking a coordinated approach to transportation regulation. In 1932, the Wharton School's Emory Johnson chaired another U.S. Chamber of Commerce committee whose report urged that rail carriers be allowed to engage in water and highway transport and that all transport be treated the same under federal policy.[63] Also in late 1932, a committee of truck and rail executives convened by the National Highway Users Conference agreed in principle to the concept of coordination. William J. Cunningham, a former railroad manager who joined the Harvard Business School faculty in 1916 as the first James J. Hill Professor of Transportation, shaped the committee's report. Committee members could not agree on regulating freight rates, suggesting that truckers and railroad managers defined coordination in different and self-serving ways.[64]

Perhaps the most important advocate of coordination was Harold Moulton of the Brookings Institution. A graduate of the University of Chicago, Moulton earned a Ph.D. in economics for his dissertation that argued waterways were almost always a product of politics, not rational decision making. In 1929, he repeated that argument in his study of the hydropower and navigation project proposed for the St. Lawrence River. Moulton's most important report on this theme was a review of American transportation launched in 1932.[65] He assembled a committee and shaped the structure and content of a national study, which he presented as driven by the concerns of institutional investors about the financial health of railroads. Moulton persuaded former president Calvin Coolidge to chair the committee, which included as members financier Bernard Baruch, former Democratic presidential nominee Alfred E. Smith, publisher of the *Atlanta Constitution* Clark Howell, and International Harvester president Alexander Legge. Brookings transportation economist Charles L. Dearing assembled the book-length document, which concluded that "the United States has no unified national transportation policy." Moreover, the committee concluded that American transportation agencies worked "at cross purposes," adding, "instead of a unified program of regulation designed to promote a common objective, we have a series of unrelated and often antagonistic policies carried out by a variety of government agencies." The committee's solution sounded very familiar—let those forms of transportation best suited in terms of cost do the job. Their report also pressed for an end to government subsidies and unequal regulation.[66]

By 1933, in the depth of the Depression, the weight of expert opinion favored this approach to the problems facing American transportation, although the actual definition of coordination (intermodal firms vs. common regulation, for example) varied widely. Even ICC commissioners

FIGURE 12. Harold G. Moulton, first president of
the Brookings Institution (1928–1956), was deeply
involved in transportation policy debates during
the 1920s and 1930s as an advocate of the policy of
transportation coordination. Source: The Brookings Institution Archives. Used with permission.

endorsed the basic concept of coordination. In 1930, they had launched a
second study of motor vehicles and federal regulation, conducting hearings
in seventeen cities. Many railroad officials pressed the ICC for specific
authority to utilize motor transport. As an editorial writer for *Railway Age*
summarized the testimony of an executive of the St. Louis Southwestern
Lines in 1930, "The modern railroad must offer a co-ordinated rail, bus, and
truck service." By establishing a bus subsidiary, his line had "stopped a passenger revenue leak so great that revenues threatened to reach the vanishing
point in 1933." This official concluded that rail, bus, and truck service "must
be consolidated as one system."[67] The ICC's attorney-examiner agreed, concluding that "the national transportation machine cannot function with progressive efficiency, part regulated, part unregulated." Railroads no longer
exercised a monopoly in transportation, he argued; indeed, shippers should
remember that they had a stake in maintaining financially healthy rail carriers. Many witnesses considered equal regulatory treatment essential to
achieving this end, but the ICC report concluded that legislation governing
motor vehicles need not stifle new modes of competition. The ICC examiner offered no detailed answers, proposing instead a period of "wide latitude for experiment, trial, and test."[68]

The economic plight of transportation firms of all types in the early 1930s added real urgency to conversations about transportation regulation and policy. As the Depression worsened, railroads faced staggering losses. Equally, trucking executives complained about the unfettered competition from independent truckers—the detested "gypsy" truckers—with a single vehicle who undercut posted prices in order to secure a load. Against this backdrop, the venue for conversations about transportation coordination shifted from academic publications and ICC hearing rooms to the Congress and, increasingly, to the office of the president. For example, members of Congress convened hearings on railroad holding companies, a tempting arena for politicians seeking to explain to constituents the causes of the deepening depression.[69] During the early 1930s, congressional distrust of the railroads still foreclosed consideration of genuine changes in regulatory policy. Those members interested in transportation were preoccupied by the framework and features of the Transportation Act of 1920, as seen by the prolonged debates over the repeal of the recapture clause (the section setting the maximum profit a railroad could earn) and the seemingly endless valuation project. Not even the economic disaster facing the railroads, including widespread bankruptcies, could free Congress from the grip of railroad history.

Less bound by history, President Hoover carved out a greater role for the executive branch in shaping transportation policy. He continued a pattern he had begun as commerce secretary for Presidents Harding and Coolidge, involving presidents in shaping the structure of American transportation. The dire economic straits of transportation firms prompted even greater levels of federal involvement, including direct assistance to rail carriers. In late 1931, Hoover pressed Congress to create the Reconstruction Finance Corporation (RFC) primarily to stabilize railroad finances. In January 1932, the RFC became the lender of last resort for the railroads and other industrial corporations. By November 1934, RFC officials had loaned $512 million.[70] Starting in early 1932, Hoover also supported negotiations between railroad managers and union leaders that reduced wage rates by 10 percent for a year. Although never passive in the face of the Depression, Hoover only modestly extended his style of using voluntary direction from the federal government by embracing RFC loans and negotiated wage reductions.[71]

President Franklin D. Roosevelt further shifted the locus of transportation discussions toward the executive branch and toward coordination. In a campaign speech delivered in Salt Lake City in September 1932, Roosevelt announced that railroads comprised a vital part of "our national economic life," and given the importance of railroad securities to banks, insurance companies, and citizens alike, they could not be allowed to collapse. One source of railroad distress, Roosevelt asserted, was wasteful competition between rail carriers that led to needless duplication of facilities. Individual firms worked at cross-purposes, Roosevelt believed, rather than as parts of a national transport system. As part of a program to "to do what it takes to get things moving," Roosevelt promised to conduct a national transportation survey for the purpose of developing new national policies. The RFC loans then available were only a stopgap, he noted, so Roosevelt mentioned several possible actions. He proposed a government promise to stand behind railroad securities, ICC regulation of competing motor carriers, simplification of the process for abandoning railroad mileage, consolidations of rail systems, regulation of railroad holding companies, and "a freer hand for railroad management and labor."[72]

In the fall of 1932, "getting things moving" was a political metaphor that applied to the entire nation and conjured up images of restored prosperity. Rail executives reacted positively to Roosevelt's speech, but action came more slowly. During the remainder of the campaign, candidate Roosevelt never returned to the subject of transportation and offered no additional ideas for revising the regulatory regime. After his election, he held private conversations with ICC commissioner Joseph Eastman and several railroad executives. Roosevelt apparently promoted the idea of moving the ICC into the Commerce Department—a pet idea he returned to several times during the 1930s—until Eastman vigorously defended the independence of the commission. In the end, Eastman and W. M. W. Splawn, counsel for the House committee on interstate and foreign commerce and after 1934 an ICC commissioner, drafted a bill that Congress passed quickly in May 1933.[73]

The Emergency Railroad Transportation Act was a modest proposal. It could hardly have been otherwise. Conversations with railroad labor leaders such as Donald Richberg, counsel for the Railway Labor Executives Association, and railroad presidents Carl Gray (Union Pacific), J. J. Pelley (New Haven), and F. R. Williamson (New York Central), had highlighted for the president the deeply rooted labor-management antagonism that complicated the task of proposing any measure designed to restore profitability to the transportation industries. The emergency bill overturned a couple of minor elements of the Transportation Act of 1920, authorized the ICC to regulate railroad holding companies, and, most importantly, established the Office of the Federal Transportation Coordinator to study the transport situation and propose detailed solutions and reforms. Roosevelt's top officials emphasized that the coordinator was not a dictator who would possess overriding authority; and just as important in winning congressional approval, railroad union leaders had secured a clause prohibiting any actions that cost the jobs of railroad workers.[74] In less than two months in office, Roosevelt

FIGURE 13. Joseph B. Eastman served as a member and leader of the Interstate Commerce Commission from 1919 to 1944. He not only served as Federal Coordinator for Transportation from 1933 to 1936 and as director of the Office for Defense Transportation, but was a leading advocate of the policy of transportation coordination. Source: The Collection of the University Archives, Amherst College. Used with permission.

had moved transportation policy from the domain of Congress to the White House.

In June 1933, FDR appointed Joseph Eastman, until then his informal adviser on rail matters, to the new post of Federal Coordinator of Transportation. An ICC commissioner since 1919, Eastman had been appointed by Woodrow Wilson after a career as a reformer involved in municipal utility regulation in Boston. He was a protégé of Supreme Court Justice Louis Brandeis, and during the 1920s enjoyed a sometimes stormy relationship with railroad executives and fellow ICC commissioners because of his willingness to consider nationalization of the railroads. By 1933, however, the diligent reformer from Boston had won the respect of almost all parties, railroad executives included, and Eastman was the obvious choice for the coordinator's position. Eastman never entered Roosevelt's inner circle of advisers, however, no doubt because of his uncompromising defense of the ICC's independence from the chief executive.[75]

Coordinator Eastman assembled a staff for three regional offices, in the process irritating Postmaster General James Farley by failing to consult leaders of the Democratic Party about appointments. Eastman hired several railroad executives to study the nation's transportation system and identify opportunities for greater efficiency. Lacking authority to reorganize the railroad industry, Eastman instead emphasized his desire to accomplish cooperatively changes already suggested by others. As he phrased it, "[A] more descriptive title for the position might, therefore, be Federal Co-ordinator of Railroads and Doctor of Transportation."[76] Echoing the position of transportation economists such as Sidney Miller, Harold Moulton, and Emory Johnson, Eastman argued that transportation should be conceived as a coordinated system, not as separate technologies embedded in individual industries. "The ideal to be achieved," he wrote, is "a transportation system which will utilize each agency in the field for which it is best fitted and discourage its use where it is uneconomical or inefficient."[77] In particular, Eastman hoped to encourage coordinated rail/truck interactions, especially at rail terminal operations. He added "[T]his work is by no means a mere attempt to bolster up the railroads at the expense of the trucks," but an attempt to develop better transportation. For the same reason, Eastman favored regulation of transportation by a single federal agency as the best way to foster coordination and avoid partisan and competitive struggles between railroads, motor vehicles, and other forms of transport. Like the old Progressive-era reformer that he was, Eastman believed objective cost data, not political considerations, should determine technical choices. The echoes of Harold Moulton's ideas here are not surprising, for the two men were close friends who played squash and occasionally went bird watching together.[78]

To coordinate an efficient transportation system based on real cost data, Eastman relied heavily on surveys distributed to shippers, travelers, the public, and transportation executives, earning the nickname "Questionnaire Joe." For instance, Eastman's staff distributed a Merchandise Survey asking about one hundred shippers and receivers of freight about less-than-carload freight services and express agencies. A freight survey went to railroad officials, while additional surveys gathered data on railroad passengers and marketing. Later surveys examined railroad research activities and explored the possibility of pooling freight. Yet another questionnaire asked state regulatory commissioners what they were doing about motor transport regulation, the problems they faced, and the need for federal regulation. Still others asked for views on the pivotal issue of governmental subsidies for transport, and on the regulation of highway transport. Altogether, from 1933 through 1936, the coordinator's staff conducted some five thousand studies.[79]

Eastman's staff made slower progress turning the mountain of data into policy recommendations. In his first annual report to Congress in January 1934, Eastman asked for and received a second year to prepare recommendations. Eastman had learned that special protection granted railroad workers in the 1933 emergency legislation created a thorny obstacle, for efficiency improvements almost by definition affected the jobs of railroad workers. Even though as an ICC commissioner he had usually supported labor's views on many issues (such as company unions), Eastman now expressed occasional frustration at the active resistance to his office by union leaders. He hoped to encourage rail managers to try new approaches, but union leaders blocked most technical changes. In fact, railway labor leaders sought unsuccessfully to place railroads under the jurisdiction of the National Recovery Administration and noisily advocated a six-hour workday with no wage cut. Eastman supported unions where possible, but in one private letter he contended that "Labor executives are drunk with power!" More damaging to Eastman's relations with labor leaders were his public comments that shorter workweeks were the "counsel of despair."[80]

By the spring of 1934, Eastman had concluded that transportation problems grew from "a policy of encouraging an oversupply of transportation service." Shippers might save money, but the resulting social costs were high. Repeating a position economists had first adopted in the late 1910s, Eastman wrote, "Unregulated competition may be quite as much of a public evil as unregulated monopoly." He continued to endorse coordination and to urge uniform regulation by the ICC of all forms of transport. In May 1934, he told members of the National Association of Mutual Savings Banks that it was time to abandon wasteful competition between railroads, trucks, and barges. Coordinating the efforts of all forms of transportation would "make the national railroad system more efficient and economical."[81]

Historian William R. Childs observes that "numerous political causes prevented serious consideration" of Eastman's plans during 1934, including resistance from railroad labor leaders and growing impatience among railroad executives for regulation of commercial motor vehicles. Representative Sam Rayburn attempted to use hearings on a motor vehicle regulation bill to set the stage for Eastman's legislation, but leaders of the American Trucking Associations attacked the bill as a trick to put truckers out of business. Roosevelt renewed the coordinator's appointment a second time, but Eastman offered no plans during the remainder of 1934. President Roosevelt spoke little about transportation policy, and his occasional offhand remarks on the possibility of nationalizing the railroads offered no help. Compared to Hoover's active intervention Roosevelt exhibited much less interest in transportation, apparently content to allow Eastman time to prepare ideas for improving transportation.[82]

Eastman was, in fact, diligently building support for transportation coordination plans that included the regulation of commercial motor vehicles and water transportation by the ICC. In November 1934, a writer in *Railway Age* explained, "Mr. Eastman has added to and perfected his legislative program and in numerous public addresses he had done much to pave the way for a sympathetic consideration of the program for co-ordinated regulation of all forms of transportation."[83] Finally, in his 1935 state of the union address, Roosevelt mentioned permanent transportation regulation, and Eastman sent the president nine bills that proposed extensive alterations in the regulation and organization of American transportation. The most important measures extended federal regulation to commercial motor vehicles and water transportation, reorganized the ICC (an issue that the commissioners themselves had grappled with since the 1920 legislation), established a permanent transportation coordinator, provided benefits to employees affected by changes in the railroads, and altered federal transportation subsidies. Eastman rejected the idea of creating a Department of Transportation, falling back on an old Progressive reformers' argument. "Transportation is essentially a technical subject and should be dealt with accordingly. It is vital that it be kept out of politics, so far as possible."[84]

In February 1935, the president transmitted Eastman's legislative program to Congress, where it quickly ran into opposition. Individual representatives and senators singled out many items for criticism, including a clause allowing railroads to charge less for long hauls than for short trips (the old long haul/short haul bugaboo). In mid-April 1935, members of the Senate interstate commerce committee voted to send to the entire Senate Eastman's proposal to regulate commercial motor vehicle rates and routes, but only after Eastman and others persuaded Senator Burton K. Wheeler that the bill was not a railroad plot to weaken motor competitors. As before, the deep-seated distrust of railroads had snagged plans for this pivotal feature of transportation coordination. In response, Eastman had scaled back his vision of coordination from the original goal of genuine intermodal cooperation. Instead, he accepted language that directed ICC regulators to "recognize and preserve the inherent advantages of each" mode of transportation. With this clause in place, motor vehicle regulation passed the Senate easily, but the bill took longer to work its way through the House. Not until August 9, 1935, could President Roosevelt sign into law the Motor Carrier Act of 1935.

Commentators at the time gave Eastman substantial credit for the bill's passage, although historian Childs concludes that the American Trucking Associations' acceptance of regulation and significant role in working for the bill was as important.[85] The principle of coordination appeared most prominently in the decision to place regulatory authority over both railroads and commercial motor vehicles in the hands of ICC commissioners. Even so, inclusion of the clause directing the ICC to protect different forms of transportation reflected the lobbying efforts of the truckers, as well as the practical limits of the principle of transportation coordination.

If the Motor Carrier Act had fallen short of Eastman's original goals, he still hoped that passage of the remaining bills would advance the purpose of creating a coordinated transportation system. For that reason, Eastman urged Congress to consider the most important bills as a package. In the end, however, members of Congress passed only one other proposal drafted by Eastman—a bill on railroad reorganization that simplified cumbersome railroad receiverships. The president himself may have damaged prospects for the other bills by not sending a message of support to Congress until five months after his state of the union address. Without Roosevelt's specific arguments about the merits of the bills, supporters of alternatives to Eastman's plans and vision took advantage of the void in the debate. At Senate committee hearings on water transportation, for example, supporters of inland waterways offered testimony full of traditional antirailroad vitriol. And Eastman's ICC colleagues opposed the coordinator's plan to reorganize the commission. In the end, Eastman failed to overcome the opposition to his package of legislation. By the mid-1930s, not even a modest level of presidential leadership could bring harmony to the realm of transportation.[86]

Coordinator Eastman sought additional time to continue working for the package of bills, but President Roosevelt denied the opportunity to him. By mid-1935, support for Eastman had waned among railroad executives and railroad labor leaders alike. The following year, Roosevelt chose not to reappoint Eastman as Federal Coordinator for Transportation, allowing him to return to the ICC. The move marked a diminishing commitment by the administration to the guiding principle of coordination. Even though the federal government financed highways and waterways, and already regulated railroads, Roosevelt succumbed to the orthodox conviction that trains, trucks, barges, and airplanes were independent industries rather than interconnected parts of a coordinated and unified transportation system.[87]

THE UNRAVELING OF TRANSPORTATION COORDINATION

No sooner had President Roosevelt endorsed regulation of trucking by the ICC in his 1935 state of the union address than he began to favor independent regulation of airlines. Like many such changes, this shift in Roosevelt's position had its origins in another government committee, this one operating outside Eastman's direct charge.[88] In the wake of the airmail scandal of 1933–34, the president had appointed Clark Howell, editor of the *Atlanta Constitution,* to chair a committee to investigate aviation policy. As had Eastman's staff, members of Howell's aviation committee gathered extensive information, traveled widely in the United States and Europe, and in the end issued a report at almost the same time as Eastman. The aviation report in effect challenged the core principle of Eastman's plans for coordination, for Howell's primary recommendation was to establish an independent Civil Aeronautics Commission to oversee aviation regulation. The aviation committee explicitly rejected assigning such duties to the ICC, claiming the ICC was too busy and too inclined to compare airlines to railroads. Only after airlines rested on a sound financial footing, members of the group asserted, could aviation be integrated into the larger transportation system.[89]

Chairman Howell expressed surprise when Roosevelt initially rejected the aviation report's proposal of an independent regulatory agency. Although he forwarded the report to Congress, the president echoed Eastman's views, adding, "We should avoid the multiplication of separate regulatory agencies in the field of transportation."[90] This stance led the primary Senate booster of aviation, Patrick A. "Pat" McCarran, to introduce a bill assigning aviation regulation to the ICC. At hearings in July 1935, Eastman testified in support, but officials from the Post Office and Commerce Department long responsible for aviation policy opposed the bill. In turn, McCarran amended the committee's version to include a separate aviation commission. The modified bill stalled in committee.

With Roosevelt's cabinet officials in obvious disagreement about the virtues of a single regulatory agency for transportation, administration support for coordination soon faded. An important signal was the president's decision not to fight the mounting opposition to continuing Joseph Eastman as Federal Coordinator of Transportation. In spite of Eastman's efforts on their behalf, reports historian Ellis W. Hawley, railroad managers lost enthusiasm for Eastman and his energetic office when the emergency conditions of 1933 began to ease. Moreover, the formation of the Association of American Railroads in 1934 provided the industry with its own coordinating mechanism, and rail executives increasingly viewed the coordinator's office as an intrusion upon managerial rights. Once union leaders secured job security provisions from the railroads, ironically negotiated by Eastman, they also abandoned support for the coordinator's office. Additionally, Eastman's unwillingness to bend the ICC or his office to the president's will was a final factor in Roosevelt's decision in June 1936 to send Eastman back to the ICC as a regular commissioner. Finally, Hawley determined that Roosevelt's decision reflected the general ambivalence of many Americans to national planning during the New Deal.[91]

Without Eastman, coordination had no champion within the administration, and advocates of separate modes increasingly dominated the policy deliberations. Thus in 1936, the president signed the Merchant Marine Act that created an independent agency to govern coastal and ocean shipping.[92] The real litmus test of Roosevelt's commitment to transportation coordination and regulation by a single agency came in the area of aviation policy. In 1937, congressional debate over aviation regulation and federal support resumed. Members of both houses considered a flurry of proposals that differed mainly in where they located regulatory authority for the young airline companies, with the ICC or in an independent commission. At the outset, the leading congressional figures on transportation, Senator Pat McCarran and Representative Clarence F. Lea, favored a bill originally prepared by Eastman and members of the Air Transport Association and endorsed by the president that would have given the ICC regulatory oversight for aviation. Kenneth D. McKellar, the powerful senator from Tennessee, however, advocated an independent regulatory agency, but debates were inconclusive. With commercial airlines still struggling financially, Roosevelt decided to create an Interdepartmental Committee on Aviation Policy to draft a new administration bill. The committee included assistant secretaries from the U.S. Post Office, the Commerce, State, Treasury, and War Departments, and the ICC.[93] A key figure was the director of the Commerce Department's Bureau of Air Commerce, Fred Fagg, who persuaded the committee to support an independent regulatory agency for aviation. FDR still preferred regulating airlines through the ICC, but according to the author of one account, his son persuaded him to accept the new bill. Another account credited Fagg with persuading Roosevelt to change his mind, while a third has it that the president was simply weary of this issue. It may have helped that the new bill directed the president to appoint not only the members of this Civil Aeronautics Authority, but also the chair, in effect giving the president greater control over the new agency than he had over the ICC, where commissioners elected their own chair. Whatever the precise circumstances, in January 1938 the president called Senator McCarran to the White House for a discussion of an independent regulatory agency for aviation. By May, members of the House and Senate had passed similar bills along that line, and differences were resolved in a conference committee. On June 23, 1938, the president signed the McCarran-Lea Civil Aeronautics Act.[94]

Clearly, the formation of the Civil Aeronautics Authority undermined fundamentally the vision of coordinated transportation supported by Eastman and academic economists such as the Brooking Institution's Harold Moulton. Pat McCarran later noted that his bill rejected coordination on the grounds that an agency devoted solely to aviation would bring "wholesome, progressive regulation" that better served the industry and the nation. Eastman's plan of regulating air from the ICC was undone by the claim that a Civil Aeronautics Authority could develop "a more intimate touch and knowledge of the needs" of aviation.[95]

The passage of the final transportation policy measure of the 1930s—the Transportation Act of 1940—confirmed that lawmakers, regulators, and transportation executives had stepped back from their earlier support for the concept of coordination as the foundation on which to build American transportation policy. Yet in another way, approval of the Transportation Act of 1940 proved to be a significant departure from previous efforts to enact transportation legislation, mainly because of President Roosevelt's extensive involvement in its development. A shift in the locus of authority was underway, one in which the president emerged as an equal to the members of Congress in shaping transportation legislation. Perhaps accidentally, in December 1937 Roosevelt launched the push for major transportation legislation at a press conference. A reporter, prompted by a meeting between Roosevelt and banker Jesse Jones, who chaired the Reconstruction Finance Corporation, asked about problems facing the railroads. Roosevelt at first deflected the query by asserting that the ICC was responsible for railroads, adding that he had no plans to reinstate the coordinator. Then Roosevelt noted that while government ownership was not an option, the railroads could not operate forever under receivership. They were not earning enough to pay for their capitalization, they suffered from unnecessary duplication of facilities, and they confronted "competition for the sake of competition." Where traffic now moved by highway, suggested the president, it made sense to consolidate rail carriers and allow abandonments of unprofitable lines. Federal subsidies to railroads were not the answer, Roosevelt observed; such a development would persuade leaders of every other troubled industry to seek federal assistance.[96]

When the recession of 1937 dragged into the next year, the president could no longer avoid the problems facing the nation's transportation firms, especially the beleaguered railroads. As another sign of his increasing engagement with efforts to structure American transportation, during 1938, President Roosevelt directed members of two different advisory committees to develop proposals for a national transportation policy. In mid-March, Roosevelt assembled the first committee, a blue-ribbon group of distinguished individuals from government and industry, at the White House to discuss the troubled situation of the nation's railroads. The debate, lively at times, extended over the course of three days. Banker Henry Bruere, for example, told committee members that they failed to appreciate the depth of the crisis; he advocated direct federal action, not more studies. Future Supreme Court Justice William O. Douglas, then an attorney at the Securities and Exchange Commission, proposed an $800 million rehabilitation plan, with funds distributed to those railroads by a three-person examining board appointed to insure development of a sound, coordinated transport system.[97]

Following this lengthy discussion, Roosevelt asked three members of the full committee (ICC chairman W. M. Splawn, Eastman, and ICC financial expert Charles Mahafie) to turn the deliberations into a report containing "complete, definite, and factual recommendations for immediate action by Congress in regard to the whole railroad situation, which is critical." Roosevelt gave the three men a week to produce the report, prompting hasty meetings with railway executives and shippers. Splawn reviewed the committee's progress directly with the president. Jesse Jones, who had participated in the initial conference, commented, "There has to be a correction of the competitive situation—not only between railroads, but between all transport agencies." Private industry, Jones had concluded, could not make the necessary adjustments on its own. The so-called Splawn committee's sixty-page report adopted a similar position. Members proposed immediate relief for the railroads, perhaps in the form of a $300 million loan for railroad equipment purchases. They recommended ending government discounts for shipping on railroads—so-called land-grant rates—and proposed reducing railroad wages, as in 1932. For the long term, the committee proposed the appointment of a Federal Transportation Authority, whose three members could recommend steps aimed at eliminating wasteful competition, including consolidation. The committee also recommended that Congress finally repeal the 1920 requirement that the ICC shape railroad consolidations, and instead allow the ICC to approve any consolidation deemed to be in the public interest. Finally, Splawn's committee called for investigations of the relative economy of trucks, buses, and water carriers in order to restrict destructive competition and to learn the extent of government subsidies. The report proposed additional studies to focus on railroad financial abuses. All told, the committee's prescriptions resembled ideas that Eastman had started to develop in 1933, so much so that some observers judged the proposed three-person board a substitute for the abandoned coordinator's office. Eastman's legacy of support for coordination was most apparent in the suggestion concerning "[t]he desirability of subjecting all important forms of transportation to equal and impartial regulation by a single agency of the government." On April 11, Roosevelt sent the report and a draft bill to Congress.[98]

By April 1938, however, the administration's commitment to this core element in transportation coordination—regulation within one agency—was wavering. First, members of Congress and the administration were already shaping civil aeronautics legislation resting upon independent regulation. Equally, other parties to the transportation debates now voiced objections to transportation policy resting on coordination—or at least to its implementation. George Harrison, a railway union leader, contended that railroad employees wanted nothing more to do with coordinators, although they would not oppose a three-person board with a limited mandate. Harrison favored legislation to guarantee the operating income of rail carriers. Expressing disappointment in what he called overly cautious measures, Secretary of the Treasury Henry Morgenthau Jr. advocated formation of a federal department of transportation with immediate authority to order coordination.

President Roosevelt himself proceeded indecisively. In mid-April, editors of *Railway Age* complained that, "The President [had] dumped the railroad problem and his gleaning thereon into the lap of Congress with a 'do-with-these-as-thou-will' message." Indeed, Roosevelt offered guidance to Congress on only three issues—he opposed government ownership; rejected direct subsidies to the railroads; and claimed (dubiously) that the ICC's "purely" executive powers were unconstitutional. This last point renewed FDR's long-standing effort to reign in independent agencies, but in June 1938 Congress adjourned without acting on the president's report.[99]

Beginning later that year, Roosevelt undertook a more direct role in preparing transportation legislation. In September 1938, he convened a second, smaller advisory committee labeled the Committee of Six to distinguish this group from the earlier Splawn committee. Composed of three railroad executives and three railway labor leaders, members of the Committee of Six worked in surprising harmony. In December, all six men unanimously presented recommendations to the president that reflected a much narrower view of the transportation problem. Joseph Eastman later observed that the Committee of Six had emphasized competitive conditions facing the railroads, while the Splawn committee had considered the internal efficiency of all carriers. The two reports had many similarities, including calls for ICC regulation of waterway transportation, repeal of the 1920 consolidation clause, an end to land-grant freight rates, and several ideas about short-term aid to rail carriers. The Committee of Six report differed primarily in asking for a statement of national transportation policy and a clause giving the ICC final authority over the rates charged by all providers of interstate transportation.[100] Like many federal transportation reports before and for decades to come, the Committee of Six document sought improvements in the financial conditions of the nation's rail carriers. Intriguingly, committee members embraced a core idea of supporters of transportation coordination who hoped to strengthen the railroads—centralize regulatory authority over all types of transportation firms in one agency.

Because of the president's continued involvement, the Committee of Six report provided the initial basis for congressional action on transportation in 1939.[101] In the Senate, Burton Wheeler, who had been so critical of the Van Sweringens earlier in the decade and skeptical of Eastman's plans in 1935, prepared a package of legislation, relying heavily upon the Committee of Six document. In January 1939, members of the House interstate commerce committee held hearings on an Omnibus Transportation Bill that chairperson Clarence Lea assembled by combining elements from the reports submitted by both presidential committees. Senate hearings began after the House committee finished work in April. The usual transportation leaders testified at both hearings, voicing predictable concerns couched in familiar terms. Waterways supporters from midwestern and Great Plains farm states stridently charged that the ICC would never regulate inland water transportation fairly. With equal urgency, railroad executives demanded such regulation. Air transport officials opposed a provision returning authority to set air rates to the ICC and found several senators who agreed. Eastman appeared on behalf of his fellow ICC commissioners, testifying that none of them favored a reorganization of the commission.

For at least fifteen years, such divergent opinion usually had stymied efforts to adjust the nation's transportation policy. Now, however, President Roosevelt's consistent participation made a noticeable difference in the development and passage of legislation. Not only had Senator Wheeler and Representative Lea developed bills using the recommendations of the president's two advisory committees, each also reported that Roosevelt had directly requested and supported their efforts. Once hearings began, the president invited the chairpersons and members of those committees to meet at the White House at least three times during the spring of 1939. These expressions of presidential interest may have helped both houses of Congress pass transportation bills—the Senate in May and the House in July. Members of Congress had amended both measures significantly, yet they retained basic similarities. The rhetoric of transportation coordination seemed to influence the assignment of regulatory authority, for both measures directed the ICC to regulate water transportation. In addition, both bills created three-person study boards to examine various transportation problems. The two measures repealed the old consolidation plan called for by the Transportation Act of 1920, and proposed yet another study of freight rates; both opened with a statement of national transportation policy. The conference committee had many specific details to reconcile, but members of Congress adjourned in late 1939 before completing their work.

When Congress reconvened in January 1940, transportation problems seemed overshadowed by the war in Europe. With Joseph Eastman pressing the conference committee to complete its work, the conferees at first made reasonable progress. Then several typical congressional difficulties delayed final action on the transportation bills. First came the release of a letter from Secretary of Agriculture Henry A.Wallace, Secretary of War Harry Woodring, and Chairman Emory S. Land of the U.S. Maritime Commission, announcing their opposition to ICC regulation of waterways. Unlike the practice adopted in later presidential administrations, Roosevelt's appointees still publicly exercised independent judgment. This situation forced Roosevelt to intervene quickly, and he used a press conference to undo the damage by making clear his support for anointing the ICC as the single transportation regulatory agency. Next a handful of representatives criticized House conference committee members for abandoning several elements of the House's original legislation. Disgruntled members won a vote to recommit the bill to the conference committee, throwing the prospect of passage into question. Finally, a disagreement regarding the operation of freight forwarders (also known as consolidators) threatened to disrupt the bill's progress through Congress. Forwarders served as shipping middlemen, accepting small batches of packages which they consolidated into larger lots for shipment. These agencies made their profit by charging more than the railroads for carload shipments, but less than shippers would have paid the railroads directly at less-than-carload rates. Developing policies that applied to the operations of freight forwarders proved enormously contentious. Carriers and regulators were not always happy about the existence of the forwarders, but many shippers enjoyed these services, which definitely operated at a crack in the ICC rate regulatory structure. Indeed, questions about freight forwarders remained an object of constant and intense lobbying and litigation into the 1970s. Not surprisingly, in 1940, members of Congress could not resolve this complicated issue and adopted instead the temporary expedient of creating another commission to study this issue along with the equally divisive question of the extent and impact of government subsidies for transportation.[102] With these issues set aside, in August Congress passed the Transportation Act of 1940 and Roosevelt signed the bill into law.[103]

This newest transportation legislation contained only one substantial innovation—placement of regulatory control of water transportation under the ICC. ICC commissioners now regulated rail, truck, and water transport, apparently accomplishing one of Eastman's primary aims as coordinator. A number of observers, including members of the Committee of Six, judged the preamble of the act at least as significant as unification of regulation under the ICC. This preamble stated that Congress "declared to be the national transportation policy" that all forms of transportation shall be fairly and impartially regulated "to the end of developing, coordinating, and preserving a national transportation system by water, highway, and rail. . . ." This language also seemed to represent a victory for Eastman and others, including many economists who had long supported transportation coordination. In fact, the Transportation Act of 1940 ended attempts for five decades to define coordination as one of the aims of American transportation regulation.

When the rhetoric is stripped away, this legislation offered only lip-service to the concept of transportation coordination. Thus included in the bill was language similar to that in the Motor Carrier Act of 1935, which required ICC regulators to "recognize and preserve the inherent advantages of each" form of transportation. That this mandate was repeated in 1940 in regard to water carriers affirmed an approach to regulation incompatible with genuine coordination, by which the actions of the commissioners, not economic efficiency or some other form of expert judgment, decided the fate of each form of transportation. Thus after 1935, ICC officials developed a Motor Carrier Bureau that soon became a largely autonomous office regulating trucking without regard for the railroads or any other form of transportation. After 1940, ICC regulation of water transportation unfolded in a similar fashion. In other words, regulators and legislators, as well as truckers, barge operators, and airline executives, still envisioned the technology they operated as defining separate industries, or modes. The idea that these technologies formed potentially complementary forms of transportation gave way to the weight of railroad history, more traditional images of competition, and the weight and momentum of business and political leaders' increasing interest in fostering development of independent (as opposed to integrated) transportation industries.

Ironically, however, this style of regulation defined by separate modes did not operate reciprocally for the railroads. ICC staffers and commissioners eventually interpreted the clause requiring attention to the "inherent advantages" of each mode differently when it came to the railroads. Since the mid-1920s and in the absence of specific prohibitions from the ICC commissioners, railroad executives had developed motor vehicle divisions or wholly owned subsidiary firms. Many transportation economists endorsed such steps and urged regulators to allow rail carriers such latitude. Railroad-owned truck and bus subsidiaries expanded steadily through the late 1930s, and Brookings Institution economist Harold Moulton continued to argue that effective coordination meant corporate managers should be allowed to choose which "mode" delivered the most efficient transportation service. The new law did not prohibit outright the development of motor vehicle enterprises by railroad corporations, as some in the Senate had proposed in 1930.[104] Even so, after 1940 ICC commissioners steadily restricted railroad utilization or ownership of motor vehicles in commercial service. Eventually they denied rail carriers permission to acquire existing bus and trucking companies, a major blow since this was often the only way to acquire the certificates of convenience and necessity that were the basic requirement for operating regulated transportation services. First come, first served, prevailed here, and many railroads were blocked by the slowness with which they had recognized the utility of motor vehicles in the early 1920s.[105] Consistently, ICC commissioners ruled against railroad operation of motor vehicles in competition with independent operators already in business. These rulings effectively foreclosed not only the possibility of intermodal transportation firms, but eventually the operation of motor vehicle subsidiaries by railroads. As economist Emory Johnson observed in 1947, the 1940 legislation kept "railroad participation in motor transportation, and the co-ordination of rail and motor transportation, within narrow limits."[106]

Ultimately, the continuation and reinforcement of the separation of transportation into modes was the primary accomplishment of New Deal administrators during the Depression era. Despite extended discussion of an integrated conception of transportation by experts such as Eastman, Moulton, and Johnson, the legislative efforts of the 1930s failed to embrace regulatory coordination, much less operational cooperation. Officials of the new Civil Aeronautics Administration showed no interest in the railroads, its founders having won the battle to remove the ICC from aviation policymaking. The Motor Carrier Act also circumscribed the activities of railroads, and especially their motor vehicle subsidiaries. The authors of the 1940 legislation thus ended for decades any possibility of transforming railroads into full-scale transportation companies. Transportation coordination survived largely as a rhetorical exercise that took the form of the bill's preamble. In reality, the traditional political calculus of one mode at a time remained firmly in place after 1940. The strength of the standard view of transportation modes was quite evident whenever the politically charged subject of transportation subsidies arose. For example, many executives in various transport industries criticized Eastman's last report as coordinator, a four-volume study on "Public Aids to Transportation" released between 1938 to 1940, for suggesting that subsidies were not only deeply rooted in transportation, but served to skew transportation economics. The nation's policies in transportation had caught up to the transportation innovations such as long-distance trucking that had disrupted transportation policy set in place in 1920, but coordinated federal actions on highways, airways, and waterways were not part of the adjusted regulatory regime. Put another way, federal policy rested on a preference for distinct transportation industries and distinct transport markets rather than the ideal of cooperation and coordination.[107]

The Transportation Act of 1940 also marked the final rejection of the Progressive-era emphasis on neutral expert authority in the realm of transportation policy. In the years between the wars, experts had proposed two conceptual foundations to guide American transportation policy—railroad consolidation and transportation coordination. Backed by academic transportation economists of note, each idea attracted substantial support within the transportation community for a time, as ways of addressing serious difficulties facing the nation's transportation system. Harvard's William Ripley and the Wharton School's Emory Johnson, among others, conceived of consolidation of the nation's rail carriers into a smaller number of larger regional firms as the policy solution for the 1920s. During the 1930s, Johnson along with the Brookings Institution's Harold Moulton, Harvard's William Cunningham, and the ICC's own Joseph Eastman promoted a unified transportation—and regulatory—system that encompassed multiple modes of service, a conception of transport not necessarily defined by single-technology industries or firms. Both approaches rested on the assumption that railroads no longer exercised a monopoly over transportation and that regulation should address the unhealthy structure of competition between rail carriers, or between railroads and buses, trucks, and inland waterways. By 1940, however, both seemingly neutral expert policy visions lost out to a combination of older visions of predatory railroad behavior and now-traditional political considerations in which leaders of interest groups such as truckers, airline executives, and barge operators and their political allies such as Senator McCarran worried about themselves alone.[108] Writing decades later, transportation economist James C. Nelson argued that the Motor Carrier Act of 1935 and the Transportation Act of 1940 demonstrated that "economics was largely disregarded by the congress and the ICC."[109] Despite substantial and intimate involvement in the policy process, Eastman, President Roosevelt, and transportation economists failed to reshape the basic structure of American transportation between 1920 and 1940. Rather than redefining the foundations of transportation policy, the legislation adopted during the 1930s served instead to reify the positions of the four main and independent modes of transportation delivered via rails, roads, air, and inland waterways.

By 1940, the segmentation of transportation activities into distinct truck, bus, air, and waterway industries had been granted the weight and authority of the government of the United States. Moreover, operators of barges, airlines, and commercial motor vehicles had joined rail executives, shippers, labor leaders, and regulators as participants in the legislative scene. In fact, transportation executives in each area had determined it better to gain official standing as a mode and official protection of rates and routes, even if it meant accepting federal regulation as part of the bargain. For many transport executives, federal regulation also included the likelihood of a nurturing state prepared to spend lavishly on waterways, roads, and air service.

Unlike transportation policy in earlier decades, however, American presidents during the interwar years had taken a direct hand in framing industries and markets. In 1922, Warren Harding had almost apologized when he had entered transportation policy debates. Herbert Hoover's involvement in a range of transportation issues as Commerce Secretary and then as president marked the beginning of greater levels of engagement. Hoover nonetheless had remained one step removed from railroad policy except for the formation of the Reconstruction Finance Corporation. Although the pattern was far from consistent, Franklin Roosevelt was the first president who sought to mold transportation policy in detail. While Roosevelt often exhibited only limited intervention during Joseph Eastman's tenure as federal transportation coordinator to recast the structure of transportation during the mid-1930s, he played a much more direct and active role in the passage of the act of 1940 than earlier presidents had taken in transportation legislation. Through such devices as the formation of advisory committees, contact with congressional committee chairs, press conferences in which he detailed aspects of his proposals for the press, Roosevelt presided over the movement of key transportation legislation through Congress. He had launched a fundamental shift in the locus of authority over transportation policy.[110]

Between 1920 and the 1940s, then, federal officials, including the president of the United States, had determined to regulate waterways, airways, and trucks and buses as distinct entities separate from railroads, each with their own sets of regulators, interested congressional committees, and self-centered professional and lobbying groups like the energetic American Trucking Associations. Now there were four main modes of transportation, known popularly as transportation industries. After 1945, members of each of these industries emerged as full-blown actors on the political scene. By that point, no one, including the truckers or any of the others, wanted to remember their own births at the hands of the state. Nor did they wish to be reminded that, as economist Nelson observed in 1987, transportation markets as well as transportation industries were distinctly and solely political creatures.

Over the next three decades and more, the basic policy features of the Transportation Act of 1940 remained relatively unchanged, even as the specific policies for individual modes changed enormously. World War II proved to be only a temporary interlude in which railroads were restored for a time to positions of dominance within the American transportation system because of the demands of war. Joseph Eastman actually came close to realizing elements of his policy of coordination as he once again directed the nation's transportation systems as director of Defense Transportation from 1941 until his death in 1944. Once the war ended, however, concern for the coordination of railroads, motor carriers, and inland waterways again faded from the scene.[111] Up to the 1970s, the politics of transportation in the United States focused around the efforts of leaders in sharply defined rail, truck, and airline industries to defend and expand the boundaries created for them by the Motor Carrier Act of 1935, the Civil Aeronautics Act of 1938, and the Transportation Act of 1940. At the same time, every president of the United States beginning with Dwight D. Eisenhower and concluding with Jimmy Carter sought to bring about deregulation of transportation prices and services. Following a chapter on airline politics after World War II, we turn to the unceasing efforts of leaders of rail and truck corporations starting in the mid-1950s to protect and expand their prerogatives. In this struggle, all assumed, lobbying and litigating would deliver what a politically constructed marketplace could not. Thereafter, we turn to the politics of presidential deregulation.

Curiously, the cold war exempted the airline industry from the daily give and take of transportation politics. For three decades following World War II, members of no transportation industry prospered more under federal tutelage than leaders of the nation's certificated airline firms. With soon-storied names such as Trans World Airlines and Pan American World Airways capturing popular and political imaginations, officials at the Civil Aeronautics Board (CAB) regulated airline rates and routes, simultaneously protecting these firms from competition at the hands of upstarts such as nonscheduled carriers. At the same time, however, CAB officials also induced executives of the great firms such as American Airlines to lower fares, fostering creation of a "mass" market for air travel. By the early 1970s, with popular consumerism reaching a high point, the clamor among politicians was for still-cheaper fares. Once a protected industry structured largely by politicians and immune from earlier deregulatory efforts, by the mid-1970s even the airlines political mentors were demanding deregulation.

CHAPTER 3

Constructing Commercial Aviation, 1944–1973

In the [postwar] regulatory environment . . . there was no room for nonscheduled carriers.
—Historian Roger D. Launius, 2000

DURING THE THREE DECADES following the end of World War II, federal officials yoked the airline industry to national defense. It was essential, contended members of the U.S. Congress and every president of the United States, for the nation to maintain a substantial fleet of airliners capable of ferrying troops and other passengers to trouble spots around the world. Commercial airlines, all judged, occupied a pivotal position in planning for the nation's defense. Airline executives as well as their regulators functioned within this larger policy objective, which did not dissipate until the conclusion of the Vietnam War. Up to that point, the crises of the airline industry comprised another phase of the many crises of the cold war era.[1]

Starting in 1938, when Congress and President Roosevelt approved the Civil Aeronautics Act, federal officials regulated and promoted aviation separately from truck, rail, and waterways transportation. Officials at the Civil Aeronautics Board (CAB) also protected routes from competitors and determined the rates charged by "certificated" airlines; doing so, it was thought, protected America. In their well-secured position, policy controversies such as the effort by federal officials during the mid-1950s to bring about limited deregulation of trucking and railroading did not touch executives of the airline carriers such as United and Eastern Airlines. In the mid-1960s, when President Lyndon B. Johnson and members of his senior staff planned transportation deregulation alongside efforts to create a department of transportation, airlines still held positions of indispensability that kept them outside the purview of would-be deregulators. As the glamorous child of war and cold war, airlines occupied a privileged position in federal policy and in the imaginations of politicians, regulators, and ordinary Americans.

Beginning in the early 1970s, however, air travel and the airlines lost part of their luster. In turn, political leaders chose airlines as the first target for deregulation.

Officials of the U.S. Civil Aeronautics Board fostered the growing popularity of air travel. Soon after World War II, CAB officials such as James M. Landis approved development of inexpensive service by nonscheduled airlines. A decade later, during the early days of the "jet" age, another group of officials at the board aggressively pursued popularization of air travel with rules about lower fares and more competition, even when leaders of a reluctant industry objected—until 1969, when recession struck. By the late 1960s, many Americans were flying on "cheap" fares and had grown accustomed to the prospect of additional fare "discounts." After 1970, politicians and popular writers increasingly judged airlines as simply another transportation business, like the railroads and trucking, whose prices appeared unreasonably high. In addition, political and business leaders began to emphasize the idea of fighting economic decline by eliminating regulation. By that point, few remembered (or cared) that federal officials had sought to develop air travel as an industry servicing a "mass" market. From beginning to end, the American airline industry was a child of an American state that promoted national defense, a consumer society, and a growing economy.

PERFECTION OF ENTRY CONTROL: THE AVIATION OLIGOPOLY, 1944–1958

In 1938, at the insistence of hard-pressed airline executives, Congress had enacted the Civil Aeronautics Act, which created the Civil Aeronautics Administration (CAA). Members of Congress had rejected the vision of Joseph Eastman and other transportation experts that airlines were simply another form of transportation that the ICC should oversee. Instead, Congress treated aviation as a unique form of transport requiring special attention. CAA officials regulated airlines without regard to railroad and trucking firms or their passengers and freight. Under this legislation, moreover, the CAA controlled air navigation and the pricing of airline services. Equally important, only the CAA could authorize an airline company to carry passengers through the award of a certificate of convenience and necessity. In the language of the regulatory regime, airlines holding those permits were said to be "certificated." At the outset, such certificates were granted to only sixteen airlines. In 1942, as a wartime measure, the Civil Aeronautics Board was split off from the CAA. Appointed by the president, members of the new CAB still controlled the prices airlines charged, the number of certificated airlines, and the routes they flew.[2] In a nation rhetorically committed to price and service competition, federal officials and their counterparts in the executive offices of the nation's airlines had called an oligopoly into existence.

Airline executives and their well-to-do customers shared the fruits of oligopoly. Between 1945 and 1957, airline service developed mostly (but not entirely) as an elite institution. Airline executives modeled their service along lines offered first-class patrons on the nation's best railroads. Between 1949 and the latter 1950s, passengers wealthy enough to fly on a Boeing-377 Stratocruiser (based on the C-97 Stratofreighter and the B-29 Super-fortress, both aircraft built for the Army Air Corps during World War II) descended a spiral staircase from the upper to the lower deck, which included a beverage lounge seating up to fourteen persons. In this era, almost all passengers were businessmen (family travel, though much pro-moted, took off only in the mid-1950s). After 1949, certificated airlines launched coach service; until 1953, however, coach passengers always flew on all-coach aircraft. Only rarely did first-class passengers encounter their lowly fellow travelers. Instead, first-class ticket holders ate meals from china plates with silverware and linen napkins. Airline publicists added to the glamour of air travel with images of luxury, modernity, and pampering for the special few.[3]

Regardless of equipment and images, however, officials of the Civil Aeronautics Board mostly protected air carriers from the vicissitudes of price and service competition. After the war, as before, those same sixteen "certificated" airlines still carried most of the passengers. Even on major routes such as New York to Chicago, moreover, passengers rarely had more than two or three carriers from which to choose—and their choices almost always included American Airlines, United Airlines, Eastern Airlines, Delta Airlines, or TWA. Airlines flew current or former "airmail routes" (complete with federal subsidy until 1954). Airline executives could fly new routes only after securing a "certificate of convenience and necessity" from the CAB, a difficult task. On certificated lines, passengers completed 12 million trips in 1946 and 45 million in 1957. As early as 1951, however, economist Lucile Sheppard Keyes had pointed out that entry foreclosure (a CAB rule that prohibited other airline firms from serving main routes) served as the key-stone of federal aviation policy.[4]

Between 1940 and 1948, airline officials had latitude to experiment with expanded service. As World War II ended and the cold war began, many in the industry felt free—or even obligated—to indulge in extravagant expan-sion dreams. These dreams found expression in equipment purchases. By 1947, however, airlines were foundering. During the first sixteen months

FIGURE 14. James M. Landis, dean of the Harvard University Law School, served during 1946–47 as chair of the Civil Aeronautics Board, creating regulations that fostered the first steps in converting the industry from service for a comparative few to a "mass" transportation. Source: Art & Visual Materials, Special Collections Department, Harvard Law School Library. Used with permission.

after the war, executives of the certificated carriers spent more than $235 million on new planes and equipment, but lost $4,340,000 in 1946 and well over $20 million in 1947. CAB chair James Landis blamed a "spirit of speculation." Certificated airlines blamed everything else. With the single exception of Eastern, certificated carriers could not survive in the 1940s without the "air-mail subsidy."[5]

Airline officials bewailed most loudly competition from unregulated carriers, known popularly as nonscheduled airlines and more idiomatically as the "nonskeds." (Technically, CAB officials characterized these nonskeds as Large Irregular Carriers, or LICs.) Never able to join the Air Transport Association of America (ATAA), a trade association composed of the sixteen certificated carriers, executives of the nonskeds formed their own trade association. Within a few years of war's end, regulation had fostered creation of an "in" and an "out" group in airline transportation. Writing in 2000, historian Roger D. Launius characterized exclusion of the nonskeds from the meetings of the Air Transport Association of America as "a subtle form of aviation apartheid that permeated the minds of those in control of commercial aviation . . . during the first two decades following World War II."[6]

A "loophole" in the 1938 act had permitted entry for nonscheduled airlines (by exempting from regulation "unscheduled" flights). During World War II, GIs learned to fly and, after the war, the government began to sell off planes. According to an estimate made by CAB officials, before 1949, some 3,600 airline firms started or announced operations. Few actually flew passengers, and far fewer survived any period of time. In 1951, the nonskeds' best year, Korean War military contracts helped them boost their market share to 7.5 percent of air passengers and 21 percent of air freight. With war-surplus planes and ex-GI pilots, owners and managers of nonsked airlines exploited markets the certificated airlines largely ignored, including coach service and air freight, and made inroads into both regional markets and profitable transcontinental service.[7]

Wary of a flood of postwar "GI carriers" that would imperil the certificated carriers, CAB officials tried to niche the nonskeds where they would have least impact. Remembering the financial chaos air carriers had experienced during the early 1930s, in May 1946, the board issued a ruling that required full reports of nonscheduled carrier activities and submission of minimum rates. As part of these new rules, CAB officials attempted to restrict the nonskeds to ten or fewer trips per month between any two points. Irregular service, the board wrote, was "that which neither directly nor indirectly leads the public to believe that between given points a reasonably certain number of flights . . . may be anticipated." This CAB dictum would eventually prove to be a death sentence for the nonskeds. The standard DC-3 aircraft, purchased in large numbers by scheduled and nonscheduled airlines alike, was too costly to be kept ready for service and yet used only a few times a month. "In the [postwar] regulatory environment . . . ," reports historian Launius, "there was no room for nonscheduled carriers."[8]

Former GIs and other entrepreneurs were not so easily discouraged. In 1946, these ex-military pilots claimed an organization five thousand strong. During those heady days, leaders among the nonskeds even explored potential collaborations with executives of ocean shipping interests and the American Trucking Associations. (Not subject to rules of certificated carriers that kept them apart from other types of transportation, nonsked executives once again raised the promise and threat of creating transportation companies.) By autumn 1946, CAA Act coauthor Senator Pat McCarran was denouncing restrictions on nonscheduled carriers as contrary to the intent of Congress.[9] The image of the daring GI pilot was of great value in the early political battles surrounding nonsked air carriers, just as it had been for Charles A.Lindbergh and others during the 1920s.

Enthusiastic veterans had not established the major nonsked carriers. The president of Transair, one of the early giants, was a banker and railroad director who had served in the war as special assistant to Army Air Corps General Henry ("Hap") Arnold. Yet another nonsked, the all-cargo Slick Airways, was founded when twenty-five-year-old Earl F. Slick, heir to an oil fortune, bought seventeen C-46s in a fifteen-minute transaction in mid-1945; his airline prospered.[10] Nonskeds also had powerful political allies. Until 1947, the administration of President Harry S. Truman did little to discourage them.

In 1947, however, the certificated airlines such as United and American Airlines suffered large financial losses. Lobbyists for the Air Transport Association, the trade association of the certificated carriers, blamed CAB chair Landis, and continued to do so long after President Truman declined to renew his appointment that December. With his professed interest in unsubsidized competition, Landis had irritated and frightened executives of the certificated carriers.[11]

During the late 1940s, however, CAB officials were still willing to entertain applications for additional service submitted by cargo operators. In July 1949, the CAB granted five-year certificates to executives of four cargo carriers, permitting them to carry freight among points linking four territorial clusters. The authorization, said the CAB, was "primarily promotional in character and relates to developmental rather than to purely regulatory processes." These authorizations represented the CAB's first and final flirtation with permissive entry, one urged by defense department officials to expand the reserve fleet.[12]

At the same time, CAB officials launched a process of shutting down the nonscheduled passenger carriers. After August 6, 1948, the CAB accepted no new applications for exemption from the rule against passenger flights by noncertificated carriers. On May 20, 1949, past exemptions were effectively revoked. Now, CAB rules required nonsked operators to apply for certificates of convenience and necessity and to become "certificated." In mid-1951, moreover, the Civil Aeronautics Authority began applying strict new safety rules to nonscheduled carriers. That autumn, CAB officials denied a final set of "new" applications made by transcontinental coach operators.[13] With their often-dismal safety records, including accidents bunched together at Newark Airport, safety was one reason to shut down the nonskeds.

CAB officials also wanted to rescue certificated carriers from their own postwar extravagance and simultaneously to rationalize the airline industry—arguments first advanced during the 1920s and 1930s. In 1950, nonscheduled carriers ranked fifth in passenger-mile production, and captured a significant share of the long-haul market. "By the early 1950s," reports one scholar, "approximately 63 so-called large irregulars routinely transported passengers, some of them duplicating air-line routes at drastically reduced fares." In the CAB system that prevailed between 1945 and 1978, however, long-haul runs granted to major carriers were expected to "cross-subsidize" unprofitable short trips imposed on the same carriers. So the nonscheduled "cream skimmers" had to go. As part of their emphasis on rationalization of carrier services, CAB officials also pressured certificate holders to merge complementary route systems—an idea that Congress and the ICC had attempted to impose on railroads during the 1920s. At the same time, the CAB asked carriers to expand coach service.[14] Thus, in the airline business, government again appeared as both patron and quasi-manager—reprising in some respects the apparently discredited industry-stabilization efforts of Postmaster General Brown twenty years earlier.

Entry foreclosure was not accomplished easily. Several nonskeds had built impressive records. In California, where long distances and major cities made unregulated intrastate service practical, nonskeds like California Central showed up regulated service by offering Los Angeles–San Francisco rates half those of the certificated carriers. Executives of the nonskeds such as S. J. Solomon of Atlantic Airlines also produced innovations such as passenger luggage carry-ons in 1946.[15] In the consumerist decade of the 1970s, low fares offered by California- and Texas-only airlines served as a key argument for deregulation.

Although they shook up airline business practices with their innovations during the 1950s, the nonskeds also engaged in self-destructive behavior, especially with regard to safety. Pilot and flight-attendant experience varied widely and maintenance was sometimes marginal. In the winter of 1951–1952, four crashes in rapid succession near Newark Airport caused the temporary closing of that facility. Although two crashes involved certificated craft, "nonskeds" received much of the public blame. President Truman quickly created an Airport Commission under James H. "Jimmy" Doolittle. During World War II, Doolittle, who was awarded the Congressional Medal of Honor, had served as a bomber pilot and then as commander of the Eighth Air Force during the period of the Normandy invasion. Doolittle and members of his commission effectively sealed off debate and contained the public outcry over airport safety.[16]

Truman also demanded a final drive against the nonskeds. In January

1952, he wrote CAB chair Donald Nyrop: "I'd like very much to have some concrete action . . . more for the safety and for saving lives than for any other reason." In April 1952, the CAB and CAA together imposed new safety rules on the remaining uncertificated carriers, requiring them to meet the operational standards of certificated lines.[17] By the time Truman left office, courts had given the CAB all the power it needed to end the nonscheduled experiment. Yet Landis and his successors had hesitated.

Like Roosevelt and Truman, President Dwight D. Eisenhower and his senior administrators continued to treat commercial aviation as an industry apart from other transportation industries. In 1953, its first year, the Eisenhower administration created the President's Advisory Committee on Government Organization (PACGO), headed by Nelson A. Rockefeller—a "liberal Republican" and former adviser to Truman. The PACGO recommended presidential appointment of the ICC chair and centralization of the ICC's administrative (but not regulatory) functions—ideas earlier voiced by Franklin Roosevelt. But members of the PACGO did not address aviation. Neither did Eisenhower's commerce secretary, Sinclair Weeks, who headed a drive during 1955–1956 to deregulate railroads and trucks. As had been true in transport policy debates in the 1930s, aviation was a separate matter. In this case, aviation was left to members of the Air Coordinating Committee, Eisenhower's continuation of a Truman-era body. During 1953 and 1954, members of this committee merely froze in place the policies developed in the 1951–1952 crackdown on nonscheduled air carriers.[18] Throughout the 1940–1958 period, commercial aviation remained part of the foundation of America's defense. Only members of the executive branch of government could act effectively on air policy, and even they could act only where the demands of new jet technology and the needs of defense and commerce intersected.

THE EARLY JET AGE AND THE DEBACLE OF REGULATION, 1958–1971

The arrival of commercial jets challenged traditional concepts of airline economics. Using "old style" thinking, airlines continued to purchase propeller-driven planes until 1956, shortly before placing their first jet orders. Fast "write-off," encouraged by the Office of Defense Mobilization with the aim of keeping the Civil Air Reserve fleet at a desired minimum of six hundred aircraft, enabled this rapid construction and then destruction of millions of tons of aluminum and steel. Another reason for rapid equipment turnover was airline competition on the basis of minimal differences in speed. Finally, in October 1955, Juan T. Trippe's Pan American World Airways broke the prop-or-jet equipment logjam with an order for twenty Boeing 707s and twenty-five Douglas DC-8 jetliners. The new planes were 157 percent faster than the fastest long-range nonjet; in coach configuration, they carried 147 percent as many passengers. Transcontinental airtimes were expected to fall by at least 40 percent and—an implicit recognition of the meaning of this massive new capacity—virtually all jetliners were ordered with mixed first-class and coach seating, a layout first used with propeller-driven planes only in 1955.[19] Jets could complete three trips for every two made by a DC-7, carrying 363 persons in the time the fastest "prop plane" moved 204. "Overcapacity" inevitably returned with the jet age.

Once airline officials put their first jets into service, operational efficiency improved. The first jets were a "wonder." Once everyone had jets, however, they offered no competitive advantage—only increasing efficiency. Introduction of subsequent generations of jets put additional pressure on airline executives to keep up with competitors. In the year 2000, a thirty-five-year-old DC-9 was still a viable (if not very attractive) aircraft, but the idea of a major airline competing in 1970 with planes constructed in 1935—essentially DC-2s—was absurd on the face of it. During the 1960s, entire fleets were scrapped or sold within five to fifteen years of purchase. And then came "jumbo jets." Never again would capital pressures of such enormity be exerted on the aviation industry—and all of this pressure took place in a period of rapidly rising consumer militancy, cynicism, and growing distrust of protective regulation. Airlines' preparation for the jet age in the 1950s necessarily focused on finance, facilities, and technology: it did nothing to ready the airlines for the rapid transition of their industry from elite to mass transportation. Short of cash, "front-end" financing was a problem in the early jet age. American Airlines, with one of the industry's most advantageous cash positions, bought its first twenty jets with a loan that would mature in 1996.[20]

Meanwhile, airline executives and their regulators faced more immediate questions—business questions. In summer 1958, Harvard economist Paul W. Cherrington reported to the White House that the CAB's target profit rate of 8 to 9.5 percent appeared far too low to attract the necessary investment. And the situation worsened. Between 1955–1958, a drive by CAB officials for regulated competition generated more service and lower profits. In 1954, 60 percent of the nation's top four hundred airline markets were served by only one airline; by 1958, competition existed in 87 percent of them. Three or four airlines competed in the top dozen nonstop markets—more than in 2003 following twenty-five years of deregulation.[21] Airline executives entered the jet age prepared for some of the technological challenges of 500-mile-per-hour aircraft; for their economic consequences, however, they were scarcely prepared at all. In the meantime, CAB officials pressed airline executives to broaden markets and introduce a degree of price competition.

The jet transformed air transport. Starting in 1958, the sale of coach seats zoomed. As early as 1960, coach seating accounted for more than 50 percent of scheduled airline capacity. Equally evident by 1960, commercial aviation faced real, not imagined, overcapacity and capital crunches. In 1955, debt service consumed one-tenth of 1 percent of certificated carriers' revenues; in 1960, 2.5 cents per dollar went to debt service. Profits collapsed from a 9.4 percent return on investment in 1956 to 2.9 percent in 1960—a profit margin similar to that which would terrify railroad executives in the 1950s. Members of the aviation community also (mistakenly) came to believe that perennial rounds of reequipment were inevitable.[22] Less visible but still determinative amid all the buzz surrounding profit margins and exciting jet aircraft were members of the Civil Aeronautics Board and their decisions regarding routes, subsidies, and fares.

In 1960, CAB members reacted to jet-induced overcapacity by applying a utility-like "rate of return" criterion, seeking to maintain the desired return by pressuring airlines to adjust supply to demand. The rate specified was 10.5 percent for the "big four" (American, Eastern, TWA, and United), and 11.25 percent for the remaining eight "trunkline" carriers. Under this formula, as the transition to jets drove debt to record highs, fare increases of 10 percent (1958) and then, in 1960, 5 percent were implemented.[23]

The "jet age" intersected with a new CAB drive for more competition in airline service. Between 1961–1969, CAB officials tried to lower fares and broaden the air travel market, and do so over airline protests that the market had a natural limit. Under Presidents John F. Kennedy and Lyndon B. Johnson, CAB chairs Alan S. Boyd and, later, Charles S. Murphy led the market-broadening movement. Crucially, the CAB's democratizing role was not evident to the public. CAB procedures were cumbersome and resulted in ever-longer rate-case delays.[24] The market-broadening, fare-shrinking policies of the 1960s CAB anticipated the demands of the consumer movement a decade later. Although these policies earned the agency little public credit, they set a norm that led consumer advocates to react strongly when CAB commissioners returned to a protective mode in the early 1970s.

Simultaneously, CAB commissioners under Kennedy and Johnson moved to abolish direct subsidies. For big airlines, subsidies declined from 6.2 percent of revenue in 1950 to 0.1 percent in 1965. Even for local service carriers, subsidies dropped from 49.9 percent of revenue in 1959 to 6.5 percent in 1970. Airlines responded to these disappearing subsidies and to overcapacity with authentic price and service competition.[25] Indeed, in "real dollars"—measured against inflation—airfares declined. In current (1960–1969) dollars, fares rose by 12.8 percent between January 1960 and September 1969, with 4.3 percent of this increase in 1969. Meanwhile, the consumer price index rose by 21.4 percent. Real fares could fall because of jet productivity: between 1960 and 1968, airlines' net savings (productivity savings minus labor, fuel, equipment, and other operations cost increases) totaled $1.5 billion, with $215 million in savings in 1968 alone.[26]

Throughout this period, CAB officials pressed for more coach service and lower fares to broaden the market. In 1961, President Kennedy had appointed CAB member and longtime state regulator Alan Boyd as CAB chair. Boyd worked to expand the air travel market within the framework of regulation. He encouraged youth standby and other promotional fares and a range of market expansion and (arguably) price-lowering ploys. In these actions, Boyd's CAB followed—or paralleled—the work of Kennedy's presidential task force on aviation goals ("Project Horizon"), which issued its first report on June 27, 1961. Also in keeping with this report, Boyd urged marketing of air travel to the 90 percent of the U.S. population who, in 1960, had never flown.[27]

With few exceptions, however, airline executives held that air travel was not price-elastic. Coach and special discount fares, airline managers continued to argue, merely diverted traffic—six airline presidents told Boyd as much in October 1961. But major airlines filed the first youth standby fares and major coach reductions, and only a few refused to join the fracas.[28] As in the postderegulation days a generation later, a fare reduction by one line meant a reduction by all. The jet had introduced a level of overcapacity that challenged the cold war ideal of stability, just as nonskeds and overoptimistic trunkline route expansions had challenged that ideal after World War II.

Then there was Continental Airlines, whose practices haunted the industry until the end of regulation. As historian Michael H. Gorn notes, Continental began with just the sort of route system major airlines found unprofitable in the1930s, when earnings had come from airmail subsidies and long-haul runs. Continental first flew between Colorado Springs and El Paso. In the jet age, President Robert F. Six made a major success of this unlikely airline. Continental's compact, regional route system permitted an early version of "hub" scheduling: Continental executives kept their aircraft aloft almost two more hours per day than the industry average and economized on everything but service frills. In the autumn of 1961, Continental's managers flew in the face of "overcapacity" by applying to offer

Chicago–Los Angeles service with bottom prices 25 percent below others' regular coach rates. Continental carried just 3 percent of scheduled airline traffic in 1960, but fare competition was real, and had to be met where it arose.[29]

Yet airline executives often failed to appreciate the vast changes in airline pricing and use that both CAB officials and executives like Robert Six were introducing. In the early 1960s, the airlines' own "scientific marketing" studies "showed" that airline travel was linked to the general economy (and thus to the fate of the cold war boom), and was not directly competitive with the automobile. Most major airline executives still agreed with United's William A. Patterson, who contended that air travel was "naturally" first-class travel. Coach as well as discount fares, Patterson contended, simply diverted traffic.[30]

Pressured by the CAB and by occasional bouts of real price competition, throughout the 1960s airfares trended downward. Airlines filed "excursion" fares for long-haul flights, seasonal cuts, and shuttle rates in a variety of markets. By 1970, nearly half of all coach passengers traveled at a discount, and bargain fares accounted for up to 44.8 percent of all revenue air-passenger miles. As Boyd pointed out, when the CAB resisted lower fares, it was combating a chaotic rate structure—de facto price deregulation—not market expansion: "We are not seeking stability of fares," he advised in early 1964, "[we simply want to keep] the chaos under control."[31]

Jet economics had made profits possible with a smaller proportion of seats filled than in the piston-engine era. Still, airline officials realized that in the long run, they needed to fill most of the seats they flew. Between 1962 and 1968, they raced to do this, while insisting that low fares and promotions did not increase ridership. In the amazing mid-1960s, airlines profited while fares and load factors fell. Despite what airline executives asserted, they acted as though the market was elastic. In turn, airline passengers became accustomed to the fare gimmicks and began to take these special fares as a matter of course when thinking of air travel.

In 1962, airline executives knew that, within two years, a second wave of jets would cause capacity to increase again. Douglas DC-9s and Boeing 727s would replace almost all piston and turboprop aircraft, creating new efficiencies—and a new seat surplus. But immediate prosperity blinded all. Trunk airline earnings averaged over 10 percent in 1964, and moved higher in 1965. CAB chair Boyd warned early that year that, should earnings continue above the "appropriate" level established by a 1956–1960 investigation conducted by the CAB [GPFI-1960], "we would have to take some action." The board recommended a range of special fares and simple fare cuts that made sense only in terms of a price-sensitive market.[32]

Airline officials responded to Boyd's jawboning, and airline traffic rose 14 percent in 1964 and 1965. This boom gave weak carriers access to credit, and raised profits—and hopes. Eastern Airlines rejoined the ranks of significantly profitable carriers, and TWA paid its first stock dividend since 1936.[33] Intensified competition reflected the CAB's goals for the 1960s— that more persons could fly more frequently at more affordable prices. In July 1965, Boyd left the CAB to join the Department of Commerce, where he worked with President Johnson's top officials to create a new cabinet-level Department of Transportation.

Charles S. Murphy, another advocate of lower fares and market expansion, succeeded Boyd. More fare cuts ensued as the CAB acted on its General Passenger Fare Investigation (1960), which suggested a "reasonable profit" figure of 10.5 percent. Studies conducted by the CAB, much disputed by economists working for the airlines, suggested that still lower fares would expand the air travel market.[34] This crucial position was thus staked out by regulators themselves, well before the deregulation drive that started in the 1970s.

Airlines complied with CAB directives via a range of what National Airlines' president Louis B. Maytag called "gimmick" fares. In December 1965, American and then United inaugurated the "youth standby fares" that would bedevil the industry for five years. By 1966, youth, "Discover America," and other standby and advance-purchase fares were everywhere, and full-fare coach passengers made up just over half of all coach travelers. "Gimmicks" were the airlines' preferred response to CAB calls for general fare cuts—at least a traditional fare structure remained alongside the many special fares.[35] By 1967, however, reequipment costs and wage and price inflation had begun, and the air travel boom was about to end.

THE DEBACLE OF REGULATION, 1967–1971

By 1971, airline prosperity was but a memory. Although the market for air travel had greatly expanded, the companies in existence were the same old set, operating under a version of the same old rules. During the early 1970s, moreover, when airlines raised fares, charter carriers reemerged as the consumer's friend. Much of this period's chaos developed in arenas where the airlines had real choices. The airlines' equipment-purchase and labor-contract decisions during the golden years of 1966 and 1967 had led them by the 1970s to behavior that consumer-oriented politicians and journalists increasingly judged absurd.

As before, new equipment promised both greater savings and greater capacity. From 1958 to 1963, piston-engine planes were replaced on long flights by large, four-engine craft like the Boeing 707 and Douglas DC-8. Between 1964 and 1973, two- and three-engine DC-9s and Boeing 727s and 737s displaced the remaining propeller-driven planes on flights under one thousand miles. Such planes added capacity through speed as well as size. Then, in mid-April 1966, Juan Trippe's Pan American contracted for twenty-five Boeing 747 aircraft, each capable of carrying 490 passengers and priced at just under $20,000,000. Even in 1966, some competitors foresaw a dangerous equipment race (the 747 was defined as a luxury craft, not a producer of economies of scale). Critics had long urged that "overcapacity" arose largely from management error, not competition.[36] Forced by competitive pressures, airline managers had purchased airplanes that provided more "seats" than could be sold. Once the premier international airline had opted for the 747, the others (Northwest and TWA) had to do the same. Both carriers had many domestic routes, leading to another equipment race involving every major airline.

For a time, new aircraft created new inefficiencies. Both wide-body craft (like the European Airbus, the McDonnell-Douglas DC-10, and the Lockheed 1011), and the earlier, narrow-body craft (specifically the Boeing 737) relied for their attraction on lower seat-mile costs. Airline executives expected such planes to usher in another era of rising productivity. New aircraft, however, entered a scheduling and planning world left over from the pre-jet age. Before 1968, airline officials had quite literally worked out schedules and equipment purchases and allocations with pencil and paper.[37] In this context, faster and larger aircraft only added to expenses, not to income. In fact, both airline and CAB officials had introduced overequipment and route duplication—classic noneconomic forms of competition. The CAB did nothing to discourage massive equipment orders. (For example, in 1968 alone, 474 new aircraft were delivered to scheduled airlines.) Between July 1966 and the end of 1970, the CAB also awarded 241 new "route segments." Existing carriers won all these routes. Although the CAB had not awarded certificates to additional carriers, it had met its own aim of creating more competition.[38] Only a continuing aviation boom could have justified airlines flying more routes with larger planes.

In order to keep flying during the boom of the mid-1960s, airline officials also accepted costly labor agreements. In summer 1966, five major airlines ended prolonged negotiations with the International Association of Machinists (IAM), representing mechanics and some other ground crew workers. The affected airlines together supplied over 60 percent of domestic passenger service; thus, their settlement set the pattern for the industry. Fully alert to the "wage-price spiral," IAM officials called for a one-way inflation escalator clause. After five months of negotiations, nothing could persuade the IAM or its members to give up the escalator clause. The union struck the five airlines, imperiling not only the summer travel season but also Lyndon Johnson's war effort in Vietnam.[39]

IAM workers settled for a 4.9 percent raise, with a cost-of-living adjustment provision that would force raises to meet expected inflation. The agreement did not permit wage cuts if the cost of living fell. Over three years, the base wage increase was 6.76 percent. Between 1962–1966, the overall urban cost-of-living increase amounted to 6.6 percent; and it would rise another 7 percent over the life of the contract (1966 through 1969). Thus the contract's one-way cost-of-living provision was a time bomb that would subject airlines to major wage increases in the later 1960s and (by contract extensions) the early 1970s—at a time when business fell and overcapacity and fuel costs peaked. The 1966 settlement's real impact hit as the contracts expired in the midst of early 1970s inflation and recession. Labor costs increased 15 percent between 1968 and 1970—substantially faster than capacity or employment. After declining to 42.6 percent of total costs in 1963, labor costs resumed their piston-age proportion (about 46 percent of all costs) by 1970.[40]

After 1966, CAB officials moved slowly back toward protection. Airlines pressed for and, by the end of 1967, received increases in "excursion fares." By 1970, many airlines were losing money. Losses proved especially devastating for large, railroad-like carriers such as United and TWA, whose routes were mostly located outside the newly developing South and West. CAB officials were also strikingly ineffective in "selling" protection of large airlines in an era of consumerism that idealized "small" entrepreneurial businesses. Executives such as George Spater at American Airlines reacted to spreading pools of red ink with service innovations such as piano bars, including crooners. In 1971, moreover, airline officials made the same plea voiced by railroad executives, seeking rate freedom via a "zone of reasonableness" in fares. They failed to use the power when they got it. But the major theme of 1968–1971 was a regulatory system that increasingly appeared "anticonsumer" in a period of rising public expectations and a foundering economy.[41]

Indeed, outdated airline ideas of competition exacerbated the situation. Faced with losses, airlines scheduled more flights to steal each others' passengers. Regulated carriers' domestic passenger miles flown rose 15.9 percent from 1967 to 1968, but capacity grew nearly 25 percent. By 1969, the four largest lines' load factors fell to 49.4 percent from 53 percent the preceding year—*before* the arrival of jumbo jets. In 1970, only three midsized regional carriers (Northwest, Continental, and Delta) reported a profit.[42] In battling recession and overcapacity, old tools did not work.

Airlines saturated long, dense routes with service. In early 1971, American, United, and TWA offered thirty-five one-way flights per day between New York and San Francisco; fewer than in 1970. Yet jumbo jets had increased the number of seats by 38 percent. During 1970, major airlines offered 153 one-way flights each day between New York and Chicago. Among the few areas of discretion available to airline managers under terms of CAB regulations, however, overcapacity and the purchase of still more equipment were built into the thinking of airline executives.[43]

"Amenities" competition in this period also reached a zenith. Battlegrounds included seat width, fold-down "middle" seats that created tables or "a seat and a half," five-across seating in coach, and floor-level carry-on baggage compartments for last-minute check-ins. Food, too, was a point of competition; exotic and expensive cuisines were featured. In 1971, American Airlines introduced a "Coach Lounge," which was basically a stand-up bar. In all, airline executives continued to "sell" service elements that had little to do with transportation. None of these efforts did more than shift passengers from one line to another. Nor could amenities competition reduce airline costs, which between 1967 and 1970 rose faster than consumer prices—8.6 percent faster in 1970 alone. Meanwhile, real gross national product growth slowed to a mere 2.4 percent. In this context, the plea of airlines executives for a fare hike produced two unintended results.[44]

The first result was a study by CAB staff published in 1968 showing that fares in competitive markets were "frequently lower" than fares in uncontested markets. This report coincided with an onslaught of congressional consumerism. California representative John E. Moss and nineteen of his colleagues in the U.S. House opposed any airfare increase, demanding better service as a condition of higher fares. For the first time, airline consumer issues had moved into the political arena.[45]

As a second consequence, the CAB report also provided a telling argument against fare increases. Authors noted that "a fare level set well above cost, based on a reasonable load factor, may contribute to the operation of excessive capacity . . . [and] long haul jet coach fares are quite high in relation to cost of service even at the relatively low load factors prevailing."[46] If high-priced, long-haul fares encouraged overcapacity, which created a need for higher fares, airlines had a difficult case to make for fare hikes.

In the summer of 1969, airline officials filed for a round of fare increases. The new chair of the CAB, Secor Browne, inherited the downside of the 1961–1968 CAB legacy of cutting fares. An MIT aerospace engineering professor who believed airline profitability should be high on the CAB priority list, Browne came to the CAB from the new Department of Transportation, where he had served as assistant secretary since March

1969. On September 12, 1969, the CAB approved a major fare increase, with the largest increases applying to shorter hauls. The new fare schedule immediately made Browne the focus of Congressman Moss's outrage.[47] Opposition from Moss, followed shortly by that of consumer advocate Ralph Nader, then at peak popularity, presented CAB officials with a truly serious problem.

Supported eventually by thirty-one House members, Representative Moss argued that fares should be directly related to cost of service, and that minimum load-factor standards should be imposed as a test of any fare increase. Echoing the opponents of the railroad's "value of service" rates during the 1920s, Moss took his case to court. The District of Columbia federal district court overruled the CAB on procedural grounds and rolled back airfares. During the hearings, however, Ralph Nader joined the battle, calling the CAB a "shill for the airlines." Regulation's credibility had begun to dissolve.[48]

CAB officials reacted belatedly and clumsily to the rise of consumerism. Early in 1972, the board created a "Consumer Advisory Commission" and announced an attack on overbooking, a process by which airlines sold more tickets than seats, figuring that many passengers would fail to appear. Core consumer concerns, however, were price and service; and on both fronts, the CAB did not—and indeed could not—meet the expectations of early 1970s' consumerism. CAB opposition to wide coach seats and five-across seating inevitably seemed "anticonsumer." So did CAB efforts to limit charter flights (a drive that led to a congressional investigation of the agency). When the board ended Discover America, youth standby, and family fares, its action could easily be interpreted by members of the 1970s generation as a revocation of consumer entitlements.[49]

While the airline industry passed through its most severe crisis since the 1930s, the CAB conducted a new "Domestic Passenger Fare Investigation." This study covered almost all aspects of regulation from general fare levels and fare structure through depreciation, valuation, and return. Meanwhile, in 1970, domestic scheduled passenger traffic actually declined at the same time that capacity continued to increase, and certificated airlines lost $168,700,000. The industry was capitalized at roughly $5.5 billion. At the beginning of 1970, however, outstanding contracts for flight equipment totaled $4.7 billion.[50]

Seemingly oblivious to consumerism in their panic over rising levels of debt and massive losses, airline executives sought remedies in measures sure to alienate politicians and ordinary Americans even more. By 1970, it was clear to airline officials that the CAB would act to link fare increases to cost of service and load factors. Perhaps in order to meet anticipated CAB fare hike criteria, in late August 1970, executives of American, United, and

TWA agreed, without CAB authorization, to cut capacity on fifteen routes they largely controlled.[51] By 1972, CAB officials had approved these "capacity control agreements." Thus again the board might seem to exist only to support greedy airlines.

In early 1971, airline officials urged their own version of "deregulation." Leaders of the Air Transport Association of America, the industry's trade association, sought legislation removing the power of the CAB to suspend rates except in extraordinary circumstances. Although disagreements were evident within the airline community, a solid front was expected at Senate hearings in February. "Some of the most vital decisions affecting the airlines' economic health are beyond the control of airline management," ATAA president Stuart G. Tipton told the Senate Commerce Aviation Subcommittee on February 2.[52]

Tipton and a parade of airline presidents recounted the usual ATAA terror tale. Like railroad managers complaining about bus lines, or trucking firms lamenting "gypsy" truckers in the early 1930s, airline executives complained that supplemental air carriers were a major cause of regulated carriers' losses. Equally, ran the argument of airline officials, second-generation jet purchases would cost $5.9 billion in 1970–1972 alone. Sounding like a railroad executive from the 1920s, Tipton asked for legislation to prevent CAB suspension of any rate that would result in returns under the 10.5 percent recommended by the CAB's "General Passenger Fare Investigation," issued in 1960. He also asked for restrictions on airline labor's right to strike, tougher restrictions on charter carriers, and an assortment of other measures. For the most part, members of President Richard M. Nixon's administration backed the ATAA.[53] Everything the airlines and their regulators said and did appeared contrary to the image of consumer-friendly expansion and fare cutting.

As in the 1960s, Continental Airlines and its president, Robert Six, helped nail shut the coffin lid on airline regulation as a public good. Representing perennially profitable Continental, Six told the story the public wanted to hear. "Most of the statements being made about the ills [of] the industry," he told members of a Senate committee, "go beyond gloom. They approach hysteria." The "real worry," Six contended, was that government might adopt some of the measures advocated by frightened carriers. Mergers and capacity controls, for example, could demolish the good effects of competition. Even the sickest carriers might profit if they used their aircraft as efficiently as Continental and employed fewer persons. There was no need for less competition. The press delighted in Six's remarks, as industry leaders cringed.[54]

Robert Six and Continental Airlines did not bring about airline deregulation. Indeed, the argument that transcontinental systems could easily be made profitable was not self-evidently true. With certain other carriers, like Pacific Southwest (PSA) and Delta, that challenged the ATAA's conventional wisdom, however, Continental became a symbol for what could be achieved with more efficient management and more entrepreneurial outlooks. In retrospect, Six's remarks highlighted the poor timing of the ATAA's initiative.[55]

In 1971, Congress produced nothing new. CAB officials issued a series of rulings that upheld most of their own traditions, yet offered one remarkable new opportunity for the survival of regulation. First, the CAB followed the advice of officials at the new Department of Transportation (DOT) and voted to set load-factor standards to be met by any carrier seeking a fare increase. The CAB endorsed DOT's conclusion (also drawn in its own 1968 study) that "the higher the fare level in relation to cost, the more capacity carriers will offer." The board now required an overall 52.5 percent load factor of any carrier seeking the increase granted in the same proceeding, while future increases would require load factors ranging up to 55 percent. The CAB's standard was a rough average of trunk airline load factors in the middle 1960s.[56] CAB officials thus put in place a policy that encouraged more crowded aircraft just as consumer expectations and organization were on the rise.

Critically, the CAB action placed part of the fare-making process in the carriers' hands. After lengthy discussion of market elasticity, the board tentatively accepted American Airlines' proposal that fare levels be stated as maximums. Despite its concern that fares would sink to the lowest economic level, since "a carrier generally cannot afford to have a higher fare than that of his competitor," CAB fare orders thereafter were stated as maximums, not exact fares.[57]

Contemporaries observed that this CAB action was revolutionary, opening the door to at least a degree of price competition. But no one went through the door. All carriers, including Continental, filed at once for the maximum rate. "Rate wars" via special fares continued, but the CAB could not create price competition in 1971. It is not simply obvious, however, that the CAB in 1971 prevented price competition. Air profits rebounded between mid-1971 and the end of 1973; regulation itself, however, received no more real chances to prove its effectiveness.[58]

CONCLUSION

Having set out in the 1930s to popularize air travel and create a stable airline system that served defense and supported itself from fares rather than subsidies, by 1971 several generations of CAB officials had actually achieved most of their goals. Right after World War II, limited service nonsked operators had created the first generation of "mass" airline passengers. Equally, CAB officials had fostered "youth" and other fares that added to that growing market for cheap airfares. Only a generation later, however, the board, whoever the members, gained a reputation as protector of a monopolistic big business and an enemy of consumers and of price competition. Failing to identify earlier and contemporary efforts to expand airline travel, critics of the day and scholars of regulation described the CAB as a captive of airline executives. Although they had forced some competition, officials of the CAB had also helped air transport develop as an industry afraid of the winds of competition—so much so that when the CAB opened the door to price competition—at the request of at least American Airlines' executives—leaders of the remaining carriers ran in the opposite direction, with executives of American and the maverick Continental keeping pace with their rivals. Protective regulation had failed—not because it always prevented competition, but because the public of the 1970s identified the CAB with higher airline ticket prices, and because the CAB and federal policy in general had produced a sheltered, insecure industry, afraid of the vast changes it had wrought. Airline executives of the 1960s liked to compare themselves to the bold aviators of the past. In truth, the industry that they and CAB officials had created was an oligopoly; and the leaders of that industry were programmatically opposed to providing low-cost airfares demanded by consumers and their congressional representatives. In some respects a more apt comparison for those postwar airline managers might have been to the experiences of railroad executives during the 1920s and 1930s. The contexts of airline and railroad regulation were certainly different, yet both the CAB's independent regulation of aviation and the ICC's oversight of the railroads meant that the basic shape and operation of transportation firms and the nature of transportation markets were creatures of politics and public policy.[59]

Airlines and the Civil Aeronautics Board comprised only one segment of the American transportation system. Following World War II, railroads remained large and well-capitalized, but faced financial challenges as well as the challenge brought by aggressive truckers seeking to take away railroad traffic. In turn, rail executives were adept at bringing their messages of financial decline and unfair competition with truckers to the attention of consumers as well as the nation's political leaders. Just as important, however, members of no group proved as energetic as truck operators in defending the regulatory regime. In 1955, Secretary of Commerce Sinclair Weeks—with the support of President Dwight D. Eisenhower—introduced the idea of limited deregulation of truck and railroad rates based on the idea of rate minimums and maximums. Also, Weeks was willing to contemplate route competition between truckers. Not an ideologue but a practical politician, Weeks sought above all to rescue the nation's declining railroads.

In the mid-1950s, neither members of the Interstate Commerce Commission nor members of Congress were prepared for anything as risky for constituents and themselves as rate and route deregulation of surface transportation. Among truckers, Weeks's proposals for partial deregulation set off a period of frantic organizing and lobbying that extended up to termination of the regulatory regime in 1980. Weeks's proposals pushed truckers to freeze in place a defensive strategy and rhetoric that also extended up to 1980. Why deregulate, truckers asked themselves and politicians for the next thirty-four years, when the United States already possessed "the best transportation system in the world"? Among railroad officials, failure to adopt Weeks's proposals encouraged another round of mergers, which this time went by the name of merger "mania."

In 1970, following bankruptcy of Penn Central, the largest merger, President Nixon made deregulation the centerpiece of presidential transportation policy. A few years later, President Gerald R. Ford added airlines to the growing list of industries that would be subjected to "regulatory reform." Between 1978 and 1980, President Jimmy Carter presided over deregulation of airlines, trucking, and railroads. In bringing deregulation to the center of American politics, Presidents Nixon, Ford, and Carter relied on ideas that had their origin with rail officials and with politicians such as Weeks and Eisenhower who had sought to thwart the postwar decline of the railroads.

RUN-UP TO DEREGULATION: SURFACE TRANSPORTATION, 1949–1970

THE REPORT OF SECRETARY OF COMMERCE SINCLAIR WEEKS WAS "PIOUSLY IN FAVOR OF GOOD SOUND COMPETITION."
—NEIL J. CURRY, PRESIDENT, AMERICAN TRUCKING ASSOCIATIONS, 1955

WITH APPROVAL OF the Transportation Act of 1940, members of Congress and President Roosevelt had put in place a system for regulating the nation's surface transportation systems. Henceforth, federal judges and officials at the Interstate Commerce Commission ruled on politically charged matters such as disputed rates, mergers, and even railroad efforts to own trucking firms or launch piggyback service. Equally, leaders of rail and trucking firms would rely on their own rate bureaus to determine rates charged customers. In principle and in law, trucking, rail, barge, and air carriers were members of distinct industries. In all, political leaders and industrial executives committed in the abstract to the idea of competition had instead embraced creation of a complex regulatory regime.

Within a few years of approving this regime, however, federal officials launched an effort to dismantle parts of it. Motivated by concerns about profitability and ultimate survival of the railroads similar to those voiced during the 1930s by Joseph Eastman, the emphasis among several officials was on eliminating regulation. In 1949, for example, Charles Sawyer, secretary of commerce under President Harry S. Truman, recommended partial deregulation of freight rates. Again in 1955 and 1956, President Dwight D. Eisenhower supported Sinclair Weeks, his secretary of commerce, in calling for modified deregulation, starting with limited price competition between truckers and railroaders. Eisenhower worried about consumer prices; and nearly every federal official worried about the declining financial condition of the railroads. In 1956, however, the notion of restoring competition to truckers and railroaders enjoyed few friends in or out of Congress. In the context of the transportation regulatory regime established in 1940, partial restoration of price competition was a peculiar and unpopular idea. Nonetheless, the earlier efforts of Sawyer and then of Weeks and Eisenhower marked a key moment. Once endorsed by such top officials, especially Eisenhower, a limited version of "free markets" in transportation became politically "thinkable."

In 1956, failure to achieve limited deregulation encouraged rail and trucking executives to take distinct courses of action that also had their origins in the transportation debates of the 1930s. Facing rising costs and declining revenues, rail leaders launched service and legal innovations. Still not finished with the dieselization of their locomotive fleets, in 1954 rail executives started piggyback service (haulage of truck trailers on railroad flat cars) aimed at winning back freight business from aggressive truckers. As part of an effort to reduce costs, moreover, those same rail executives created a period of merger "mania," returning to a version of the idea of consolidation that had been part of railroad legislation and expert discussion during the 1920s. In 1968, rail executives including Alfred E. Perlman and Stuart T. Saunders even merged the great Pennsylvania and New York Central Systems, creating the Penn Central.

Unlike their railroad counterparts, who embraced the idea of a modest level of rate-making freedom, truckers judged deregulation an especially frightening prospect. Authors of the Motor Carrier Act of 1935, which framed the regulation of trucking, had created specialized operating rights and other advantages for truckers. Two decades later, many who had participated in the effort to secure those advantages stood as influential figures in trucking politics. Those longtime activists and their younger counterparts remained committed to protecting and even extending those advantages. In 1955 and 1956, Neil J. Curry and other leaders of the American Trucking Associations (ATA) took the fight for the status quo to Congress and to President Eisenhower. Particularly important to those truckers was protection of operating rights, which limited competition with railroads and other truckers to certain types of commodities, and protection of rate bureaus, which minimized price competition. Truckers characterized rate bureau activities as a process of collective rate making.

Starting in 1956, success in blocking implementation of Weeks's deregulation initiative reinforced the determination of trucking attorneys such as Peter T. Beardsley and trucking leaders such as Vee Helen Kennedy and Robert J. McBride to maintain aggressive political and legal action as a standard way of conducting business. During the 1950s and 1960s, lawsuits and political action under the direction of leaders such as Beardsley, Kennedy, and McBride proved successful in protecting both rate bureaus and operating rights against marauding rail executives and detested freight forwarders.

Success in the short run, however, also encouraged those same truckers and their ATA attorneys to continue time-tested legal and political strategies that later proved brittle, and easily cracked, when President Richard M. Nixon and his successors revived the deregulation battle. As frequently as rail officials litigated with truckers about the boundaries of their respective industries, and as much and as often as truck executives brought lawsuits against rail executives and one another regarding rates and routes, up to the end of the 1970s, each and all of them operated within markets and within industries determined by federal rules and federal regulators. Not even appearances before congressional committees by leaders of the mightiest railroad corporations or their big budget for lobbying could introduce substantial changes in transportation markets or in the structure of the transportation industries. This was the period of the regulatory regime.

REPORT OF THE WEEKS COMMITTEE

President Eisenhower's endorsement of rate freedom had its origin in the efforts of railroad officials and political leaders during the administration of President Harry S. Truman to formulate a policy solution to railroad decline. Since the 1920s, truckers had been taking high-value and profitable freight from railroads. Between 1940 and 1953 alone, rail's share of domestic freight tonnage fell from 61 to 51 percent, a whopping loss despite the temporary revival of rail traffic during World War II. Part of the problem was that truckers served retailers and manufacturers who were themselves moving to the suburbs, and to the southern and western parts of the country. With little new rail mileage constructed after 1920, railroads were unable to serve those businesses. During the late 1940s, as truckers plied the vast highway network that federal and state officials had financed and were still constructing, rail track maps still had a 1920s look. At the same time, rail passengers continued the flight to automobiles that had started in the 1910s, accelerated during the 1920s, and revived after World War II. For the rail industry as a whole, general passenger deficits topped $500,000,000 in every year after 1946.[1]

Rail leaders had long blamed truckers for their many woes, but after World War II railroads proposed a new remedy. The calls of rail executives during the 1930s for equivalent regulation had failed to produce the desired results, achieving instead only price regulation that favored truckers for their many woes. As early as 1949, Henry F. McCarthy, vice president of the New York, New Haven & Hartford Railroad, adopted a different solution when he called for "deregulation." Many will object to deregulation on the ground that it will bring "chaos," McCarthy added, "but for twenty-five years we have been going through chaos in one form or another." In reality, rail leaders never wanted a measure as drastic, threatening, or difficult to achieve as total deregulation of rates. Instead, rail leaders such as McCarthy began to advocate the idea that ICC officials set minimum and maximum rates for rail and truck operators, allowing for real price competition. The area between the minimum and maximum was the "zone of reasonableness," in which, argued one rail official, "the free market rather than regulation should govern."[2] With this approach, then, federal officials would construct a market, but this market, such as it was, would operate only within a yet-to-be-determined zone or range of price minimums and maximums. By the late 1940s, no rail executive doubted the central role of federal officials in shaping that market, or the centrality of those officials in securing the profitability of rail, both ideas first embraced in the Transportation Act of 1920.

In 1949, Charles Sawyer, President Truman's secretary of commerce, fused the concerns of rail and political leaders about the declining position of the nation's railroads. Sawyer issued a report advocating significant reliance on competition. "If another type of carrier or another carrier of the same type can perform the service at a profit," Sawyer contended, "it is entitled to the business." Still locked in the language of the 1930s with its emphasis on carrier "types" (and the idea that each transportation "mode" should perform the services for which it was "best" suited in terms of economic efficiency), Sawyer nonetheless had suggested that price competition might not be a bad thing. Reflecting the growing interest among political and rail leaders in achieving a modicum of deregulation, in June 1949, editors of *Fortune Magazine* published an article titled "The Coming Crisis in Transportation," in which the author urged that "railroads must be deregulated and allowed to compete."[3] No later than 1950, then, the idea of deregulation had entered the conversation of business writers, senior federal officials, and railroad executives. What deregulation lacked, however, was presidential, congressional, and ICC leadership.

In January 1953, Dwight Eisenhower took office as president. Not until 1954, however, did Eisenhower's administrators turn their attention to deregulation of surface transportation. On March 1, Eisenhower learned from advisers that railroads were "now getting close to collapse, unable to withstand the competition of subsidized airplanes, trucks, busses, and ships." As one response, Eisenhower created the Presidential Advisory Committee on Transportation Policy and Organization. Secretary of Commerce Sinclair Weeks headed the committee, which journalists, politicians, and many critics soon called by his last name.[4] Although the Weeks committee had its origins in the immediate rail crisis of 1954, the ideas put forward emphasizing partial creation of a "free market" resonated back to the late 1940s with the recognition by Secretary Sawyer and business writers of rail's rapid decline, and further echoed the debates about transportation coordination of the 1930s.

In April 1955, Secretary Weeks issued his report. Weeks and members of his committee determined that widespread use of trucks and airplanes during the preceding generation had produced a "transportation revolution" resulting in genuine competition between rail and truck. Regulations created in an earlier period to protect consumers against unfair rail practices were not simply obsolete, but, so it was argued, actually prevented the most efficient allocation of traffic. Weeks urged creation of a process he called "dynamic competition." Not some arcane idea of an economist, dynamic competition was Weeks's formulation for rescuing the railroads. "Recommendations [of the committee]," a journalist reported in the *New York Times* on April 19, "were interpreted as giving railroads a better chance to compete in the growing and varied rivalry of trucks, airplanes and water carriers." In short, regulation was now bad for the railroads and for all of American business. In practice, Weeks advocated limiting ICC regulation of rail and truck rates to minimums and maximums, preventing predatory practices on the one side or price gouging on the other.[5]

Weeks's call for price deregulation was a stopgap, not a long-term transportation policy. Unlike Harold Moulton and Joseph Eastman, who had surveyed a similar terrain in the 1930s, nowhere did Weeks and members of his committee link their remedy—modest price deregulation—with limitations on federal funding of waterways and highways. Ironically, at the same time federal officials were then preparing budget projections and legislation to fund construction of the costly Interstate Highway System that would certainly open the way for rapid, coast-to-coast trucking service.[6] With one report, however, Weeks had elevated the railroad idea of partial deregulation (through creation of the awkward-sounding zone of reasonableness) from the obscure discussions of political leaders, business writers, and transportation and policy experts to the center of American politics.

At a press conference in early May, President Eisenhower proclaimed the Weeks report "a brilliant piece of work." Rather than take up details of the report, Eisenhower focused his remarks on its potential benefits for the economy as a whole. Journalists learned that "the purpose ... [of the Weeks report] is to make competitive influences more governing in our ... transportation system." Eisenhower perceived rate deregulation as a step toward lower prices throughout the economy. "The person to remember," Eisenhower added, "is the general consuming public." No doubt recognizing that organized truckers would object to any plan promising fiercer competition with one another and with railroads, Eisenhower expected "heated discussion" of the Weeks report.[7] Consistent with earlier presidential efforts extending as far back as Warren Harding and Calvin Coolidge, Eisenhower treated transportation as a topic of strategic importance for the economy as a whole.[8]

No single factor did more to galvanize truckers' commitment to protecting the boundaries of their regulatory victory of the 1930s than the report of the Weeks committee. In 1955, Neil J. Curry inherited the task of defending the interests of organized truckers against Weeks and others who supported destruction of what Curry and his counterparts regularly characterized as "the best transportation system in the world."[9] A trucking company executive, Curry was serving his term as president of the American Trucking Associations, a nationwide trade association headquartered in Washington, D.C., that included several types of truckers. Like his predecessors, Curry's responsibilities as ATA president included representation of members in countless appearances before congressional committees, state and federal regulators, and at meetings of truck operators. More than any other responsibility, the president of the ATA mobilized members for political battles that seemed never to end.

Curry took the lead in converting economic ideas about regulation into preparation for action against the Weeks report. Late in April 1955, Curry called members of the ATA's executive committee into special session to hear presentations on the significance of the Weeks report from the ATA's managing director John Lawrence and members of ATA's legal team. Trucking executives spoke of the centrality of "transportation costs" in determining "the difference between success and bankruptcy for the farmer, merchant, and manufacturer." Under threat, normally hard-edged truckers reimagined themselves as consumer advocates. Given what they called "this basic reason," members of the executive committee concluded that "strong federal regulation to protect the public is imperative." Even more, a member of the ATA's legal staff seemed to revive fears of tranportation coordination, warning that implementation of the Weeks report could serve as a "wedge for rail entry into trucking."[10]

During early May, ATA president Curry brought these messages of consumer protection and of rate and rail competition to meetings of business and transportation executives in Detroit and Washington, D.C., where he met with two governors one day and with President Eisenhower on another day. As part of what an ATA publicist described as an "unending mission," Curry made speeches to a luncheon meeting of the Georgia Motor Truck Association and to the Traffic Club of New Orleans. Labeling arguments in favor of deregulation "as phony as a three dollar bill,'" Curry adopted 1930s-style rhetoric to warn listeners in Savannah that Cabinet Secretary Weeks had proposed giving the railroads "the right to conduct an all-out rate war on trucks." Members of Curry's audience in New Orleans learned that Weeks had based his report on the "fictitious and unrealistic" assertion that railroads were suffering financially. The Weeks report, Curry added, was well written and "piously in favor of good sound competition," raising the troubling prospect that "a good many worthy people are going to be taken in by it."[11]

By April 1956, long-awaited hearings before a House subcommittee only created an opportunity for truckers, railroad executives, Secretary Weeks, and others to say in public what they had been telling one another at meetings and conferences for the past year. "The whole premise of our proposal," declared Secretary Weeks, the first witness, "is that if a given segment of the transportation industry can give a better rate, then shippers are entitled to that rate." In brief, Secretary Weeks affirmed the perceived reasonableness of competition. Yet an attorney for the ATA declared that competitive rate making actually represented "the complete antithesis of both free enterprise and dynamic competition." On the other side, Jervis Langdon Jr., chair of the Association of Southeastern Railroads, once again "emphatically endorse[d]" the report of the Weeks committee seeking greater reliance on competitive rates. A headline writer for *Transport Topics,* the ATA's weekly newspaper, characterized pending legislation as "rail tinted." According to Anthony F. Arpaia, chair of the ICC, transportation leaders were taking a "snail's eye approach" by which each "urged a selfish and narrow solution of their own particular competitive problem regardless of how temporary or illusory such a benefit could be."[12] Given this lack of agreement among transportation officials and the unwillingness of President Eisenhower to take a more active and visible role in seeking partial deregulation, during 1956 legislation supporting Weeks's proposals stood no chance of winning approval in Congress. Just as in the 1930s, rail leaders could not overcome traditional anti-railroad rhetoric and build support for actions that appeared to help their industry. Rules and processes established fifteen and twenty years earlier now seemed immutable.

Few besides Secretary Weeks and several railroad executives supported his deregulation proposals. Nearly everyone (not including railroaders) for whom transportation represented a livelihood or an important service perceived the idea of deregulation as a personal attack. Members of the ICC and of the U.S. Senate and House shared those now-traditional fears; and with senators and congressmen and ICC officials as featured speakers at truckers' meetings and as celebrants of regulation, the system of rail and truck regulation as a whole was probably never in real danger. Still, trucking executives remained cautious. "We have a breathing spell," a top official told delegates at the ATA's annual meeting held in New York City late in October 1956, "on . . . the determined attempt of our railroad brethren to hamstring the trucking industry's competition by changing the fundamental rules."[13]

Characterized as a breathing spell rather than as the victory that it was, publication of the Weeks report and the subsequent scare it brought ATA members encouraged a formalization of trucker politics. First, the already overheated rhetoric of truckers congealed into a couple of memorable, battle-tested, and repeatable phrases. Whether at luncheons, banquets, conferences, congressional hearings, or in their own publications, leaders of the trucking industry repeated identical phrases about the political economy of trucking, phrases that would have been familiar to Joseph Eastman. Regulation was prerequisite to competition, they maintained. In language that retained the predatory images of the nineteenth century, moreover, trucking executives still asserted that railroad leaders were planning to use rate competition to force truckers to "bleed themselves to death," after which prices would increase to monopoly levels. Equally, arrival of the Weeks report reminded ATA leaders and their members that politics offered the best and only protection for the growth and profitability of trucking operations. "Presentation of our interests in any given situation," the new ATA president announced in October 1956, "is our responsibility." Accordingly, he added, "we need political strength."[14]

Even before arrival of the temporary "breathing spell," Curry and his associates had already convinced themselves that only larger doses of passionate rhetoric and "political strength" could offer truckers the protection they needed and deserved as operators of the "best transportation system in the world." The purpose of political strength was to protect the regulatory regime and the highly nuanced position of truckers within that regime. In particular, Curry and every ATA leader before and after him worked energetically to protect their government-created authority to determine rates charged customers through their own rate bureaus and to keep one another and potential "outsiders" such as railroad executives and freight forwarders from invading the protected zones of regulated trucking. Starting in the late 1930s and extending up to deregulation in 1980, the conference system served as among the most important of the bureaucratic and political institutions that surrounded and protected truckers' operating rights.

PROTECTING OPERATING RIGHTS THROUGH THE CONFERENCE SYSTEM

Clearly, truckers thought only about their activities, and not transportation as a whole. Truckers' strong desire to draw hard boundaries around their firms and industry started with their system of operating rights. Under terms of the Motor Carrier Act, which had thwarted Eastman's effort to achieve coordinated transportation in 1935, truckers held certificates issued by the ICC to provide specific and very limited types of service. Like their counterparts in the airline industry, truckers were also "certificated." In 1937, two years after passage of the Motor Carrier Act, the ICC published a classification of operating rights. The ICC's list followed a system long understood and practiced among truckers, including categories based upon whether the firm held common, contract, or private carrier rights, and whether service took place along regular or irregular routes. In addition, ICC officials further categorized truckers according to seventeen types of commodities carried, as for instance household goods, heavy machinery, refrigerated solid products, and so forth. Each classification, moreover, carried with it a letter and numerical code such as common carrier, class C-2, which stood for truckers holding operating rights to haul household merchandise over irregular routes in radial service.[15]

Beginning in 1937, distinctions among truckers that had been informal carried the force of law and the supervisory support of the ICC. Complex on the surface, this classification scheme allowed trucking executives, their watchful attorneys, and ICC officials to protect, say, a firm carrying heavy machinery from competition by more aggressive heavy-machinery carriers, or by members of other trucking groups. Uniform classification also allowed ICC officials to promise uniform treatment to each type of shipper. As had been true of railroad rates since before 1900, the classification scheme facilitated the bureaucratization of regulation in the hands of ICC officials. Throughout the period of truck regulation extending up to 1980, the type or types of operating right(s) held defined a firm's position in the trucking system and consequently the ability of that firm's executives and sales teams to solicit traffic.

In turn, truckers created specialized organizations to protect holders of each type of operating authority. In the language of the day and industry, truckers labeled these organizations conferences, as for instance the common carrier conference. In practice, the history and contemporary workings of these trucking conferences and the operating rights that they protected were closely tied to the decisions made by founders such as Robert J. McBride. Between 1939 and the mid-1950s, McBride dominated the politics of the Regular Common Carrier Conference (RCCC). In 1939, founders of the regulated trucking industry, including Walter Mullady, Maurice Tucker, and others, asked McBride to serve as director of their newly created Common Carrier Division, which was also a constituent group of the American Trucking Associations. The Common Carrier Division (later

Regular Common Carrier Conference) included truckers holding operating rights as common carriers—as opposed to the contract and private carriers, whose operating authorities were more limited in scope. Like the truckers he now represented, McBride's background included experience with railroads, railroad regulation, fierce competition with other truckers including contract carriers, and a reputation as a transportation expert in an industry in which expertise could be converted into political influence.[16] The governing idea, all realized, was to prevent potential competitors such as railroads, contract carriers, freight forwarders, and private truckers from seeking business inside of the potentially lucrative region set aside under the regulatory regime for holders of common carrier operating rights.

During the mid-1950s, Robert McBride was still fighting these battles. In January 1955, for example, he met with members of his board of governors at a hotel in Miami. Two cases were at hand, both of which reflected the continuing efforts of railroad leaders to develop services in line with the 1930s vision of coordinated transportation. In one, McBride reported that an ICC examiner had recommended authorizing executives of the Southern Pacific Railroad to extend their trucking service from an auxiliary to railroad operations to regular trucking service that would compete head to head with members of the Regular Common Carrier Conference. McBride promised to file exceptions to the official's report with the ICC. The second case that concerned McBride also focused on perceived railroad invasion of territory set aside for truck common carriers. Attorneys for the Kansas City Southern and the Louisville & Nashville railroads were asking the ICC to remove what were known as "key points" restrictions from their trucking operations. As McBride's listeners well understood, key points restrictions limited rail operation of trucks to service that was supplementary to rail operations. Up to that point, ICC regulations had prohibited railroads like Kansas City Southern from offering truck service between larger cities, the now-contested key points. McBride asked members of his board whether they perceived any "compromise in these two areas of rail attempts at unrestricted rate competition and unrestricted right to enter the trucking business." He answered himself with the observation that "we have only one alternative," which was to "mobilize our collective strength and to fight tooth and nail to maintain our right to serve the people."[17]

McBride had to remain vigilant against potential encroachments not only by railroad executives, but by another group of truckers, the contract carriers. Substantial differences separated the two types of truckers. Briefly, common carriers represented by McBride picked up merchandise and carried it to recipients, often unloading and reloading smaller shipments at their own terminals. Contract carriers, however, moved merchandise directly between a shipper and a recipient. Direct service and lower overhead allowed contract carriers to charge shippers a lower rate for each delivery. During the mid-1950s, McBride responded to contract carriers' attempts to invade the common carrier field with lawsuits, ICC filings, and lobbying members of Congress, the same tactics he used to resist aggressive railroaders. Even the efforts of contract carriers to convert to common carrier authority merited resistance. By June 1955, according to McBride's top assistant, one case had already cost the common carriers "a great deal of time and money in opposing it." Yet these major investments in lobbying and legal services never guaranteed favorable outcomes. "If we hope to protect our operating authorities," McBride's assistant reported to truck operators, "we must make a record on which the Commission can justify a denial."[18]

Early in 1956, attorney Albert B. Rosenbaum succeeded Robert McBride as general manager of the Regular Common Carrier Conference. (McBride, then sixty-eight years of age, continued his legal and political work for the RCCC, using a more elevated title.) Like McBride, Rosenbaum defined the work of the common carrier conference as essentially defensive in nature. For example, at a meeting of the Board of Governors of the common carrier conference held in Palm Springs, California, early in 1956, Rosenbaum warned that only two of eleven members of the ICC had served more than four years in office, creating the possibility that what he characterized as a "new" idea could materialize.[19] Like McBride, Rosenbaum's job was to prepare for the arrival of new and old ideas that might threaten his members' operating rights.

In August 1957, Rosenbaum and McBride gained an important legislative advantage against the contract carriers. Always fearful that contract carriers would increase the number of customers served to the disadvantage of members of his regular common carriers, Rosenbaum and McBride persuaded Congress to modify the Motor Carrier Act. In the future, holders of contract carrier authority could serve no more than eight shippers. Known in the industry as "the rule of 8," in principle, McBride and Rosenbaum had finally erected a barrier that would secure existing common carrier loadings for their members. No wonder that in October 1958 a writer for *Transport Topics* named Robert McBride "Mr. Common Carrier."[20]

Vee Helen Kennedy represented contract carriers in these deliberations. Since 1943, Kennedy had served as executive secretary of the Contract Carrier Conference, the counterpart position to that held by McBride and later Rosenbaum. Unlike McBride and Rosenbaum, who were both attorneys and men long immersed in the rituals and competitive strivings of unregulated and regulated trucking, Kennedy secured her position by following the narrower path that during the 1940s and 1950s was available only to a few women in the transportation field. Born around 1900 in Washington, D.C., Kennedy attended a local high school, where her courses included typing and shorthand. For two years during the early 1920s, she studied English at George Washington University, and then accepted a full-time position at the American Automobile Association. By the mid-1930s, Kennedy worked as secretary and administrative assistant to the auto association's executive vice president. In 1943, the first executive secretary of the Contract Carrier Conference resigned to devote more time to his prospering law firm. In turn, Charles P. Clark, one of the founders of the contract carrier group and a former executive at the auto club, recommended Vee Kennedy as its second executive secretary. Chance and talent had converged. By the mid-1950s, Kennedy was known among industry leaders as the "'first lady' of trucking."[21]

By October 1958, more than a year after McBride prevailed upon members of Congress to limit the number of customers a contract carrier could serve, Kennedy asserted that the contract carrier industry had reached "a state of transition." Approximately six hundred contract carriers, she reported, "are in litigation . . . for conversion to common carriage." Kennedy predicted that "many cases will be carried to the courts, [with] the conference participating in all lead cases in these fields which may establish precedent to protect the rights of contract carriers." Kennedy also promised to intervene before the ICC on behalf of contract carriers "to see that . . . the amendatory language is followed."[22] Even if Congress had redrawn the legal barriers separating contract and common carriers, Kennedy intended to bring her members to the edge of those barriers, and perhaps breach them. Longtime participants in the transportation industry such as Vee Kennedy and Robert McBride understood that few protections for their members' operating rights were permanent, or impermeable. Because ownership of operating rights guaranteed the right to solicit a particular type of trucking business in a particular territory, ownership of those rights also governed the merger and growth of trucking firms.

OPERATING RIGHTS AND PROTECTED GROWTH
THROUGH MERGER

Whether working as a common or contract carrier, possession of ICC-awarded operating rights offered a method for truck operators to enlarge the scale of their operations inside boundaries guarded by legal and political watchdogs like McBride, Rosenbaum, and Kennedy. Truckers had long experience with consolidation. Between 1940 and 1955, the number of trucking firms had declined from more than twenty-six thousand to around eighteen thousand. In 1956, one observer determined that "the great majority of this decrease was due to motor carrier unification proceedings."[23]

Examination of two mergers highlights the central and expected role of operating rights and ICC decisions in guiding the way in which executives undertook mergers. During the mid-1950s, the six Bonacci brothers owned and operated the AAA Trucking Corporation. Founded in 1931, the firm had remained limited in fleet size and operating rights for more than two decades. The brothers drove the trucks and handled freight at their only depot in Trenton, New Jersey. Not even the firm's common carrier rights into New York, New Jersey, and as far south as Philadelphia guaranteed growth in hauls and revenue. According to a writer for *Transport Topics,* who most likely relied upon the Bonacci brothers for information, AAA "grew slowly, nurtured by enthusiasm, hard work and long hours of truck driving."[24]

ICC examiners had no obligation to encourage growth. In 1953, the Bonacci brothers asked the ICC for permission to transport syrup in tankers between Kearny, New Jersey, and plants in Pennsylvania and New York. At that point, the Bonacci brothers held operating rights to transport syrup in containers over those routes, but not in tank cars; this was the authority requested. According to a report in *Transport Topics,* commissioners determined that "necessity did not require common carrier operation between the points." Fortunately for the Bonacci brothers, executives of Coca-Cola created that sense of necessity, which led the ICC to authorize the Bonaccis to carry flavoring syrups in tanks from Kearny to New York City and liquid syrup from Brooklyn to Kearny.[25]

In 1957, when the Bonaccis purchased the operating rights of Garford Trucking, the brothers expanded their operating authority as far north as Boston and south to Baltimore and Washington, D.C. As part of the approval process, the Bonaccis showed ICC examiners that their merger would lead to more economical operations, especially by eliminating the costs of interlining freight with competitors such as Garford. In addition to the potential for cost reductions, ICC officials also evaluated whether combining these firms would create new operating rights for the Bonaccis. Evidence of an earlier period of interlining with Garford was required to show the potential for economy rather than creation of a new service. In October 1958, the Bonaccis placed an advertisement in *Transport Topics* that featured a sketch of their expanded routes and a photo of a young man whose pants and jacket appeared too short. The caption for the advertisement read "AAA Trucking is . . . Really Growing."[26] Under rules of the regulatory regime, ownership of operating rights offered protection against interlopers. Given the dependence of truck executives on the ICC for prior approval of each modification of operations, including mergers, those same operating rights could also place limits on growth.

The same ICC rules that limited growth also offered truck executives one of the few paths toward achieving a substantial increase in fleet size, tonnage carried, and revenues earned. This process of merging operating authority—the term within the industry was "tacking"—meant that truckers purchased operating rights from another firm and aligned or "tacked" them together, extending their service territories and providing single-line service over a longer distance. By the mid-1950s, executives at Pacific Intermountain Express (PIE) had built one of the nation's largest trucking firms through the process of tacking operating rights.[27] Unnoticed by most truckers was the extent to which the rules of the regulatory regime had permeated to each detail of company ownership, organization, operations, and proposed avenues of growth.

In 1926, founders of the company that later took form as PIE launched service in Pocatello, Idaho. By 1937, they had merged several trucking firms and extended service to such major points as Salt Lake City, Denver, Los Angeles, and San Francisco. Just as importantly, as writer Harry D. Wohl later pointed out in an adulatory article in *Transport Topics*, by 1937, founders had "established the grandfather rights of the present PIE."[28] From the outset, operating rights bestowed by the ICC added value to the PIE franchise.

In 1939, a new group of executives took charge of operations at Pacific Intermountain Express. Again according to Harry Wohl, a senior writer for the ATA's weekly *Transport Topics*, these executives "saw many small lines working under financial handicaps and dependent upon each other for tonnage to balance their hauls." One of those executives, Abner S. Glikbarg, an attorney who had worked for several years in private practice before joining PIE, took principal responsibility for handling the company's business before the ICC.[29] In the trucking business, where the ICC was necessarily a close associate in any effort to achieve growth through merger, those who spoke the language of ICC examiners and commissioners stood to prosper.

During World War II, a boom in truck transportation brought an immense increase in tonnage and a regular flow of cash to the new company. Beginning in 1944, officers of PIE leased the equipment and operating rights of another firm. In 1946, they purchased those rights and equipment, opening the way for regular service between Chicago and St. Louis and major cities on the Pacific Coast including San Francisco and Los Angeles.[30] War and public policy had created favorable conditions for Glikbarg and his associates to expand PIE's operations.

In the late 1940s, the growth-minded Glikbarg offered to purchase Keeshin Motor Express. At that point, the Keeshin firm owned more equipment than Glikbarg's PIE. Keeshin was also operating in bankruptcy. (Unlike the CAB stew l p of the young airline industry, ICC regulators never attempted to guarantee the profitability or service continuity of any one trucking firm.) The real advantage of purchasing Keeshin lay in acquisition of its route system. Keeshin held operating rights for regular, common carrier service between Boston and Washington, D.C., in the east and Minneapolis, Des Moines, and St. Louis in the west. By tacking their operating rights, PIE executives would preside over coast-to-coast service of more than twenty-six thousand miles.[31]

ICC officials and pesky railroad attorneys got in the way of Glikbarg's planned expansion. In November 1950, ICC officials disapproved the merger with Keeshin. At hearings held by the ICC, attorneys for the railroads argued that authorizing PIE officials to create a transcontinental firm would lead to a loss of rail's highest value traffic. Approval of the PIE-Keeshin merger, asserted railroad attorneys, would weaken the railroads, undermine the economy, and pose a threat to the nation's military strength. On grounds that echoed the transportation coordination supporters of the 1930s, namely "preserv[ing] the inherent advantages of each" type of transportation, ICC commissioners endorsed the railroads' arguments, even asserting that rail executives could not meet the needs of economy and nation "unless . . . [they] continue to receive a sufficient traffic volume to maintain their plants and services." As late as 1950, ICC commissioners charged with maintenance of the regulatory regime had determined that protection of the railroads' boundaries took precedence.[32]

In the mid-1950s, Glikbarg launched another program of acquisitions. In September 1955, PIE took control of West Coast Fast Freight, which operated from Spokane and Seattle, Washington, and Missoula, Montana, to Los Angeles. PIE officials also purchased Orange Transportation Company. The idea in making this purchase, Wohl reported, was to "bridge the gap for PIE between intermountain and eastern points and the Pacific Northwest." In the absence of opponents such as railroad attorneys or competing truckers, ICC officials permitted Glikbarg to expand from regional to national operations. For the second quarter of 1956, Pacific Intermountain ranked third in the trucking industry in gross revenues and first in net income.[33] Under terms of the regulatory regime, a sharp increase in revenue had to start with the ICC-approved tacking of operating certificates.

By the early 1960s, Glikbarg and his associates at Pacific Intermountain Express had built a large and profitable firm based on their operating rights, a growing economy, savvy management, and ICC rules and rulings. ICC rulings had also kept Keeshin Motor Express outside of Glikbarg's domain and had limited the growth of the Bonacci brothers' firm. Yet in an industry in which lawsuits were only another element of conducting business, neither the fabulously successful Glikbarg nor the more modest Bonacci brothers brought lawsuits to limit or abolish regulation. Equally, truck operators had a long and successful history of political action, but not one of them appeared at hearings to demand the reduced regulation that Sinclair Weeks had sought in 1955 and 1956. Instead, truckers such as the Bonaccis and Glikbarg paid dues to the ATA, subscribed to *Transport Topics,* and presumably invoked phrases such as the "best transportation system in the world" at appropriate moments. In reality, right up to the end of the 1970s, truckers with backgrounds like the well-known Abner Glikbarg at PIE and the little-known Bonacci brothers at AAA Trucking participated in the ATA's political action committees aimed at protecting operating rights. Away from the hustle-bustle of getting freight delivered and frequent huddles with attorneys, the Bonacci brothers and Abner Glikbarg and his associates had no reason to doubt the centrality of federal law and ICC rulings for undergirding their operating rights and for creating the ability of lawyers such as Robert McBride to mount aggressive defenses against railroaders. Truckers such as the Bonacci brothers and Abner Glikbarg were equally energetic in defending the right of their rate bureaus to determine shippers' charges.

RATE BUREAUS

Rate bureaus protected the truckers' system of collective rate making. In brief, rate bureaus allowed truckers to gather in one place and determine the rates charged to shippers, avoiding some of the vicissitudes of unconstrained markets with their occasional bouts of wild price and profit fluctuations. In spring 1948, Congress passed over President Truman's veto the curiously named Reed-Bulwinkle Act. Authors of the act had exempted rate bureaus from antitrust legislation. Starting that year, federal law shielded truck and railroad operators from daily price competition. As with virtually every institutional fixture of the nation's transportation system, truckers' rate bureaus (and railroaders') were firmly grounded in public policy.

Like the conference system built by Robert McBride and Vee Kennedy, those rate bureaus had their origins and early development in the actions of specific persons; Lewis A. Raulerson was one of those persons. In 1930, Raulerson and a partner organized a trucking company and began hauling automobiles and parts for the Ford Motor Company out of Charlotte, North Carolina. In 1933, they started another firm, Atlanta-Florida Motor Lines, a common carrier between Atlanta and Jacksonville. Through a series of purchases and consolidations, by the early 1950s, Raulerson's Great

Southern Trucking Company emerged as the largest common carrier in the Southeast.[34]

Raulerson harbored apparently contradictory views about relationships between government agencies and business firms. According to the author of a nonscholarly account of Raulerson's early days in the trucking industry, Raulerson "and his colleagues deplored the unions and railroads with equal vigor." Following World War II, moreover, Raulerson joined that group of Americans who expressed concern about "statism, socialism and communism." Nevertheless, Raulerson supported the growth of a network of organizations that brought federal legitimacy and legal protection to the business practices of truck operators. He was a founding member of the Florida and American Trucking Associations, organizations whose leaders from the outset were dedicated to the maintenance of the regulatory regime. Raulerson was also a founding member of the Southern Motor Carriers Rate Conference; for eleven years he served as its president and treasurer.[35]

Starting in 1948 with the Reed-Bulwinkle Act, congressional protection against antitrust litigation allowed truck operators such as Lewis Raulerson. Abner Glikbarg, and the Bonaccis to impose routine on the activities of their rate bureaus. Depending upon the extent of their operating authorities, truckers paid an admission fee plus a percentage of their gross revenues to join a rate bureau. Around 1951, monthly fees paid by truckers ranged between $3.50 and $325.00 at one rate bureau. Fees for the sale of published rates augmented bureau revenues. In turn, rate bureaus employed full-time managers and clerical personnel who among other tasks provided uniform rate information to members. Raulerson's Southern Motor Carriers Rate Conference, with headquarters in Atlanta, served truckers located between eastern Louisiana, Florida, and portions of Virginia and West Virginia. In one peculiar arrangement, the Central States Motor Freight Bureau published rates for a vast territory across the Midwest, but had no direct members. Instead, truckers joined local bureaus in Pennsylvania, Ohio, and adjoining states. Never a precise activity, a few of the territorial rate bureaus also published rates for shipments outside their territory.[36] The rate bureau system offered members the advantage of considerable flexibility in determining prices to charge shippers; those rate bureaus also served as another legal and institutional layer bringing stability and predictability to rates, regulations, and trucking operations.

On the surface, the work of trucking rate bureaus assumed a straightforward, bureaucratic quality. In 1951, transportation professor Charles A. Taff was able to describe "typical" procedures in "representative motor carrier rate bureaus." Much of the work at a rate bureau, Taff reported, revolved around the filing, adjustment, and publication of freight rates. Each proposed rate change, he reported, "is placed on a monthly public docket and also published and distributed to members." Still wider dissemination of proposed rates took place through industry-wide newspapers such as *Transport Topics.* As one example, on January 3, 1955, managers of the Central States Motor Freight Bureau published a list of proposed rate changes in *Transport Topics,* including a proposal submitted by operators of a trucking firm carrying candy or confectionary from Chicago to New Castle, Pennsylvania, and seeking a revised rate on a minimum shipment of twenty thousand pounds. By the mid-1950s, large rate bureaus such as the Central States and Raulerson's Southern Motor Carriers Rate Conference handled around one hundred such rate proposals each week.[37]

Supported by federal law, several rate bureaus achieved considerable size and legal weight. In June 1955, the Middle Atlantic Conference—a rate bureau—employed ninety-five persons and paid annual expenses amounting to nearly $300,000. At hearings on rates, the peripatetic writer Harry Wohl observed that "all concerned have the right to say their say." Yet the reality of the matter was that members of the standing rate committee—the regular staff—settled most rate disputes. "In the absence of an appeal," noted Wohl, "the recommendation of the standing rate committee is final." Thereafter, bureau employees filed the recommended rate with the Interstate Commerce Commission, which bolstered the legitimacy of the rate committee's decision. "Unless someone complains," Wohl observed, "the rate seldom is suspended by the Commission."[38] The achievement of bureaucratic regularity in rate bureau operations meant that senior employees exercised considerable authority in determining prices charged to shippers.

Managers of the Middle Atlantic Conference also brought top-notch legal talent to their negotiations with the staff at the Interstate Commerce Commission. Members of the Middle Atlantic's senior staff each enjoyed between thirty and forty years' experience in the transportation field. Most senior staffers were also attorneys or practitioners registered to bring cases before the ICC. Legal and statistical experts employed at the American Trucking Associations' headquarters in Washington, D.C., supplemented the work of rate bureau staff members, including the staff of the Middle Atlantic Conference. According to Wohl, senior officials at the Middle Atlantic Conference—as attorneys and ICC practitioners—could "take common action and engage in common defense of the members."[39]

Altogether, rate bureau executives marshaled political clout for dealings with federal officials and legal weight for dealings with shippers and competitors. Up to 1970, these activities represented the key contributions of rate bureaus to the workings of the regulatory regime. During the 1970s, however, consumer advocates and politicians, including each of the presidents of the United States, sought to deregulate trucking by eliminating rate bureaus' antitrust immunity. Even before the 1970s, however, neither rate bureau officials nor ATA attorneys were successful in reducing or eliminating the dangers to their rate making and operating rights posed by the much-disdained freight forwarders.

FREIGHT FORWARDERS' THREAT TO OPERATING RIGHTS

Freight forwarders built transportation businesses in the spaces formerly ignored by railroads and truckers. On the face of it, the freight forwarding business was uncomplicated. As one example, Harry M. Baker, president of Coast Carloading Company of Los Angeles, a freight forwarding company, arranged for pickup of small shipments in his own fleet of trucks. From headquarters in Los Angeles, drivers working for Baker consolidated these small shipments into much larger ones, delivering boxcar loads of merchandise to railroads and trailer loads to trucking firms. The small shipper paid the small shipment rate to Baker. Yet Baker, because he had delivered a boxcar or trailer-sized load, paid a much lower rate to the railroads and trucking firms with whom he contracted for services. The difference between the two rates was his profit. Baker wrote a member of Congress, moreover, that the rates he charged shippers were lower than those charged by regular truckers, lower in one example by 20 percent. By the early 1970s, Baker directed operations in nine states and Canada.[40]

Although day-to-day activities of freight forwarding firms were simple, freight forwarders had failed to achieve a legitimated standing within the transportation community. One textbook writer described freight forwarders as "a hybrid in the transportation field." Freight forwarders were also an anomaly in the regulatory regime. Although freight forwarders had existed throughout the twentieth century, the position of forwarders had been a highly contested issue in debates leading up to the Transportation Act of 1940. Not until 1942 did Congress and the president extend the protection of rate and territory regulation by the Interstate Commerce Commission to the freight forwarding industry. At that point, freight forwarders gained the protection of public policy. Yet freight forwarders still lacked many of the legal rights accorded regular truckers, particularly the right to establish lower rates with railroads on long-distance and especially piggyback service. In 1956, leaders of freight forwarding firms had testified with truckers in opposition to rate competition sought by Secretary of Commerce Weeks. At that same hearing, the president of the Freight Forwarders

Institute, the industry's trade association, asked for the right to handle portions of the fast-growing piggyback business at the lower rates available to certificated truckers. That request never went beyond the hearing stage. As late as January 1968, then, the chair of the ICC could still inform members of a congressional committee that "freight forwarders have a distinctly different status . . . than other forms of transportation."[41] Like their counterparts in railroading and in the diverse segments of trucking, during the years after World War II, freight forwarders had boundaries to protect and boundaries to expand.

By the late 1960s, freight forwarders were ready for another effort to expand their operating authority. In the middle of a period of fast economic growth, small shippers were complaining to Congress about inadequate service. In 1967, Giles Morrow, attorney for the Freight Forwarders Institute since 1940, asked Congress to consider legislation that would allow freight forwarders to negotiate rates with railroads for long-distance shipments. Morrow had the support of ICC commissioners; and an official in the new U.S. Department of Transportation characterized Morrow's bill as "bring[ing] greater equality of regulation among all of the various surface modes of transportation."[42] Late in January 1968, members of the House Committee on Interstate and Foreign Commerce held hearings on Morrow's bill. In opposition stood certificated truckers and several of their allies, hoping to keep regulatory boundaries as they were—or perhaps to roll them back.

Most of the witnesses Morrow had lined up to testify in favor of his bill worked as owners and senior managers at small manufacturing firms. These owners and managers shipped in small lots, and their plants were located in remote places. One of Morrow's witnesses, Milton Strickland Jr., worked as office manager of the Kex Plant of Callaway Mills in La Grange, Georgia, which manufactured industrial wiping cloths. Strickland and the others made nearly identical observations about the lower charges and higher-quality service provided by freight forwarders. Strickland urged passage of the bill "in order to maintain this service and enable the freight forwarder to hold the line on increasing costs and rates." Railroads serving his area, Strickland reported, "have discontinued accepting small . . . shipments," and approval of this bill would "insure us a continued good service for our small shipments."[43]

Each of Morrow's witnesses argued for equality of legal treatment for freight forwarders relative to common carriers. Both freight forwarders and regular carriers operated trucks and delivered merchandise to the railroads and elsewhere. Existing law, however, limited the ability of freight forwarders to contract with the railroads for shipments beyond 450 miles. Holders of common carrier certificates faced no such mileage restrictions.

Strickland wanted Congress to "authorize the freight forwarder to enjoy the same privileges motor carriers have been enjoying for some time."[44] Morrow's witnesses affirmed the principle of equality of treatment and the desire to retain or gain some economic advantage.

No one spoke more forcefully about guiding principles and trucking profits than executives and attorneys representing the American Trucking Associations, the national trade association. Despite decades of disagreement between their member groups, including Robert McBride's common carriers and Vee Kennedy's contract carriers, ATA officials still recognized freight forwarders as an enemy in common. "This bill," the ATA's senior attorney Peter T. Beardsley told a congressional committee in January 1968, "would enable freight forwarders to enter into contracts with railroads . . . at rates below those charged shippers for the same service." In other words, Beardsley worried that freight forwarders, by promising large shipments, could demand that railroad executives offer especially low rates, rates that might prove lower than those available to his trucking common carriers. Passage of Morrow's bill, contended Beardsley, would "multiply . . . the opportunities for forwarders to take advantage of the carriers who transport their traffic." Granting this additional authority to freight forwarders, he added, would "intensify an already-evil situation. . . ."[45]

Participants in American transportation politics often used counterattack as a legislative strategy. In this case, attorneys for disgruntled leaders of the ATA urged legislation that would strip freight forwarders of their already limited operating authority. In particular, Beardsley wanted members of Congress to eliminate the right of freight forwarders to contract with truck operators for what he characterized as "unconscionably low rates." Such repeal legislation would eliminate the legal underpinnings of the freight forwarder industry, leaving "all shippers on an even keel." According to the president of a trucking firm located in Tampa, moreover, defeat of Morrow's bill and enactment of legislation stripping freight forwarders of their (constricted) operating authority would actually "produce the most equitable situation . . . possible for the benefit of the shippers and receivers of freight in all parts of our country."[46] Consistent with the "lessons" truckers had drawn from their historical experiences, whenever their operating rights were threatened, truckers went on the legal and political attack.

Shippers came forward in support of Beardsley and his common carriers, not Morrow and his freight forwarders. One of those shippers was Sam Hall Flint, the vice president for distribution at Quaker Oats, a large manufacturer of breakfast cereals. Flint also served as chair of the National Industrial Traffic League, a shippers' organization. Flint invoked images of "excessive pressures" that forwarders would impose on railroads to achieve lower rates for themselves, leaving remaining shippers (perhaps including shippers like Quaker Oats) to "pay . . . substantially more than the freight forwarders for the same transportation services from the railroads."[47]

In reality, the legislative situation had been deadlocked from the start of the hearings. Few with experience in American transportation politics could have believed that members of Congress would actually follow Beardsley's advice and strip freight forwarders of their operating authority. Introduction of that bill, which truckers secured from a willing member of Congress, advertised the potential weight and authority of the federal government behind the insistence of truckers and shippers that they, not the freight forwarders, were the long-standing victims of discriminatory legislation. That was the symbolism of the moment.

Equally decisive early in 1968 was the decision of railroad executives not to endorse Morrow's efforts on behalf of the freight forwarders. As one rail executive explained to members of the committee dealing with Morrow's bill, freight forwarders made extensive use of the railroads' piggyback service, and the fear among rail executives was that forwarders would use that volume as "a means for negotiating lower rates." Award of contractual rights to freight forwarders, he feared, "will deteriorate into a system of give-and-take bargaining," creating a situation that "can only lead to a reduction in railroad revenues." According to the handwritten notes of a member of the house committee, rail executives "opposed . . ." contract rates out of concern that "FF [freight forwarders] could play one R.R [railroad] against another." In short, legislated boundaries separating forwarders, common carriers, and railroads appeared essential to maintenance of railroad and trucker revenues. When it came to freight forwarders, moreover, rail leaders were in no mood to approve so threatening an idea as "give-and-take bargaining. . . ."[48]

Morrow's bill was dead. On January 17, 1968, Fred H. Tolan, chair of the legislative committee of the National Industrial Traffic League and a consultant to western shippers, wrote clients that "western railroads yesterday rescinded their support . . . that had earlier been obtained under freight forwarder pressure." Earlier, reported Tolan, executives of southern and eastern railroads had decided not to support Morrow's bill. So convinced was Tolan that this bill would languish that he was not even planning to make a statement before the House committee. Only if the bill "reaches the Senate," Tolan informed clients, would he "request time to appear."[49]

This victory by Peter Beardsley and his ATA members over Giles Morrow representing freight forwarders added one more anecdote to the conviction among postwar politicians and journalists that truckers were unbeatable in American politics. Whether it was the truckers' success in securing approval of the Reed-Bulwinkle Act or in turning back Weeks's idea about creating a "zone of reasonableness" in which markets would determine shipping prices, no one at the time doubted the ability and willingness of trucking organization leaders to mobilize members and legal talent for another fight in Congress or another presentation before the ICC or a federal judge. Excellent at protecting their boundaries, truckers, for all their legal and political weight, could not extend them outward to shove aside the much-disliked freight forwarders. Put in place between 1935 and 1940, during the postwar decades the trucking industry's structure lacked political malleability and its submarkets (freight forwarders and common and contract carriers, for example) were largely impermeable from inside or outside the trucking industry. In this legal and political climate, railroad executives enjoyed little ability to move boundaries of the regulatory regime in their own favor.

RAILROADS IN THE AFTERMATH OF THE WEEKS REPORT

In 1955, leaders of the Association of American Railroads (AAR) produced a leaflet titled "Mrs. Kennedy's Five Pounds of Sugar." (Like the American Trucking Associations, the AAR served as the trade association for the nation's rail executives.) The leaflet featured a photograph of a middle-aged woman with her left hand on top of a box of granulated sugar. The woman was engaged in an animated discussion with the grocer in the checkout lane. Presumably, that conversation was focused on the high price of sugar in her home city of St. Louis. The leaflet's authors pointed out that railroads could bring sugar to Mrs. Kennedy from New Orleans at a reduced rate, but "*the proposed rate reduction is never put through*" (emphasis in original). Regulation of railroad rates and service, a railroad publicist wrote, "denies the public the benefits of the most efficient form of transportation."[50]

Railroad executives had published "Mrs. Kennedy's Five Pounds of Sugar" as part of their effort to secure approval in Congress of reduced regulation of rates as recommended by Secretary Weeks. Like President Eisenhower and the rhetorically adept truckers, railroad leaders had taken up the cause of the consumer. The broad intent of rail executives was to operate in a less fettered manner when it came to determining rates and determining whether they could extend trucking services. In fields as litigated and lobbied as railroad use of trucks and railroad rate making, however, that railroad leaflet portraying Mrs. Kennedy's concern about sugar prices represented only a fraction of the printed and spoken words prepared during the postwar decades to influence legislators and ordinary citizens regarding the adverse effects of the regulatory regime on consumers and on railroad profits, employment, and service.

Ultimately, the effort of railroad leaders to win support for Weeks's proposals proved ineffective. In response to the Weeks plan, energetic truckers had mounted, as we have seen, a united campaign aimed at persuading members of Congress that only regulation could protect "the best transportation system in the world." In June 1956, a writer for the *New York Times* reported that railroad executives were engaged in "soul-searching" regarding "repeated political defeats—defeats that are reflected in balance sheets and income statements."[51] In short, the failure of Weeks and Eisenhower to bring about partial deregulation reconfirmed what rail executives had believed since 1920 or before—that politics and public policy guided railroad operations, and guided them adversely.

In retrospect, the importance of "Mrs. Kennedy's Five Pounds of Sugar" rested less on its failure to persuade in this one instance than on the leaflet's symbolic and literal connections to the strenuous efforts of railroad managers to reduce costs, improve service, and avoid future defeats, especially defeat of plans for deregulating railroad managers. During the 1950s and 1960s, leaders of the nation's railroads also expended vast amounts of capital and energy to complete the dieselization of their fleets, launch substantial piggyback service, and merge operations, including the costly and time-consuming merger of the gigantic New York Central and Pennsylvania systems. In the 1950s and 1960s, rail executives attempted both to reduce regulation (when it suited their interests) and at the same time to run successful businesses within the narrow confines that the regulatory regime made available to them. Both strategies resembled elements of earlier policy options that had failed to secure broad support among railroad leaders or public officials—transport coordination in the 1930s and railroad consolidation in the 1920s.

DIESELS AND PIGGYBACK

Conversion from steam locomotives to diesel electric engines proved the most important mechanical innovation of the postwar era in railroading. The diesel engine possessed greater pulling power, operated at a lower cost, and led to fewer maintenance problems than old-fashioned steam engines. Up to 1945, operation of more than 2,800 diesel units had provided railroad management with substantial evidence of diesel's many advantages.[52]

After World War II, rail executives launched full-scale conversion to diesel motive power. As historian Albert J. Churella explains, "[R]ailroads . . . understood that, in order to achieve the full economies of dieselization, they would have to eliminate *all* of their steam locomotives, along with related service and repair facilities, as quickly as capital constraints would allow" (emphasis in original). Even rail executives whose lines handled shipments of coal switched to diesel. In 1956, executives of the Louisville & Nashville Railroad, a line that carried vast amounts of coal, retired their last steam engine in favor of an all-diesel fleet of locomotives. Within a decade and a half following World War II, executives of every railroad had completed the process of dieselizing the American locomotive fleet. In 1960, fewer than eight hundred steam engines remained in service. At that point, reports railroad historian John F. Stover, "it was almost easier to find a steam locomotive in a museum than one operating on a railroad."[53]

Widespread use of diesel engines reduced operating expenses and boosted railroad productivity. Diesel engines cost $125,000 to $200,000 each, approximately twice the price of steam engines. Officers at the mighty Pennsylvania Railroad determined, however, that diesel locomotives produced cost savings ranging between 20 and 40 percent. "Most of these savings," Churella finds, "accrued from the replacement of inefficient steam locomotives with a smaller number of more reliable . . . diesels." Equally important, steam engines at the Pennsylvania and at every other railroad had required maintenance on a daily basis, which meant that rail executives operated service facilities such as water-supply equipment across their lengthy systems. Unlike those cumbersome steam engines, diesel engines remained in operation for thousands of hours without service, eliminating the need for daily repairs and far-flung maintenance centers. According to Stover, then, the diesel locomotive "brought a revolution to the nation's railways."[54]

Just as the diesel was the most important innovation in railroad locomotives, the trailer-on-flatcar (TOFC) represented a key change in freight service. Basically, the trailer-on-flatcar, known popularly as a piggyback car, represented a simple innovation. Trucks still picked up freight from shippers. Instead of carrying that freight to recipients, however, drivers brought it to a railroad depot, where railroad employees loaded the trailer portion of the truck onto a railroad flatcar. In turn, the railroad carried that trailer long distances, where it was unloaded, connected to another truck tractor, and delivered locally. Trailer-on-flatcars provided more rapid and more economical handling of general and specialized freight. Piggybacking also "proved," asserts Stover, "that railroaders could serve truck shippers."[55] Even more, full implementation of piggybacking held out the promise that railroads might yet secure a dream dating to the 1920s and emerge as transportation companies, escaping the rigid confines of ICC rules.

The idea of a flatcar carrying a truck or container was an old one in railroad circles. As early as 1833, editors of *Niles' Weekly Register* reported that the Baltimore & Ohio offered piggyback service. During the 1920s and

1930s, executives of several railroads, including the Pennsylvania and the New York, New Haven & Hartford, offered piggyback service on a limited basis as part of efforts to make themselves into transportation companies. Only in the mid-1950s, however, did rail executives develop piggyback operations throughout their systems. Although an industry publicist later judged trailer-on-flat-car "the transportation story of the decade," up to that point not even awareness of piggyback principles and their practical application at the hands of managers at the well-known New York, New Haven & Hartford (hereafter the New Haven) had fostered its widespread adoption.[56]

As with most innovations in the transportation industry, political and legal factors had impeded implementation of piggyback service. For years, as a retired rail and piggyback executive explained in 1962, "there was a fear on the railroads that establishing trailerload rates would hasten the conversion from carload [a railroad vehicle] to trailer [a truck vehicle], producing little actual increase in volume." Early in 1954, however, attorneys for the Chicago & North Western Railway (C&NW) sought permission from the Interstate Commerce Commission to offer door-to-door freight service to multiple points between Chicago and Green Bay, Wisconsin. They proposed using 100 percent railroad-owned equipment. Officials of the C&NW had crossed the sacred line into the "field" of "another carrier." In June 1954, leaders of six eastern railroads, several of which had first experimented with trucks and trucking in the 1920s, filed to engage in wholly-owned, piggyback service. In response, attorneys for the American Trucking Associations filed a protest, arguing that the railroads would be engaged in highway transportation without certification, violating the operating rights of ATA members. Nonetheless, ICC officials determined to permit this "experiment" to begin and took the entire question under extended study.[57] Until the 1950s, another of those interminable boundary disputes that characterized most of the politics of the regulatory regime had delayed introduction of trailers-on-flatcars. In this instance, however, officials of the ICC relocated the boundary.

With this boundary moved in their favor, rail executives quickly inaugurated service. By 1959, fifty-seven railroads offered piggyback operations. Without doubt, railroads earned the greatest revenues when they solicited traffic from shippers and picked up merchandise in their own trucks, bringing it to flatcars. Under the new ICC guidelines, however, rail executives also accepted piggyback shipments from truckers. As early as 1960, about 25 percent of piggyback volume consisted of trailers owned by trucking firms. Regardless of the truck's ownership, the idea of piggyback service gained attention among railroad executives and observers as a method for boosting rail income in a period of fierce—and often unsuccessful—competition with truckers. Even though this experiment fit neatly with the late 1920s and 1930s dreams of several rail leaders and transportation experts who had sought to promote coordinated ground transportation through transportation companies, in 1960, sober economists such as John R. Meyer and his colleagues at Harvard University described piggyback as "not simply a trailer on a flatcar but a new concept in railroading." Regardless of the origins of piggyback, in 1967, an industry writer predicted that "the word for piggyback's growth well into the '70s will also be 'spectacular.'"[58]

Much of the growth in piggyback service came not from hauling general freight, but from solid increases in specialty shipments such as automobiles. In 1959, railroads carried 8 percent of the nation's automobiles from manufacturers to dealers. Beginning around 1960, executives at lines such as the Louisville & Nashville Railroad (L&N) launched a program of aggressive solicitation of automobile business. As a start, they mounted trilevel racks on flatcars, allowing carriage of twelve standard-size automobiles and up to eighteen imported vehicles. Soon, L&N trains made daily trips from the Ford Motor Company's assembly plant in Louisville to Nashville. Yardmen connected that train with another carrying automobiles manufactured in St. Louis, creating a lengthy and lucrative run to ports such as New Orleans. L&N sales personnel had also solicited import car business that filled its trains' racks for the return trip. Between 1960 and 1962, L&N's automobile business experienced a phenomenal increase of 3,800 percent. A publicist in Louisville headlined the L&N operation as "piggybacking at full throttle. . . ." By 1966, moreover, the average cost of shipping an automobile from the Midwest to the West Coast fell from $280 to $120. As railroad carriage of automobiles continued on the upswing, that same year optimistic editors at *Railway Age* headlined that the "Growth of Auto Traffic Shows What Rails Can Do."[59]

In reality, the first decade of trailer-on-flatcar service never delivered loads and profits comparable to the inflated predictions of railroad observers and executives. Up to the mid-1960s, piggyback operations generated only a small portion of railroad revenues—less than 2 percent in 1960 and only about 5 percent in 1966, a boom year. Among participants and observers in an industry unaccustomed to positive news, however, piggyback service held out the promise of recovery, perhaps even the return of a solid prosperity. "For the first time in 18 years of declines," observed Daniel P. Loomis, the president of the Association of American Railroads, in January 1965, "the railroads' share of total intercity freight volume has leveled off at 43 percent." According to Loomis, "[T]he piggyback surge has been crucial to the railroad renaissance."[60] In the railroad business, even a leveling off in the rate of decline was reason for self-congratulation.

During the mid-1950s, railroad managers completed the dieselization of their locomotive fleets and simultaneously launched piggyback service. Such innovations promised cost reductions and service improvements that many rail officials hoped would make up for limits on operations imposed by ICC regulations. Yet not even strenuous lobbying campaigns, including the efforts of Sinclair Weeks, had convinced Congress to change most of those regulations. Nonetheless, optimistic railroaders, journalists, and politicians told themselves and one another that even without reduced regulation, innovations such as dieselization and piggyback would help restore the competitive position of the nation's railroads. During the 1950s and 1960s, many in and out of the railroad business also believed that mergers would lead to a restoration of profitability. At one point, so many mergers had been consummated or planned that contemporaries described the merger movement as a period of "mania."

MERGER MANIA

Mergers were another component of the postwar effort to restore profitability and luster to the nation's declining railroads. Rhetoric of the period resembled that of another time of stress for the railroads—the period after World War I, when members of Congress wrote consolidation into the Transportation Act of 1920 as the solution to multiple problems. This time, advocates asserted, mergers would reduce costs. Consolidated operations, advocates further argued, would eliminate time-consuming transfers at railroad interchanges, leading to more rapid flows of merchandise between sellers and buyers. According to railroad observers, regulators, and executives, then, merged railroads would have greater success in meeting the fierce competition for long-haul traffic brought by barge operators, airline managers, and aggressive truckers. If ICC commissioners, truckers, and politicians could block Sinclair Weeks's proposals to reduce railroad rate regulation, and if again ICC commissioners, truckers, and those same politicians could prevent railroads from owning aircraft, steamships, or fleets of trucks, then at least newly merged railroads, many contended, would provide long-distance and uninterrupted service—at a profit.[61] Like piggyback service and dieselization of locomotive fleets, moreover, mergers, even the largest mergers, kept railroad managers strictly inside the railroading domain that ICC officials and politicians had allocated to them. Ironically, every merger had to begin and conclude with the approval of ICC commissioners, and sometimes with the approval of leading members of Congress, presidents of the United States, and justices of the U.S. Supreme Court.

In 1957, merger of the Nashville, Chattanooga & St. Louis Railway into the Louisville & Nashville Railroad kicked off the period of "mania." In 1961, promises of improved service and cost savings, especially in yard work, underlay the reasoning as leaders merged the Erie Railroad with the Delaware, Lackawanna & Western Railroad, creating the Erie Lackawanna Railroad. In 1963, a similar logic guided proponents of a merger between the gigantic Chesapeake & Ohio Railway and the equally mammoth Baltimore & Ohio Railroad. The combined firm included eleven thousand miles of track and a hefty level of debt. In 1966, an observer concluded that "merger madness has reached a peak."[62]

Rather than allowing the movement—or madness—to peak and taper off, rail executives pursued additional mergers. Like consolidation efforts in the 1920s and 1930s or the mid-1950s, each new merger in the mid-1960s built on the hope and promise of reduced costs and improved service. "We've got a route now that nobody can beat," an executive at the recently merged Seaboard Coast Line Railroad reported to *Railway Age* in July 1967, and "we're going to give the truckers a fit." Early in January 1967, a writer listed seventeen actions underway that involved the merger, control, and consolidation of more than forty railroads.[63]

Ultimately, the merger movement, like virtually every organizational and operational feature of American transportation, took place as a child of the regulatory regime. In a system that had been constructed by public policy and by the politics of the day, one must not be surprised that shippers, railroad executives, union leaders, and politicians had much to say about proposed mergers. As noted above, railroad executives described mergers in terms of improved economies and improved service, and the process, unlike in the 1920s, was driven directly by the carriers' executives rather than by ICC experts. Even so, railroad executives could not act alone to merge operations. Merger negotiations and subsequent filings with the ICC threatened economic and political relationships, including those of shippers located along the rights of way, merchants interested in low-priced and predictable deliveries, and employees, whether at the railroads or in plants, warehouses, and shops along those same rights of way. As one example, in January 1965, an assistant U.S. Attorney asserted that the proposed merger of the Great Northern Railway Company and the Northern Pacific Railway Company with the Chicago, Burlington & Quincy Railroad "would entail a basic and irreversible change in one of the most significant influences upon the economic life of this area, upon its farm production and marketing [and] its industrial production." Against matters of such obvious weight and magnitude for the millions of Americans living between Seattle and Chicago, the U.S. Attorney insisted that the promised benefits of the merger in the form of cost savings for the railroads and service improvements for shippers appeared quite modest.[64]

With the stakes of larger mergers raised so high, politicians inevitably represented the financial, employment, and transportation needs of their districts and states. Members of the U.S. Senate and House heard often both from voluble merger enthusiasts and from those whose opposition was equally passionate. These conflicts spilled into preliminary negotiations surrounding a merger and extended though court filings and appeals. With so many hurdles, the execution of railroad mergers sometimes extended over the course of a decade or longer. In February 1965, publicists for the Association of American Railroads described the merger process as "costly and often painful." Indeed, attorneys representing the Great Northern and other roads had filed preliminary merger papers with the ICC in 1961. Not until February 1970, however, did the U.S. Supreme Court finally approve the proposed merger, creating the Burlington Northern.[65]

Penn Central Merger

Efforts to merge the New York Central and the Pennsylvania Railroads proved especially lengthy, conflicted, and politicized. The Penn Central, reports historian Richard L. Saunders Jr., was "the big merger." On November 1, 1957, at the beginning of the period of "mania," the presidents of the New York Central and Pennsylvania announced from New York City and Philadelphia their plans to launch "'further studies'" regarding a merger. The combined road, if it came into being, would hold assets of $5 billion, making it the nation's tenth-largest corporation. With 184,000 employees and revenues of $1.5 billion annually, the new firm would dominate railroad traffic in its region. Despite their large revenues and immense scale of operations, however, during 1957 the Pennsylvania and New York Central each earned less than 1 percent on their invested capital. Naturally, the two presidents emphasized the immense savings that would materialize through joint rather than competitive operations. In January 1959, the president of the New York Central, with his "merge" button still affixed, called off merger talks, handing what historian Saunders describes as a "humiliating rebuff" to James M. Symes, the president of the Pennsylvania.[66]

In September 1961, Alfred E. Perlman, the president of the New York Central, restarted merger talks with a telephone call to Symes. Merger of the two lines still held out the prospect of creating a successful railroad. Now, managers promised savings of more than $60 million a year, freeing up funds for new investments; they hoped to create what historian Saunders characterizes as "a sleek technological machine that would drive all others to the wall." As complex negotiations and the inevitable litigation got underway, managers at both lines ordered costly and important improvements at the New York Central's freight yards in Buffalo, Detroit, and elsewhere, and at the Pennsylvania's key Conway Yard near Pittsburgh.[67]

Like the proposed merger of the Great Northern and Northern Pacific with the Chicago, Burlington & Quincy, the real business of combining the Pennsylvania and New York Central rested not only with company executives, but also with politicians, union leaders, ICC officials, and judges. In March 1962, attorneys representing the Pennsylvania and New York Central filed for approval of the merger with the ICC. Hearings extended over 129 days and included 463 witnesses and appearances by 338 attorneys who altogether produced 25,000 pages of testimony and another 100,000 pages of correspondence, exhibits, and so forth.[68]

The purpose of producing such an immense body of information and opinion was not to persuade with fact, logic, or sheer volume. Nor was anyone asked to achieve mastery of the information produced in the hearings. More important, reports historian Saunders, was "how their ox was going to be gored." As one example, leaders of weak railroads such as the Erie Lackawanna and the New Haven sought inclusion in the proposed merger with a view toward protecting already weak routes and assets. Once the Pennsylvania and New York Central merged, freight that the Pennsylvania had formerly delivered to the New Haven would remain on combined Penn Central operations, leaving the New Haven out in the cold. As far back as 1961, aides to President John F. Kennedy had sought a solution for the New Haven's many problems, highlighting the importance of that road for the politics and economics of the New York region. On January 5, 1966, New Haven trustees accepted an offer of stock, bonds, and cash from Pennsylvania and New York Central executives to take control of the New Haven's freight operations (but not its passenger service). The New Haven's trustees had managed to dispose of what historian Saunders describes as a "cadaverous railroad running up annual deficits of $15 million." Later, a member of the ICC described the merger as "a big grab bag," suggesting perhaps that crafty New Haven trustees had helped their sagging railroad to a handful of undeserved resources. As much as railroad leaders liked to portray themselves as under siege from truckers and others outside of railroading, the truth was that mergers also encouraged venality and competition from within, especially when regional politics created such a strong position from which to demand a payout.[69] Much of the remaining history of the Penn Central merger is a history of persons and organizations who possessed some clout and a willingness to use it to nail down their share of the supposed profits, protections, and luster that the new firm was going to provide.

Leaders of railway labor had jobs to protect. In 1959, future Pennsylvania president Stuart T. Saunders had been president of the Norfolk & Western Railway, a Pennsylvania subsidiary. Merger negotiations he was conducting with leaders of the Virginian Railroad drew the antagonism of union leaders, whereupon Saunders negotiated an "'attrition agreement'" with them. Following the merger, the company might transfer an employee to another job, but Saunders agreed to rule out future layoffs. On May 20, 1964, Saunders (since October 1963, the CEO of the Pennsylvania) signed a similar agreement with leaders of Pennsylvania and New York Central unions. Like the earlier deal, Saunders and his union counterparts determined that management could transfer an employee to another worksite, but layoffs or dismissals were not permitted. Saunders also agreed that persons laid off between the date of the agreement and the actual merger were entitled to reemployment. "Labor and its political allies had been silenced," writes historian Saunders of the merger, leaving it to politicians to protect other workers and other politicians.[70]

Politicians defended the perceived economic interests of their constituents, sometimes even before those constituents realized those interests needed a defense. The mayor of Newark, New Jersey, sought a stop for passengers at South Newark and assistance with the city's urban renewal program. The governor of Pennsylvania and the mayor of Philadelphia worried that executives of the merged Penn Central would eliminate railroad service to the Port of Philadelphia. In 1964, however, Pennsylvania Railroad officials promised continuing service to the port, which left only the objection of Philadelphia's mayor, who feared loss of the Pennsylvania headquarters to New York and consequent reduction in jobs and diminution of the city's prestige as a corporate center. With all the prosperity that the combined railroad was going to spread around, was it not possible for both cities to retain important Penn Central offices? Once again, Pennsylvania and New York Central officials paid the price asked. The combined Pennsylvania and New York Central would maintain its executive offices in Philadelphia along with general offices in both New York City and Philadelphia.[71]

Maintenance of commuter service into New York City by the bankrupt New Haven represented the largest problem facing politicians. "Commuters on the New York and New Haven," reported a *New York Times* journalist, "have long been subjected to uncomfortable rides in trains that have deteriorated badly and often just break down completely." With the opening of the Connecticut Turnpike in 1959, moreover, additional commuters drove to work, at once reducing revenues for the New Haven and increasing the financial burden of repairing deteriorated equipment. In 1962, consultants for the trustees had recommended that "no more federal funds, over and above those already committed, will be advanced . . . to meet operating deficits." In 1965, however, seven members of the U.S. Senate—all from states in which the New Haven maintained commuter service—introduced legislation to provide federal subsidies for continuing operation. The federal and state governments subsidized highways, waterways, airways, and airlines, John O. Pastore, one of those senators, told a hearing on March 2, 1965, while "the New Haven has been required to maintain its own track, roadbed and other facilities and to pay taxes on its holdings." Pastore insisted that "there is nothing wrong with the New Haven that cash won't cure."[72]

For all of the pressures exerted, side deals arranged, and senatorial rank brought to bear, commissioners of the ICC still exercised first authority over mergers. On April 27, 1966, more than four years after the filing, members of the ICC voted unanimously to approve the merger of the Pennsylvania and the New York Central. Commissioners ordered the entire New York, New Haven & Hartford included in the new Penn Central, not just its freight system, but permitted managers to discontinue a number of its passenger lines. Commissioners also ordered payments to the Erie Lackawanna and two other railroads for traffic that would be lost. Appeals by disappointed holders of New Haven bonds to the federal courts and eventually the Supreme Court served to delay the actual merger until February 1, 1968, boosting the period between filing and merger to nearly six years. As part of their finding in favor of the merger, justices cited the importance of maintaining New Haven operations.[73]

Local observers and participants found much to celebrate in creation of the Penn Central. With promised savings of millions a year and no job losses, editors of the *New York Times* perceived "a new era in rail transportation." Managers of the Penn Central, predicted editors, would "be in a position to slug it out with truck and air carriers." Politicians representing homeowners located along the New Haven's right of way were especially excited. With the Penn Central financing part of the New Haven's operations and with direct federal aid and funds from New York State bonds, no longer would thousands of commuters have to worry about elimination of their daily transportation to New York City. No longer, moreover, would local politicians and developers have to fear for the economic vitality of fashionable suburbs such as New Rochelle in the event the railroad collapsed and those commuters sought residence elsewhere. Executives of the Pennsylvania and the New York Central predicted costs savings, upgraded facilities, maintenance of service on the New Haven, and no diminution of freight over former Pennsylvania and New York Central tracks. Looked at over the long history of efforts to achieve integration of railroad firms and their disparate, competitive, and uneconomic operations, historian Saunders concludes that the "dream[s]" of "Albert Cummins to Louis Brandeis to Walker Hines to Joseph Eastman . . . would now be realized in the Penn Central merger."[74]

The Penn Central merger realized only financial and political disappointments. In part because of poor planning, confusion characterized freight deliveries. Often, shipments ran days or even weeks late, and Penn Central managers had trouble locating behind-schedule deliveries for anxious shippers and receivers. According to historian Saunders, Penn Central "computers were asked . . . to locate twenty cars known to be on the system, [and] couldn't find any of them." "Penn Central's service failures," observed a reporter for the *Wall Street Journal* on July 12, 1970, "include[d] every type of complaint ever registered, and in greater numbers than ever encountered on any other line." Products undelivered meant that wholesalers and retailers lost business. Products arriving late (rather than not at all) such as "'stale'" beer encouraged shippers to take their business to the Erie Lackawanna or to a trucking company.[75]

Only after the merger did company officials discover that the much-celebrated computer system at the New York Central was incompatible with its less well known counterpart at the former Pennsylvania Railroad. Incompatible computer systems also meant that financial data essential to sound management were often incomplete, in error, or simply missing. According to historian Saunders, "unsettled accounts went from $57 million shortly after the merger to $87 million in January of 1970, to $101 million in March 1970."[76]

Employees also judged themselves incompatible with one another. Whatever the new name, employees thought of themselves as Pennsylvania or New York Central, not Penn Central. Conflicts led to resignations of talented and energetic executives. Following the merger, more than ninety members of the well-trained and successful marketing staff assembled at the former New York Central resigned. Employee morale remained low, especially among those who attempted to make a poorly planned merger work for shippers and riders.[77]

Starting in late 1969 and into early 1970, a declining economy contributed to the woes of Penn Central managers. The harsh winter of 1969–1970 added more costs to a fast-growing list of expenses. On June 12, editors of the *Wall Street Journal* published an article titled "How Decaying Service, Bickering Officials Led to Penn Central Crisis." On June 21, 1970, directors of Penn Central sought the protection of bankruptcy, at that time the largest in American history. Company directors cited a "severe cash squeeze . . ." and the inability "to acquire from any source additional working capital." In keeping with the political dimension of rail operations, a *New York Times* writer reported that President Richard M. Nixon rejected the request of Penn Central executives for a loan guarantee of $200 million on the grounds that the "political risks were too great."[78] Whether the Penn Central would have survived in a less hostile and less self-interested regulatory environment or in a faster-growing economic environment is unknown, and unknowable. In 1970, politics and public policy informed virtually every activity at the Penn Central, including its bankruptcy application and requests for last-minute resuscitation.

In 1955, leaders of the nation's railroads had launched their final drive for deregulation with leaflets such as "Mrs. Kennedy's Five Pounds of Sugar." Deregulation, they believed, was vital to successful competition with aggressive and savvy truckers. Unable to alter the structure of the transportation industries and prohibited from reaching into markets dominated by truckers, rail executives such as Alfred Perlman completed the dieselization of their locomotive fleets and launched ambitious piggyback programs. No effort to reduce costs and overtake truckers held out more hope for railroad leaders than the great merger movement, the "mania." Rail executives young and old believed that mergers promised cost savings and service improvements. That mergers were inconsistent with the professed commitment of rail executives to restored competition was one of those inconsistencies that never attracted much attention.

CONCLUSION

During the years after 1956, the Weeks report and the earlier report of Commerce Secretary Sawyer took their places on the dusty shelves of research libraries along with previous schemes to revamp the nation's rail system. Nevertheless, Weeks's report and President Eisenhower's endorsement of it had caught the attention of economists, transportation executives, and politicians. Among those industry and policy activists, the exhilarating and frightening ideas contained in the Weeks report reverberated through policy circles up to the partial deregulation of the trucking and railroad industries in 1980. For a quarter-century, however, everyone with something to protect (such as truckers) were enraged at the prospect of price competition inside of a "zone of reasonableness"; and everyone with something to gain (such as railroad executives and railroad workers) wanted some limited form of freedom—the zone of reasonableness—within which to adjust rates and operations.

The battle about the organization of the transportation industries and regulation of the many transportation markets assumed several forms, again depending on whether one stood to gain or lose. Truckers wanted to protect the rate bureaus through which they engaged in collective rate making that Congress had exempted from antitrust scrutiny in 1948. Truckers also sought to protect their operating rights, which in effect were licenses awarded by the ICC that allocated territories and commodities to individual firms within distinct fields of trucking such as Robert McBride's common carriers and Vee Kennedy's contract carriers. The system of operating rights and rate bureaus founded by truckers like Lewis Raulerson set the terms for every aspect of trucking operations. This system of operating rights enforced by the ICC placed severe limits on the ability of the Bonacci brothers to increase their scale of operations. Equally, the system of operating rights, including the "tacking" of those rights, had framed the growth strategy that Abner Glikbarg and his associates employed to create the gigantic Pacific Intermountain Express. Ultimately, ICC enforcement of the system of operating rights and rate bureaus established boundaries that defined common and contract carriers as regular players in the system, and that left little room for freight forwarders, who remained as peculiar outsiders. Savvy truckers and their attorneys, such as Neil Curry and Peter Beardsley, took the fight to preserve the boundaries of this regulatory regime to the courts, Congress, and to the White House. Between 1955 and the early 1970s, they defended "the best transportation system in the world." Starting around 1970, however, as political leaders focused increasingly on the high prices paid by "consumers," truckers' rhetoric, litigiousness, and political tactics—which had served them so well during the previous four decades—began to seem battle-weary and fragile.

As early as 1949, railroad leaders sought partial deregulation, even coining the term "zone of reasonableness." Those same rail leaders continued the drumbeat of rate-deregulation talk with publication of catchy flyers such as "Mrs. Kennedy's Five Pounds of Sugar." Given the difficulty of modifying, let alone abolishing, the regulatory regime, rail executives such as James Symes at the great Pennsylvania Railroad introduced costly changes in equipment and service with a view toward boosting profitability. Complete dieselization of their locomotive fleets comprised one part of that competitive strategy. Piggyback service was another favored device for improving returns. So was the much-touted period of merger "mania" that started in the mid-1950s and culminated in 1968 with merger of the gigantic Pennsylvania and New York Central lines, creating the Penn Central. Piggyback service and mergers were among the few profit-seeking innovations permitted to railroads under rules of the regulatory regime. Indeed, architects of each merger and especially the great Penn Central merger had to take account of the myriad stakeholders along the way, including politicians and workers seeking security or a payout.

Every president after Eisenhower also took up aspects of industry structure, rates, and "free markets" that Sawyer and Weeks had sought to change. Put another way, President Eisenhower had launched a process whereby elimination of barriers between truckers and railroads (and other "modes") and elimination of politically constructed transportation submarkets such as contract and common carriers became part of the institutional office of the president. Subsequent presidents and their staff members, moreover, did not delve into the details of or even much care about rate bureau operations or about the extended efforts of truckers to defend their operating rights against one another or freight forwarders. Instead, each president and his staff perceived transportation as part of a broader canvas—a canvas in which the president of the United States assumed overall responsibility for the functioning of the nation's economy. During the 1960s, President Lyndon B. Johnson and his senior officials took up the deregulatory idea with a view toward "fine-tuning" the American economy. Starting in the 1970s, Presidents Richard M. Nixon, Gerald R. Ford, and Jimmy Carter looked to deregulation of transportation and other industries as a device that would reduce the costs of production and consumption in an economy characterized by fast-rising prices and fast-rising unemployment—the dreaded stagflation. Ironically, bankruptcy of the great Penn Central in June 1970 set President Nixon on the path toward deregulation. President Nixon made deregulation thinkable again. During the 1960s and 1970s, deregulation was largely a presidential initiative. For President Lyndon B. Johnson and his senior aides, deregulation, once achieved, would not only fine-tune the economy, but help construct a presidential nation.

CHAPTER 5

TRANSPORTATION IN A "PRESIDENTIAL NATION"

PROPOSALS TO SEEK "BROAD-SCALE DEREGULATION [HAD TO BE] CONSIDERED CAREFULLY IN LIGHT OF THE STRONG POLITICAL REACTION."
  —ALAN S. BOYD, UNDERSECRETARY OF COMMERCE FOR
  TRANSPORTATION, 1965

ON NOVEMBER 22, 1963, Lyndon B. Johnson became president of the United States, replacing the assassinated John F. Kennedy. In November 1964, Johnson was elected president by a vote of forty-three million to twenty-seven million. Johnson believed that his tremendous victory rested upon popular enthusiasm for the details of his domestic agenda, labeled the Great Society.[1] Stripped to the bone, however, much of the public relations hoopla surrounding Johnson's Great Society amounted to an effort by senior federal officials to substitute a memorable and quotable phrase such as the Great Society for the old and messy business of centralizing federal agencies and approving new policies that would hasten the pace of economic growth.[2] As part of efforts to boost economic growth, Johnson intended to revamp the federal government's transportation programs. During the Johnson years, economists and journalists described the process of seeking faster economic growth as "fine-tuning."

In July 1965, Johnson asked Joseph A. Califano, his top aide for domestic policy, to oversee efforts to create a Department of Transportation. In turn, the new secretary of transportation—a presidential appointee—would centralize control of planning and spending on federal promotional programs such as runway, highway, and waterway building and simultaneously start the process of eliminating regulation of transportation firms. In the short run, moreover, Johnson and Califano sought authority for the president to appoint the chair of the Interstate Commerce Commission. Yet Johnson's Great Society for transportation was not only a program of centralization and deregulation. Eventually, top officials in the proposed transportation department would guide private truck, rail, air, and water-carrier firms in the direction of national systems of transport, leading to easier movement of persons and merchandise from ship to rail, air, or truck. Here, then, was the rebirth of the idea of federal transportation coordination that Joseph Eastman and others of the Depression era had promoted. By the 1960s, however, creation of a department of transportation comprised not only one part of building the Great Society, but also one part of building what Califano later described as "a Presidential Nation."[3]

Several of Johnson's proposals for bringing the Great Society and its economic fine-tuning to transportation encouraged solid opposition among trucking and barge management and leaders of their unionized workforces. Since the late 1930s, trucking industry leaders such as Abner Glikbarg and the more smaller Bonacci brothers had built firms and shaped relationships with suppliers, employees, and customers inside the confines of the regulatory regime. As we have seen, Glikbarg and the Bonaccis and every other certificated trucker regularly endorsed the workings of the ICC in protecting their firms from severe price competition that might follow a diminution of operating rights or the loss of antitrust immunity for their rate bureaus. At the same time, politicians and especially senior members of the U.S. Senate and House were accustomed to exercising solid influence in writing complex formulas that dished out the cash for highway and runway construction, shipbuilding, and river navigation projects directed by the U.S. Army Corps of Engineers.

In October 1966, members of Congress approved creation of the U.S. Department of Transportation, bringing scattered programs such as the Federal Highway Administration and the Federal Aviation Agency into one agency. As the price for congressional approval, however, Califano and Johnson had dropped demands for deregulation, direct presidential control of spending on transportation improvements, or even inclusion of the Maritime Administration in the new department. Not even Johnson's proposal to have the president appoint the chair of the ICC survived congressional fear of centralized authority, or at least centralized authority that many judged threatening to regulated carriers, their employees, and congressional prerogatives. Although Johnson and Califano created a Department of Transportation, they could not win authority to undertake the larger goals of reorganizing the transportation industries and restructuring transportation markets. As late as 1968, however, Alan S. Boyd, the new Secretary of Transportation, still spoke in optimistic terms about fostering deregulation and improving coordination among participants in the nation's transportation systems.

PRESIDENT KENNEDY AND AMERICAN TRANSPORTATION

In November 1960, president-elect John F. Kennedy started this particular search for deregulation and administrative centralization. Like Johnson after him, Kennedy sought to speed up the pace of economic growth, and more efficient transportation was part of that overall goal.

Following his election, Kennedy asked James M. Landis to prepare a report on the state of the nation's regulatory agencies, reprising to an extent the efforts of Joseph Eastman for Franklin Roosevelt. Landis was a brilliant legal thinker with wide administrative experience, including prior services as dean of the Harvard Law School and chair of the Civil Aeronautics Board. In December 1960, Landis reported to Kennedy that the Interstate Commerce Commission "lacks positive direction" and that the methods of the Civil Aeronautics Board produced "inordinate delay" and "a failure to do forward planning" that "promote[ed] . . . air commerce." According to historian Thomas K. McCraw, "in less than six weeks" Landis had produced a "merciless dissection of the commissions' failures."[4]

No one solution or even several, Landis believed, could remedy the many problems that encumbered regulatory agencies. At the outset, however, he recommended administrative changes, including the often-discussed idea that Congress empower the president to appoint the chair of the ICC. In turn, Landis hinted at creation of a department of transportation that would enhance presidential authority. "Evolution of a national transportation policy," Landis asserted, "must have a close and intimate relationship to the President." Equally, Landis urged Congress to authorize mergers "within and between different modes of transportation." Although Landis did not say so specifically, he had to realize that permitting mergers between, say, truck and railroad corporations would lead to creation of transportation firms that would compete with or even supercede companies that provided only truck, rail, or even air services. Although Dean Landis had served as one of the architects of the regulatory regime, in 1960 he presented one of the first systematic attacks upon its existence.[5]

Historian McCraw finds that Landis's "powerful arguments for regulatory reform found a receptive ear at the White House." On April 5, 1962, President Kennedy sent a Special Message to the Congress on Transportation. Kennedy complained about the presence of "a chaotic patchwork of inconsistent and often obsolete legislation and regulation." Kennedy wanted "less federal regulation and subsidization"and he also urged "a more coordinated federal policy and a less segmented approach."[6] Presidents Hoover, Roosevelt, and Eisenhower had made similar recommendations. By the early 1960s, moreover, members of a new and rising generation of transportation economists, including Paul W. MacAvoy, John R. Meyer, and George W.

Hilton were urging deregulation of the transportation and other industries.

In the short run, Kennedy and Landis failed to create a department of transportation or bring about deregulation of the nation's transportation industries. In 1962, neither members of Congress nor leaders in the transportation industries were prepared to award additional authority to the executive branch based upon the urgings of a president or the say-so of Dean Landis and a few professors of economics. McCraw finds, however, that Kennedy's legislative recommendations had the effect "for a season . . . of draw[ing] the public's attention to the seriousness of long-neglected problems."[7]

PRESIDENT JOHNSON AND CREATION OF A DEPARTMENT OF TRANSPORTATION

Beginning in mid-1964, President Johnson took his turn at trying to bring about deregulation and build a transportation department.[8] Johnson sought to make transportation firms and federal transportation agencies part of his Great Society and part of a presidential nation. Like President Eisenhower, Johnson also chose to avoid conflict with truckers and others who liked most aspects of regulation. Ultimately, the politics of the day encouraged Johnson and his aides to award first priority to assembling a transportation department rather than seeking deregulation. Johnson's search for legislation leading to the transportation portions of the Great Society started with the report of his Task Force on Transportation Policy.

In June and July 1964, President Johnson created fourteen task forces. Reports of these task forces, Johnson told his cabinet on July 2, would "provide the background for discussion among the Cabinet agencies and the White House in formulating the 1965 legislative program." In short, Johnson's task forces would create outlines for legislating the Great Society, but done in the Johnson way. Johnson insisted that members of these task forces deliberate in secret. According to political scientists Emmette S. Redford and Richard T. McCulley, secrecy encouraged "candor, even boldness" among task force members, qualities that the president found lacking in federal officials "dedicated to preserving the status quo." Just as important, secrecy allowed the president to "consider . . . policy options and . . . political feasibilities." Secrecy, according to Redford and McCulley, made it possible for President Johnson to "maintain . . . his mastery of the process."[9] At the outset, shaping the details of the Great Society was also part of the process of shaping a presidential nation.

During mid-June 1964, Kermit Gordon, director of the Bureau of the Budget, prepared an initial list of names of members of the Task Force on

Transportation Policy. As had often been the case in efforts to define and shape transportation policy, the aura of "objective" expertise retained a special appeal to politicians, and each person on Gordon's list was an economist. This pattern reflected the growing perception among policy leaders, including Gordon, that economists really could articulate ideas leading to national economic growth. As a member of the President's Council of Economic Advisers during 1961–1962, moreover, Gordon would have been keenly aware of the scholarly and policy preferences of his junior colleagues. In turn, Gordon selected members of a younger generation of economists who had already begun to criticize government regulators and government regulations. As early as 1959, John R. Meyer (and several colleagues), a Harvard University economist and one of the persons selected for the committee, had recommended "a substantial reduction in government regulation of transportation and heavy reliance on the forces of market competition to insure services and rates." Gordon himself described George W. Hilton, the task force's future chair, as an "economist with emphasis in transportation regulatory problems."[10] By selecting George Hilton and John Meyer and other economists for membership on the transportation task force, Gordon had largely predetermined the task force's orientation toward the prospect of changing federal transportation policies.

Budget director Gordon also determined the agenda of the transportation task force. He sought "better cost data" on rail, truck, and other freight operations. Data on costs, he contended, would help determine "areas in which the possibilities of intra-modal competition make deregulation desirable." Anyone in the trucking industry would have recognized that intramodal competition meant that Vee Kennedy's contract carriers and Robert McBride's common carriers would be permitted to compete directly with one another. As another part of the agenda he had in mind, Gordon wanted members of the task force to report on "the charter of the new Department of Transportation," which, when operating, would "lay the groundwork on which a basic re-evaluation of Federal transport policy could be evolved." Members of Hilton's transportation task force would focus on both deregulation of freight rates and enhanced coordination of federal investment in transportation facilities.[11] At the outset, Budget Bureau director Gordon had sketched a program of transportation coordination and deregulation more ambitious than anything prepared by Joseph Eastman for Franklin Roosevelt or by Sinclair Weeks. Gordon and other members of the Johnson administration knew what they wanted by way of policy changes, and now it was up to Hilton and his associates to deliver.

On November 16, 1964, members of Hilton's task force submitted their report to the president. At the core of large number of proposals stood the same two ideas that Gordon had recommended months earlier. First, Hilton and his colleagues advocated deregulation of freight rates and easing of entry requirements into fields such as trucking. "Entry" was the word that policymakers and transportation officials often used to describe the system of operating rights that limited common and contract carriers to certain commodities on certain routes, and that shut out others such as freight forwarders from soliciting for that business. If Hilton and his committee members had their way, moreover, the federal government would repeal the Reed-Bulwinkle Act permitting rail and truckers' rate bureaus to determine prices. The nation's transportation system, they contended, would "best serve the Great Society if it operates . . . with highest attainable efficiency." Creation of markets following elimination of rate and entry regulations, committee members added, could lead to railroad ownership of trucking companies, a course of action they described as consistent with their goals of "flexibility and experimentation."[12] Again, here was a plan for reorganizing transportation industries and restructuring transportation markets.

Hilton's task force also endorsed Gordon's second goal, creation of a department of transportation. Leaders of the department, as the committee reported, would coordinate federal investment in transportation such as highways and ports and allow the secretary of transportation to present a single point of view to regulatory agencies dealing with rates and operating rights. As presently constituted, Hilton's committee reported, federal transportation policy appeared "not a policy but many fragments of a policy." During the mid-1960s (as in previous decades), one way to solve a political dilemma was to create a federal agency, hoping that centralized administration by nonpolitical experts would foster presidential authority and eliminate the give and take of ordinary politics. Curiously, members of the transportation task force had found achieving consensus difficult, which ought to have suggested the greater difficulty ahead in writing a program that satisfied truckers and others with deep stakes in a fragmented-regulatory regime.[13]

Early in July 1965, Lyndon Johnson asked Joseph A. Califano to find the next level of agreement. Califano, then thirty-four years old, had graduated from the College of the Holy Cross and Harvard Law School. Before moving to the White House as coordinator of Johnson's domestic policy agenda, Califano worked directly under Secretary of Defense Robert S. McNamara as a systems analyst. Califano carried ideas about systems from discussions among military, engineering, and business leaders to the offices of presidential aides.

Beginning in July, Joseph Califano served as the White House staff officer in charge of coordinating construction of what he subsequently labeled a "presidential nation." A presidential nation for transportation, Califano

FIGURE 15. Joseph A. Califano directed President Lyndon B. Johnson's effort to create a Department of Transportation. Johnson and Califano sought to centralize the federal government's transportation activities and simultaneously foster deregulation of railroads and truckers. Source: Lyndon B. Johnson Presidential Library. Used with permission.

later wrote, consisted of a "single executive [who] had the authority to shape and conduct a coherent policy that promoted the public's interest in modern, cheap . . . and fast transportation." At the outset, Joseph Califano sought centralization of $6 billion in federal transportation spending and one hundred thousand federal employees in the office of the president. In Califano's version of a presidential nation, the president would take responsibility for "fine-tuning" the American political economy.[14]

Califano turned to another committee for advice on how to assemble the transportation components of that presidential nation. Members of this committee included senior officials assigned to the Council of Economic Advisers and the Departments of Commerce and Treasury. Alan S. Boyd, formerly chair of the Civil Aeronautics Board and recently appointed by Johnson to the post of Undersecretary of Commerce for Transportation, served as chair. On August 12, only eighteen days in office, Califano directed Boyd to prepare a report on the "pros and cons" of creating a Department of Transportation and on how to bring about "greater flexibility in the regulation of transport rates." Califano also charged Boyd and members of his committee to examine the recommendation of another task force that the president appoint the chair of the Interstate Commerce Commission. In all, Califano sought "a vigorous and imaginative program for consideration by the Second Session of the 89th Congress."[15]

Whatever Califano's preferences for an imaginative program, he relied for a detailed set of recommendations on federal officials long steeped in the politics of regulation. No idea carried more weight in their deliberations than the often-repeated admonition that truck operators liked regulation and would energetically oppose deregulation. Given that perception, the best for which Califano could have hoped was a cautious set of recommendations. On August 27, now one month into his new assignment, Califano dropped the demand for imagination and vigor in favor of "concrete proposals and goals toward which the Great Society can move."[16] In this iteration, the Great Society appeared as a legislative program capable of securing a majority vote in Congress.

On September 2, Boyd submitted the report of his committee to Califano. In principle, Boyd endorsed "more flexibility in regulation . . . [and] greater reliance on competitive market forces." Yet proposals to seek "broadscale deregulation," he advised, had to be "considered carefully in light of the strong political reaction." Even on the question of creating a department of transportation, Boyd urged restraint. Agreement among senior federal officials for creation of a transportation department appeared "widespread." Boyd, however, judged that it "would represent a major legislative effort." The one idea Boyd endorsed without reservation was that of making the chair of the ICC a presidential appointee.[17]

Early in September, Califano had an unambiguous recommendation for only one of his "concrete goals," that of presidential appointment of the ICC chair. On September 11, Arthur M. Okun, a member of the President's Council of Economic Advisers, found Boyd's proposals "sure-footed, slow-paced, [and] cautious," adding that "they pussyfoot particularly on deregulation." President Johnson, Okun believed, "is going to be disappointed, unless something is done to break the traffic jam." On September 13, a senior official in the Bureau of the Budget characterized the state of deliberations as that of "transportation chaos."[18]

Once again, Califano took charge of planning for transportation legislation. On September 22, Califano wrote Johnson that he would meet in a few days with Boyd and another senior official and "ask them to consider and prepare papers," leading to creation of a department of transportation (or some reorganization of the executive transportation functions) and a "program of deregulation to make transportation rates more competitive and rational." At the bottom of that memo, Johnson wrote "Hooray."[19] In Califano's hands, administrative centralization and deregulation remained the orders of the day.

By mid-October, now having served three months as the president's domestic policy adviser, Califano had presided over a process of consolidating and limiting the scope of proposals for changes in federal transportation policy. A program described by economist Okun a month earlier as "pussy footing" in the area of deregulation had nonetheless begun to congeal. On October 12, however, Califano characterized his recommendations for President Johnson as "streamlining our government and getting us out of the old, outmoded regulatory structure." During the next year, he added, with transportation and other legislation in place, "the President and the Congress should be the Great Managers, the Great Administrators—the architects of efficient, effective government." Altogether, he asserted, this legislation, including transportation legislation, constituted a process of "organizing our Government for the Great Society." According to historian Robert Dallek, President Johnson already believed that "consolidation of control in the executive assured greater economy and efficiency."[20] Whatever the mix of flattery and policy recommendation, by October Califano had redefined the Great Society as an organizational phenomenon.

Early in December, Califano launched negotiations with railroad executives and with senior officials of barge and truck firms. The idea, he told President Johnson, was "to explore the views of everyone interested on a totally confidential and off-the-record basis." In addition, Califano asked Johnson's permission to talk with Senator Warren G. Magnuson, chair of the commerce committee. Califano wanted to "get Magnuson's agreement to keep an open mind before any interests (particularly the trucking interest) get to him."[21]

Among executives and politicians associated with the transportation industries, however, rare were the persons who had not adopted a point of view. For example, Stuart Saunders, president of the Pennsylvania Railroad, told Califano and presidential aide Lee C. White that he wanted "an integrated transportation set up." In the sometimes arcane language of the transportation industries, that phrase since the 1920s had meant that "railroads should be permitted to acquire trucking companies." Leaders of trucking firms, however, reported that rail ownership of trucking operations served—as always—as an area of "great anxiety" for them. Truck operators also perceived "plenty of vigorous competition in the industry today," and expressed concern that "any movement to deregulate would bring a return to chaos and irresponsibility." Provided no changes were made in regulatory policy, however, truckers expressed willingness to approve creation of a department of transportation, leading President Johnson in an optimistic moment to tell Califano that "'we're going to get our Department of Transportation.'"[22]

Discussions with Senator Warren Magnuson and Representative Harley O. Staggers reinforced the view that creation of a department of transportation might prove politically feasible, but that deregulation had no supporters. On January 10, 1966, Lee White learned that Magnuson was "strong" for creation of a department of transportation and for presidential appointment of the chair of the ICC. In these areas, Magnuson was so favorably disposed that he even wanted to introduce the legislation. Similarly, Staggers endorsed the idea of creating a transportation department. On January 25, Staggers also told White that he "had no difficulty" with the idea that the president would appoint the chair of the ICC. As for proposals to deregulate the transportation industries, Staggers "predicted bitter opposition and controversy over them." Equally, Magnuson, according to White's memo to the president, "believe[d] that they should not be submitted and that they won't get anywhere if they are." According to political scientists Emmette Redford and Marlan Blissett, "the bold and imaginative program [originally sought by Johnson and Califano] had become, for the moment, two structural reforms—a department of transportation and a presidentially designated chairman of the ICC."[23]

On March 2, President Johnson sent a message to Congress urging creation of a department of transportation and presidential appointment of the chair of the ICC. Despite the scaled-down program he was proposing, Johnson invoked the idioms of centralized control and rapid economic growth. "We must clear away the institutional and political barriers which impede adaptation and change," he told members of Congress. At the same time, Johnson, sounding like President Roosevelt and Joseph Eastman, asserted that "we must coordinate our transportation agencies in a single coherent instrument of government." Such a program, he contended, would "strengthen the national economy as a whole."[24]

Early on, political and business leaders joined in expressions of enthusiastic support for Johnson's proposals. Citing opportunities to achieve what he labeled "effective leadership" and "vigorous administration," Governor Mark O. Hatfield of Oregon urged members of his state's congressional delegation to vote in favor of the transportation bill. Equally, on March 23, members of the executive committee of the American Trucking Associations held a special meeting to consider the pending legislation. Truck executives "applaud[ed]" what was described as "the President's recognition" that regulatory agencies "should remain unaltered." Those same trucking executives did voice concern about the contents of Section 7, an obscure portion of the bill dealing with the authority of a secretary of transportation to determine what were known as transportation investment standards. On balance, however, trucking leaders notified the press that they favored creation of a department of transportation. "I am . . . gratified," the savvy executive director of the ATA wrote Califano on March 30, "to officially stand up and be counted."[25]

No sooner had truckers and maritime officials finished endorsing Johnson's proposals in general than they and others organized to block approval of several parts of it. The ensuing legislative struggle often revolved around arcane matters. For example, leaders of the American Trucking Associations had gone along with Califano and Johnson's plan to create a department of transportation. ATA leaders, however, disliked the section in Johnson's transportation department bill that would permit a future Secretary of Transportation to determine transportation investment standards. Equally troublesome was Johnson's proposal to include the Maritime Administration as part of the new transportation department.

Opposition to presidential determination of transportation investment standards—known as the Section 7 controversy—appeared first. In short, the question was whether Congress would permit the secretary of transportation, a presidential appointee, to coordinate federal construction of airports, roads, and waterways, including projects undertaken by the influential engineers at the well-funded Federal Highway Administration and U.S. Army Corps of Engineers. As early as March 29, 1966, Senator Magnuson had expressed concern about replacing "able individuals like the heads of the FAA and the Bureau of Public Roads . . . with planners." On April 29, Mike N. Manatos, Johnson's liaison to the Senate, reported to Johnson on his conversation with the staff director of the Senate Committee on Government Operations, a committee chaired by the powerful Senator John L. McClellan. Members of the committee, Manatos reported, were engaged in "negotiations . . . to find language with which 'the committee could live.'" If Johnson agreed to delete Section 7, Manatos had learned that "you'd have a bill almost immediately."[26]

By mid-May, others among President Johnson's top officials were predicting legislative doom, unless Johnson agreed to drop the unpopular Section 7. On May 11, Alan Boyd, one of the bill's principal architects, wrote commerce secretary John T. Connor that amendments to Section 7 proposed by members of Congress would "leave the Secretary of Transportation with less freedom than he would have in the absence of Section 7 altogether." With the presence of Section 7 now placing "the entire bill . . . in jeopardy," Boyd urged its elimination.[27]

Inclusion of the Maritime Administration in the new department of transportation comprised a second area of contention. The Maritime Administration provided construction and operating subsidies to owners of the nation's shipping fleet. Labor leaders had long joined with their counterparts in executive offices in supporting those subsidies, creating a formidable coalition in meetings with congressional and presidential leaders. In this instance, labor and management opposed inclusion of the Maritime Administration in the proposed department of transportation. Sounding like airline executives fighting possible regulation by the ICC during the 1930s, maritime leaders feared a loss of clout if the federal government's vast water-borne shipping programs were subsumed in a much larger agency less susceptible to their immediate and combined influence. In turn, a loss of influence, management and labor officials had concluded, might mean construction of fewer ships and creation of fewer jobs. Participation in a unified department of transportation with emphasis by administrators on transportation coordination threatened maritime autonomy and finances. Altogether, report political scientists Redford and Blissett, "the real issue . . . [was] money." On May 12, one of President Johnson's aides reported "growing pressure on you to 'do something' in the maritime field."[28]

The struggles regarding the Maritime Administration and the arcane Section 7 controversy comprised only the most visible portions of a growing concern among congressional and transportation officials about the loss of control of federal subsidies for highway building and other construction and safety programs related to transportation. The best way to maintain control of programs, argued critics of Johnson's proposal, was to transfer agencies such as the Federal Highway Administration directly into the new department of transportation. Members of Congress and leaders in the transportation industries described this desire for the continuing independence of their favorite transportation agencies with phrases such as "legal entity" and "modal autonomy." Whether called a legal entity or any other name, the idea was to transfer agencies such as the Federal Highway Administration and the Federal Aviation Agency directly into the new department of transportation. Senator Mike Monroney, nicknamed "Mr. Aviation," was also insisting on Senate confirmation of agency heads. As Monroney complained during hearings, he did not want agency administrators (such as the administrator of the Federal Aviation Agency) "report[ing] to the secretary [of transportation] 'through a barricade or layer of assistant and under secretaries.'"[29] In 1966, Monroney stood four-square behind the policy of continuing the Civil Aeronautics Board and the aviation industry as separate and distinct from railroading, trucking, and waterway carriers. Whether or not he knew the history of American transportation policy, Monroney also stood foursquare behind a continuation of the fragmented transportation programs and policies put in place in 1940, and scorned during the 1960s by James M. Landis, by budget bureau director Kermit Gordon, and by members of George Hilton's task force.

Leaders of trucking, barge, or railroad firms rarely or never conceptualized in such abstract terms as legal entities, vesting, or presidential nation. These executives and their union counterparts knew, however, what they liked, and what they feared. They feared deregulation and they liked the way federal policy had fostered creation of separate and distinct air, rail, barge, and truck industries, including the many subcategories of trucking such as common and contract carrier. In turn, truckers and nearly everyone else associated with one of these distinct transportation "modes" feared enhancement of presidential authority at the expense of federal officials such as the Federal Highway Administrator and officials of the Corps of Engineers, who had long supported generous programs of road building, airway guidance, and river improvement. Within a few weeks of hearing Johnson's message, transportation executives organized to protect the autonomy of federal agencies upon which their firms and industries had come to depend. For example, on March 16, W. J. Barta, president of the Mississippi Valley Barge Line, expressed concern to about 150 transportation executives regarding what he had identified as a new transportation policy. That new transportation policy, Barta contended, raised the prospects of rate deregulation and railroad ownership of barge companies. Equally, an executive of a trucking company raised questions about such matters as investment criteria fixed by a secretary of transportation and inclusion of the Bureau of Public Roads in a transportation department. Truck operators had long supported the autonomy of the Federal Highway Administration with its emphasis on highway spending, especially spending to complete construction of the high-volume Interstate Highway System. At this point, the Section 7 controversy—who would determine investment standards for waterways, roads, and airport runways—had become merged with the legal entity debate. By April 6, as members of a house subcommittee opened hearings on the transportation bill, editors of *Traffic World* published an article reporting "More Doubts on Dep't of Transportation."[30]

Califano and Boyd agreed to delete many of the aggravating sections. As early as May 24, Califano had told Senator McClellan "that there would be no problem on Section 7." On May 30, Califano accepted relative autonomy for each of the agencies scheduled for transfer to the new department of transportation. The revised transportation bill would "designate . . . four modal Administrations—Aviation, Highway, Maritime, and Rail." As long as these modal administrators reported to the secretary of transportation, Califano and Boyd believed that they had preserved the principle and perhaps the long-run potential of enhanced presidential coordination of transportation activities as a whole.[31] As Joseph Eastman had learned in 1935 when attempting to bring all transport regulation inside the ICC, consolidation of authority was very difficult.

House and Senate leaders wanted more than these partial concessions. Congressional leaders continued to talk about vesting and the transfer of legal entities. As before, the real question was whether day-to-day authority in an area such as highway construction would reside (vest) with the Federal Highway Administrator or with the secretary of transportation. No one supported vesting with agency administrators more than Senator Henry M. "Scoop" Jackson of Washington. During the first weekend in August, Boyd and three other members of the administration met with Senator Jackson's aide in a room on the second floor of the White House. Whatever their doubt or doubts about vesting, they thrashed out an agreement providing that in areas of safety, decisions of the rail, air, and other administrators were "administratively final and not subject to Secretarial review." Apparently, the phrase "administratively final" provided the precision judged lacking in vesting, the older phrase meant to carry the concept of modal autonomy. "Senator Jackson is delighted with the draft language developed over the weekend," Boyd wrote Secretary of Commerce John Connor on August 9, "and accepts it as his own." Recognizing the limits he had accepted, on August 30 Califano wrote President Johnson that *"safety* can be so broadly defined that it can embrace virtually every function" (emphasis in original).[32]

Still looming was a determination about whether Congress would approve movement of the Maritime Administration from the Department of Commerce into the proposed Department of Transportation. Between August 23 and August 25, aides to President Johnson, including Califano, negotiated with members of a joint group of ship operators and union leaders. On this issue, executives of shipping firms and their union counterparts spoke as one. While Califano and other administration officials articulated the promise of enhanced efficiency and coordination that would follow creation of a transportation department, leaders of the joint labor-management group invoked images of "a ghetto of relative insignificance" for the nation's shipping industry. According to notes prepared by an assistant to Califano, members of the maritime group sought "a preferred position for the Maritime Administration in the new Department," especially creation of a "subsidy board." Despite Califano's promise of "a new maritime program" as the "first order of business" once the transportation department was launched, by the morning of August 25, a union negotiator had determined "that there can be no deal short of the Maritime Administration as a separate independent agency."[33]

Maritime leaders also possessed the clout to secure a portion of what they wanted. On August 30, members of the U.S. House of Representatives voted 190 to 63 not to move the Maritime Administration to the Department of Transportation. According to historian Dallek, George Meany, President of the American Federation of Labor-Congress of Industrial Organizations, had "effectively pressured House members into excluding merchant shipping from department control."[34] In all, members of Congress and industry leaders had supported creation of a department of transportation, but not one that included the Maritime Administration, deregulation, or the now-infamous Section 7. Congress had even refused to award the president authority to appoint the chair of the Interstate Commerce Commission. For the moment, the operating rights and rate bureaus that truckers so prized remained safe from the presidential grasp. In addition, the idea of the 1940 transportation act—that each "type" of transportation enjoys its own regulation and its own promotional agency—remained secure in federal law.

On October 15, 1966, Johnson presided at a signing ceremony for legislation creating the U.S. Department of Transportation. On Johnson's orders, leaders of the Maritime Administration were not invited. Johnson told guests that the transportation department would "have a mammoth task—to untangle, to coordinate, to build the national transportation system for America that America is deserving of." In the language of rural America that politicians sometimes invoked, Johnson added that creation of the department represented "another coonskin on the wall."[35]

Only the day before the signing, an official of the Bureau of the Budget had reminded Johnson that the pending legislation left out the maritime administration and placed "*restrictions on the authority of the Secretary*" (emphasis in original). On balance, that official recommended that the president sign the bill, contending that it "will allow the new Secretary of Transportation to assume leadership in formulating and executing our national transportation policy." The rhetoric of the Great Society and a presidential nation was that of administrative coordination. Not even Johnson's invocation of rustic metaphors, however, could obscure the impressive triumph won by his opponents who had advocated the continuing autonomy from the presidential grasp of federal transportation agencies and the privately owned transportation firms that enjoyed specialized operating rights and antitrust exemption.[36]

Following the bill signing, Califano resumed his efforts to place additional authority over transportation spending, regulation, and coordination in the president's hands. Perhaps with more energy on his part, Califano reasoned, members of Congress and transportation officials would concede the importance of centralized management aimed at speeding the pace of national economic growth. On October 25, Califano created another committee, this one under the direction of John Connor, the secretary of commerce. Califano directed Connor to plan transportation legislation for the next Congress. Once again, Califano wanted plans that were "vigorous and imaginative" and that included presidential appointment of the chair of the

Interstate Commerce Commission. Califano also wanted proposals that would lead to enhanced flow of merchandise and passengers from one transportation system to another, as for example the fast-growing business of transferring containers from ships to rail and truck.[37]

By late 1966, however, appointment of another committee and the use of overworked and overblown phrases such as "vigorous" and "imaginative" proved only an exercise. Califano and Johnson had exhausted their negotiating skills and resources. "The Transportation Department bill had been the toughest legislative fight of the 89th Congress," Califano reported years later. That fight, he added, had consumed "perhaps 15 percent of my time in 1966 and required almost daily presidential attention." Altogether, Califano concluded, "we could not afford an effort like that again."[38] At or near the peak of his authority as president, not even Lyndon Johnson possessed sufficient clout to create a transportation department, including a secretary, authorized to coordinate among leaders of truck, rail, air, and barge industries or break open to the many submarkets of transportation such as Vee Kennedy's contract carriers and Robert McBride's common carriers.

Appointment of senior officials to the new Department of Transportation might still yield a part of what Congress had refused. As a start, Johnson appointed Alan Boyd as the first secretary of transportation. Before taking up the post of undersecretary of commerce for transportation in 1965, Boyd had enjoyed years of experience in managing large and complex transportation systems, including service as a member and chair of the Civil Aeronautics Board and as a member of the Florida Railroad and Public Utilities Commission. Whether as an undersecretary or as the secretary-designate, however, Boyd had long disliked the reality of transportation as a mishmash of trucking firms, railroads, barge lines, air carriers, and as yet another mishmash of federal programs for road building, waterway development, or aides to airlines. Instead, Boyd envisioned the nation's transportation in terms of interconnected systems that would deliver materials and personnel from ship to rail to truck or air in a nearly frictionless fashion. In turn, Boyd looked forward to the prospect of guiding the nation's transportation systems and investments in the direction of newly emerging concepts such as logistical science and away from a process perceived as endless negotiations and litigation among regulators, shippers, and carriers about such mundane and self-serving matters as operating certificates, rights-of-entry, rate bureaus, or whether railroads could own trucking companies. Sounding like Joseph Eastman, Boyd judged those deliberations "picayune."[39]

The presence of the large Department of Transportation whose officials, including Alan Boyd, emphasized ideas such as systems and intermodalism did foster diffusion of those concepts among business and political leaders.

On January 31, 1968, approximately eight hundred transportation executives and political leaders gathered for a meeting and luncheon at the Waldorf Astoria Hotel in New York City. Presentations at the meeting revolved around topics such as transportation logistics and methods for improving the coordination of freight between surface, water, and air carriers. The luncheon speaker, Senator Monroney, who had so energetically supported relocation of agencies to the transportation department as "legal entities," alerted his audience to dramatic changes coming to transportation politics. "In the not too distant future," Monroney contended, Congress will "wrestle with such issues as deregulation of rates, intermodal ownership, and removal of entry controls." As it was, he contended, "existing statutes militate against a system approach to transportation." Monroney added that "I do not relish the legislative fray that will occur."[40] Even in his use of the new language of systems and intermodalism, Monroney (as well as every truck operator) expressed a preference for the traditions and security of the regulatory regime that had been given its final legal form in 1940. In the midst of the prosperity of the mid- and late 1960s that was buoying up revenues for large segments of the rail, air, and trucking industries, moreover, no one, it appears, wanted to enter that fray.

Beginning in 1969, members of the administration of President Richard M. Nixon assumed direction of the nation's political economy, including its transportation networks. During the 1960s, President Johnson had dealt with transportation as part of the politics of managing growth. During the 1970s, Nixon and his successors dealt with transportation and other industries as part of the politics of economic decline—a decline marked simultaneously by rising levels of unemployment and rising levels of inflation. Like Johnson, Nixon sought to build a presidential nation. Consequently, Nixon followed Johnson in urging greater centralization of authority in the office of the president. Nixon even secured congressional approval for presidential appointment of the chair of the Interstate Commerce Commission. Rather than using his new and existing authority to "fine-tune" the American political economy, however, President Nixon and his senior advisers settled on deregulation as the cure for the problems of transportation and for many of the problems of the economy as a whole. Not until the late 1980s did senior political figures return to Johnson and Califano's efforts to use federal authority to foster coordination and intermodalism. Instead, the 1970s started with bankruptcy of the Penn Central and ended late in 1980 with deregulation of railroads, trucks, and airlines.

CHAPTER 6

RICHARD M. NIXON AND PLANNING FOR DEREGULATION, 1970–1974

PROSPECTS [FOR ACHIEVING DEREGULATION] ARE BEING DIMINISHED BY WHAT IS BEING PERCEIVED AS A FAILURE ON THE PART OF THE ADMINISTRATION TO BACK THE BILL.
  —PRESIDENTIAL AIDE DAVID M.GUNNING TO PETER M. FLANIGAN,
    MAY 11, 1972

IN RESPONSE TO the Penn Central bankruptcy, President Richard M. Nixon launched a sustained effort to deregulate trucking firms and railroads. Deregulation, if it came about, would shift authority in this field of ground transportation from the Interstate Commerce Commission—and the president, who appointed its members—into the hands of executives of rail and trucking companies. In the face of rising prices and declining employment, moreover, Nixon abandoned difficult-to-achieve goals such as fostering improved coordination among truckers, railroaders, and operators of other "modes" in favor of the more straightforward task of diminishing or eliminating barriers among transportation markets, as for instance between common and contract carriers. During the early 1970s, however, Nixon could not identify a constituency who would join him in lobbying Congress for deregulation. When heads of trucking firms along with Frank E. Fitzsimmons, leader of the powerful International Brotherhood of Teamsters, refused to support deregulation, Nixon, like Eisenhower and Johnson before him, chose not to press the matter with members of Congress. By 1972, electoral politics took precedence over the politics of deregulation. Although Nixon ultimately failed to support his own deregulation proposals, he had nonetheless helped move the idea of deregulation from the realm of the thinkable—where Eisenhower and Kennedy had left it—into the mainstream of American politics.[1] Equally, by securing approval from Congress for presidents to appoint the chair of the ICC, Nixon also placed a powerful tool for deregulation in the hands of his successors.

NIXON AND DEREGULATION

As had happened with Presidents Roosevelt, Truman, and Eisenhower, a railroad crisis encouraged President Nixon to focus on transportation and, in this case, to restart the drive for deregulation. On Sunday, June 21, 1970, attorneys for the gigantic Penn Central Railroad entered federal court seeking the protection of bankruptcy. "The biggest and most heralded merger in railroad history," reported the *Wall Street Journal*, "has turned into a disaster." Stuart T. Saunders, former chair of the board of Penn Central, told members of the Senate commerce committee that the railroad industry, including Penn Central, had "been hit hard by the recession, inflation, tight money, and high-interest rates." Bankruptcy at Penn Central, he added, had come to pass not because of "mismanagement," but because of "problems which were unmanageable."[2]

As historian Allen J. Matusow explains, Nixon's senior economists thought that the economy was "tottering" and that bankruptcy of the Penn Central Company, if it came, "just might bring it down." Not just another large railroad in declining economic health, contemporaries calculated that collapse of the Penn Central would boost unemployment by several hundred thousand and affect shipments for nearly half of the nation's factories. Even before the official announcement of the bankruptcy action, President Nixon was prepared to take action. On June 4, according to notes taken in secret by presidential aide John D. Ehrlichman, Nixon told members of his inner group of advisers that "this railroad must be saved." Nixon authorized a package of federal loan guarantees for Penn Central, which would keep the firm operating. Nixon instructed his staff, however, that Secretary of Transportation John A. Volpe, not the White House, should "carry" the loan package to Congress. Otherwise, the president told aides that he wanted the company's debts paid off, nonrailroad assets sold, and Saunders "kick[ed] . . . out as president and executive."[3] Rhetorically at least, Nixon was appointing himself to the post of acting receiver for the Penn Central.

The Penn Central bankruptcy and its potential for upsetting the nation's economy and the federal budget also encouraged Nixon to consider innovative policies. Nixon sought to accomplish more than a quick fix for railroad finances such as the loan guarantees. At a meeting held on March 5, 1970, (more than three months before the Penn Central filed for bankruptcy), Nixon had directed senior officials in his administration to review the idea of deregulating trucking firms and railroads. (In 1970, airlines still retained their special status as the first line of defense in the cold war.) At that meeting, Nixon urged study of the railroad problem "on a broad basis." As part of that broad review, Nixon instructed transportation secretary Volpe to "see

[the] Council of Economic Advisers." Like their predecessors and a growing number of contemporary economists, members of the council advocated deregulation of transportation.[4]

Volpe's meeting with members of the council turned into another government committee. This one, however, was focused on deregulation. Early in May, two months after the president's directive to Volpe, members of a group entitled the Subcommittee on Transportation held their first meeting. Hendrik S. Houthakker, a member of the Council of Economic Advisers, served as chair of the committee, which included senior officials located in the Departments of Transportation, Commerce, Labor, Justice, and the Office of Management and Budget. At the outset, members of the committee had the appearance and ideological commitments of Presidents Eisenhower, Kennedy, and Johnson's earlier task forces and committees that had promoted the idea of deregulating transportation.

Although Houthakker and his colleagues were disposed toward the idea of reducing government's role in transportation, a memo prepared by Peter M. Flanigan focused their deliberations on the idea of deregulation in particular. On May 4, before the committee had met, Flanigan, an assistant to President Nixon for commercial and economic matters, sent a memo to each member of the committee. The purpose of their upcoming meeting, he informed Houthakker and the others, was "to discuss how the Administration can best proceed in bringing about less restrictive regulation." As part of the memo, Flanigan included an "options paper" prepared on May 1 by a member of the committee that sketched topics such as "deregulation strategy objectives."[5] As part of their role in a presidential nation, senior aides to the president had set out the framework for committee deliberations possibly leading to reduced government regulation of transportation.

In their report, members of Houthakker's subcommittee repeated concerns about the cost and effectiveness of transportation services that had circulated among federal officials since at least Herbert Hoover, and that had prompted discussions about deregulation since the presidency of Dwight Eisenhower. On September 22, Houthakker and his associates told members of the Cabinet Committee on Economic Policy that "regulation has led to rates which are generally higher than they would be in the absence of regulation and to an inefficient utilization of national transport resources." In turn, members of Houthakker's subcommittee recommended that the administration pursue a program leading to "decontrol of transportation."[6] In 1964, members of a task force created by President Johnson had used the word "decontrol" rather than "deregulation," suggesting that six years later deregulation still lacked a political context and a historical narrative known to policymakers.

Whether described as decontrol or deregulation, leaders of the Nixon administration proceeded cautiously. Similar to leaders in the Eisenhower and Johnson administrations, the question before Nixon's top aides was whether the economic benefits of deregulation would prove worth the effort and political risk in trying to bring it about. In January 1970, before the Penn Central crisis peaked, Nixon had concluded that a broad, consumer-oriented coalition could be assembled around the idea of deregulating transportation. Nixon told his advisers that "consumerism" enjoyed a "hi [sic] public interest" and appeared "flamboyant" and "sexy." In turn, organized consumers, it was hoped, would offset the certain arguments of truckers and teamsters that deregulation would destroy operating rights and the work of their rate bureaus and was thus certain to bring financial losses and lower wages. In December 1970, however, Virginia A. Knauer, Nixon's adviser on consumer matters, reported a sense of "skeptic[ism] that the aid of the national consumer organizations could be successfully solicited" in support of a program of deregulation.[7]

In the absence of general enthusiasm among consumer organizations to lobby for deregulation of trucking and railroads, Nixon's and his top officials determined to create their own coalition of deregulation enthusiasts. This coalition, it was hoped, would be composed both of shippers and long-suffering railroad executives and their union counterparts. In that way, political risk, policy change, and a restoration of economic growth might still prove compatible. Consultations and coalition building began in June 1971, with Peter Flanigan and President Nixon serving as the lead officials.

Richard Nixon was the first president to meet with railroad managers and workers regarding deregulation. Nothing said at these two meetings had not been repeated, and repeated often, since 1949. According to notes prepared after the meeting held on June 10, railroad executives blamed union work rules and delays in bringing about mergers. "Proposed mergers," they reported, had "been delayed from seven to nine years," which appeared "inexcusable."[8] Even a year after the Penn Central bankruptcy, rail executives were still hoping to revive their companies with additional mergers.

Nixon promised to secure a speedup in merger approvals. What Nixon really wanted, however, was the help of railroad executives in building political support for eliminating or at least reducing regulation. Unlike attorneys at the U.S. Department of Justice who had delayed mergers, Nixon reminded rail leaders that members of regulatory commissions were independent, making it "more difficult to get faster action in the regulatory process." Nixon believed, nonetheless, that "most of the regulatory commissions are obsolete in the way they function." Only "a drastic overhaul" of regulatory agencies could "meet the needs of the times." Nixon urged rail leaders to help bring about that overhaul. "We need grassroots support" that would "get Congress moving on some of these things."[9]

In his meeting several days later with fourteen railroad labor union officials, Nixon learned that they blamed regulators and managers—not workers or work rules—for the many problems affecting their industry. Charles Luna, president of the United Transportation Union, told Nixon that railroad management had purchased nonrailroad firms, creating conglomerate businesses that led to *"railroading becoming secondary to the conglomerate"* (emphasis in original). As for labor's productivity, a commonplace topic in the industry, Luna asserted that "freight in transit moves only 2 hours in 24," demonstrating, he contended, "the need for better management." Railroads had to prosper, all agreed, but not, as Luna put it, "out of the pockets of the working men." Still another union president, Charles R. Pfenning of the American Train Dispatchers Association, reported to Nixon that "labor . . . [was] not the basic problem." Instead, according to Pfenning, "the heart of the matter . . . [was] unfair regulatory practices." Only a few months earlier, in fact, a leader of one rail union had told a reporter that "'we're going to have to get back to the original philosophy of free competition.'" The ICC, he concluded "should be abolished."[10] Much as Flanigan and Houthakker were hoping, leaders of railroad labor appeared ready to join that "grassroots" effort aimed at eliminating a portion of the regulatory regime.

Now that the president and his assistants had met with rail and labor leaders, executives of firms that shipped in large quantities wanted to articulate concerns about regulation at their own private meetings with presidential officials. Railroad executives, a Cargill executive wrote Flanigan on July 6, "have each had an opportunity to express themselves at meetings in the White House," adding that now it was time "that the people who pay the bills be afforded the same courtesy." Again, no one said anything that had not been said before. Always articulate and well versed in converting economic ideas into policy pronouncements, one executive supported increased competition in transportation on grounds of "ferret[ing] out some of the inefficiencies that currently plague the industry."[11] In other words, large shippers blamed regulators and regulations for high transportation costs.

By early July, members of the Nixon administration had completed this first round of "grassroots" organizing. On July 9, John Glancy, an assistant to Peter Flanigan, outlined the "probable sources of support and opposition for proposed deregulation bill." Truck operators, as Flanigan and others had learned in separate meetings at the White House (and much as everyone had expected), would "strenuously oppose" deregulation measures such as limitations on rate bureaus in setting rates or curbs on operating rights that would permit more truckers to enter a lucrative route. Equally, Glancy believed that teamster leader Frank Fitzsimmons "will probably take [a] position . . . much like those taken by the trucking companies." As for leaders of the rail unions, Glancy reported that they would support deregulation plans that permitted railroads to abandon unprofitable lines. "The rail unions," Glancy pointed out, "would like to share with the railroad companies in the pecuniary benefits from abandonments." Like their counterparts in the trucking industry, however, railroad leaders disliked the "idea of removing anti-trust immunity for some rate bureau activity." Although, as senior officials had learned, large shippers favored many of their deregulatory proposals, "smaller shippers are likely to be more timid and some will support the truckers' position on these issues." Nor could Nixon and his aides rely on leaders of farm groups to endorse deregulation, because farmers "now benefit from below-cost rail rates." Indeed, on July 9, the acting secretary of agriculture wrote Flanigan that "agriculture would be giving up a lot and getting very little in return."[12] In mid-July 1971, that "grassroots support" for rail and truck deregulation that Nixon and his aides were seeking was nowhere in sight.

Despite Glancy's pessimistic appraisal, by early August 1971 Nixon's aides had prepared draft legislation proposing partial deregulation of trucking and railroading. That bill, as Glancy explained to another senior official on August 6, aimed to "reduce regulation of surface freight transportation in certain respects," including reduced authority for rate bureaus to set rates and limiting truckers' operating rights, an idea that was increasingly described as easing entry for competitors.[13] The twin goals at this early stage of deliberations were first to rescue ailing railroads and second to boost the overall pace of the nation's economic activity by attacking price and route restrictions that every certificated trucker such as Abner Glikbarg and the Bonacci brothers had long and enthusiastically supported. The next and most important step in assembling that "grassroots" coalition was to secure the approval of Frank Fitzsimmons, general president of the International Brotherhood of Teamsters. Like truck owners, however, Teamster jobs and high wages depended on that same set of price and route restrictions.

On August 18, Flanigan and Fitzsimmons met for a period of two hours. Flanigan recognized, he told Fitzsimmons, that a "community of interest existed between the Teamsters and the Truckers." At the same time, Flanigan observed, leaders of trucking groups had entered objections to many aspects of the administration's proposed deregulation bill, such as their objection to "freedom to reduce rates and some limit on rate bureau activities." Flanigan also told Fitzsimmons that "all of the objections . . . were probably not shared by the Teamsters," suggesting that Flanigan hoped to split teamsters from truckers on part of their proposed plan of deregulation. "Fitzsimmons listened to the details of the proposal," Flanigan noted, and then "voiced two objections." Elimination of rate bureaus in determining single line (not interlined) rates, Fitzsimmons feared, could "lead to serious inequities where a [trucking] company will grant a shipper an advantage in one competitive market in order to secure its business in other markets." Fitzsimmons also worried about the consequences that would follow easing of entry rules, or what he described as "removal of geographic restrictions in certificates." Removal of those restrictions, asserted Fitzsimmons, could boost tonnage carried by larger trucking firms, but "could well spell the death bell for the local truckers."[14] Teamster leaders such as Fitzsimmons could also talk the language of truck company managers and owners who had long preferred maintenance of a rigid wall between railroads and truckers as well as maintenance of segmented trucking markets, as for instance between common and contract carriers.

On October 22, Flanigan responded by letter to the issues Fitzsimmons had raised at their meeting and later in writing. Members of the Nixon administration, Flanigan wrote, had been trying to "to work out ways of meeting the concerns you expressed." In terms of plans to reduce the immunity of rate bureaus, Flanigan explained that the goal was "eliminat[ion] of regulatory delays" that would, in turn, allow "both shippers and carriers . . . to receive the full benefits of the contemplated rate flexibility." Flanigan, moreover, promised a "floor" on rate reduction, a floor "below which no motor carrier could lawfully go." Here, then, was a modified version of the railroads' proposal dating from the late 1940s to establish a "zone of reasonableness." As Flanigan knew, however, truckers and teamsters identified terms such as "rate flexibility" as a euphemism for the destruction of their rate bureaus and for a period of rate wars, losses, and layoffs judged soon to follow. "Members of the Nixon administration," Flaningan assured Fitzsimmons, possessed "no desire to see a return to unrestrained cutthroat competition in the trucking industry."[15]

On October 22 and 23, Fitzsimmons held separate meetings with Charles D. Baker, an assistant secretary in the Department of Transportation, and with John N. Mitchell, the Attorney General. Only a month before, on September 22, a senior official had written Flanigan that legislation aimed at making it easier for truckers to enter new routes would produce "the battle of our lives." Mitchell, however, still wanted to "meet Fitzsimmons at least half way." Mitchell's reasoning was that "Fitzsimmons will be in a position to offset, to some extent, trucker opposition." What Mitchell and Baker also determined at those meetings was that "we could go ahead with the deregulation bill . . . without jeopardizing the overall relationship between the Teamsters and the Administration." On October 28, Flanigan informed top officials in the Nixon administration, including Attorney General Mitchell, that a bill seeking partial deregulation of surface transportation would go forward.[16] For now, risk taking for economic growth took precedence over legislative and electoral risk.

Politics soon took over. In a replay of Eisenhower's failure to support Weeks's limited deregulation proposal, no sooner had the bill gone to Congress than leaders in the Nixon administration failed to lobby energetically for its approval. As early as October 1971, a leader of a farm group reported that Flanigan appeared more concerned about "what the hell the carriers were going to say, rather than with the shippers' reactions." Still enthusiastic nonetheless about this proposed legislation, on October 29, John Glancy recommended that Flanigan "talk . . . with some of the key people on the Hill," including Representative Gerald R. Ford and Senator Norris H. Cotton. By November 24, however, Glancy reported to Flanigan that "I didn't leave the meeting this morning feeling very reassured about our program for pushing" the deregulation bill (and an accompanying bill providing loans and grants to railroads). Glancy complained that "we haven't yet done much with the general press or in the speech-making area." Although Glancy believed that shippers were "giving the bills some solid support," he worried that Russ Murphy, a new member of the staff, "seems to have little appetite for the job of developing contacts with the key people in the world of shippers." By May 1972, following months of inaction, Flanigan learned that deregulation-minded staff at the Department of Justice and the Council of Economic Advisers "believe that . . . prospects [for achieving deregulation] are being diminished by what is being perceived as a failure on the part of the Administration to back the bill."[17]

Truckers and teamsters were not waiting to learn whether Flanigan and his aides were prepared to "back the bill." Not only did truckers and teamsters still possess much of their celebrated clout, but they were willing to use it to block the administration's legislation. On June 30, James M. Beggs, the Undersecretary of Transportation, wrote Flanigan that "bills have emerged from both sides of the Hill" that include "no" reduction in the authority of rate bureaus to determine rates, and "no" restrictions on operating certificates, the hated liberalization of entry. Worse yet, those bills even authorized senior officials of the Interstate Commerce Commission to "budget directly with Congress without submission to OMB [the Office of Management and Budget]."[18] Such a course of action, as all understood, would have enhanced the authority of the ICC, just at the moment that a few in and out of Congress had begun to speak of diminishing or even eliminating the regulatory regime. In the time-honored tradition of the trucking industry, a threat to operating rights or the prerogatives of rate bureau officials encouraged submission of legislation seeking to expand the boundaries of protected transportation industries or modes and their many submarkets composed of railroads, contract and common carrier truckers, and the rest.

With deregulation appearing doomed, by June 1972, members of Congress were more interested in advancing $5 billion in loans to ailing railroads than in advancing deregulation. Approving grants and loan guarantees—and all that money for paying employees and suppliers—was bound to prove more attractive to members of Congress in an election year than the messy and risky business of deregulating hard-nosed truckers and their teamster allies. The popular loan program also created one last opportunity for Flanigan and other top aides to lobby for partial deregulation, if they chose to risk it. The strategy, as another Nixon official outlined it for Flanigan, was a simple one. "Tell Congressmen," went the reasoning, "that if the Administration position on . . . [partial deregulation] is accepted, the Administration will support . . . the enlarged system of loan guarantees.[19]

Shippers who were supposed to have joined the grassroots program for deregulation, were also urging approval of loans to railroads shorn of troublesome deregulation proposals. A senior official of the Transportation Association of America told Flanigan that the bill was "not perfect" but urged a spirit of "compromise." Insistence by Flanigan on inclusion of what were described as "highly controversial provisions . . . that carriers bitterly oppose" would lead to "waste by the failure of Congress to act" and could also encourage "affected groups to withdraw support and become a strong opposition force, especially in this election year." Much as Peter Flanigan's aide John Glancy had predicted a year earlier, smaller shippers had become "more timid."[20] Especially during this presidential election season, a portion of the nation's many shippers preferred the certainties of the regulatory regime—and loans to roads on whom many depended—to the uncertainties of deregulation.

At a moment during which only politics mattered, John Volpe, the secretary of transportation, recommended acceptance of the loan program—without deregulation. On August 8, Volpe sent a letter to John Ehrlichman, one of President Nixon's top two assistants. Volpe focused on "the political aspects of the transportation regulatory and assistance legislation." Volpe reminded Ehrlichman that "we already have six major railroads in reorganization," and without relief "there is little doubt that the Penn Central will run out of cash and may land in our hands." Volpe also worried about jobs lost, which he numbered at "tens of thousands of them on the railroads themselves, in addition to the literally hundreds of thousands . . . that would be affected if the Penn Central and other railroads are allowed to fall by the wayside." In a process Volpe described as "speaking politically again," he told Ehrlichman that "if we insist on the entry . . . and . . . other provisions

..., we not only miss the opportunity to save the railroads but we antagonize the truckers [and] teamsters." Failure to "compromise at this point," Volpe warned, would also signal truckers "that the Administration would be coming in next year insisting on a bill that would have entry provisions and other things they are definitely against." Support of this legislation, Volpe concluded, would allow leaders of the administration "to take credit for saving many jobs, and keeping this industry in private hands," all of which, he added, amounted to "Good Republican philosophy."[21] In August, Flanigan relented, permitting a program of loans and loan guarantees to go forward without insisting upon deregulation. In 1972, electoral politics triumphed.

Politics triumphed again in 1973. Early in the year, leaders of a small group located in and out of the federal government coalesced to support a program of deregulation. Members of this group included Hendrik Houthakker and Jack C. Pearce. In 1971, Houthakker had returned to the economics department at Harvard University. By April 1972, he had circulated a statement among twenty-five economists asking them to support Nixon's deregulation proposals. Jack Pearce formerly served as an attorney in the Antitrust Division of the U.S. Department of Justice, where he had prepared drafts of President Kennedy's legislation aimed at achieving partial deregulation of transportation firms. During 1970–1971, Pearce worked as deputy general counsel in the White House Office of Consumer Affairs. In that post, Pearce served on Houthakker's Subcommittee on Transportation that had recommended a program of deregulation to Peter Flanigan and members of Nixon's Cabinet Committee on Economic Policy. Now in private practice, Pearce's clients included shippers who had banded together under the acronym COMET, the Committee on Modern Efficient Transportation. Created in February 1972 to lobby for Nixon's deregulation bill, executives of several of the nation's largest shippers such as Sears and General Mills had joined COMET. In February 1973, a Nixon official reported that COMET officials were "independently in contact with [the new Secretary of Transportation Claude S.] Brinegar and the DOT bureaucracy." For the first time, the idea of deregulating rail and truck firms had an identifiable constituency, alongside railroad labor and management, that included a professional economist located at the prestigious Harvard University and an attorney with several large and politically savvy shippers as his clients. An official in the Nixon administration described the goals of COMET members as "'greater latitude' for carrier managements in the management of carriers' business."[22]

During early 1973, however, highway politics trumped deregulatory politics. For several years, President Nixon and his senior transportation officials had been asking members of Congress to spend money in the highway trust fund for mass transit, not just for highway building. Under terms of the Federal-Aid Highway Act of 1956, all gasoline taxes went into a trust fund; and truckers, longtime advocates of highway improvements, had regularly opposed what they described as "diversion" of those taxes from the trust fund to nonhighway projects such as mass transit. Anxious to secure approval of a limited "diversion" precisely for mass transit, on March 19 a senior official at the Department of Transportation sent a handwritten note to one of President Nixon's aides reporting "we are doing all we can *not* to aggravate the truckers right now." In 1973, moreover, few believed that Congress would pass deregulation proposals.[23] Politics was still in charge.

Fear of the power of organized truckers prevailed again in the middle of 1973. By late July, leaders of the Nixon administration had prepared yet another bill aimed at fostering deregulation. This effort, however, focused only on deregulating the nation's declining railroads, unlike the bill approved by Flanigan in the fall of 1971 that had included regulated truckers. Only one member of the cabinet, Secretary of the Treasury George P. Schultz, held out for additional legislation that would have permitted truckers carrying exempt agricultural commodities to compete for regular common carrier business. Schultz, an economist and a former dean of the Graduate School of Business at the University of Chicago, had years of experience with the lectures and publications of his university faculty such as economist George J. Stigler who opposed federal regulation of transportation and other industries. Nonetheless, Michael Raoul-Duval, one of President Nixon's new aides, joined Brinegar in opposing the addition sought by Schultz. "I concur with Secretary [of Transportation Claude S.] Brinegar's assessment," Raoul-Duval wrote top presidential assistant Melvin R. Laird, "on the grounds that it will trigger a very adverse reaction to the entire bill by the trucking industry." If Congress approves deregulation of the railroads, Raoul-Duval added, then we could "follow up with other regulatory reforms."[24] In 1973, Secretary Brinegar and DOT officials along with trucker opposition had succeeded in driving trucking deregulation from the administration's transportation agenda. Thereafter, until Nixon resigned from office on August 9, 1974, the politics of dealing with the Watergate break-in took precedence over the politics of deregulation. Politics remained in the driver's seat.

NIXON AND APPOINTMENT OF THE ICC CHAIR

Deregulation of railroads and trucking firms never had comprised all or most of President Nixon's transportation policy initiatives. Like several of his predecessors, including Roosevelt and Johnson, Nixon and his aides also pursued administrative and legislative changes aimed at centralizing transportation regulation in the president's hands. Historian Joan Hoff describes this process of centralization as one in which Nixon sought to reorganize the executive branch of the federal government to look and behave more like a corporation, with the president as the nation's chief executive officer.[25] Direct presidential appointment of the chair of the Interstate Commerce Commission comprised one of Nixon's centralizing efforts. In 1969, Nixon sought authority from Congress to appoint the ICC chair. Three years earlier, in 1966, members of Congress had denied that identical authority to President Johnson, just as members of an earlier Congress had stopped President Roosevelt from tampering with the ICC. Up to the late 1960s, then, commissioners rotated the chair among themselves on an annual basis, creating a collegial form of governance. Presidential responsibility for economic performance, however, had suggested to Nixon and his predecessors at least as far back as Roosevelt the desirability of enhancing presidential control over each of the federal levers of economic activity, including regulatory agencies such as the ICC.

No doubt aware of Johnson and Califano's failed effort, Nixon and his senior aides chose a different path to control the ICC chair. Rather than asking Congress to approve legislation allowing the president to appoint the Chair—Johnson and Califano's chosen tactic—Nixon sought that authority through a process called administrative reorganization. On January 20, 1969, in his first message to Congress, Nixon asked for a two-year renewal of the president's authority to reorganize the federal government, which had lapsed at the end of 1968. On March 27, members of Congress approved the extension.[26] Rather than having to seek legislation allowing presidential appointment of the chair of the ICC, now the president was asking for authority to make that appointment subject only to a resolution of disapproval voted by a majority in each house of Congress within a period of sixty days.

Despite the change in tactics, Nixon's reasoning in seeking to appoint the chair of the ICC was identical to that of Califano and Johnson. On July 22, 1969, in a message to Congress urging approval of the reorganization (as it was now labeled), Nixon cited the importance of "firm and clear legal responsibility for management of the Commission's . . . affairs." As Nixon phrased it, "no modern business . . . would tolerate the practice of annually rotating its chief executive." Authors of Nixon's reorganization plan also spoke of vesting authority in the chair of the ICC.[27] In 1966, however, opponents of Johnson's plan for centralizing transportation authority in the Office of the Secretary of Transportation had spoken of vesting authority with the administrators of the modal agencies such as the Federal Highway

Administration. Now, Nixon wanted to vest authority with the chair of the ICC for such crucial matters as appointment of personnel, budgeting, and the allocation of workloads and responsibilities among remaining members of the commission. By the late 1960s, the language of corporate managers was emerging as a routine part of the language of politicians.

Nixon's proposed reorganization still had to avoid congressional disapproval. As before, leaders of the National Industrial Traffic League, a large organization of shippers, opposed presidential appointment of the chair. They cited the importance of the ICC's autonomy. In this context, what traffic league officials meant was that they feared the potential of a strong chair who might vote to permit higher shipping rates or allow truckers and railroad executives to stop making deliveries to remote places. Among those such as small shippers who often talked about the advantages of markets, regulation of transportation rates and mandated delivery still had their uses. Leaders of the Association of American Railroads, however, supported presidential appointment of the ICC chair. In a letter to the house committee appointed to review the president's plan, the president of the AAR spoke of "pav[ing] the way for improved management and increased efficiency." In short, railroad executives wanted higher rates, additional mergers, and less frequent service to small towns. Equally, the head of the Air Freight Motor Carriers Conference, a group of truck operators who brought freight to and from air carriers, endorsed the idea of presidential appointment of the ICC chair. The attorney for that group advocated "intermodal coordination," which was, he asserted, emerging as a "reality." That reality, asserted the attorney, now required improved coordination among federal regulatory agencies. Even the chair of the house subcommittee had discovered a "need for closer . . . working relationships in the area of regulation."[28] Nothing in Nixon's plan mentioned or hinted at enhanced federal coordination, higher or lower transportation rates, or less or more service to the nation's remote areas. Altogether, here was another illustration of the customary scramble among leaders in the transportation industry to promote a favored outcome, or to head off one that was undesirable, uncertain, or unknown. Among activists in the politically constructed transportation industries, the effort to protect or expand the boundaries of industries and markets extended back over many years, and sometimes over many decades.

Whatever shippers, carriers, or members of Congress imagined about the likely outcomes of presidential appointment of the ICC chair, the fact that Nixon had sent it forward under the renewed Reorganization Act placed the burden on Congress to vote it down, which it determined not to do. Perhaps Nixon benefited in this matter from a congressional inclination not to refuse a presidential request early in his term. Beginning in January

1970, the president of the United States possessed the authority to appoint the chair of the Interstate Commerce Commission. In turn, the chair would possess authority over such weighty matters as the ICC's budget and the workload of remaining ICC members. In an instant, Congress awarded President Nixon what it had denied President Johnson. In 1969, the politics of centralization and administrative coordination could still command a wide allegiance.

CONCLUSION

Since 1945, every president of the United States has recognized his special responsibility for boosting employment and earnings. In 1955 and 1956, President Eisenhower and Secretary Weeks proposed partial deregulation of rail and trucking firms with a view toward rescuing failing railroads and the businesses and travelers who still depended heavily upon them. President Johnson created the Department of Transportation and contemplated deregulation of railroad and trucking firms with a view toward accelerating the pace of economic growth. Members of that 1960s generation of political and business leaders described the process as one of "fine-tuning" the economy. Whether in the 1950s or the 1960s, the goal of would-be deregulators was to reduce or eliminate politically contrived barriers between transportation industries and markets, again as for instance between railroaders and truckers, whether common or contract carriers.

President Nixon inherited an economy in the early stages of a lengthy period of decline. Like Johnson, however, Nixon's response to economic downturn was to seek both centralization of federal regulation in the form of presidential appointment of the ICC chair and deregulation of transportation prices and services. Historian Hoff describes a process whereby Nixon sought "centralized planning and structural decentralization in domestic affairs." Nixon himself described this paradoxical situation with great clarity. Years after leaving office, he told Hoff that "bringing power to the White House [was necessary] in order to dish it out."[29]

By taking risks, President Nixon had made deregulation a regular if sometimes unpopular topic of conversation among leaders in transportation and politics; and by taking additional risks, Nixon had secured authority for the president to appoint the chair of the ICC. In 1972 and 1973, however, the politics of reelection (and especially the politics of not offending temperamental truckers and teamsters) caused Nixon to hold back on deregulation efforts. Starting in 1973, the politics of the Watergate break-in eroded and then destroyed Nixon's presidency. Beginning in 1973, the politics of the Watergate break-in also undercut Nixon's deregulatory efforts and limited his ability to bring additional centralization and coordination to transportation agencies. Because plans for centralization of transportation (and other federal agencies) were so negatively associated with President Nixon, his successors had only deregulation (the opening of transportation's many submarkets) remaining as a tool in the presidential arsenal of devices for dealing with railroads, trucks, and airlines in a declining economy. Not for another two decades did the idea of coordination among rail, airlines, and trucking return to the top of the federal list of priorities. By then, proponents of coordination operated under the newly fashionable idea called "intermodalism."

Starting in 1974, President Gerald R. Ford and Senator Edward M. Kennedy began the lengthy process of transforming deregulation into an increasingly plausible idea for restoring growth without inflation to the American economy. As part of that process, Kennedy and especially Ford also launched a process of identifying and recruiting a constituency for deregulation. In 1979, President Jimmy Carter started deregulation of trucking on an administrative basis, relying on his ability to appoint the chair of the ICC. Not only were American presidents such as Eisenhower and Kennedy among the earliest and most visible advocates for deregulation of rail and truck, but later presidents starting with Nixon and extending to Ford and Carter used the growing authority of the presidential office to bring that deregulation into being. Ford's first step was to discredit the regulatory regime; and his next was to use the authority of the Department of Transportation to approve railroad loans as a lever to bring about partial deregulation.

CHAPTER 7

GERALD R. FORD AND PRESIDENTIAL DEREGULATION, 1974–1977

FORD IS NOW FURTHER OUT ON THE DEREGULATION LIMB THAN KENNEDY,
JOHNSON AND NIXON EVER ALLOWED THEMSELVES TO GET.
   —LOUIS M. KOHLMEIER, *NATIONAL JOURNAL*, 1975

Between 1974 and 1980, Presidents Gerald R. Ford and Jimmy Carter presided over deregulation of the nation's air, truck, and rail systems. Ford and Carter took different approaches to the process of bringing about that deregulation. Ford attempted to foster deregulation first by discrediting the seemingly bizarre rules and the many rule-makers who worked at the ICC and other regulatory agencies. Once having diminished regulations and regulators, Ford introduced legislation aimed at deregulating railroads, trucks, and even airlines. Only because bankrupt railroads were in desperate need of loans and grants, however, was Ford able to secure a limited railroad deregulation as the price for award of government credit and cash.

Jimmy Carter also wanted to eliminate all or most of the regulatory regime. At the outset of his term beginning in January 1977, Carter and his aides relied less on legislation and more on administrative measures to foster deregulation. Carter appointed deregulation-minded economists to chair the Interstate Commerce Commission and the Civil Aeronautics Board. In turn, those economists, such as Alfred E. Kahn, began the process of dismantling the regulatory regime. At the same time, Carter recognized that eventually deregulation would have to enjoy legislative approval. For that task, he employed talented and energetic aides such as Mary Schuman, Richard M. Neustadt, and Stuart E. Eizenstat. They organized a coalition of proderegulation business leaders to offset the strenuous efforts of airline executives, truckers, and teamsters who sought to maintain regulation. In 1978, President Carter and his aides secured deregulation of airlines; and in 1980, they brought about deregulation of trucking and further deregulation of railroads.

Despite these modest differences in their approach to deregulation, Ford and Carter had much in common. Senator Edward M. Kennedy was a competitor with both Ford and Carter for the presidency. Throughout this period, however, Kennedy cooperated with Ford and Carter's efforts to bring about deregulation. Equally, both Ford and Carter (and several of their top aides) recognized—always in private—that the much-touted studies by deregulation-minded economists were in fact limited in scope. As the attending physicians for the American political economy, Ford and Carter had determined nonetheless to run the risk of prescribing deregulation of truck, rail, and airline firms as their recommended cures for rising levels of unemployment and inflation. Unlike President Johnson's desire to use deregulation to enhance presidential authority and then "fine-tune" the economy, Ford and Carter tied the remote concept of deregulation to economic problems understood and felt by every American. Discrediting regulation and regulators came first.

DISCREDITING REGULATION AND REGULATORS

Gerald Ford served as president between August 1974 and January 1977. During that period of two and a half years, Ford brought deregulation front and center as a main topic in a large number of public addresses. Ford launched this rhetorical war on the regulatory regime soon after taking office. Inflation loomed as a major problem, he told members of the U.S. Senate and House of Representatives at a joint session of Congress held on October 8, and government was a key source of that inflation. The federal government, Ford asserted, "imposes too many hidden and too many inflationary costs." As a start, Ford urged Congress to create a National Commission on Regulatory Reform. Members of that group would provide a "long-overdue total reexamination of the independent regulatory agencies" aimed at "eliminat[ing] existing Federal rules and regulations that increase costs to the consumer without any good reason." Members of Congress failed to create Ford's regulatory reform commission. Within two months of taking office, however, Ford had linked the presence and activities of those regulatory agencies with his own efforts to "whip" inflation, which the president described as a threat to "our country, our homes, our liberties, our property, and . . . our national pride."[1]

During the next two years, President Ford spoke often about the apparent links between inflation, unemployment, and government regulation. In each talk, Ford highlighted the problems that regulation had reportedly brought about, and urged members of his audience to mobilize for reform.

For example, in his speech on October 15, 1974, to participants at the annual convention of the Future Farmers of America in Kansas City, Missouri, Ford asserted that regulations of the Interstate Commerce Commission caused "many, many trucks [to] return empty." Ford drew direct links between high costs faced by farmers and regulations prepared by a distant federal agency, asking audience members "to work with others to eliminate [these] outmoded regulations that keep the cost of goods and services high."[2]

During spring 1975, Ford's attacks on regulation contrasted federal rules with his own efforts to restore prosperity. On April 18, for instance, Ford highlighted restoration of "economic health" with a proposed reduction in the size and scope of the federal bureaucracy. In an address to participants in a White House Conference on Domestic and Economic Affairs, held in Concord, New Hampshire, Ford asserted that "more than 100,000 people are employed by the Federal Government for the sole and exclusive responsibility of writing, reviewing, and enforcing some type of regulation." It was true that some fifty federal regulatory agencies, including the now visible ICC and the less visible Commodity Futures Trading Commission, employed approximately one hundred thousand persons. Whether President Ford or anyone else had actually determined the precise role of each senior and junior employee or each agency as a whole in bringing about inflation mattered less in this context than the image of those one hundred thousand federal workers described by Ford as residing in a "bureaucrat's dream of heaven." Heaping further blame on federal regulation and regulators for the economic downturn, on June 17 Ford told members of the National Federation of Independent Business that "a big businessman is what a small businessman would be if the Government would ever let him alone!" Rather than trying to explain often difficult-to-understand institutions such as rate bureaus or the rigid distinctions in federal law and regulatory rules between common and contract carriers, Ford instead attempted to mobilize a constituency for deregulation by invoking the language of productivity and growth in an age of economic decline.[3]

As Ford made these speeches, Senator Edward M. Kennedy added to the emerging political drama of transportation deregulation. Kennedy focused on the airlines. In spring 1975, he held much-publicized hearings on intrastate airfares under the direction of Stephen G. Breyer, a new member of the Harvard Law School faculty. Kennedy asked witnesses to explain why unregulated airlines operating only in California and Texas could charge lower fares and still provide frequent service at high load factors. Kennedy's questions, contends business historian Richard H. K. Vietor, "posed . . . inexplicable contradiction[s] or, worse, . . . [were] simply unanswerable." President Ford, citing reports of the Kennedy hearings and especially the finding that airline fares in Texas and California were "as much as 40-percent lower than those controlled by the CAB," concluded that "something must be wrong." In May 1975, Louis M. Kohlmeier, a writer for the *National Journal*, observed that "Ford is now further out on the deregulation limb than [President] Kennedy, Johnson and Nixon ever allowed themselves to get."[4]

Unlike Presidents Eisenhower, Kennedy, Johnson, or even Nixon, however, President Ford wanted to create the impression that government never had a valid reason to deny the unambiguous virtues of competition between truckers, railroaders, and other transportation firms. Without doubt, the regulatory regime, including the Civil Aeronautics Board and the Interstate Commerce Commission with their emphasis since the late 1930s on separate and distinct transportation industries such as airlines, railroads, and trucking and their intricate submarkets such as common and contract carriers, were and remained creatures of the federal government. Again, rather than using his speeches to explain the complex politics of regulation, Ford chose instead to represent himself as the chief economic officer of the national economy. Like his counterparts at large, vertically integrated firms such as Sears and General Motors, Ford imaged the regulatory regime in the form of recalcitrant middle managers at the CAB and ICC who through ineptitude, stupidity, or downright malevolence had slowed the flow of merchandise from production to distribution and consumption. In the corporate state, as in the corporation, top executives oversaw a process of ratcheting up production, simultaneously closing down units and terminating the services of those who blocked the visible hands of senior managers such as themselves.

Ford's message got through to journalists. Prior to the Kennedy hearings and President Ford's many speeches, deregulation had remained in the provinces of economists such as Hendrik Houthakker and presidential advisers such as Joseph Califano and Peter Flanigan. As an example, between 1970 and 1974, editors of the *New York Times* never used the words "regulation" or "deregulation" in the title of a news story. During 1975, however, those same editors published thirty-six stories containing the word "deregulation" in the title. In 1976, editors of the *New York Times* ran another thirty-five stories employing the word "deregulation" as part of a story's title.[5]

Not every newspaper editor published stories with the word "deregulation" in the title. Even so, editors of newspapers and magazines with widespread readership, such as the *Christian Science Monitor*, the *Los Angeles Times*, the *Chicago Tribune*, and *Time*, ran stories about economic conditions and about the rhetorical and legislative efforts of Senator Kennedy and President Ford to reduce or eliminate federal regulation of transportation and other industries. What Kennedy and especially Ford accomplished with their antiregulation rhetoric was to launch a process whereby Americans not familiar with the principles and details of government regulation began to associate remote and perhaps unheard-of agencies such as the Civil Aeronautics Board and the Interstate Commerce Commission with concrete problems such as unemployment, energy shortages, and high prices for air travel, food, and package delivery. In May 1977, editors of *U.S. News & World Report* published just such a story. Repeating President Ford's count of more than one hundred thousand persons working in federal regulatory agencies, a writer added that the decisions of those regulators "affect the food that people eat, the cars they drive, the fuel they use, the clothes they wear, the houses they live in, the investments they make, the water they drink and even the air they breathe."[6] Long before economists such as Alfred E. Kahn took charge of the Civil Aeronautics Board, President Ford, Senator Kennedy, and many journalists had set about the task of educating ordinary Americans and their representatives about the apparent costs imposed on them by government regulators and their regulations and about the presumed advantages of transportation deregulation.

President Ford's next step was to convert images and rhetoric into legislative action. The railroads came first. Starting in March 1967 with the Central Railroad of New Jersey, by mid-1974, executives of eight railroads now including the once-mighty Penn Central and the more modest Lehigh & Hudson River Railway had sought the protection of bankruptcy. Trains still operated, but sometimes at speeds no greater than ten miles per hour, a condition brought about by federal speed limits on tracks and bridges in poor condition. As part of a ruling on consolidating those eight railroads into one, in December 1974, justices of the U.S. Supreme Court found "a rail transportation crisis seriously threatening the national welfare." Several of the weakest railroads, moreover, were located in the Northeast and Midwest, regions in which rising costs for heating oil during a severe winter had added to inflationary pressures and unemployment. Equally important, those railroads carried coal and freight. Delivery of those items not only created jobs for railroad workers, but also sustained many more jobs in nearby factories and then down the economic line among wholesalers and retailers. Directly and indirectly, countless households depended on bankrupt and weakened railroads for jobs and supplies. We now face the "grim reality," transportation secretary William T. Coleman wrote Ford on April 12, 1975, of "a major breakdown of our rail freight system."[7]

Cost, history, and politics added to the complexities of starting railroad deregulation. Late in 1973, members of Congress and President Nixon had approved the Regional Rail Reorganization Act, bringing into existence the United States Railway Association (USRA). Headed by an eight-person board of directors, Congress charged officials of the USRA to prepare a plan for managing the assets and maintaining the service of Penn Central and the other bankrupt railroads. On May 29, 1975, directors of the USRA voted to create the Consolidated Rail Corporation, soon known popularly as Conrail. In turn, officers of Conrail would assume responsibility for day-to-day rail operations, presumably keeping shipping costs low through competition with other railroad lines. As part of the USRA's focus on the maintenance of low-cost shipping, moreover, officers of two profitable rail-roads, the Chessie System and the Norfolk & Western, would assume control of parts of the bankrupt lines. Members of the USRA board gave this plan the technical name "Three Carriers East," which journalists popular-ized as the "Three-system plan." Both names bore a striking resemblance to the "three-system East" plan conceived in the late 1950s by James M. Symes, president of the Pennsylvania Railroad. The USRA plan and the earlier Symes plan were part of the legacy of numerous plans for railroad consolidation that had consumed so much attention among railroad execu-tives, ICC regulators, and academic economists between 1920 and 1932.[8]

The three-system plan, like those earlier consolidation schemes, con-tained elements certain to make nearly everyone jittery, or angry. Abandon-ments, some seven thousand miles worth—and still more unemployment—loomed in the future, unless some public entity, presumably the federal government, subsidized maintenance and service on those less-used tracks. Indeed, much of the trackage likely to be abandoned carried little freight. Even so, observes historian Richard Saunders Jr., "as long as the railroad was there [in small towns located in areas facing especially difficult economic times including western Pennsylvania, portions of Ohio and Michigan, and sections of upstate New York], there was hope that the factories would come and the young people would stay." Early in February 1975, U.S. senator James Buckley of New York described plans to abandon railroad mileage as "shocking and intolerable." Already, the American landscape contained many cities such as Camden, Ohio, and Ligonier, Pennsylvania, that design-ers of the Interstate Highway System had bypassed and from which railroad executives had withdrawn service during the recent past. In this environ-ment of decline that had occurred and fear of worse to come for residents of another group of cities and towns, on June 7, governors of seventeen states met with President Ford to express concern about proposed abandonments.[9]

Nor was there enthusiasm about the three-system plan at the executive offices of the Chessie System and Norfolk & Western. Presidents of the two railroad firms liked the idea of gaining a few lucrative routes, especially in the Philadelphia and New York City areas. But they did not want to acquire the less profitable routes—as for example the Erie Lackawanna Railway's line from Buffalo to the New York terminal area in New Jersey—or those requiring lots of expensive upgrading—unless the federal government would pay for the upgrades. Equally, the USRA plan provided $250 million to pay laid-off railroad workers, leading Chessie executives to seek assurance that the federal government would "cover" all former-employee costs. Even more, one Chessie System official worried that a planned federal payout to Penn Central bondholders would prove insufficient, eventually leading a court at some future date to impose a deficiency judgment on the Chessie. Creditors and Penn Central officials also wanted more money from the federal government. Writing in 1975, economist George W. Hilton characterized the organization and funding of Conrail as "an extreme example of denying a market test."[10]

Costs of creating Conrail loomed large among Ford's top aides. Based only on the formal plan, they informed the president of their estimate of $4 billion in federal loan guarantees and another $1.6 billion in federal grants over a ten-year period. Worse yet, one aide told Ford that Conrail "will not be financially viable at any foreseeable time." The president of the Chessie System took essentially the same view of Conrail's likely costs, rendering his judgment in the rhetoric of privately managed enterprise. Conrail, he told a reporter for the *Wall Street Journal*, appeared a "political rather than an economic solution," leading him to conclude that what was taking place was "changing the ownership [and] changing the name of the rathole." Perhaps as a consequence of years of conversation and problem solving in the transportation industry, senior federal officials and their counterparts at the railroads shared the same negative outlook regarding government management of large enterprises such as the railroads.[11]

On May 19, 1975, President Ford sent omnibus railroad legislation to Congress linking loans with deregulation. In his accompanying message, Ford stressed that a proposed loan program would lead to "speedy and rational restructuring of the railroads" and removal of "regulatory restrictions" deemed "excessive and antiquated." What was now called railroad "revitalization," Ford promised, was only the first step of an "overall program to achieve fundamental reform of transportation regulation." In short, restructuring and deregulating the railroads would serve as the opening round in a much lengthier campaign of restructuring and deregulating the nation's transportation industries. A draft of the president's message even described a process whereby deregulation of transportation would help "revitalize our entire free enterprise system." Increasingly, the essence of government in the 1970s and beyond was not that of facilitating a return to much-discussed markets but was instead an effort to create those markets.[12] Implementing such a grand design brought federal officials right back into the thick of politics.

Members of Congress had no intention of leaving so important and contentious a set of matters as railroad loans and reorganization solely in the hands of creditors, USRA trustees, railroad executives, or the president of the United States. Anticipating problems that would emerge following publication of the Final System Plan, in 1973 members of Congress had guaranteed themselves sixty legislative days to approve the plan, or disapprove it. A majority in the Senate or the House could exercise a veto. Given the congressional recess in August, a journalist reported that action was not "expected . . . until late Fall."[13]

Representative Brock Adams also planned to exercise clout in the realms of railroad funding and deregulation. Born in 1927, Adams had served in the U.S. Navy during World War II. Returning to civilian life, in 1949, Adams graduated from the University of Washington with a degree in economics. In 1953, he earned a law degree at Harvard University. In 1961, early support for John F. Kennedy's presidential ambitions helped Adams secure appointment as U.S. Attorney for the Western District of Washington. In 1964, Adams won election to the U.S. House of Representatives. His district and nearby areas in Seattle and Tacoma included truck depots; an airport and seaport that had long served as transportation hubs for domestic and international traffic; several major railroad lines such as those of the Great Northern Railway and the Northern Pacific Railroad; a large number of unionized-transportation workers; and the Boeing Company, a gigantic manufacturer of commercial and military aircraft. In September 1973, as negotiations on rail legislation neared conclusion, a staff member to the New England Congressional Caucus described Adams as "the most knowledgeable member of the House Sub-Committee on rail issues."[14] Smart and likeable, Brock Adams had decided to make railroad legislation into one of his areas of specialization.

Brock Adams was also a practical and ambitious legislator. Academic proponents of deregulation, he told an audience of airline executives in November 1975, were "theorists and 'other-world economists.'" Fond of publicly extolling concrete solutions over the still-untested proposals of economists, Adams was in fact prepared to go along with many of President Ford's recommendations aimed at loosening regulatory constraints on railroad management. Loan guarantees for the railroads appeared satisfactory,

Adams judged, as did the prospect of "using the financial leverage created by government financing to promote regulatory reform . . . [and] a more rational system through mergers of railroads." By mid-1975, with many once again fearing collapse of the railroads and ensuing federal ownership, these ideas enjoyed standing as evidence of practicality. Perhaps word during August 1975 from Woody Price, Adams's senior legislative aide, that reaction of "folks" to the Final System Plan appeared "sullen but not mutinous" emboldened Adams to run the risk of taking a leading position on railroad consolidation and deregulation.[15] Beginning in August 1975, Adams coalesced with members of Congress and leaders of the Ford administration to help write that omnibus bill. Probably without realizing it, Adams was following the steps of John Esch and Albert Cummins, also practical legislators who through study and inclination had played pivotal roles in shaping the Transportation Act of 1920.

With so many jobs, railroads, and associated businesses at stake, negotiations between Secretary Coleman and leaders in Congress proved difficult and lengthy. On October 23, Woody Price sent a gloomy report on prospects for passing railroad legislation. "Neither labor nor management," Price wrote Adams, "are very enthusiastic about the bill." Each was "frightened by the quickie merger and restructuring provisions." Mergers and restructuring raised the specter of abandonments that would in turn foster a loss of service and jobs. Leaders of railroad unions wanted guarantees of wages for laid-off workers, a deal already included in the legislation that had set up Conrail in 1973. "This bill has more problems than a dog has fleas," Price warned, adding that one person had retitled the omnibus bill as the "'ominous' bill."[16]

Secretary Coleman was already dissatisfied. President Ford was prepared to spend or guarantee loans for $5.8 billion. Free-spending members of the Senate commerce committee, Coleman wrote the director of the Office of Management and Budget on November 24, had approved a total of $9.7 billion. Although the "pricing flexibility" Coleman and Ford sought for railroad executives had survived the vote of a House committee, Congressman Adams "has tried in subcommittee to weaken the regulatory reform . . . and may continue his efforts in full committee." On December 19, Coleman publicly announced the threat of a presidential veto. He cited a "significant increase in the federal deficit" and what he characterized as the "frustration" of his deregulation program that would "revitaliz[e] . . . the nation's railroads." An aide to a member of the Senate characterized Coleman's position as that of "'veto, veto, veto unless you give me exactly what I want exactly the way I want it.'"[17]

Threat of a presidential veto produced results. Although members of the

Senate and House had passed a common bill, Senate leaders did not enroll their legislation. The promised veto, Coleman and other senior officials wrote Ford late in December, had now created "a willingness to pursue a compromise with the Administration." William Coleman directed the administration's negotiators through his undersecretary and senior staff in the Department of Transportation; and because members of the House and Senate left negotiations in the hands of their assistants, Brock Adams exercised influence through Woody Price, his legislative aide. Never far from negotiators and their principals stood shippers, truckers, and railroaders—both management and labor. Members of Congress remained nearby as well, always concerned about federal spending for loans, grants, and improvements and about whether deregulation would lead to abandonments of service in their districts and states. Formal negotiations began January 2, 1976, and continued up to January 15, a few days before Congress reconvened.[18]

On January 14, Coleman reported to senior officials that "negotiations have gone well." Now, the federal government would make loans and grants totaling $6.098 billion, including money for Conrail, for subsidizing operations on lines scheduled for abandonment, and for track and bridge improvements on the Conrail system. Coleman also liked the "substantial improvements to the regulatory provisions of the bill," which included enhanced rate-making authority for railroad executives and limits on the pricing authority of their rate bureaus.[19] In the mid-1970s, the award of substantial pricing authority to railroad managers went under the awkward-sounding name of a "no-suspend zone," which was identical in practice to the peculiar-sounding "zone of reasonableness" that Commerce Secretary Weeks had sought in the mid-1950s for rail and truck executives.

By whatever name, President Ford and Secretary Coleman had prevailed upon Brock Adams and his colleagues to award limited-pricing discretion to rail managers. As the principal advocates of deregulation, Coleman and Ford had created their first market, in this case the market that would take place within the newly designated zone of reasonableness. The price Ford and Coleman paid included federal loans, branchline subsidies, job guarantees, and federal payments to the railroad workers who would be laid off. Limited deregulation of rate making and some shrinkage of service was a deal that members of Congress were willing to make with Ford in order to guarantee federal spending, jobs, and (diminished) railroad service, including start-up of Conrail on April 1, 1976. All in all, however, remaining institutions of the regulatory regime including rate bureaus, ICC regulations, and the concept of independent transportation modes had survived presidential speeches, meetings, and legislative arm-twisting. Only billions for "revitalization" in an environment of inflation and unemployment and the threatened shutdown or nationalization of part of the railroad system had brought William Coleman, Brock Adams, President Ford, and railroad labor and management that far. Such were the politics of the Railroad Revitalization and Regulatory Reform Act of 1976 (4-R), which President Ford signed on February 5, 1976.

Approval of 4-R also represented the high-water mark in Ford's efforts to deregulate American transportation. By late February 1976, only a few weeks after Ford signed the 4-R Act, a portion of the deal aimed at restoring competitive railroad service to the New York and New England areas was coming undone. Executives of the Southern Railway and Chessie System had agreed to purchase approximately twenty-two hundred miles of track formerly owned by the Reading Railroad or the Erie Lackawanna, two among the bankrupt carriers whose properties and employees were to be transferred to Conrail. Union leaders representing Erie Lackawanna and Reading employees, however, refused to accept work rules offered by Chessie executives, even if those rules were the same ones under which current Chessie employees worked. Union officials preferred both the older work rules and employment by the new Conrail management—backed by Congress—and had no reason to change their minds. Editorial writers invoked phrases such as "union rigidities" and a "booby trap . . . set by the friends of organized labor."[20]

Secretary Coleman still hoped to rescue the purchase of those twenty-two hundred miles. He scheduled a meeting with leaders of the Chessie and Southern railroads and their union counterparts for February 25. Even with Coleman's pressure, no one budged. On April 1, 1976, Conrail started operations, including operations on the former Erie Lackawanna lines. Employee desire for job security trumped the desire of politicians and Chessie officials for railroad competition in the New York region.[21] Airline executives, teamsters, regulators, and members of Congress also held their own in the contest with President Ford and Secretary Coleman.

INABILITY TO DEREGULATE AIRLINES AND TRUCKING COMPANIES

During 1974 and 1975, President Ford regularly articulated the advantages of deregulation, including the advantages of securing deregulation of trucking and airline firms. In 1975, as Congress took up rail legislation, Ford's senior officials, including Secretary Coleman, shaped legislation to deregulate the airline and trucking industries. Because deregulation—or regulation—were never unitary concepts, officials dealt with administrative, legal, and political problems, including such esoteric matters as the extension of pricing flexibility to airline and trucking company managers and elimination of antitrust immunity from their air and truck rate bureaus. Every discussion of deregulation also included the politically difficult idea of "freedom of entry." The very point that had enraged truckers when first advertised in 1955 by Secretary Weeks, freedom of entry portended easy movement of would-be competitors into lucrative routes, reducing or eliminating the ability of truck operators and rate bureau officials to determine prices charged both by the gigantic Pacific Intermountain Express and the tiny AAA Trucking Corporation owned by the Bonacci brothers. Freedom of entry also portended a loss of their valuable operating rights long protected by leaders of national trucking associations such as the American Trucking Associations and the Regular Common Carriers Conference. Since the start of the regulatory regime for truckers in 1935 and for airlines in 1938, jobs and profits rested on the protections offered by rate bureaus such as the Southern Motor Carriers Rate Conference, on attorneys such as Robert McBride at the Regular Common Carriers Conference, and on always watchful members of the Civil Aeronautics Board and at the Interstate Commerce Commission. Starting in 1955, moreover, announcement by Weeks of his plan to seek limited "freedom of entry" and pricing flexibility had energized truckers and their union counterparts to undertake new levels of political organizing and self-protecting litigation. Late in 1975, an official of the Teamsters Union described Ford's plans to deregulate the trucking industry as "the most destructive legislative proposal in the last 40 years."[22]

Like his predecessors, President Ford worried less about the gripes of any one group such as truckers and teamsters and more about the overall functioning of the economy. In turn, Ford's administrators served the president and his goals. Shorn of arcane deliberations about how to deal with entry rights or rate bureaus, Ford's senior administrators sometimes thought of themselves as doing for business executives what those executives ought to have done for themselves. Economist George C. Eads, a Ford official active in the airline deregulatory effort, had determined that airline executives posed the chief impediments to eliminating those inefficiencies. "To be blunt," he wrote another administration official on June 19, 1975, airline executives appeared "afraid that they have guessed wrong about the type of service that even the business executive would prefer." The problem, as Eads had it, was that airline officials were "afraid to test that possibility." What was required to bring about "operational changes," asserted Eads, was "increased flexibility in both entry and exit."[23] Whether the remedy for those "inefficiencies" included changes in entry policy or some other set of

FIGURE 16. President Gerald R. Ford meeting with members of his Task Force on Airline Reform, October 8, 1975. Prominent in this photo (from left to right) are President Ford, William T. Coleman (shaking hands), and John W. Snow. Source: Gerald R. Ford Library. Used with permission.

proposals, senior officials in the Ford administration defined themselves as the authors of enhanced competition and lower prices in the transportation industries—ground and air.

In practice, airline deregulation came first. The Kennedy hearings earlier in the year had brought substantial attention to low-priced fares available in California and Texas. As was shown in the chapter on airlines after World War II, by the early 1970s, federal leaders no longer identified the nation's air fleet as the key factor in cold war preparations. Altogether, airlines had joined trucks and railroads as likely targets of these would-be deregulators and market-builders. During the mid-1970s, however, airlines still retained much of the glamour of their early years. Even silly promotions such as equipping larger aircraft with piano lounges and crooners only added to the popular association of airlines with affluent lifestyles, especially among the business and professional persons who flew regularly in first class. Airline deregulation, if it came about, promised fare reductions that those business and other flyers would recognize, and could serve as a first step in the larger effort to deregulate other industries such as trucking and even banking and telephony. "The air bill," a senior official in the Office of Management and Budget wrote President Ford on September 29, "is the most publicly visible in that it deals with a direct consumer service and pocketbook issue." The idea, then, was to "assure increased consumer attention to the legislation."[24]

Beginning early in 1976, that effort to deregulate the nation's airlines shifted from the arena of press conferences and internal memos to the arena of political organizing. In mid-February 1976, President Ford and Senator Kennedy exchanged letters employing phrases such as "leadership," "thoughtful efforts," "cooperation," and Ford's stated conviction that "consumers and businessmen alike stand to gain from prompt and positive legislative action." One presidential aide, Edward C. Schmults, had advised Ford on February 18 that a letter to Senator Kennedy "would play an important part in building the bipartisan coalition needed for enactment of the air bill."[25]

President Ford assigned John W. Snow to assemble that coalition. In 1976, Snow was serving as a senior official in the Department of Transportation. Holder of a Ph.D. in economics from the University of Virginia and a law degree from George Washington University, Snow harbored none of the fears often expressed by airline officials that opening routes would increase financial problems, or bring ruin. In December 1975, for example, Snow had written Secretary Coleman that opening of entry to competitive airlines would lead to creation of an "efficient . . . financially sound . . . industry." Snow further believed that increased demand for air travel would "moderate the effects of competition," leading another senior member of the Ford administration to write in hand on her copy of the memo, "not really sure about this." In the mid-1970s, as many senior officials and members of Congress such as Brock Adams recognized, proposals to deregulate airlines or trucking rested more on conviction or on economists' hypotheses than on a large and solid empirical base. "'Deregulation' had entered the national vocabulary only recently," observes historian McCraw, "and so far there was little besides bombast to stand behind it."[26] For John Snow, however, deregulation of American transportation, starting with the airlines, represented an opportunity to extend an academic conviction into a policy outcome. Unlike Sinclair Weeks or Dwight Eisenhower, for whom limited deregulation of trucking and railroads appeared a pragmatic response to railroad decline, John Snow and his colleagues in the Ford and later administrations advocated construction of transportation markets as their major form of political expression.

Snow launched this coalition-building by organizing Ford's senior officials into liaison teams. Next, Snow directed team members—including William Coleman, the secretary of transportation—to "brief" members of Senate and House committees and their staffs. Snow himself anticipated conversations with fifty members of Congress, a figure in addition to the twenty-two members of the Senate and House and their staffs with whom he had met since the previous October. Most likely, Snow had identified those seventy-two members as his core constituents for deregulation. Next,

Snow assigned Ford personnel to meet with editors of major newspapers and magazines such as *Business Week,* the *Denver Post,* the *Chicago Sun Times,* and the *Wall Street Journal.* Snow directed others to conduct research on topics such as airline safety and the increasingly vexing matter of service to small towns. Preparation of testimony, which Snow wanted completed a week before hearings started in April, was to include "defense" of airline deregulation against such anticipated charges as "decrease[d] safety," "damage . . . [to] smaller communities," and that it would "result in industry chaos and financial ruin." Altogether, Snow estimated that twenty-four persons would expend more than seven hundred hours in conducting briefings and research and in identifying likely supporters in Congress.[27]

Snow also ordered team members to conduct a process labeled "liaison with interest groups." Those interest groups included the Consumers Union and several others identified as "consumers" and three environmental groups such as the Sierra Club. Although few women occupied senior posts in the Ford administration, Snow assigned them to meet with members of the consumer and environmental groups. Snow directed other top-level staffers, all male, to meet with leaders of groups identified as "economists," "financial community," and "banks," including Walter B. Wriston, chief executive officer of the Chase Manhattan Bank. Snow himself would "handle all contacts" with executives of three regional airlines such as Air West.[28] In the event that Congress permitted regional carriers to enter the more lucrative routes held by United and the other major carriers, executives of firms like Air West had much to gain. Just as efforts to protect regulation consisted of defending a federally drawn line, proponents of deregulation aimed to restructure transportation industries and reduce transportation prices by redrawing that same line in someone else's favor.

On May 11, John Snow testified before the House subcommittee on aviation, restating the key points that members of his teams had been making all spring. "The present regulatory system," Snow announced, "has become a major obstacle to the provision of air service at the lowest cost." Snow urged a program of "price competition" that would lead to creation of "a healthy air transportation industry." Legislation introduced by Senator Kennedy, Snow reminded the committee, "also includes an increase in pricing flexibility as one of its key features." As early as January 1976, officials of United Airlines had signaled a willingness to accept some degree of price competition, but remained concerned that easing of entry threatened "a sound system of financially healthy air carriers." Snow, however, told members of the House subcommittee that easing of entry requirements would "police . . . behavior," encouraging carriers to "keep prices at a level low enough to forestall entry of competitors." As for fear that deregulation would encourage airlines to quit small towns, Snow contended that, by eliminating restrictions "the proposed legislation would result in more, not less, air service." Rather than the "'market chaos'" promised by airline executives in the event of deregulation of entry and prices, Snow once again turned to one of the key findings of the Kennedy hearings, pointing out that "there is no chaos" in the California and Texas markets.[29]

Briefings by members of Snow's liaison teams and his own assurances of lower prices and continuing service to small towns could not overcome doubts about diminished service to those same small towns, or about economic "chaos" among airline corporations. In March 1976, Secretary Coleman offered a potential sweetener in the form of promised subsidies to airlines serving small towns.[30] At that late date, however, few paid attention. During summer and fall 1976, as political party conventions met and the presidential campaign got underway, neither President Ford nor his opponent, Georgia governor Jimmy Carter, talked in detail about airline and truck deregulation. According to journalist Richard E. Cohen, "the momentum for regulatory reform . . . [had] stalled." The basic problem, Cohen observed, was that "neither of the principal candidates believes that there is a readily obtainable constituency." Departure of John Snow to serve as director of a federal agency, Cohen thought, added to "the sense of enervation on the part of the Ford regulatory reform program." During the fall, moreover, with the campaign in full swing, one of Ford's top officials warned him about "alienat[ing] truckers and teamsters" and urged the president to "low-key our support" of trucking deregulation in public remarks.[31] Beginning in mid-1976, President Ford substituted electoral politics for the politics of deregulation and national economic management.

As they prepared to leave office, leaders in the Ford administration published a postmortem account of their unsuccessful efforts to bring about deregulation of the airline and truck industries. On the one hand, they blamed leaders in the trucking and airline industries. "Airlines, trucking firms . . . , and some labor unions," reported authors of the administration's account, "have been highly critical of any attempts to change the economic regulations which govern their operations." As examples, they reported that pilots had "registered complaints against the Administration's air bill, and the Teamsters objected to proposed changes in regulation of motor carriers." According to Ford's senior officials, "labor and management have generally been on the same side of the economic issue." On the other hand, Ford's administrators reported "disappointment that organized consumer groups were not more helpful in encouraging the Congress to act."[32] In other words, opponents of deregulation remained articulate and well organized, and the much-sought-after coalition of deregulation supporters had not materialized.

Failure to secure deregulation was a more complex phenomenon than Ford's officials admitted or understood. At the outset, one must not underestimate the ability of pilots, teamsters, and executives of airline and trucking companies to make concerns known to members of Congress. Union leaders represented thousands of members located in virtually every congressional district; and union leaders such as Frank Fitzsimmons possessed years of experience in dealing with federal officials, whether members of Congress or presidents of the United States. At the same time, Ford and his top administrators had made choices that helped predetermine the outcome of deregulatory efforts in the airline and trucking industries. In short, leaders in the Ford administration had not taken account of likely winners and losers in the politics of deregulation.

Comparison of Ford's strategy in securing partial deregulation of the railroads is instructive. Ford and Coleman had insisted on a direct linkage between "regulatory reform" and the expenditure of more than $6 billion for loans, loan guarantees, and outright grants of funds for purchase of up-to-date equipment. In July 1975, an interviewer with *Railway Age* asked Secretary Coleman whether he was "willing to give any money without the regulatory package," to which Coleman responded that "I am not going to take public money and throw it down the drain."[33] Eager to maintain railroad employment and rail service to constituents, members of Congress located in the Midwest and Northeast accepted the dose of regulatory reform that Ford measured out. Ford's program of deregulation produced no immediate winners, but did hold out hope—and cash—that the deteriorated and precarious situation among many shippers and perhaps millions of workers in the Northeast and Midwest would not grow worse.

In proposing deregulation of airlines and trucking firms, however, President Ford had failed to identify and mobilize clear winners, and limit the number of self-identified losers. Teamsters and airline employees, the frontline workers, feared their jobs were at stake. Ford might have offered airline employees the same deal that Brock Adams and others had offered railroad workers in 1973, which amounted either to a guaranteed job or what was described as a "monthly displacement allowance." In the process of shaping the program of airline deregulation, however, President Ford ruled out assistance to airline workers facing job losses in the event of shutdowns at Pan American or the other ailing carriers. In mid-March 1975, one of Ford's aides had prepared notes for the president's use in an upcoming meeting with Secretary Coleman focused on transportation deregulation. The president would tell Coleman that the administration expressed "sympathy and compassion for owners and employees of [airline] companies in financial difficulty." At the same time, Ford expected Coleman to "do everything possible to limit Federal financial exposure except in the most extreme cases."[34] Brock Adams had supplied railroad workers with sweeteners. President Ford, however, chose to defend the budget, leaving employees to stand alone at the precipice.

Nor were the winners clearly identified and persuaded of the benefits of deregulation. President Ford and Senator Kennedy promised flyers that airline deregulation would bring less expensive airline tickets. Cheaper tickets, if they materialized, would translate into lower personal expenses, higher corporate profits, or aggregate savings. Airline passengers and other "consumers" remained unorganized, however, failing to appear on behalf of Ford's deregulation efforts. President Ford and Secretary Coleman had also promised shippers that deregulation would lower the costs of conducting business. The amount of those savings, however, remained more asserted than demonstrated. Again, lacking the sweeteners offered railroad workers, Ford's plans to deregulate trucking asked shippers to run the risk of higher prices in a deregulated environment. Equally, Ford's plan for deregulation of trucking asked shippers to jeopardize relationships with truck operators and drivers built up over years or even decades.

Nor had President Ford and his senior staff convinced small-town shippers and travelers—and their numerous representatives—that deregulation of truck and airline firms would not mean lost service, bankrupt firms, and still higher levels of unemployment. In an economy and polity, moreover, that were increasingly national and international in scope, loss of transportation services presaged further diminution of small-town economics, prestige, and political leverage. Rather than being attracted by the promise of efficient markets at work, small-town workers, owners, and politicians identified deregulation as one of those political contrivances that would hasten the pace at which they became losers. Again, one must not underestimate the tireless efforts of airline and truck executives and union leaders in defeating Ford's deregulation bills. Yet Ford's efforts to deregulate trucking and airlines in 1976 also failed because they posed risks—for shippers, for air and truck workers, for residents of small towns, for business owners and their employees, and for politicians. After mid-1976, even President Ford had chosen not to run the risk of irritating airline and trucking company employees or the many others who figured that they stood to lose in a program of deregulation.

Had President Ford secured a second term, however, perhaps he rather than President Jimmy Carter would have supervised deregulation of the nation's transportation industries. In 1974, deregulation was an esoteric topic discussed among economists, senior presidential aides, leaders in

Congress, and solid opponents such as truckers and teamsters. By early 1977, President Ford and his staff, along with a few others such as Edward Kennedy, Brock Adams, and journalists and pundits, had converted deregulation into a topic enjoying widespread attention in newspapers and magazines, a guaranteed place on the agenda of Congress, the sustained attention of regulators, and a small but increasingly savvy constituency. One of the keys to Carter's subsequent success was the organization and management of that constituency for deregulation, a political program that proponents now regularly described using the more engaging term of regulatory reform.

CHAPTER 8

JIMMY CARTER AND DEREGULATION OF THE "BEST TRANSPORTATION SYSTEM IN THE WORLD," 1977–1980

REGULATION SUDDENLY ASSUMED A POLITICAL IMPORTANCE IT HAD NOT
ATTAINED SINCE THE PROGRESSIVE ERA.
— HISTORIAN THOMAS K. MCCRAW, 1984

IN THE MID-1950s, President Dwight Eisenhower and Commerce Secretary Sinclair Weeks had launched the deregulation drive, seeking legislation that would partially deregulate trucking firms and railroads. Every president after Eisenhower advocated deregulation in some form. As part of his effort to bring about deregulation, President Johnson had created the Department of Transportation; and President Nixon had secured from Congress authority to appoint the chair of the Interstate Commerce Commission. Deregulation was part of the institutional office of the president, and the tools of deregulation, including the power to appoint the ICC chair, were part of the patrimony that presidents bestowed on their successors. Every president engaged in this lengthy effort had urged federal construction of transportation markets as part of efforts to save railroads, "fine-tune" the economy, or later, during the 1970s, to rescue railroad service and the overall economy from inflation and unemployment. Not until 1976, however, had President Ford achieved limited deregulation of the nation's railroads, creating the long-sought-after "zone of reasonableness."

Beginning in January 1977, President Jimmy Carter took his turn at trying to deregulate the nation's transportation industries. Carter made use of his immense powers to appoint like-minded persons such as economists Alfred E. Kahn to chair the Civil Aeronautics Board and Darius W. Gaskins Jr. to chair the Interstate Commerce Commission. Under President Carter, moreover, deregulation of airlines and trucking and the hoped-for creation of trucking and airline markets began as administrative rather than as legislative initiatives. First having launched deregulation on an adminis-

trative basis, Carter next relied on his talented staff and especially Mary
Schuman, Richard M. Neustadt, and Stuart E. Eizenstat to assemble a
coalition of shippers, consumers, and breakaway truckers who supported
legislation aimed at making those newfound markets permanent.

In 1978, President Carter presided over deregulation of the nation's airlines; and in 1980, he supervised deregulation of trucking and further deregulation of the still-ailing railroads. As often happened in the past, during the
1970s, politicians such as Gerald Ford and Jimmy Carter found economists
useful as experts and as heads of regulatory agencies. Whether by administrative or legislative action, however, the drive toward deregulation and the
simultaneous creation of transportation markets began and ended as presidential—and political—initiatives.

JIMMY CARTER AND AIRLINE DEREGULATION

Jimmy Carter brought no original ideas or experience to deregulation. In
1976, presidential candidate Carter had endorsed "greater federal aid to the
railroads in order to reduce their tax burdens." Equally, Carter sought "closer . . . coordination at the federal level" of the nation's transportation systems. Yet at the same time, Carter wanted to "mov[e] decisively to reform
regulation of airline industry."[1] Candidate Carter had adopted the mix of
centralizing and decentralizing proposals advocated during the 1970s by
Richard Nixon and Gerald Ford. As president, however, Carter determined
to bring about deregulation of the nation's truck, rail, and airline industries.

Airline deregulation came first. Many still judged airline travel glamorous, which meant that journalists reported regularly on air travel. Equally
important, if airline deregulation actually led to lower fares, business executives who flew regularly would see savings immediately, presumably adding
to the political momentum for truck and further rail deregulation. Within a
month of taking office, moreover, Carter's top advisers reported that several
members of Congress had already introduced bills aimed at deregulating the
airlines. Consequently, Stuart E. Eizenstat, who served as Assistant to the
President for Domestic Affairs and Policy, did not want Carter to endorse a
bill, since "endorsement of one . . . would needlessly alienate the sponsors of
others."[2] Under those circumstances, one must suspect that Carter's
appointment of the flamboyant economist Alfred E. Kahn to the Civil
Aeronautics Board and his enthusiastic and successful promotion of airline
deregulation was part of an effort to foster deregulation without "needlessly

alienat[ing]" anyone. Instead, Kahn launched the process of deregulating the nation's airlines on the basis of administrative rulings rather than on the basis of legislative change. In the politics of airline deregulation, Kahn's ideas and personality mattered.

Like many presidential advisers who had dealt with transportation issues over the years, including William Ripley, Joseph Eastman, James Landis, and John Snow, Kahn now had the opportunity to merge academic expertise with policy leadership in the field of transportation. Although Kahn lacked familiarity with details of airline operations and management, in 1971 he had published a study that included a section on the economics of airline pricing. Anticipating the revelations of the Kennedy hearings by four years, Kahn asserted that reduced prices offered by an airline in California had brought about an increase in the number of passengers, and higher revenues.[3] Again, the California and Texas findings rested on a small and not-representative sample of unregulated air travel and prices. In the hands of presidential advisers, editorial writers, and now Chairman Kahn, the limited validity of Kennedy's findings nonetheless emerged in editorials and press conferences as hard, irrefragable, and universal facts that only a selfish opponent could fail to recognize and endorse. Beginning in 1977, moreover, Kahn also possessed the full weight and authority of the chair's office to bring about regulatory change. No longer a professor of economics studying the promise of deregulation to create transportation markets, Kahn and members of the CAB could now order it.

When Kahn arrived at the CAB, he inherited seventeen years of on-again, off-again fare discounting. As early as 1961, members of the CAB had authorized special fares, as for instance family fares. Beginning in 1972, CAB officials eliminated the family fare and other special fares. By early 1977, however, Kahn's immediate predecessor as chair of the CAB had voted with his colleagues to permit executives of American Airlines and several others to reintroduce promotional fares. According to historian McCraw, "with Kahn on the scene, the dike burst." By a vote of 5–0, members of the CAB, including Kahn, authorized airline managers to lower prices as they judged wisest. Soon, airline officials created a variety of discount fares with catchy names such as "Super Coach" and "Simple Saver." By mid-1978, about half of all coach passengers flew on discount tickets. Although ticket prices had declined for many passengers, profits for the major airlines were double those earned in the previous year. A temporary revival in the American economy contributed to airline traffic and profits, but deregulation proponents argued that rising patronage and rising profits illustrated the advantages of deregulation.[4] During the late 1970s, few recalled that between 1945 and 1953, members of the CAB, with their temporary policy of allowing the "nonskeds" to offer airline service, had helped usher in the first stages of mass market air travel.

Kahn went further, insisting that airline executives compete for business on routes formerly assigned to competitors. Executives of trunk carriers such as Delta, however, feared unlimited entry of competitors into "their" routes even more than they feared price competition. Earlier CAB officials had regularly approved additional routes, but only for members of that small group of certificated carriers including Eastern, Delta, and American. One of Ford's top staffers, John Snow, had attempted to win legislative support for easing entry rules. Now, Kahn and his colleagues simply authorized additional competition. In one case, Kahn and his board members granted authority to two applicants to fly from Chicago's small Midway Airport, creating competition for older carriers flying from their hub at busy O'Hare. No longer, moreover, were CAB officials going to look after the financial health of the airline firms, which earlier boards had occasionally done in order to keep the weakest carriers such as Northeast Airlines flying. During a hectic period of about a year and a half, Kahn and members of his board believed that they had "'introduced unprecedented substantive and procedural innovations.'"[5] Following World War II, members of the CAB such as Chair James Landis had permitted several fare innovations. In the context of the late 1970s, however, Kahn's innovations such as handing out long routes to regional carriers were fostering another round of price competition and the first steps in airline deregulation.

Despite the many changes in pricing and entry policy that Kahn and his colleagues had brought about, leaders of airline unions and airline corporations such as Frank Borman at Eastern Airlines still resisted the prospect of rate and route deregulation. In addition, those opponents had access to the courts, to members of Congress worried about service to their own communities, and to members of a CAB appointed by a future president perhaps less interested in deregulation. According to McCraw, Kahn himself recognized that "the real fight . . . had just begun." What was needed, Kahn observed, was legislation that would "'secure these advances against a change of agency policy.'"[6] Possessing a smart and amusing wit and having won the affection of journalists, Kahn played an important part in persuading members of Congress about the value of deregulation.

From the first days of the Carter administration, however, Stuart Eizenstat and his senior aides had taken charge of day-to-day efforts to enact that legislation. Mary Schuman was in charge of those efforts. Prior to her position as one of Eizenstat's top assistants on the Domestic Policy Staff, Schuman had worked for the Senate commerce committee, where she coauthored portions of an early airline deregulation bill sponsored by Senator Howard W. Cannon and Senator Kennedy. In November 1977, Schuman moved to the Carter/Mondale transition team and then to the Domestic Policy Staff. A recent graduate of the University of Washington law school, Schuman was an activist for airline deregulation. In March 1977, she announced that deregulation would bring "a healthier industry because you won't see half-empty planes in the skies with all the frills we see now." Like John Snow in the Ford administration, Mary Schuman came to Washington convinced of the efficacy of deregulation and determined to create a vibrant market for airline operations.[7]

Schuman also brought great energy to her new job as a member of Eizenstat's team. During the summer of 1977, Schuman spoke to business and civic leaders in sixteen cities. Self-confidence added to Schuman's central role in the effort to achieve "reform." Schuman was at ease telling journalists in every city on her tour about the advantages of deregulation. In August 1977, one of those newspaper writers who liked the idea of deregulating airlines described Schuman as "a singularly attractive and brainy lady." Schuman was also comfortable telling airline executives that they had to talk with her about deregulation, not with President Carter. In November 1977, a writer for *Business Week* observed that "reaction to Schuman might be different if she were a 35-year-old male and if she were pushing a policy that was agreeable to more transportation executives." Again like John Snow, Schuman was in charge of assembling that coalition in and out of Congress in favor of airline deregulation. Ten years later, political scientist Dorothy L. Robyn described Schuman as "Washington lobbyists' choice for the single individual most responsible for passage of the airline bill."[8]

Even a savvy operative like Schuman soon discovered that an emphasis on tough rhetoric and use of euphemistic phrases such as reform had their limits. In mid-1977, most airline executives still opposed deregulation. Delta's leaders especially disliked the prospect of opening "their" routes to competitors. "It is my intention," the chair and chief executive officer of Delta Airlines wrote President Carter on August 8, "to expend whatever energy and resources we have available to us to fight deregulation in its present form."[9]

Nor was there uniformity and certainty among leaders in Congress and the administration regarding important details of deregulation. Like the railroad bill signed in 1976 by President Ford, many, including the powerful Senator Warren Magnuson as well as Carter's Secretary of Transportation Brock Adams, sought protection for airline employees in the event that large-scale layoffs followed deregulation. Adams, moreover, expressed concern about loss of service to small towns, telling a journalist early in March that persons who had prepared studies showing that deregulation would bring no diminution of service "were economists and people who dealt with theoretical aspects of it as opposed to people who've been out in those communities and saw what happened."[10]

Schuman's first task was to maneuver Brock Adams into a public endorsement of most aspects of deregulation. At the request of Adams and his top officials at the Department of Transportation, Schuman and others had agreed to present legislation that would phase in deregulation of airline entry and pricing over a period of two or three years. Although Schuman judged the lengthier phase-in "good on the merits, and politically it is desirable because Congress is more likely to go along with it," on March 18 she reported to Eizenstat that no further advance was possible to accommodate Adams. Reviewing testimony that Adams and other transportation officials had prepared for Congress, Schuman found their remarks "totally negative [and] spoke only of predation, bankruptcy, large carriers squeezing out small ones, etc." Schuman returned the testimony to Adams, telling him and his aides that "testimony must be positive, and that the negative aspects of the issue could be covered in questions and answers."[11] Mary Schuman was as confident and as direct with cabinet secretaries as with airline executives.

President Carter and Stuart Eizenstat handled the next stage in dealing with Adams. "We are concerned," Eizenstat wrote Carter on March 23, "about the testimony of Brock Adams." In turn, Carter told Eizenstat in a handwritten note to "give me a brief tabulation of points from testimony so far [and] I'll send it to Brock for quick comment." Carter's determination to make deregulation policy, a journalist had reported earlier in the month, "reveals that it is the White House, not the Transportation Department, that is calling the signals on CAB reform."[12]

Presidential intervention secured results. "DOT's testimony is near great!" Schuman wrote Eizenstat on March 31, "the tone is very positive." Adams was prepared to testify in favor of "pricing flexibility . . . [and] entry and exit liberalization." Nonetheless, Adams would not relent on guarantees for small-town airline service or on job protections for airline employees.[13]

President Carter was willing to risk a diminution of small-town service. "Claims" that smaller cities "would be left without service," Eizenstat wrote Carter on March 25, "have been shown to be totally without foundation." Perhaps uncertain about the accuracy of the few and limited studies reporting no harm to smaller cities following deregulation, Carter wrote by hand on one of the versions of the memo of March 25, "hope this is true." Similarly, in December 1975, a senior official in the Ford administration had written "not really sure about this" in reaction to the high hopes for airline service following deregulation. Nevertheless, within two months of taking

FIGURE 17. Discussion of airline regulation, Oval Office, May 4, 1977. (From left to right) Stuart Eizenstat, Charles L. Schultze (seated, back to photographer), Mary Schuman, Brock Adams, Frank Moore, Jack Watson, and President Jimmy Carter. Each president of the United States, starting with Dwight Eisenhower and concluding with Carter, made transportation deregulation a centerpiece of his policy agenda. Deregulation of transportation began and concluded as a presidential initiative. Source: University of Washington archives. Used with permission.

office, the limited findings to come from the Kennedy hearings and the results of studies by several economists such as Paul W. MacAvoy on "deregulation effects" had emerged among many or most in the Carter administration (and earlier among many or most in the Ford administration) as fact and prophecy with universal applicability. With Adams's testimony now complete as part of a nearly uniform endorsement by senior Carter officials of deregulation and its many benefits, Schuman planned to "launch a good lobbying effort on the Hill to counteract the industry."[14]

Good luck intervened. By early June, Senator Kennedy and several colleagues in the Senate had revised their bill to provide a continuation of small-city airline service. Up to that point, the federal government had paid subsidies to regional carriers serving smaller cities and towns. Under the revised bill, as Schuman and Eizenstat explained it to President Carter, "the current federal subsidy program is reformed to *guarantee* service for 10 years to all small communities currently receiving service." Because the program of subsidies "is steamlined," they added, "there will be no increase in federal subsidy."[15] Like railroad deregulation under President Ford, members of

Congress offered a program of straightforward sweeteners to residents and leaders of small cities and towns worried that deregulation would convert them into losers. In case economists such as Alfred Kahn and Paul MacAvoy were proven wrong about the beneficial effects of deregulation for all, the state would subsidize the small-city airline market that Mary Schuman and others were planning to create for airline service.

In mid-June, Schuman launched her lobbying campaign among members of Congress, featuring President Carter as the lobbyist-in-chief. Schuman had scheduled a meeting for Carter on June 20 with leaders in Congress. A public briefing would follow, with the congressional meeting described as a "photo opportunity" and the public briefing described as "open to press coverage." In a memo listing "talking points" for these two events, Schuman and Eizenstat wanted Carter to reemphasize the "guarantee" that "no small community now receiving service will lose it for 10 years." Otherwise, Schuman and Eizenstat scripted Carter to sound like President Ford, asking him to repeat the well-known findings of the Kennedy hearings that "fares are much lower in Texas and California where the CAB does not regulate."[16]

By late July, Mary Schuman had immersed herself in the details of legislation. She reported to Eizenstat that Kennedy's revised bill now provided "automatic route entry" for large and small carriers and a "'zone of reasonableness'" permitting airline management to raise fares up to 5 percent for the first two years after the bill passed, and to lower fares up to 55 percent. More problematic was a section of the bill easing entry by carriers, including regional carriers, into one another's routes. "Our strategy at this point," Eizenstat learned, is to *hold on to* the entry provisions in the bill" (emphasis in original), subverting an effort by members of the Senate committee "to eliminate the automatic route entry section and replace it with a requirement that the Board implement its own."[17] Because the regulatory regime had long consisted of numerous administrative and legislative items such as entry requirements, pricing policy, and small-city subsidies, the process of securing deregulation consisted of an equal number of administrative and legislative innovations.

In late September, Schuman reported "some good news . . . on the airline markup." By a vote of 13–5, members of the Senate commerce committee had defeated an amendment aimed at eliminating automatic entry by airline management into one another's routes. By more than two to one, members of the committee had affirmed the opening of airline routes, overturning one of the central pillars of the regulatory regime. Open entry promised substantial price competition, which was precisely the reason airline executives had opposed it. Curiously, the market-oriented Senator Barry M. Goldwater was one of the five who favored a continuation of limited entry. "The votes today," Schuman told Eizenstat and several others, "should get the bill moving."[18] "Good!" Eizenstat wrote on his copy of the memo.

During succeeding months, Schuman and Eizenstat turned often to Carter for additional assistance in negotiations with Brock Adams or recalcitrant legislators. For instance, on September 27, Schuman wrote Eizenstat and other top officials that Senator Warren Magnuson was "against us" on opening of airline routes to new competitors. On October 24, Eizenstat reported to Carter that Magnuson "has been filibustering." At Eizenstat's urging, Carter telephoned Magnuson, leading to the positive report by Carter that Magnuson "wants us to help him get a quorum Thursday."[19] Efforts to modify airline entry and price policy started with President Carter and his senior officials.

Carter could not always control each detail of legislation. In late May 1978, members of the Senate voted to provide salary payments for up to three years to airline employees who lost their jobs, or whose salaries were reduced by the onset of hard times for airlines. Federal payments would even include relocation expenses and compensation for the sale of a house below market value. Members of the house voted for six years worth of benefits. "The principle of equal treatment of unemployed workers is violated," a senior official in the Office of Management and Budget wrote Eizenstat on May 26, "when a small group is singled out for extra-ordinary Federal benefits for which their unemployed neighbors are not eligible." On September 27, as the airline bill headed for a Senate-House conference, Eizenstat and another senior official nonetheless assured President Carter that "recent events show that airline employees benefit from airline competition, so the prospects for having to invoke this provision are not great."[20] By October 1978, Carter's desire to deregulate the airlines immediately mattered more than economists' predictions, justice in the abstract, or the prospect of making comparatively modest payouts to unemployed workers sometime in the future.

Luck intervened one more time. President Ford had sought to bring about a change in CAB policy through a program of what political scientists Martha Derthick and Paul J. Quirk characterize as "appointments and exhortation." Nonetheless, Ford's primary focus was on legislating deregulation. By appointing Alfred Kahn as chair of the CAB, Carter had launched deregulation on an administrative basis, achieving quick and substantial results. Early in 1977, however, neither Carter nor his top aides such as Mary Schuman and Stuart Eizenstat had foreseen the dramatic effect that Kahn's actions would have on airline executives and their earlier opposition to deregulation. By early 1978, airline executives, including those at

Delta, no longer opposed deregulation. By late 1978, airline executives actually sought deregulation. "The deregulatory activism of the commission," report Derthick and Quirk, "gave the airline . . . industr[y] compelling reasons to prefer some sort of statutory result, to want that result to be reached quickly, and if necessary, to accept broad procompetitive provisions to get it." On October 24, President Carter signed the Airline Deregulation Act. Members of the House had approved the conference report 356–6, and the Senate had approved it 82–4. Again like the zone of reasonableness pricing concept Secretary Weeks had advocated for trucking and railroad, airline executives could now raise and lower fares within a broad range; and open entry, formerly detested by airline and union managers, was now a matter of public policy. Beginning on January 1, 1985, the CAB would go out of existence. As President Carter observed at the signing ceremony, early in 1977, "[T]his bill had few friends. I am happy to say that today, it appears to have few enemies."[21]

Although mostly in the background, President Carter in particular had played a key role in bringing about deregulation. Not only had Carter appointed Alfred Kahn to chair the CAB, starting the program of administrative deregulation. It was Carter alone, as president, who made the decision to pursue legislative deregulation. Sometimes, moreover, Carter provided straightforward instructions to senior staff members regarding his preference for deregulation. During April and May 1978, as negotiations with congressional leaders seeking antinoise legislation for airports as part of deregulation grew more intense, Carter sent handwritten memos to Stuart Eizenstat and others exhorting them "to hold to maximum deregulation" and "support all deregulation."[22] Since the Eisenhower administration, deregulation had rested in presidential hands.

President Carter, along with Mary Schuman, Stuart Eizenstat, Alfred Kahn, and Senator Kennedy, had installed a new doctrine for airline operations. No longer would presidential appointees at the Civil Aeronautics Board and their staff of experts determine routes and rates and no longer would those officials take responsibility for the financial and organizational security of the industry or its member firms. In turn, Carter, Kennedy, and the others hoped that the experience of several airlines operating in Texas and California could be replicated in the form of service, pricing, and organizational innovations among many more airlines operating nationwide networks. Never one to doubt his research findings or the perceived experience of deregulated airlines in two states, CAB chair Kahn announced that soon "the airlines . . . will be knee deep in the free-enterprise system and not returnable." In the short run, moreover, airline deregulation would serve as the first step in a much larger campaign to deregulate trucking and other industries and help reduce inflationary pressures. Nevertheless, congressional leaders protected some of their best organized constituents, agreeing to subsidize small-city service for ten years, and also to pay the salaries and moving expenses of displaced workers for up to six years—were that action to become necessary. In the event airline deregulation produced negative results, protection of airline employees and small-city residents also protected members of Congress from their anger. Brock Adams well understood the fears of his former colleagues in Congress and the aspirations of his former constituents in Washington State. Despite having conceded these points to Adams, Magnuson, and others, Carter, his staff, and Senator Kennedy worked as a group described by political scientist Anthony E. Brown as "'policy politicians' united by their commitment to deregulation." Altogether, the success of these policy politicians rested on dissatisfaction among sections of the polity with inflation, unemployment, and with government itself, and on the still-untested idea that so simple an act as deregulating airlines and the subsequent appearance of this latest round of government-created price and service competition would reduce inflation and unemployment, reversing the dreadful effects of stagflation.[23] Carter and his staff of policy politicians also led the effort to deregulate the trucking industry.

DEREGULATING TRUCKING

Carter's goal in fostering deregulation of trucking and railroads was identical to that of Ford and Nixon. If the prices charged by truckers and railroads could be reduced, ran the argument, then in an era of inflationary pressures the price of every other commodity would also fall. On February 7, 1979, Eizenstat told a meeting of consumer groups that "the costs of regulated surface transportation are borne by . . . consumers as reflected in the price of virtually every product available in the marketplace." In 1955, Secretary Weeks and President Eisenhower and the railroads' fictitious "Mrs. Kennedy's Five Pounds of Sugar" had made the identical point. At the outset of this latest drive to deregulate trucking, moreover, keen observers of transportation politics judged that teamsters and truckers still possessed formidable defenses. In mid-1979, according to a writer for the *Wall Street Journal*, directors of the American Trucking Associations could rely upon a staff of lobbyists and the combined efforts of more than seventeen thousand trucking-company members. Leaders of the Teamsters Union and their six hundred thousand members, ran the reasoning, would stand "side by side [with employers] against deregulation." Similar to the effort of each president since Eisenhower, however, Carter, Eizenstat, and Schuman planned to rely on what Eizenstat characterized as "strong leadership from grassroots groups throughout the country."[24]

As Mary Schuman learned in a series of meetings with leaders of trucking companies, moreover, many executives remained united around the time-honored defenses of trucking regulation. At those meetings held late in 1977, trucking officials, and especially truckers holding operating rights as common carriers, spoke of low rates, predictable employment, and predictable service. Again like their contemporary counterparts in the airline industry, these same truckers spoke often and voluminously about maintenance of reliable service to small cities and towns. "The current system," an executive of Southeastern Freight Lines told Schuman, "is basically sound." Deregulation would lead to rate increases of 20–30 percent on less-than-truckload shipments, the head of Georgia Highway Express told her. "Open Pricing and free entry," argued an official of Briggs Trucking Company, "would return the industry to the cutthroat competition that existed prior to 1935." Changing the nation's trucking industry, he predicted, "would have sociological impacts that would boggle the mind." Leaders of African American truck owners also joined in celebration of the regulatory regime. According to notes of a meeting held on November 18, 1977, African Americans operating trucking firms told Schuman "that the rules should not be changed just when minorities are entering the game." Schuman wrote Eizenstat that truckers "made precisely the same arguments the airlines made against deregulation early in the airline debate."[25]

Not familiar with the long history of regulation and deregulation, Schuman could not have recognized the degree to which truck operators in the late 1970s were actually repeating the proregulation arguments they had been advancing since the 1930s. Starting in 1948 with congressional approval of the Reed-Bulwinkle Act, leaders of the American Trucking Associations and especially managers of common carrier firms such as Briggs had identified the antitrust immunity of their rate bureaus as a key feature of the legal and ideological underpinnings of the regulatory regime. Nor would Shuman and her associates have been aware that in 1955, following Sinclair Weeks's proposal to bring about partial deregulation of trucking and railroading, truckers' rhetoric and behavior had congealed into a series of set phrases such as the "best transportation system in the world," and into several decades of lawsuits and aggressive lobbying at the hands of industry leaders such as Robert McBride, Albert Rosenbaum, and their uncompromising attorneys and lobbyists. In 1979, as before, managers of common carriers such as Briggs and Southeastern were prepared to defend their operating rights and the right of their rate bureaus to determine prices charged shippers.[26] As Schuman was in the process of discovering, among truckers and again especially among executives of common carriers such as Briggs and Southeastern, history (and powerful lobbying efforts, often in conjunction with the Teamsters) really mattered.

At those meetings, however, Schuman also learned that leaders of competing trucking organizations were now open to the idea of limited deregulation. Since the late 1930s, differences between contract carriers formerly led by Vee Kennedy and common carriers formerly led by McBride and Rosenbaum had been part of trucking politics. McBride and Kennedy and the many truckers they represented had long cooperated and competed with one another. Contract carriers could offer lower rates than common carriers, but were limited to handling door-to-door deliveries in bulk and further limited to serving no more than eight customers. If, however, legal distinctions between contract and common carriers were reduced, or even abolished, as the chair of the Contract Carrier Conference now recommended to Mary Schuman, then contract carriers, such as Don and Al Schneider's Schneider National, could move into areas of the trucking business long dominated by common carriers.[27] Once again, trucking politics, like transportation politics as a whole, consisted of efforts to move a federally drawn line in one's favor, and against the interests of competitors.

With the opening created by Carter and Schuman, moreover, in the late 1970s officers of several firms operating their own trucking fleets—the private truckers—joined the assault on the regulatory regime. With their trucks often returning empty from deliveries, officers of corporations that operated their own trucking fleets, such as textile manufacturer West Point-Pepperell, asked Schuman to help them secure authority to transport not only their own merchandise, but the merchandise of other firms.[28] Owners of private truck fleets wanted to continue to operate as private carriers part of the time, and as contract carriers at other times. Again, deregulation proposals resonated not in the abstract, but because they offered a concrete opportunity to redraw competitive lines.

Even the long-disparaged freight forwarders joined the antiregulation fray. Freight forwarders handled small shipments through other truckers and railroads. During the post–World War II years, as often as forwarders and their attorney Giles Morrow had attempted to expand their operating rights, leaders of common and contract carriers blocked those efforts in Congress. In 1977, Schuman learned that those forwarders still "opposed general deregulation . . . ," but hoped to secure the ability "to make contract rates with . . . railroads and to operate pickup and delivery service outside their terminal areas."[29] In short, freight forwarders, private truckers, and contract carriers wanted federal officials to bestow upon them what was already bestowed on their competitors.

Late in 1977, however, leaders of the freight forwarders and other segments of the trucking industry, including the loyal Teamsters, were not prepared to overturn the regulatory regime for some unspecified and uncertain
system labeled regulatory reform. Instead, leaders of each of these groups
such as the freight forwarders wanted maintenance of rules that advantaged
their segment of the industry, and abolition of rules that did not. With luck,
they were reasoning, the passion of Senator Kennedy, President Carter, and
Mary Schuman for deregulation might yet be refocused to bring about the
kind of deregulation that offered business opportunities for themselves and
that with the same stroke disadvantaged competitors.[30]

In 1978, however, deregulation-minded commissioners of the ICC
opened the door to a rupture in the formerly united front of truckers opposing deregulation. In *Toto Purchasing and Supply Company, Inc.,* commissioners determined that private carriers such as West Point-Pepperell were entitled to carry freight for others, and to charge them for the service. Naturally,
leaders of the Teamsters and the American Trucking Associations and their
attorneys made an effort to undo *Toto,* asking Congress and the federal
courts to provide relief. Leaders of the Private Carrier Conference, however,
joined Carter's aides in seeking to codify *Toto* in federal legislation. Again,
the idea at this point among private truck operators was not to overturn the
many elements of the regulatory regime, but to enhance their own share of
the action inside of it.[31]

The *Toto* decision created an opening for contract carriers to join the
deregulators. As early as 1976, when President Ford and Senator Kennedy
were launching the truck deregulation effort, Thomas Callaghan, the managing director of the Contract Carrier Conference (earlier directed by Vee
Kennedy), wanted the rule of eight overturned. "We could argue," he later
told political scientist Dorothy Robyn, "that it was unfair to limit the number of customers contract carriers could serve and thereby punish them for
their success. The issue," he added, "was appealing to the membership and
an easy story to tell to the outside world."[32] By the mid-1970s, the self-inter-
est of contract carriers coincided with the general commitment of business-
oriented politicians and ordinary Americans to reward successful managers
and entrepreneurs.

Long experience had also taught truckers that political action had to
coincide with the telling of their apparently easy or engaging stories.
Callaghan also took the bold step of establishing "the Kennedy connection"
in support of their joint efforts to deregulate common carriers. Callaghan
testified before Kennedy's committee and even appeared at a press conference at which Kennedy announced his plan to repeal antitrust immunity
granted rate bureaus in the Reed-Bulwinkle Act of 1948. "Normally,"

Callaghan told political scientist Robyn, his members would "never have established a political connection with Teddy Kennedy, but they were peeved and feeling feisty." By themselves the partial defection of the private carriers and the total defection of the contract carriers would not have proved sufficient to undo the clout of the ATA and its energetic core of common carriers such as Southeastern, Briggs, and Consolidated Freightways, who in good times had profited handsomely from the workings of the regulatory regime. Those defections, however, limited the ability of ATA leaders to appear at congressional hearings and in congressional offices making claims of industry-wide unity in their opposition to deregulation.[33]

Disagreements among trucking industry leaders created an opportunity for President Carter to exploit. On May 15, Carter sent a handwritten note to Stuart Eizenstat, "Stu, Move—Very Good." With that note, Carter and his senior staff, including Mary Schuman and Richard "Rick" Neustadt, formally launched the effort to deregulate trucking.[34]

Like President Ford, public appearances came first. On June 21, Carter hosted a ceremony in the White House Rose Garden to announce the kickoff of efforts to deregulate trucking. Senator Kennedy was the first to speak, reflecting Carter's decision to submit a joint deregulation bill. Like the contract carriers, President Carter found value in establishing his own Kennedy connection. The ceremony also provided a large audience for Senator Kennedy's announcement that deregulation of trucking would eventually "sav[e] consumers and business men and women $5 billion." Still others invited to the reception included leaders of Sears, the American Farm Bureau, Consumers Union, the U.S. Conference of Mayors, and the Private Truck Council, the trade organization of the private truckers who were anxious to get into commercial trucking.[35] The announcement ceremony put on public display for ATA officials, teamsters, and members of Congress the size and diversity of the trucking deregulation coalition assembled by Mary Schuman—the coalition for which every president since Dwight Eisenhower had been searching.

Beginning around September 1979, however, Mary Schuman no longer served as the person in charge of day-to-day coalition management and legislative maneuver. At her request, President Carter appointed Schuman general counsel of the Civil Aeronautics Board, the agency that she, Carter, Alfred Kahn, and others had set for abolition in 1985. Schuman's job at the CAB, one suspects, was to insure a continuing emphasis on deregulation, rather than a return to the regulatory regime in place up to early 1977. In turn, Richard Neustadt and a few senior officials at the Department of Transportation assumed Schuman's responsibilities for the legislative component of trucking deregulation. Neustadt was the son of Richard E. Neustadt, professor of government at Harvard University, who himself had served as a member of President Truman's staff and later as an adviser to President Kennedy. Before joining Carter's Domestic Policy Staff, "Rick" Neustadt, an attorney, had worked as a political writer for CBS News. A decade later, political scientist Robyn reported that "Neustadt was regarded as one of the brightest young minds in the White House."[36]

Beginning in June 1979, Neustadt and his colleagues at the Department of Transportation made plans for the legislative use of their newly created constituency for deregulation. This process was complex and lengthy. Senior officials at DOT worked from a "basic list of supporters, including major shippers, business and agricultural groups and others." Rather than make a general appeal to persons and corporations on the list, however, the first step was to select shippers who resided in "targeted states and districts," represented by members of key congressional committees. In addition, an administration official wanted those shippers "to advise their employees of the benefits to their firms resulting from the bill and to encourage them to write as well." The goal was to "mobiliz[e] their stated support [that] could effectively neutralize much of the trucker opposition."[37]

President Carter used his authority to appoint the chair of the Interstate Commerce Commission and two additional members to accelerate the process of neutralizing truckers. In mid-May 1979, Carter penned another note to Eizenstat, "p.s. Let's move on ICC member appointments." With that note, Carter combined the search for legislative deregulation of trucking with a search for deregulation-minded appointments to the ICC.[38]

For chair of the ICC, Carter elevated Darius W. Gaskins Jr., a member since early 1979. Gaskins was professor of economics at the University of California at Berkeley, and more recently had worked for Alfred Kahn at the CAB as director of his newly created Office of Economic Analysis. Gaskins enjoyed professional experience in assessing transportation markets and in the politics of achieving administrative deregulation. At his confirmation hearing in June, Gaskins told members of the Senate commerce committee that deregulation of the airline industry suggested "that there may be substantial advantages to relying on competition."[39]

Starting in October 1979, Gaskins and Carter's two other appointees to the ICC eased rules on entry, rates, and routes, the same tactic that Kahn had used at the Civil Aeronautics Board two years earlier. As a start, Carter's new members permitted truckers to offer service on routes assigned to competitors, the dreaded opening of entry. Since approval of the Motor Carrier Act of 1935, those seeking to serve new routes had to prove that existing service was inadequate, a difficult task. In December, moreover, Gaskins and his colleagues allowed truckers to make pickups and deliveries at all points in their certificates, not just at designated points such as Chicago and then New York. In February 9 , Gaskins told members of the board of governors of the Regular Common Carrier Conference (with members including Southeastern Freight Lines, Briggs Trucking, and Consolidated Freightways) that Congress was "almost certain" to remove "privileges" such as "broad antitrust immunity [and] strict control over entry." Members of his audience, Gaskins urged, ought to "step forward and make the choices which best serve your interests," including "greater ratemaking freedom . . . [and] a parallel reduction in the remaining entry barriers and antitrust immunity" of their rate bureaus. In short, Congress and the ICC were eliminating portions of the regulatory regime, and truckers had reached the last moment to seek "new and valuable freedoms that might be made available to your fellow businessmen [such as private and contract carriers] in other segments of the industry."[40]

By early 1980, President Carter and his senior staff had shaped most of the legislative and administrative measures supporting trucking deregulation. Darius Gaskins and Carter's other appointees at the ICC issued rules that partially deregulated trucking, a strategy pursued in earlier efforts to deregulate airlines. In addition, the president's staff starting with Mary Schuman and continued by Richard Neustadt had assembled a large coalition of enthusiasts for deregulation, including major shippers such as executives at Dow Chemical and others who represented retail-level consumers. By promising relief from rate bureaus and removal of limits on intercorporate hauling, moreover, Schuman and Neustadt had added contract and private carriers to the coalition (a tactic first attempted by members of the Ford administration). By 1980, Schuman's many interviews and conversations extending back to 1977 started to pay dividends in the form of carefully orchestrated legislative and administrative assaults on portions of trucking regulation.[41]

Furious teamsters and unhappy truckers made a strenuous effort to protect the shrinking boundaries of the regulatory regime. On March 1, 1980, Bennett C. Whitlock Jr., president of the American Trucking Associations, sent a letter to his members ominously marked, "To all Persons Interested in the Survival of the Motor Carrier Industry." Whitlock reminded members of their decades-old conviction that "sound entry controls and collective rate-making are essential to a workable motor carrier system." Equally, Whitlock worried that "small towns and small shippers would either see a reduction in service or an increase in rates." In the absence of the classic specter of the evil railroad, Whitlock was reminding members and politicians of the time-honored idea that small-town service represented a truckers' gift to the nation, in return for which the use of rate bureaus to make rates was only common sense rather than a legally bestowed privilege. On March 21, Whitlock issued another notice to members, telling them that "this is it." Again, Whitlock listed perceived threats built on the memory of political and legal action extending back decades, as for instance "elimination of antitrust immunity . . . [that] would spell the end of ratemaking and . . . the end of regulation." Once more, Whitlock wanted members to come to Washington "during this crucial period," adding that "there is no substitute for personal, eyeball-to-eyeball contact with your Senators." And once again, several hundred trucking company executives went to Washington.[42] As during their struggle in 1955 and 1956 against the Weeks proposals and in favor of the Interstate Highway System, truckers still relied on "political strength" and on the conviction that every sentient observer recognized their contribution to the "best transportation system in the world." Among truckers anyway, history still mattered.

The Teamsters' message was more strident, less historical, but just as political. "Don't Destroy Our Jobs," ran the headline in the *Ohio Teamster* for April 1980. Authors of a flyer prepared by the Ohio Conference of Teamsters announced that "the Kennedy-Carter Deregulation Bill is a Union Bustin' Tactic!!!" Particularly disturbing was the prospect of free entry by nonunion trucks into routes that the ICC had assigned years earlier to their employers. "Jobs will be lost," warned the author of an article in the *Ohio Teamster*, "to non-regulated companies and operators who are going to bypass the established firms having Teamster contracts."[43]

Like their counterparts in management, Teamster officials relied upon a large turnout of drivers to visit members of Congress. Visible in their royal blue union windbreakers, teamsters glared at members of a congressional committee who were supportive of deregulation. In the event members could not travel to Washington, union officials urged members to "take pen or typewriter in hand and let your Senators and Congressmen know how you feel about having your livelihood kicked around by the fun loving deregulators." The basic message was that "if you take away our jobs now, we will take away your jobs at election time."[44] Teamsters (and trucking company executives) never doubted the centrality of state officials in structuring the transportation industries.

In mid-March 1980, however, truck owners sought to negotiate a conclusion to legislative and administrative deregulation. "The truckers are caving in," a senior administration official wrote Eizenstat on March 19, adding that "the ATA . . . [had] offered a deal." Fearing both pending legislation and the possibility of even more stringent action by Darius Gaskins and his new colleagues on the ICC, top trucking executives were willing to accept a modest level of deregulation in return for political certainty in their future business operations. One truck operator complained that Gaskins and the ICC were "cutting off our tails an inch at a time," and that it "would be easier to lose it in one fell swoop."[45]

Starting after July 1, then, authors of the Motor Carrier Act of 1980 provided for greatly eased entry into trucking routes. Rather than requiring applicants for a new route authority to show that trucking service was needed, now those who held that authority and objected to the application of a newcomer would have to demonstrate that the proposed service was "'inconsistent with the public convenience and necessity.'" In the past, the burden, usually insurmountable, had rested on the applicant; and in the future, the burden, likely difficult, would rest on the incumbent. Equally, truck operators could raise or lower prices by up to 10 percent each year without seeking ICC approval, once again creating the zone of reasonableness recommended in the Weeks committee report of 1955. Sounding like economist Alfred Kahn, at the signing ceremony on July 1, President Carter announced that deregulation would "help to control inflation and give us an opportunity to use the free enterprise system."[46] Put another way, Carter and his top officials, including Mary Schuman and Richard Neustadt, had created one market for all truckers, replacing distinct submarkets including one for common carriers, another for contract carriers, and yet another for private carriers.

Senior officials at the American Trucking Associations had nonetheless managed to secure some ambiguity for themselves in the new era of deregulation. For example, antitrust immunity for rate bureaus—provided by the Reed-Bulwinkle Act of 1948—remained in effect until 1984, and could even be extended for another six months. Not only did rate bureaus retain their antitrust immunity, Congress in 1980 created another study commission to investigate their operations and report to Congress before the end of that immunity. As political scientist Robyn points out, truckers believed in the efficacy and fairness of the regulatory regime, giving them hope that eventually "the 'truth will out.'"[47]

Teamsters came away from deregulation with less than their employers. By giving way on entry, trucking company owners and senior managers had given away the protection of greatest concern to teamsters. In turn, teamster leaders asked Congress and ATA officials to support legislation providing a right of first hire in the event of layoffs; and Teamster leaders also wanted Congress to create a $100 million fund to pay benefits to laid-off drivers. Owners and managers objected to these protective measures. Many did not want to be compelled to hire teamsters first, and many feared that unionized drivers would seek to organize their nonunion firms. Instead, teamsters settled for the limp provision that the secretary of labor would maintain a list of regulated carriers with job openings, and, in some unspecified way, assist displaced drivers in their search for new positions. Such was the limited and tentative nature of the trucker-teamster alliance, a relationship described only a year earlier by a *Wall Street Journal* writer as one in which management and labor were prepared to stand "side by side." Exactly like truck owners and managers who relied on the American Trucking Associations for their political weight, the overrated clout of teamster leaders such as Frank Fitzsimmons was always an artifact of a highly regulated transportation regime.[48]

In reality, truck managers and teamsters were not a natural alliance, and never had been. At least since the 1950s, employers had perceived their drivers as useful allies in legislative battles, but not as social and political equals. Cartoons in ATA publications such as *Transport Topics* routinely imaged drivers as unshaven, uneducated, and in need of instruction and supervision by managers, who in turn appeared at work cleanly shaven and wearing jackets and ties. Removal of the jacket in a cartoon signified getting down to business, but not a loss of authority. Nor did illustrators show trucking company managers inside or under a truck.[49]

The social distance between managers and drivers was wide, and managers kept it that way. Truck owners and managers never invited Teamsters to join them at businessmen's clubs, at meetings of the Rotary, or at their many golf tournaments held at exclusive country clubs. Nor had truckers included teamsters in that vast network of attorneys, members of Congress, and ICC officials who talked an indistinguishable mix of business and politics at countless lunches and dinners hosted by officials of the American Trucking Associations. For their part, teamsters had brought lengthy and difficult strikes against truck operators, achieving solid pay raises. Salary negotiations and strikes only made clear that teamsters were employees, no more. During the last stages of negotiations about the Motor Carrier Act of 1980, moreover, ATA officials refused close and formal association with their Teamster counterparts, worrying that hostile members of Congress would also judge them poorly.[50] In all, teamsters and truck operators had never achieved that sense of one another as men like themselves. In so hostile an environment, teamsters received a stronger dose of Carter's newly created "free enterprise system" than their bosses.

DEREGULATING THE RAILROADS

By midsummer 1980, only the remnants of the railroad regulatory regime stood in the way of President Carter's goal of deregulating the major transportation industries. Unlike deregulation of trucking and airlines, where Senator Kennedy and presidential appointees and aides, including Alfred Kahn, Mary Schuman, Richard Neustadt, and Stuart Eizenstat, had taken the lead, at first railroad deregulation rested in the hands of Brock Adams, the secretary of transportation. Initially, Adams talked about innovative ideas such as intermodal ownership of railroads and trucking companies, ideas that politicians and experts had brought forward since the 1920s. Even Alan Boyd, the first secretary of transportation, had sought better integration of rail, truck, and airline firms and operations. President Carter, however, wanted Adams to focus on deregulation, not on complicated and difficult-to-achieve goals such as intermodalism. Regardless of his earlier preferences, in January 1978, at the start of the battle for rail deregulation, Adams accepted and endorsed Carter's insistence on a "private enterprise solution" for the plight of the railroads.[51] Driven from the national agenda in the mid-1930s by fear of the railroads and by aggressive trucker lobbying, and driven out again in the early 1970s by President Nixon's association with the Watergate break-in, not for another decade would plans for limited intermodal coordination rise to the top of the federal agenda.

On December 15, 1978, Adams delivered his basic plan for railroad deregulation to President Carter. "The Federal Government," he reported, "has been pouring over $1 billion annually into preservation of the freight rail system." Return on investment hovered below 1 percent, leaving several railroads near bankruptcy and others unable to attract additional funds or loans. According to Adams, regulation of rates and service by the ICC were among the major factors shaping these problems. Railroad executives, contended Adams, needed "rate flexibility," easing of merger rules, and authority to abandon unprofitable routes.[52] Starting with the Transportation Act of 1920, members of Congress had recommended mergers as one of the preferred cures for the lack of railroad profitability. During the 1950s and 1960s, railroad executives had launched their own period of merger "mania."

As Adams knew well from the days following the Penn-Central bankruptcy, however, threats of more abandoned lines were certain to provoke fear and hostility among small-town folks, railroad employees, and some shippers. Equally, the precise mechanism by which trucks would take the place of railroads on little-served lines was a question Adams failed to ask, or answer. In all, Adams had simply substituted the president's faith in markets for his own faith in politics and planning. In an overstatement unusual even for him, Adams nonetheless characterized his proposals as "sweeping."[53]

In explaining Adams's proposals to President Carter, Stuart Eizenstat converted them into what he labeled a "political calculus." On March 2,

Eizenstat (and Bill Johnston) alerted Carter to the likelihood that "the immediate impact of rail deregulation is likely to be less service for many communities and higher rates for many commodities." Equally, Carter learned that Adams's proposal to speed up mergers "will be threatening to many railroads as well as to some shippers and communities." Eventually, Eizenstat asserted, deregulation of rates and other measures would bolster the efficiency and health of the railroad industry and lower federal expenditures. The "political calculus," as Eizenstat phrased it, "balance[d] fears of short-term losses against hopes of long-term gains." As the president of the United States, Jimmy Carter made the decision that the calculus would work, and would be worth whatever short-term hostility that he and his administration would suffer among deregulation's likely opponents such as those who stood to pay higher transportation prices, lose railroad service, or lose their jobs. On March 6, 1979, with these choices before him, Carter penned a note to Eizenstat (and James McIntyre), directing them to "expedite railroad deregulation proposals to me." In July 1979, Carter fired Brock Adams. In turn, Eizenstat put Steve Simmons, an assistant like Mary Schuman and Richard Neustadt, in charge of the railroad deregulation effort.[54]

On November 21, 1979, Simmons reported to Eizenstat on what he had learned about the "calculus" of railroad deregulation. Rail executives still disagreed about many of the details of deregulation. In particular, they wanted the right to make contracts with shippers, altering their status as common carriers; and many of them still wanted their rate bureaus to retain authority to propose across-the-board rate increases. Shippers, however, worried about rising prices and declining service once railroad officials enjoyed rate-making freedom and the freedom to abandon service. Further, leaders of railroad unions worried about job protection for employees in the event of large-scale abandonments. As so often in the past, leaders of railroads and rail unions had never really contemplated a world without some degree of regulation. Altogether, Simmons reported, "there is *no* massive movement for deregulation" (emphasis in original). Nevertheless, Simmons believed that "if we keep pushing there is more than a 50–50 chance that by the end of this Congress we will have a meaningful railroad deregulation bill enacted into law."[55]

Given the absence of that "massive movement," Eizenstat had designated Simmons as the person who would "keep pushing" for railroad deregulation. Between November 1979 and April 1980, that activity was fast paced. For example, Simmons chaired a meeting that brought together leaders of the major railroads with top officials at the Department of Transportation, the Office of Management and Budget, and majority and minority staff members in the U.S. Senate. In addition, members of Carter's congressional liaison staff visited each member of the Senate. Now, railroad executives joined in these efforts, but conducted their own visits to senators' offices. In mid-March, Stuart Eizenstat spoke to Senate staff members assembled at the White House. Simmons also directed separate meetings, again at the White House, for large shippers such as J. C. Penney and for the representatives of smaller shippers such as the American Farm Bureau Federation and the National Industrial Traffic League. Further, Simmons created five teams composed of three presidential staff members, charging each team to visit twenty members of the Senate. As a member of the Ford administration, John Snow had used an identical setup to lobby members of Congress. Whether in meetings at the White House, in Senate offices, or in public information packets distributed to newspaper editors, Eizenstat, Simmons, and other staff members emphasized inflation, energy shortages, and declining rail service leading to bankruptcy.[56]

Early in April 1980, members of the U.S. Senate approved legislation to deregulate railroads. The vote was 91–4. The only compromise administration and rail leaders made dealt with the precise amount railroad executives could increase rates during the next five years. That topic had animated both Senator Russell Long and executives of electric utilities dependent on rail for large coal shipments.[57] With his clout and years of seniority, few in the Senate wanted to antagonize Senator Long. Equally, electric company executives represented a politically savvy and weighty component of the often-discussed captive shipper problem.

Deregulation faced slower going in the U.S. House of Representatives. In August 1980, the bill's floor manager, Representative James J. Florio, withdrew his deregulation bill from consideration. As in the Senate, the amount by which rail executives could increase rates had excited great controversy, leading to passage of an amendment by the House keeping rate increases below those allowed by the Senate. Simmons reported to Eizenstat that "intense personal lobbying by utility presidents, shippers, and the opposition of the House leadership" had led to this turn of events. On August 8, shippers and rail executives agreed on terms that were also acceptable to Simmons and to leaders of the Department of Transportation and the Interstate Commerce Commission. According to Simmons, however, "Florio flatly rejected the compromise provision."[58] Not even the momentum created by Senate and presidential approval of railroad deregulation guaranteed its ultimate passage.

Despite this setback, Simmons and other Carter appointees assembled the intellectual and legislative devices that led House members to approve railroad deregulation. Simmons believed that "all parties want the bill," which meant that Florio now stood as the only impediment. Telephone

Representative Florio, Simmons urged Eizenstat on August 21, and tell him to "move on . . . [his] position . . . [or] quite frankly we will have to consider other legislative options."[59]

Once Florio determined to "move," Simmons directed another lobbying effort aimed at members of Congress. Rather than focusing on the dangers of inflation, no doubt recognized by all, Simmons and other Carter aides spoke of railroad revitalization, especially in light of the fact that airline and trucking executives already enjoyed greater rate-making authority. As another "talking point," Simmons urged Carter's top officials, including economist and former CAB chair Alfred Kahn, to tell members of Congress that "failure to deregulate may well be the death knell for Conrail." In one sentence, Simmons was reminding members of Congress from the Northeast of the countless jobs and businesses lost following the Penn Central bankruptcy. In the case of House members who would not otherwise support the revised bill, Simmons recommended that Eizenstat tell them that "this bill is extremely important to the country and the President." By a vote of 337 to 20, on September 9, members of the house endorsed another round of railroad deregulation.[60]

On October 14, 1980, President Carter signed the Staggers Rail Act of 1980, named after Harley O. Staggers, the retiring chair of the House committee on interstate and foreign commerce. Rate flexibility, a term promoted by deregulation enthusiasts, was an important part of the Staggers Act. Like their counterparts in trucking and airline firms, provisions of the Staggers Act allowed railroad executives to lower and raise shipping rates within greatly widened parameters. In all, the railroad idea of a "zone of reasonableness" first promulgated in 1949 had found a legislative home at the hands of President Carter and his aides. Railroad executives also achieved another of their long-term goals with the right under Staggers to abandon unprofitable lines. Like their counterparts in trucking, moreover, authors of the Staggers Act permitted railroad executives to negotiate long-term contracts with shippers. Under rules approved by members of the ICC in May 1980, large shippers such as Ford Motor Company were already entering into five-year contracts for most of Ford's shipments between Ohio, Michigan, and California. President Carter characterized the Staggers Act as "the capstone of my efforts to get rid of needless and burdensome Federal regulations."[61] Approval of the Staggers Act completed the program of partially deregulating truck and rail transportation first brought to public attention by President Eisenhower and his secretary of commerce, Sinclair Weeks. No one commented on the irony that the railroads were the first regulated transportation system, and one of the last deregulated.

CONCLUSION

On July 16, 1980, a few weeks after approval of the Motor Carrier Act, ICC commissioner George M. Stafford spoke before a meeting of truck operators. Described by a writer for the ATA's *Transport Topics* as the "great dissenter," Stafford used the speech as an opportunity to celebrate the workings of the regulatory regime he had long embraced. Unlike critics who had contended that regulation led to higher prices, Stafford told members of his audience that American transportation had "prosper[ed] under regulation and benefit[ed] shippers and the public alike." Repeating a trope articulated by truckers and regulators since the mid-1950s in response to Eisenhower and Weeks's early deregulatory efforts, Stafford added that "we have the finest transportation system in the world." Stafford also used this speech as an opportunity to warn of dramatic changes that, he believed, would take place following ICC rulings and the recently approved Motor Carrier Act. "I don't hear service talked about very much anymore," he asserted, "all I hear about is competition." On August 30, Commissioner Stafford retired from the ICC. Still not persuaded that this new era of competition would provide promised benefits to truckers and shippers, Stafford told a reporter for *Transport Topics* that "the kind of regulation we had was built up over many years with a solid foundation" and yet the now-successful proponents of deregulation "were basing their views on a theory."[62]

Starting in the early 1970s, many such as Brock Adams had also worried about the eventual triumph of persons who knew only the "theoretical aspects" of deregulation. Adams's preference for intermodal coordination and his reluctance to pursue the full-scale deregulation of air, rail, and truck promoted by Mary Schuman and Jimmy Carter were factors in his subsequent firing as secretary of transportation. In communications with Stuart Eizenstat, however, President Carter expressed concern about whether airline deregulation would lead to a loss of service to smaller cities and towns. "Not really sure about this," he wrote to Eizenstat. In discussing railroad deregulation with Carter, Eizenstat predicted short-term economic costs and longer-term economic gains, expressing the matter to Carter as a "political calculus." Again, the calculus rested on faith in economists' predictions. Overall, the calculus of deregulation was whether elimination of the regulatory regime would really lower shipping prices without bringing about widespread unemployment among transportation workers, manufacturers, and eventually those same shippers. By 1980, truck and rail deregulation represented the victory of President Carter and others who, frustrated and exhausted with the workings of the regulatory regime in a period of stagflation, were willing to try something as untested as deregulation and the subsequent creation of markets for railroad and truck managers, employees, and shippers. Officially launched by President Eisenhower and Secretary Weeks in 1955 as a device for rescuing railroads in decline, during the 1960s the idea of deregulation and market creation emerged in the hands of President Johnson and aide Joseph Califano as methods for placing additional authority in the president's hands and for achieving economic fine-tuning. During the 1970s, however, Presidents Nixon, Ford, and Carter looked to convert those same ideas about deregulation and the framing of transportation markets into the nation's principal transportation policy.

During the next decade and beyond, transportation executives as well as politicians and deregulation enthusiasts had an opportunity to build their own body of personal experience and empirical evidence to explain the workings of air, rail, and trucking firms. (Still present but less visible in the decades following transportation deregulation were the guiding hands of regulators, politicians, and judges.) Starting in 1981, truck rates declined and many truckers went out of business, including several of the largest firms, such as Abner Glikbarg's Pacific Intermountain Express. Wages paid truck drivers fell, and thousands lost their jobs. Between 1978 and the late 1980s, airline executives once again reduced airfares, especially for the growing number of leisure travelers; and with fewer constraints to overcome, rail executives restarted a period of mergers that had been cut short by the bankruptcy of Penn Central and other leading railroads. In the new era of deregulation, politicians, economists, transportation officials, and popular writers attributed these changes in transportation firms and services to the extraordinary workings of markets. Falling airfares and the success of several new air carriers provided additional evidence that markets rather than ham-fisted regulators encouraged safe air travel for larger numbers of Americans. Yet another decade of railroad mergers added to the conviction that with government officials out of the way, rail officials were at last able to work out a method for providing low-cost service at a profit.

Price and service competition and sometimes attractive profit reports comprised only the most talked-about components of the new deregulatory regime. Less visible after 1980 were the remarkable changes that took place in the organization of the transportation industries. In addition to falling prices, deregulation also encouraged a process of devolution of price and service authority from federal officials into the hands of transportation company executives. Like the discredited regulatory regime that had come into being between 1935 and 1940, as we shall see, the much-celebrated market restoration of the 1980s in transportation was in reality another creature of federal policy. In a partially deregulated environment, moreover, recently empowered transportation executives and especially truckers found rate bureaus and their conferences such as the Regular Common Carrier Conference less useful. Deregulation, then, also encouraged transportation executives to begin a process of discarding the many institutions that had guided the postwar generations. Not easily spotted by observers focused on prices, wages, and employment, the processes of devolution and deinstitutionalization brought changes in the organization of transportation firms and the organization of the still-separate transportation industries. Nevertheless, starting in 1991, federal officials offered vast sums to local agencies that would build connections between air, rail, and truck operators, reversing the single-minded focus on "modes" begun in 1935. By the early 1990s, however, with the processes of deinstitutionalization and devolution more than a decade old, only rarely did transportation executives and politicians perceive a need to talk about history.

CHAPTER 9

THE AMERICAN STATE AND TRANSPORTATION, 1980–1995

STATE ACTION *ALWAYS* PLAYS A MAJOR ROLE IN CONSTITUTING ECONOMIES, SO
THAT IT IS NOT USEFUL TO POSIT STATES AS LYING OUTSIDE OF ECONOMIC
ACTIVITY.
    —SOCIOLOGIST FRED BLOCK, 1994

Starting in 1981, many of the predictions about the consequences of price
and service deregulation proved accurate. Just as politicians such as Edward
Kennedy and economists such as George Stigler and Hendrik Houthakker
had contended, prices charged by airlines and trucking firms declined during the decade and more following deregulation. Contradicting the worries
of small-town residents and politicians, moreover, managers of trucking
firms, railroads, and airlines continued to provide service. Confirming the
fears of President Carter and others, however, sharp price competition also
brought economic dislocation. Whether among airlines such as Eastern and
Pan Am or among truckers such as Abner Glikbarg's Pacific Intermountain
Express, that competition was often fearsome, leading to another round of
mergers and sometimes to the destruction of jobs, firms, and capital.[1]

The politics of American transportation also evolved in ways that few
had predicted during the decades of lobbying, litigating, and fevered
rhetoric about the virtues of regulation and deregulation. Long-accustomed
to political and legal action as reliable methods of protecting rates and
routes, during the mid-1980s truckers in particular went to Congress seeking to reestablish limited regulation. When that effort failed, however,
beginning in the early 1990s many of those same truckers dropped membership in their rate bureaus and conferences, even including the venerable
Regular Common Carrier Conference guided decades earlier by Robert
McBride and Albert Rosenbaum. In 1994, deregulation-minded politicians,
including President William J. "Bill" Clinton, and their newfound trucking

industry supporters abolished state-level trucking regulations, describing their action as federal preemption. Not content with federal preemption of state trucking regulations, in 1995, deregulation enthusiasts abolished the Interstate Commerce Commission. Starting in the period 1978–1980, then, deregulation of airline, truck, and rail operations not only devolved rate making and routing authority to transportation executives, but also fostered a process of diminishing or dissolving federal and state agencies and deinstitutionalizing business relationships that in many cases had been shaped over the course of all or most of the twentieth century.[2]

Nor had advocates of deregulation such as Mary Schuman and President Carter foreseen the emergence of firms such as CSX that managed freight shipments from ocean to rail and truck. Executives of these firms developed what were now called intermodal capabilities, carrying out portions of the long-forgotten hopes of generations of railroad executives and of regulators such as Joseph Eastman in the 1920s and 1930s and Allen Boyd in the 1960s. Beginning in 1991, moreover, federal officials finally took an active role in financing construction of intermodal connections. Under terms of the Intermodal Surface Transportation Efficiency Act of 1991, a considerable portion of federal spending for highways devolved into the hands of local politicians, who could use some of that money to bring about physical linkages between the nation's road network and its airports, seaports, and railyards.

Despite the many changes that followed the deregulatory legislation of the late 1970s, the federal government remained at the center of the American transportation industry. For example, in 1994, when members of Congress and President Clinton abolished the Interstate Commerce Commission, they transferred its remaining responsibilities to the newly formed Surface Transportation Board. After 1980, railroad officials, truck operators, airline executives, and shippers discovered, and rediscovered, that they never could free themselves of the state's spending or its regulatory embrace. Nor did they wish to do so.

Among popular writers, moreover, few apparently understood or cared that the structure of American transportation—whether as distinct modes during the 1920s and 1930s or as an evolving-intermodal system after 1980—had been and remained a creature of the American state. Nor did popular writers, politicians, and economists pay much attention to such esoteric topics as devolution and deinstitutionalization. Instead, after 1980 (as before) popular writers as well as leaders of an economy and polity seeking to understand the consequences of transportation deregulation looked to concrete measures of economic well-being such as rates, wages, and employment.

TRUCKING AFTER 1980

In the trucking industry, falling rates and rising levels of unemployment comprised the two most visible consequences of deregulation (and a depressed economy). Between 1980 and 1983, reported two academic economists, "competitive pressures and cost-cutting efforts . . . lead to rates . . . nearly 22% lower." Closer to day-to-day operations than academic economists, trucking company managers described rate cutting in identical terms. In mid-1983, truck operators in the Pennsylvania area reported that deregulation had brought dramatic declines in rates and increased layoffs. "It's hurting the trucking business," an anonymous truck operator informed a business writer, adding that "some people offer 20 to 30 percent discounts." As a result, he argued, "it's become a real cut-throat situation" that had "put some out of business and a lot of people out of work." Writing in 1986, Charles R. Perry, a professor of management and industrial relations at the University of Pennsylvania's prestigious Wharton School, characterized the period 1980–1983 in the trucking industry as a "Great Shakeout."[3]

Teamsters joined truck operators in denouncing the woeful consequences of deregulation. In a letter to the editor of the business-oriented *Wall Street Journal* published July 22, 1985, Gary Ewing, identified as a member of Teamster Local 174, contended that deregulation had fostered precisely the falling wages, lost jobs, and bankruptcies predicted several years earlier in testimony before Congress. "Since deregulation," asserted Ewing, "more than . . . 100,000 Teamsters have suffered unemployment." Not only had deregulation led to lost jobs, Ewing asserted, "but for every independent trucker working 70 to 100 hours per week at $6 or less an hour, two Teamsters who work 40 hours per week are replaced." Perry at the Wharton School calculated a figure of 6 percent unemployment among drivers in 1979, 12 percent in 1981, and 9 percent early in 1982. By 1994, however, the total number of drivers, many self-employed, had increased to 586 thousand. Nonetheless, drivers' wages continued to decline. According to a report in the U.S. government's *Monthly Labor Review,* between 1978 and 1996 the real average hourly earning (1982 dollars) of truck drivers fell 40 percent.[4]

Nor did a restoration of economic growth in 1983 foster profitability and the end of price-cutting tactics among trucking executives. The basic factor limiting profitability was the presence of additional competitors. After 1980, commissioners of the ICC no longer controlled entry into the trucking business. Contrary to the predictions of economists and ICC officials, between 1980 and the early 1990s, the number of common carriers actually declined. Even successors to Abner Glikbarg at his once-venerable

Pacific Intermountain Express consolidated operations with another firm and eventually shut down. During the decade and more following deregulation, however, truckload operators, often with few employees and using leased equipment, entered the trucking business.[5]

Competition brought by growing numbers of those truckload carriers added to pricing pressures. Additional competition at the hands of freight forwarders, railroads, the United Parcel Service, and private truck owners seeking backhauls added more pricing pressure. In 1987, the acting general manager of the Indiana Motor Truck Association estimated that the number of carriers had doubled since 1980, but that the volume of freight shipped remained unchanged in that period. In fact, the author of one study found that between 1977 and 1989, gross tonnage handled by less-than-truckload carriers such as Yellow had fallen 10 percent. Flat or declining demand and a larger number of competitors, noted a writer for *Indiana Business,* "brings the money crunch home to many a trucking firm." Deregulation was a "disaster," the president of the National Tank Truck Carriers told members of the Houston Traffic Club on January 9, 1990, adding that "price is today's killing ground."[6] By opening entry to new truckers and by permitting managers of common, contract, and common carriers to compete equally for the same business, President Carter and Mary Schuman had created conditions for a restructuring of the trucking industry and for creation of a unified rather than a segmented trucking market. Bankruptcies comprised another part of that uncertain process of industry restructuring and market creation. Starting in the early 1980s, routine reports of trucking company bankruptcies took their place alongside equally routine reports of price cutting. The failure rate of trucking firms in 1985, reported Nicholas A. Glaskowsky, a professor of management and logistics at the University of Miami in 1986, was "nearly 12 times the number of such failures in 1978." Neither the age nor the size of these firms, including Pacific Intermountain, provided certain protection against the economic vicissitudes that deregulation had brought. By the early 1990s, a writer for the *Transportation Journal* reported, only the "big three" of the largest ten trucking firms in 1979 (consisting of Roadway Express, Yellow Freight, and Consolidated Freightways) remained in business. Falling rates and bankruptcies continued into the 1990s. In 1994, according to that writer, "it . . . [was] still not clear when the industry will reach a stable equilibrium."[7]

As drivers and (many) truck owners reeled under the effects of deregulation, federal officials launched an effort to bring additional deregulation to the trucking business. Starting in the early 1980s, leaders in President Ronald W. Reagan's administration coalesced with shippers (and a few truckers) to launch an assault on trucking rates. Proponents of this deregulatory effort hoped to eliminate the Interstate Commerce Commission as well as state-level trucking regulations. Advocates of this phase of the process of regulatory reform described proposed federal legislation to eliminate state law as that of preemption. Whatever the name, like the first deregulation effort that had stretched from 1955 to 1980, this one took place over the course of ten years and the terms of three presidents. Once again, deregulation was mostly a presidential initiative.

By 1983, officials of the U.S. Department of Transportation in the Reagan administration had prepared legislation to eliminate state-level trucking regulations. Another portion of the bill, if approved, would abolish truckers' rate bureaus, which authors of the Motor Carrier Act of 1980 had permitted to operate on narrower grounds. According to a writer for *Supermarket News,* a coalition of retailers and manufacturers "applauded the administration's decision." Virtually repeating the conversations that had taken place during the Nixon administration, however, officials of the International Brotherhood of Teamsters, now led by Frank Fitzsimmons's successor, Jackie Presser, threatened to oppose Reagan's reelection if he endorsed additional deregulation. As had President Nixon in the early 1970s, during 1983 and 1984 President Reagan decided that Teamster support was more important than the apparent economic benefits of another round of deregulation.[8] Again like Nixon, for President Reagan electoral politics was ultimately in the driver's seat.

In mid-1986 a coalition made up of directors of fifteen trade associations and thirty-five corporate leaders secured the support of two members of Congress to introduce another deregulation bill. Executives of firms that shipped nationally such as K Mart, Proctor & Gamble, and Sears, Roebuck & Company stood at the heart of this coalition, but its members included directors of the Private Truck Council. In the late 1970s, leaders of that organization had supported truck deregulation, breaking from their colleagues in the American Trucking Associations. By the mid-1980s, members of the Private Truck Council were already profiting from their newly acquired backhaul business, in the process helping to drive freight rates downward and giving operators of traditional common carriers fits. Similar to legislation developed three years earlier by senior officials in the Department of Transportation, authors of this bill aimed to eliminate rate bureaus and state-level regulations. Speaking before the House Small Business Committee late in 1987, however, a senior executive at the American Trucking Associations warned that proposals to extend the scope of federal deregulation "will not lower maintenance costs, insurance prices or taxes" and "it will not end rate wars."[9]

President George H. W. Bush had no greater luck in widening the space for deregulated trucking. The vehicle for this particular effort was a bill promising billions for highway construction projects. As part of that legislation, announced Samuel K. Skinner (Bush's secretary of transportation) on February 13, 1991, "we must also relieve the industry of . . . the economic regulatory burden imposed on interstate trucking by many state governments." A Fact Sheet accompanying the secretary's press release promised "enhance[d] productivity in the trucking industry" with savings in transportation costs that "could range from $4 billion to $13 billion per year." Like President Eisenhower's endorsement of Secretary Weeks's deregulation proposal in 1955, the overarching idea for postwar American presidents was aggregate economic management, a process that presidents, their staff members, and members of Congress sometimes described as serving consumers. Predictions of the potential savings from another round of deregulation ranged widely, even wildly, recalling Brock Adams's concern that deregulation actually rested more on economic "theory" than on the results of a widely tested program. During 1991, however, neither the threat of a presidential veto nor the efforts of a new coalition of deregulation-minded business executives that now included more than one hundred trucking company executives could persuade members of Congress to abolish state trucking regulations.[10]

In 1992, leaders in the Bush administration made a final attempt to achieve greater trucking deregulation. Members of a coalition that took the name Americans for Safe and Competitive Trucking worked to pass this legislation in conjunction with Andrew H. Card Jr., Bush's new secretary of transportation. "The ICC really is a vestige of the past," Card told an interviewer for *Traffic Management* in the fall of 1992; "it is old thinking." As before, Card and others characterized federal abolition of state trucking regulations as preemption. Abolition of the ICC went under the more contemporary description of "sunsetting." New words mattered less than the weight of a growing number of trucking company executives in the coalition who were now invoking images of markets. Sounding like economists and federal officials in the 1960s and 1970s who had complained about federal trucking regulation, the president of Schneider National, a large trucking firm based in Green Bay, Wisconsin, told a congressional committee that state-level trucking regulations "'distort the marketplace and create inefficiencies that rob our industries of their competitiveness.'"[11] By the early 1990s, many truckers had joined shippers and Bush administration officials in demanding the elimination of remaining regulations.

The new deregulation drive also widened the split among members of the trucking industry. As early as 1979 and 1980, private and truckload operators (the contract carriers) had broken with executives of common carriers and ATA leaders and joined Mary Schuman in seeking to eliminate federal trucking regulations. Now during the early 1990s, the relentless process of price cutting encouraged leaders of many common carriers to quit their rate bureaus and their specialized conferences such as the Regular Common Carrier Conference (RCCC). Late in 1991, for example, managers of the gigantic Yellow Freight System and the equally large Consolidated Freightways withdrew from their regional rate bureaus. Rather than rely on rate bureau officials to develop uniform rates, managers at Yellow and Consolidated negotiated prices directly with shippers. Similarly, Yellow executives joined their counterparts at Overnite Transportation Company and several other trucking firms in withdrawing from the RCCC. According to a report in *Traffic World,* however, only Overnite (owned since 1986 by the Union Pacific Railroad—itself an idea politically unimaginable in the 1940s, 1950s, or 1970s) had withdrawn from the RCCC for "policy reasons"; the other withdrawals, ran the report, had come about due to "reasons of economy."[12] Beginning in the early 1990s, deinstitutionalization of the trucking industry was one of the unanticipated consequences of deregulation.

Deinstitutionalization of major trucking organizations also made it easier for proderegulation truckers and politicians to eliminate state trucking regulations and abolish the ICC. As before, proponents of additional deregulation still preferred to describe these activities with less threatening phrases such as "sunsetting," "preemption," and "regulatory reform." Members of the regulatory reform coalition, a writer for *Traffic World* reported in August 1994, included not only leaders of a railroad holding company, but also executives of several large common carriers, a group of shippers with more than two hundred members, and most of the larger truckload operators. This time, even leaders of the American Trucking Associations joined the fray. Between 1955 and 1980, ATA officials had led the fight to protect the regulatory regime. By reversing their opposition to further deregulation, ATA officials angered smaller truckers. So hostile were some members to relinquishing state regulation that leaders of the Oregon and Washington state trucking associations threatened to quit. "ATA realized it was more expedient to cut its losses and alienate some smaller members," reported that same *Traffic World* writer, "than to stay behind the curve and allow important legislation to pass without its input." Leaders of the Teamsters Union still opposed deregulation, as did remaining members of the Regular Common Carrier Conference. With President Clinton arguing for even greater deregulation of remaining rate bureau activity, and with the ATA neutral, in August 1994 Congress and the president agreed to preempt state-level trucking regulations. Elimination of those regulations, asserted the president of the National Industrial Traffic League in November 1994, "is a validation of the free market in trucking." In December 1995, this latest deregulation drive reached its culmination. President William J. "Bill" Clinton and members of Congress united behind abolition of the Interstate Commerce Commission, replacing it with the Surface Transportation Board, a new agency inside the Department of Transportation.[13]

The ICC had survived 108 years. In the mid-1990s, comments on elimination of the ICC took the form of reminiscences such as "fading into the sunset" rather than serious analysis of the role of the federal government and a regulatory regime that had structured transportation firms, industries, and markets for more than a century. In the incessant ballyhoo of radio and television talk shows and popular writers trumpeting the apparent triumph of markets and market enthusiasts, no one remarked or perhaps cared that with creation of the Surface Transportation Board, competitive relationships among truck, rail, and airline firms had been and would remain a creature of politics and public policy.[14] Like the trucking industry, after 1980, judges, politicians, public policies, and even commissioners of the ICC and the new Surface Transportation Board still mattered vitally in framing the organization and operation of railroad firms.

RAILROADS AFTER 1980

Following deregulation of the railroads in 1980, journalists, economists, and other observers focused attention on rates and profitability. Writing in 1991, the executive editor of *Chilton's Distribution,* a trade publication aimed at shippers, observed that "rail rates again failed to keep pace with industry cost increases." Between 1983 and 1993, railroad rates increased nearly 17 percent. Measured against inflation, however, rates had fallen nearly 20 percent. Despite their inability to achieve substantial rate increases, railroads were actually increasing loads and turning a profit. In 1990, executives of the nation's railroads reported a return on investment of 7.13 percent. In order to deliver such an impressive profit figure, ran one report, "the railroads have downsized their equipment fleets, their physical plant and their employees." Indeed, between 1980 and 1995, railroad executives reduced the number of freight cars in service from 1.7 million to 583,000, a diminution of 65 percent. During that same period, the number of railroad employees declined from 458,000 to 216,000, a drop of 47 percent. In 1990, however, railroads also carried more than 1 trillion ton-miles of freight, a new record, and did so with fewer employees and less equipment. "In the short run," contended the vice president of economics and finance for the Association of American Railroads in 1991, "the productivity curve ran ahead of the decline in rates."[15]

Less visible in these reports of railroad profitability was the reliance of railroad leaders on the federal government for the legal authority to carry out their downsizing program. Attempting to account for the railroads' improved profit picture, in April 1982 a reporter for *Barron's National Business and Financial Weekly* listed factors such as changes in federal regulation in 1976 and 1980, federal tax legislation approved in 1981, and a "more favorable government attitude toward mergers."[16] Given the dependence of railroad executives on federal officials for favorable legislation and favorable interpretation of merger rules, after 1980 politicians and judges continued to determine the basic frameworks governing railroad operations. Reminiscent of the years before 1940, shippers, railroad executives, and political leaders negotiated seriously about mergers, rates, and railroad ownership of trucking and steamship firms, ideas that had first surfaced in the 1920s but had largely been forgotten. No topic excited more negotiating and more inflamed rhetoric than rates charged members of a group calling themselves "captive" shippers.

The right of rail executives to determine rates for shippers rested on a case ultimately decided by judges of the U.S. Supreme Court. In April 1984, the Court refused to hear an appeal filed by attorneys for electric utilities, steel corporations, and other firms that shipped large quantities of coal by rail. The question before the Court was a rule promulgated in 1981 by the Interstate Commerce Commission determining that railroad rates were not subject to review unless the railroad dominated a market. Earlier, members of the federal appeals court in New Orleans had voted 8–2 to uphold the ICC's interpretation of railroad deregulation acts passed by Congress in 1976 and 1980. By refusing to consider the case, the Supreme Court left standing the decision of the court of appeals.[17]

At first glance, the case appears another victory for federal officials, economists, and the coalition of shippers and others assembled by Mary Schuman, who had sought deregulation of transportation rates. Starting in 1955 with Dwight Eisenhower and Sinclair Weeks, every president and their senior officials extending up to Jimmy Carter, Stuart Eizenstat, and Schuman in 1980 had advocated diminution or even abolition of the regulatory regime that had long shaped the organization of transportation industries, transportation markets, and the behavior of transportation executives and their union counterparts at rail, air, and trucking firms. With the decisions of the court of appeals and the Supreme Court in hand, in 1984 advocates of deregulation had brought closure within the courts as to whether rail officials really possessed the legal authority to set prices, improve service, and compete for the business of shippers. Overall, here was a situation in which creation of a market had started with congressional legislation in 1976 and in 1980, and concluded several years later before the

U.S. Supreme Court.[18]

Like their counterparts during the decades up to 1980, however, no sooner had the Supreme Court ruled than unhappy shippers turned to members of Congress in search of rate relief. "We're going back to 1887," asserted Carl E. Bagge, president of the National Coal Association early in 1985, "letting the railroads charge what the traffic will bear." In an effort to secure lower rates, Bagge and others formed Consumers United for Rail Equity, whose title and acronym CURE were presumably created to associate members with the interests of ordinary consumers in American politics. Eventually, Bagge and his group of seventy corporate members of CURE insisted that the alleged problem of high railroad rates rested not with deregulation and certainly not with markets. Rather, CURE members agreed that the absence of competition—shippers served by only one railroad—had permitted rail officials to raise rates unfairly. Invoking the language of Senator Russell Long during debate on the Staggers Act in 1980, Bagge and his associates carried the rhetorical day with their campaign to achieve lower rates on the grounds of their victimized position as "captive shippers and consumers." Even in the 1980s, the old-time image of predatory railroads still had political resonance. Adding to CURE's influence on the matter of railroad rates was the presence of Russell Long as the Senate's longest-serving member. In May 1985, a writer for *Industry Week*, a trade magazine aimed at manufacturers, asked, "Are Rails Headed for Re-Regulation?"[19]

Other shippers, equally large and savvy in transportation politics, still preferred the substantially deregulated environment in which railroads now operated. According to a writer for *Chilton's Distribution*, in April 1985 leaders of this group included "24 very large corporations . . . all of whom are heavy users of rail service for movements of chemicals, grain, automobiles, paper, oil, and steel." In a season during which everyone professed their devotion to competition and its benefits for consumers and themselves alike, members of this group organized as the Pro-Comp Committee. Early in 1985, President Reagan's secretary of transportation, Elizabeth Dole, strengthened the Pro-Comp position with her preemptive announcement that the president would veto legislation that undermined the Staggers Act. Now, Bagge and his associates in CURE faced the challenge of building a veto-proof majority on behalf of legislation that spoke not in the generalities of competition and markets but in more-complex-to-demonstrate language showing that railroads serving "captive" shippers would still earn "adequate" rates. The writer for *Chilton's Distribution* reported that the dispute between Bagge's Cure and Pro-Comp members was between those shipping high-value goods such as automobiles, where transportation costs made up a small part of the final price, and those shipping low-value goods such as coal, where transportation charges loomed much larger in determining final prices. "The first group of shippers is satisfied," asserted the writer, and "the latter is not."[20]

In May 1987, the captive shippers' dispute moved to the hearing rooms of the U.S. Congress, reprising developments of the 1920s and 1930s. Representative Frederick C. Boucher of coal-producing Virginia and Senator Jay Rockefeller of coal-producing West Virginia introduced legislation requiring railroads to reduce rates for captive shippers, a move that resembled the congressional effort to mandate lower agricultural freight rates in the mid-1920s. Echoing a long line of congressional predecessors, Senator Long once again decried the "abusive monopolistic practices" of the railroads. For their part, rail executives such as William H. Dempsey, president of the Association of American Railroads, denied the very existence of captive shippers. "The fact is," Dempsey told senators at a hearing, "that both the railroad and the shipper are captive to the markets they are competing in."[21]

Not only were rail executives talking about markets, they also had a market to protect. During the mid- to late 1980s, coal shipments produced more than 20 percent of the railroads' gross revenue. In case senators wavered in their enthusiasm for markets, late in October 1987 top rail executives visited them in their offices, raising the specter of what the chair of Conrail described as "the same type of railroad bankruptcies five or seven years out that we had in the early 1970s."[22] Only seven years into the era of deregulation, defenders of the new, market-oriented regime were finding a limited utility in history.

In November 1989, ICC commissioners updated rate rules for those much-discussed captive shippers. Following a year of solid earnings and a process described by a *Washington Post* reporter as "prodding from Congress," ICC officials determined that the Norfolk Southern Corporation had achieved revenue adequacy. Previously, the ICC had held that railroads such as the Norfolk Southern had the right to raise rates up to 4 percent above an index of costs without incurring a process known as "ICC scrutiny." Now that earnings at the Norfolk Southern and several other roads had risen to the level of revenue adequacy, they were subject to that scrutiny in rate cases brought forward by those describing themselves as captive shippers. Once again, faint echoes of past events could be heard, in this case related to the profit limitations of the recapture clause enacted in 1920. Thus, in mid-1995, the president of the National Industrial Transportation League, an organization of shippers, complained to members of a House subcommittee that "the ICC has so narrowly drawn the definition of captive shipper and adopted such ponderous, bureaucratic approaches that only a handful of large shippers have been able to seek relief from the monopoly practices of the railroads."[23] Even fifteen years after the era of regulation, the head of a large group of shippers continued to invoke powerful historical images. Equally, railroad managers serving self-styled captive shippers still contended with federal formulations that were at once protective, complex, legalistic, susceptible to political influence, and often based on rough historical analogies.

The politics of railroad mergers followed a similar path. As early as 1978, ICC commissioners had approved rules to expedite mergers. The new governing idea, marketing professor Richard D. Stone reported in 1991, was promotion of "end-to-end mergers . . . [that would provide] for greater long-term advantages with fewer risks than parallel mergers." In short, not only would there be fewer railroads, but remaining roads would provide service over larger geographic regions. This merger policy contained distant echoes of the railroad consolidation plan of the 1920s, in which ICC officials had proposed forming twenty regional systems through parallel mergers. Once again, federal officials had created the basis for a new period of merger "mania." During the period 1980–1985, the number of large, Class 1 railroads such as the Norfolk Southern decreased from forty to twenty-three. In 1982, the Norfolk Southern, combining the Southern Railway and the Norfolk & Western Railway, was itself the product of one of those mergers. By 1995, eleven much-larger Class 1 railroads remained, and in 1999, only eight, still-larger Class 1 railroads existed.[24]

The tortured path by which executives of the Sante Fe and Southern Pacific Railroads eventually merged with other rail lines illustrates the centrality of state officials in framing railroad corporations and their operations. The story began in December 1983, when leaders of the Santa Fe Southern Pacific Corporation, a holding company for two railroads, the Atchison, Topeka, and Santa Fe and the Southern Pacific, announced plans to merge their two rail operations. The Santa Fe Southern Pacific Corporation had combined office operations that same month, having been created through the merger of the Southern Pacific Company and Santa Fe Industries. At the outset, moreover, the company owned pipelines, trucks, timberlands, and mineral rights, and was California's largest private landowner. By September 1984, however, with John J. Schmidt, the chairman and chief executive officer of the holding company scheduled to appear before the ICC, a journalist writing for the *Wall Street Journal* reported the presence of "vigorous opposition by other carriers fearing the combined power of the two railroads in the West."[25] Nothing in the deregulation acts of 1976 and 1980 had diminished the willingness of competitors to invoke the prospect of a return of railroad monopolies as a tactic in the politics of American transportation.

During October 1985, government officials spoke with several voices regarding the anticipated effects of the proposed merger on shippers. Concluding that a merger of Santa Fe and Southern Pacific operations would lead to a "massive loss of competition," justice department officials asked the still-determinative members of the ICC not to approve the deal. Leaders in the U.S. Department of Transportation endorsed the merger, however, finding an adverse affect only on "geographically dispersed" portions of the combined railroad operations. Anticipating objections even to that modest loss of competition for shippers, transportation department officials suggested "possible remedies," including giving up tracks or permitting another railroad to make use of existing tracks. "The shipping public," ran the reasoning, "will be assured that an effective competitor will be introduced into the market."[26] Five years into the period of the deregulation regime, senior officials located in one part of the federal government feared monopoly pricing, while their counterparts in another federal agency both promised to frame markets and assured shippers that competitors would come forward.

Late in July 1986, ICC commissioners voted 4 to 1 against the merger. Not since 1966, when the ICC blocked the merger of the Northern Pacific and Great Northern, had commissioners failed to approve a major railroad merger. Now, however, commissioners judged that the threat of monopoly outweighed the apparent benefits to the railroads or shippers of combining operations. At a news conference held shortly after commissioners announced their decision, holding company chair and CEO Schmidt, described by a reporter for the *Los Angeles Times* as "stunned and angry," characterized the ICC's decision as "a horrible mistake." Up to that point, Schmidt and his top staff, confident of ICC approval, had refused to grant competing railroads access to their tracks. Instead, Schmidt had ordered similar red and yellow insignia applied to the locomotives of both railroads. Unable to escape the rhetoric of markets in a situation framed from the outset by federal officials, later that day Schmidt issued a statement to the press that "the proposed merger [would have] provided a private enterprise solution to a problem faced by both the Southern Pacific Transportation Co. and the AT & SF."[27]

Not only had ICC commissioners disapproved the merger, they ordered executives of the holding company to sell one or both of the railroads. On July 25, 1986, a writer for the *Wall Street Journal* reported "new speculation about the possible creation of a transcontinental railroad." According to a report in the *Los Angeles Times,* on April 20, 1987, directors of the holding company fired John Schmidt, "reportedly . . . displeased with the way the merger was handled." On June 30, 1987, commissioners made the divestiture order final.[28] Although politicians, shippers, and rail executives engaged in unceasing talk of markets, the administrative state for railroads continued to function.

Despite the order to prepare a plan for sale of the railroads within ninety days, disposal of the two roads took place over the course of seven years. As had been true since the 1920s, ICC commissioners had the power to block mergers, not to create them. By mid-1987, seven bidders, including an employee group, sought to purchase the Southern Pacific. In August 1988, commissioners approved purchase by Rio Grande Industries, which owned the Denver & Rio Grande Western Railroad. The combined railroads were suddenly the fifth largest in the nation. Sounding like a merger enthusiast of the 1960s, the president of the new firm promised "operating flexibility and new . . . clout" in the expected competition with still-larger railroads like the Union Pacific and with ubiquitous and price-cutting truckers. Finally, in September 1995, members of the nearly defunct Interstate Commerce Commission approved sale of the Sante Fe to the Burlington Northern. With combined tracks running from Canada to Mexico, a Burlington employee had earlier and characteristically described "efficiencies that will be created . . . [that will] take traffic from the highways."[29]

Not to be outdone, executives of the Union Pacific purchased the combined Southern Pacific and Denver and Rio Grande line. Turning aside a recommendation of attorneys at the U.S. Department of Justice that the proposed merger would prove anticompetitive, in July 1996, members of the new Surface Transportation Board approved that deal. The reasoning of board members, according to its chair, was that "history has shown that restructuring in the rail industry has strengthened the rail transportation system in the form of better service and lower rates." Sixteen years after approval of the Staggers Act, a federal regulator was invoking the alleged proofs of history in favor of railroad mergers. Less noticed at that moment was the fact that over the same time span regulators and rail executives had consolidated the nation's western railroads into two large systems, realizing the dreams of generations of rail leaders. Legendary owner of the Southern Pacific, Colis Huntington, for example, had once called for a national rail network consisting of only a few, or at best one, large rail enterprise. Equally, politicians and regulators such as William Ripley and the entire membership of the ICC in the early 1920s had advocated a national system of about twenty regional rail carriers.[30]

In the mid-1990s, however, shippers cared less about history or discarded plans for railroad consolidation and more about the threat of rate increases. In September 1997, a writer for *Chilton's Distribution* described many shippers as "mad as hell" about having "had to swallow three anticompetitive, megarail mergers." One of those shippers, Fred E. Schrodt, vice president of transportation for the large Farmland Industries, told a meeting of his counterparts that it was "time to sunset" the Surface Transportation Board. In place of the STB, Schrodt urged investigation of mergers by antitrust attorneys in the justice department. In the century-long tradition of the nation's shippers, Schrodt and his colleagues sought a federal solution to railroad rates always judged too high. For at least the moment, however, members of the new Surface Transportation Board, following in the tradition of the ICC of the 1920s, and the 1950s and 1960s, had determined to consolidate the nation's railroads into several large systems. Writing in August 1996, a reporter for *Purchasing* astutely observed that "STB has gone against the trend to deregulation." The fact was, ran the reporter's title, "Uncle Stays Involved."[31]

Construction of railroad-based intermodal systems during the 1980s and early 1990s was equally a matter of the administrative judgment of ICC officials and legislative judgment of members of Congress. At the outset, in December 1982, ICC officials declared an end to the decades-old prohibition on rail ownership of trucking firms and steamship lines. This proclamation finally opened the door for the creation of transportation companies similar to those advocated during the 1920s and 1930s by ICC commissioner Joseh Eastman and W. W. Atterbury of the Pennsylvania Railroad. Now changes came quickly, for by 1989, former ICC attorney and Denver University professor of transportation law Paul Stephen Dempsey reported that "the rail industry" had emerged as "an oligopoly" composed of "origin-to-destination intermodal megacarriers."[32]

Executives of the CSX Corporation were among the first to take advantage of the ICC's proclamation, linking their railroad network to truck and sea operations. Created in 1980 through a merger of the Chessie System and Seaboard Coast Line Industries, managers of the new CSX started with a base of twenty-seven thousand miles of track. As early as November 1982, a writer for *Industry Week* found CSX executives and leaders of their trucking subsidiary, Chessie Motor Express, "moving at a fast pace." In the future, the writer predicted, CSX was one of a few railroad companies that would emerge as a "super-transportation company" capable of carrying merchandise by rail, air, barge, and truck.[33]

John Snow presided over construction of the intermodal network at CSX. Following service in the Ford administration leading the deregulation effort and a stint as a Fellow at the market-oriented American Enterprise Institute, Snow joined CSX in 1977. With a law degree and a Ph.D. in economics and his experience in the Ford administration, Snow brought political and legal savvy to the politics of making CSX an intermodal competitor. During the 1980s, Snow relied on Congress and the ICC to facilitate purchase of intermodal units for CSX; and he equally relied on Congress and the ICC in a fruitless effort to prevent executives at firms such as Norfolk Southern from emerging as intermodal competitors.[34]

In 1983, CSX officials purchased American Commercial Lines, a barge company. Leaders of the barge operators trade association, the Water Transport Association (WTA), took up the cause against the CSX purchase. Citing the Panama Canal Act of 1912, in mid-1984 leaders of the WTA asserted that federal law prohibited railroads from owning barges and other water carriers. Also citing the always-present concern among shippers about the potential for higher rates and among remaining barge operators about lower rates, those same WTA executives urged commissioners of the ICC to require CSX to relinquish control of American Commercial Lines. For his part, Snow, as vice president of CSX, contended that "the barge industry is too competitive to be dominated by one large entity." In late July, ICC commissioners ruled unanimously in favor of CSX. In January 1986, a three-judge panel of the federal appeals court in Cincinnati affirmed the ICC's decision by a vote of 2 to 1.[35] As with airline deregulation under Alfred Kahn at the Civil Aeronautics Board several years earlier, the first steps in constructing intermodal firms during the 1980s rested on an administrative determination by ICC officials and on risk taking by Snow and his associates at CSX.

ICC officials proved more innovative in their ruling on Snow's purchase of Sea-Land. In 1986, Snow directed acquisition of Sea-Land, a firm that operated a fleet of container vessels. At that point, ICC rules did not permit CSX to manage oceangoing vessels in coordination with their rail and barge operations. In January 1987, Snow told a *Wall Street Journal* reporter that "we want to ... develop a one-stop approach to shipping." Again, Snow and top executives at CSX took a risk. In the Sea-Land case, moreover, in February 1987 ICC commissioners ruled 2 to 1 that they lacked jurisdiction and that Snow and his associates had no need for their approval. Overturning seventy-five years of precedent since the Panama Canal Act, the commission majority determined that Sea-Land and CSX were not competitive with one another. "The public will come out ahead," added a senior commission official, "because we'll have a more efficient, less costly transportation system."[36] By the mid-1980s, ICC officials had merged administrative discretion with the hoped-for price reductions into an official doctrine aimed at fostering rail ownership of barge and truck companies.

Beginning in the early 1990s, moreover, rail executives such as Snow were expressing as much optimism about the revenue potential of intermodal service as their predecessors of the 1950s and 1960s had expressed with the introduction of piggyback. During 1991, as trade-magazine writers trumpeted the success of joint rail, truck, and barge operations under such titles as "Intermodalism Continues to Make Inroads" and "Intermodal Service Stacks Up," Snow approved purchase of another barge line. Beginning in

December 1991, he authorized executives of CSX's intermodal unit, CSXI, to launch direct rail service from the Port of Baltimore to Cincinnati. Like similar CSXI facilities in Savannah, Georgia, and Mobile, Alabama, the idea, reported a writer for *Railway Age* in August 1992, was that "ocean carriers . . . can streamline their inland transportation operations by allowing a single service provider to transport the containers." Starting in fall 1992, CSXI executives ran trains seven days a week between California and a 350-mile area surrounding Chicago. Marketed as "Frequent Flyer" service, trains carried double-stacked containers into their Chicago terminal, from where CSXI ground personnel dispatched them with drivers and truck tractors to the docks of receivers. As in the first period of intermodal enthusiasm three decades earlier, Snow and his counterparts at other intermodal railroads still hoped, as one writer had it, to "'railroad' some business away from the trucking industry." In October 1992, editors of *Business Week* profiled John Snow and several other executives, describing them as "Masters of the Game" even "when times are tough." In the popular language of markets and the equally popular image of hard-driving executives, few in the trade or business presses recognized any direct connection between Snow's apparent successes with mergers and intermodal service at CSX and decisions made at the ICC and in the nation's courts.[37] Starting in 1978, passenger airlines also prospered and failed in an environment determined mostly by public policy.

AIRLINES AFTER 1978

Airlines were and remained more glamorous than railroads or trucks. In the two decades following deregulation, no one prepared a scholarly history of a trucking firm or the trucking industry as a whole. Three historians of railroads published books that in whole or in part documented the industry's "recovery" after approval of the Staggers Act in 1980.[38] Efforts to explain the consequences of deregulation for airline customers and employees, however, engaged a larger group of the nation's most talented scholars and journalists. Among those exceptionally talented scholars, Harvard University business historian Richard H. K. Vietor, writing in 1994, focused on the successful efforts of American Airlines' president Robert L. Crandall to reposition his firm to take advantage of business opportunities presented by termination of the regulatory regime. Starting in June 1980 with his election as the company's president, reports Vietor, Crandall focused on the "Profit Improvement Plan" that led to a reduction in the size of the fleet, development of hub operations at the Chicago and Dallas–Fort Worth

Airports, elimination of more than five thousand employees, and preparation of a "brilliant three-pronged marketing plan" that included the introduction of AAdvantage, the nation's first frequent flyer program. At the next stage, between 1981 and 1985, Crandall's innovations included purchase of new, more efficient aircraft and negotiation of revised labor agreements that created a two-tier wage structure and greater authority for managers to move personnel from one type of job to another. With these changes in hand, reports Vietor, Crandall and his associates "had set a course to become the largest and most profitable domestic airline."[39] In Vietor's account, Robert Crandall emerges as an innovative business executive who successfully shed the "contrived" service competition of the regulatory regime and adapted his large, complex firm to the vicissitudes of a market economy. Like accounts of John Snow at CSX, Vietor's Crandall appears as one of the industrial statesmen of the new airline industry. Like accounts of the postderegulation trucking and railroad industries prepared by journalists and economists, moreover, Vietor focuses on the consequences of reducing or eliminating the regulatory hand for employee wages, customer service, and airfares, and especially for American Airlines' overall profitability. Missing from Vietor's account, however, is an analysis of the market concentration that soon characterized the airline industry. Equally absent from Vietor's account was the centrality of the federal government in permitting that concentration to take place. In the market-oriented airline industry, however, federal officials and federal policy were sometimes invisible.[40] Crandall's duel with Donald C. Burr's People Express provides a glimpse of those invisible factors that were at the same time always constitutive of industries and markets.

Starting after 1978, entrepreneurs and investors started a number of new airlines. Sporting names such as New York Air, Midway, and Air Florida, executives of these firms promised low fares, predictable schedules, and minimal "frills" such as frequent flyer programs and costly meals. People Express was another of these recent entrants. Launching service in 1981 out of Newark Airport, executives at People Express led by Donald Burr paid lower wages to employees. Burr also directed personnel to perform several tasks, as for instance having pilots occasionally heft luggage and training every employee, including the chief financial officer, to work as flight attendants. Low wages and cross-use of employees kept expenses low, and permitted Burr to sell seats at cheaper prices than competitors. On flights from Newark to Buffalo, New York, Burr charged $38 for a peak fare and $25 off-peak, representing a whopping reduction from his competitor's fare of $99. In the market talk used regularly by journalists following deregulation, moreover, passengers "paid for what they wanted," whether it was fifty cents for coffee or $3 for checked luggage. Economists and business writers described the process of selling additional services such as meals and checked baggage as that of "unbundling" services. By whatever name, at its peak moment of growth during 1985, Burr's People Express served fifty cities, including flights to smaller cities such as Hartford, larger ones such as Miami, and even 747 service to London.[41]

A flamboyant figure, Donald Burr sought publicity for his airline and for himself. Journalists returned the favor by printing Burr's snappy quotes and by writing laudatory descriptions of his skills and style. "Anybody who attacks us in Newark," a *Wall Street Journal* reporter quoted Burr in March 1984, "has to be a slow wit." That same reporter quoted a banker describing Burr as "like a steamroller the size of a 747 jumbo jet coming down at you." Writing in 1995, journalist Thomas Petzinger Jr. reported that "Burr had created a stunningly large airline—and a successful one—from nothing." With these accounts, journalists merged market talk with more traditional business themes that stressed the virtues of risk taking and the importance of entrepreneurial skill.[42] That Burr had earned the MBA degree at Harvard University's Graduate School of Business Administration apparently added to his mystique among popular writers. Although Burr probably did not realize it, he and his contemporaries at Air Florida and Midway had inherited the daring of the "nonsked" operators who, during the 1940s and early 1950s, had promoted the first generation of "mass" air travel. Equally, Burr carried forward the tradition of Continental Airlines' Robert Six who, during the 1970s, had preached the virtues of more efficient use of aircraft and personnel.

Like Robert Six and managers of those audacious nonscheduled operators, Burr emerged as the enemy of executives at the traditional carriers. In March 1984, People Express featured 150 departures each day from Newark, the largest schedule of any airline in the New York City region. Burr had also ordered thirty-five additional jets, and boasted of shortly having "an operation in Newark as big as Delta's in Atlanta." In the market talk as war metaphor often used by business leaders, Burr added that his Newark base would prove "impregnable to invasions by carriers trying to add capacity there." Up to that point, however, People Express had served cities such as Buffalo and Columbus, Ohio, cities characterized by a *Wall Street Journal* reporter as "peripheral." As soon as Burr added service to cities judged more desirable, such as Pittsburgh and West Palm Beach, however, executives at Delta and U.S. Air cut fares on competing routes and boosted the number of flights. Again in the rhetoric of markets as warfare, an unnamed airline executive threatened that if Burr launched service to Chicago, "'American or United may pull out a cannon and blast them' in a fare war." Even so, Burr remained confident about plans to fly passengers from Newark to Los

Angeles at a fare as low as $119, compared to the standard coach fare of $433.[43]

Between June and November 1984, People Express executives led by Burr launched operations from Newark to Chicago, Detroit, San Francisco, and Denver, and direct flights from Minneapolis, Chicago, Detroit, and Cleveland to several cities in Florida. No longer competing for passengers against weaker airlines located in secondary cities, now Burr sought to take business from major carriers such as United Airlines and Robert Crandall's American in their primary markets. Burr also purchased Denver-based Frontier Airlines at a price of $300 million. At that point, however, Frontier executives were engaged in a fare war against United and Continental—and Frontier, a reporter later noted, "was losing." Few observers understood Burr's decisions. In November 1986, a writer for the *Los Angeles Times* invoked sports metaphors such as playing with "the big boys" and "life in the big leagues." Another writer thought that Burr both enjoyed the thrill of growth and simultaneously "lacked . . . discipline." Still another writer observed that "People Express forgot its roots." More likely, the effects of United and American's "cannon and blast" predicted earlier were already eroding bookings and revenues at People Express, and Burr and his top associates had conceived these moves into new markets as a short-run device. In this interpretation, Burr was "buying time—simply grabbing passengers any way he could" pending arrival of a computer system like Robert Crandall's at American Airlines.[44]

Early in the history of People Express, Burr had decided against purchasing an up-to-date computer system. Despite Burr's initial successes in boosting the number of flights, customers, and revenue, the absence of modern computing at People bestowed a considerable advantage on Robert Crandall and his managers at American. Crandall called his system yield management; and the computer system was named Sabre. When Burr launched service to key American hubs such as Chicago, Crandall's top yield manager, Barbara R. Amster, used data stored in Sabre to match People Express's low fares with a few seats. She held remaining seats for business customers who, Sabre reported, would likely make reservations closer to the time of departure. As one example, both American and People advertised $99 fares to Los Angeles. Every seat on People sold for $99. According to journalist Petzinger, however, "the average fare on the American plane might be $250." Better yet, the customer who actually paid $99 for an American seat also received free coffee, free baggage handling, and increasingly coveted AAdvantage frequent-flyer miles.[45]

As Burr became aware of the tremendous advantages that Sabre and yield management techniques had bestowed on American and his other competitors, he launched a crash program to develop a reservation system.

Burr hired experts from the NCR Corporation and then from American Express to construct one for him. No matter, because sophisticated programs like Sabre and Crandall's use of it to develop a program of yield management could not be tested and implemented at People Express in only a few weeks or months, or even in a year of trying. In the short run, the absence of an up-to-date computer system coupled with Burr's already antiquated telephone reservation system left thousands making repeat calls to overwhelmed personnel. Those fortunate enough to have made reservations often encountered overbooked flights, sometimes as high as 100 percent. By late 1986, People Express had acquired a large debt and was losing money daily. Years later, Donald J. Carty, one of Crandall's top executives, boasted that "we devised the fare structure that put them out of business."[46]

In December 1986, Frank A. Lorenzo purchased both People Express and Frontier for $113 million. Again, Burr had paid $300 million to purchase Frontier. In turn, Lorenzo put these two new properties under the umbrella of his Texas Air Corporation, which also encompassed Continental, Eastern, and New York Air. By early 1987, Lorenzo's Texas Air had emerged as one of the largest airline operations in the United States.[47]

Journalists explained the fast collapse of People Express with sport and other metaphors. In November 1986, a writer for the *Los Angeles Times* concluded that Burr and his associates had learned "the hard way about life in the big leagues." Switching to a metaphor drawn from popular images of urban gang warfare, the writer added that "American, United, et al., do not surrender turf easily."[48] Less a matter of turf control or other favored expressions of the day, the story of People Express and Donald Burr was in part one of entrepreneurial zeal not matched with a long-term business plan and a staff possessing the substantial resources and managerial capacity to implement that plan.

In an industry thought to be governed by fluid markets, however, popular idioms such as "turf," "big leagues," and "putting them out of business" failed to describe another part of People's demise. Like trucking, deregulation of airlines had permitted enthusiasts such as Donald Burr to launch new firms, bringing about sharp price competition and lower fares; and like trucking and railroading, leaders of airline firms such as Robert Crandall, Donald Carty, and Frank Lorenzo now directed the rapid consolidation of the airline industry. Not an isolated case, the rise and collapse of People Express was matched by the equally rapid appearance and disappearance of other airline firms. According to the results of a study by deregulation critics Paul Stephen Dempsey and Andrew R. Goetz, between 1979 and 1988 airline executives completed fifty-one mergers and acquisitions. As examples, Robert Crandall's American Airlines purchased AirCal, Delta bought

Western, Northwest acquired Republic, and U.S. Air executives purchased both Piedmont and Pacific Southwest. In 1991, Eastern Airlines, one of the industry's oldest carriers, entered bankruptcy, never emerging from it, further diminishing the number of competitors. According to Dempsey and Goetz, moreover, the fierce competition and subsequent financial losses at the hands of innovators such as Donald Burr and Robert Crandall had also encouraged airline executives to engage in their own form of merger "mania."[49]

As part of the merger process, executives of surviving airlines such as those at Delta, American, and U.S. Air consolidated flight operations at key airports. During the 1980s, Americans learned that the word "hub" meant an airport at which one or at most two airlines served most of the passengers. As examples of the consolidation of air travel into hubs, in 1977 Northwest Airlines serviced 45.9 percent of the passengers at the Minneapolis/St. Paul Airport. By 1987, Northwest executives had constructed a hub that served 81.6 percent of that airport's passengers. "At 15 of the nation's major airports," two economists reported in 1988, "one carrier controls more than half the business or two control over 70 percent of the business." Historian Vietor concludes, moreover, that "the full development of hub operations . . . created powerful barriers to entry by potential competitors."[50]

In the evolving lexicon of postderegulation airline industry, moreover, industry observers described these consolidated operations at one airport not simply as a hub, but as a "fortress hub." Writing in July 1987, a reporter for the *Wall Street Journal* pointed to changes at the St. Louis airport that had made it into one of those fortress hubs. Before 1978, he recounted, five airlines had served most of the passengers at Lambert–St. Louis International Airport. Following deregulation, an additional nine airlines competing for their share of some twenty million passengers. By mid-1987, he added, executives of Trans World Airlines "enjoy[ed] a degree of dominance . . . that any airline would have envied prior to deregulation." For instance, TWA employees in St. Louis directed 317 departures each day, compared to employees of their next largest competitor, Southwest Airlines, who managed only 22 daily departures.[51] Like their postderegulation counterparts in the truck and railroad industries, airline executives constructed large, complex, coast-to-coast passenger systems, including those fortress hubs. In retrospect, however, the period of the 1960s and 1970s under the regulatory regime was actually the moment of greatest airline choice and service (but not price) competition. The many academic experts such as George Hilton and Paul MacAvoy who had studied transportation prices before deregulation had not predicted that deregulation would also lead to creation of these fortress hubs.

Hilton and MacAvoy were participants in a century-long tradition of academic experts who advocated modification of the nation's transportation system. Starting in the early decades of the twentieth century, university faculty, including Emory Johnson and William Ripley, had advised legislators and ICC members about railroad rates and service. Along with other members of that generation of academic experts, Johnson and Ripley perceived themselves in the service of government, and often recommended greater or lesser degrees of federal regulation as a solution to railroad problems. Johnson and Ripley were among the many architects of the administrative state.[52]

In the 1960s, a new generation of academic transportation experts including Hilton and MacAvoy as well as John Snow and Alfred Kahn accepted high-level appointments in the federal government. Members of this generation of experts were less likely to perceive themselves as architects of government agencies and more likely to identify as advocates for diminished government.[53] Having reached adulthood under the regulatory regime, however, economists such as Snow and Kahn had only the limited results of unregulated airline pricing in Texas and California on which to assert the superiority of national deregulation and creation of national markets over the workings of regulators and attorneys serving truckers, railroaders, and airline executives. Despite the paucity of data available to them, members of this generation of economists, again including Snow and Kahn, nonetheless identified their federal positions as an opportunity to convert the largely hypothetical findings of graduate seminars and dissertation research into administrative and legislative directives packing consequences for millions of shippers, receivers, and consumers. Equally, at the moment that Presidents Johnson, Nixon, Ford, and Carter appointed members of this generation of economists to important, policymaking positions in the federal government, all understood that they had embarked on new and potentially risky efforts to alter or abolish the workings of the regulatory regime in favor of markets that did not yet exist. In retrospect, up to 1980, the agencies of the regulatory regime such as the CAB, the ICC, and the rate bureaus had fostered higher wages as well as higher shipping charges and (sometimes) higher airline ticket prices. Simultaneously, those agencies of the regulatory regime had also fostered predictable shipping rates, frequent and comfortable airline service, and steady employment. Nevertheless, members of that generation of economists and other academic experts—who often held lifetime tenure at the nation's leading universities—possessed immense confidence in their ability to predict that creation of transportation markets would lead to improved service at lower prices for shippers, receivers, and passengers. Ironically, their prescriptions echoed the occasional calls of an earlier generation of experts such as Harold Moulton and Joseph Eastman, who had begun to contemplate the idea of efficiency through markets during the 1930s.

After 1980, members of a new generation of academic experts (still economists, mostly) joined their aging counterparts in debates about airline ticket prices. As early as 1981, only three years after airline deregulation, John R. Meyer, a senior economist at Harvard University, and Clinton V. Oster Jr., a younger economist at Indiana University, perceived no reason to worry about high ticket prices. "A carrier withdrawing from a market because it cannot compete with a competitor's low fare," they contended, "can easily re-enter that market should the other carrier attempt to exploit a newly acquired market position by increasing fares above competitive levels." Contemporary economists labeled Meyer and Oster's idea the theory of contestable markets. Even when airlines such as Robert Crandall's American dominated traffic at a hub airport, went the reasoning among proponents of this idea, American executives would not raise prices too high out of concern that a competitor would enter that hub, or reenter it.[54] In 1981, however, Meyer and Oster were making predictions, not reporting on the concrete responses of airline executives such as Robert Crandall and Donald Burr.

By the mid-1980s, accumulating evidence of rising ticket prices had persuaded several economists that the promise of contestable markets did not always work out in practice. Between 1977 and 1983, economist Elizabeth E. Bailey had served with Alfred Kahn as a member of the Civil Aeronautics Board that bought about administrative deregulation of airlines. Reporting on a sample of two hundred airline markets, in 1985 Bailey and her coauthors reported that "the contestability benchmark does not fully hold sway in the first years after deregulation." At that point, however, Bailey judged "the degree of this market power . . . [to be] relatively small."[55]

By the late 1980s, studying the consequences of deregulation for airline ticket prices had emerged as a cottage industry among economists. In line with the conclusion that Bailey and her colleagues had reached, still other economists determined that the threat of additional airline competition had not actually led to lower ticket prices. In 1989, as one example, Thomas J. Zlatoper, an economics professor at Cleveland's John Carroll University, and Paul W. Bauer, an economist at the Federal Reserve Bank of Cleveland, concluded that "the airline industry is not perfectly contestable." In 1989, as yet a second example, Severin Borenstein, a University of Michigan economist, found that "dominance of major airports by one or two carriers . . . appears to result in higher fares for consumers."[56]

Even economist Alfred Kahn, who a decade earlier had presided over administrative deregulation of airlines as chair of the Civil Aeronautics

Board, now expressed surprise at the degree to which creation of airport hubs had permitted airline executives to boost ticket prices. Writing in the precise but sometimes opaque language of a professional economist, in 1988 Kahn noted "the diminishing disciplinary effectiveness of potential entry by totally new firms, and the increased likelihood, in consequence, of monopolistic exploitation."[57] Stated plainly, what Kahn and these other economists learned was that airline executives, including Robert Crandall at American Airlines, had created fortress hubs, trumping earlier predictions of market contestability.

By the late 1980s, moreover, politicians and journalists were also discovering that the promise of lower prices for airline tickets through a process of market contestability did not appear to be working. Less likely to employ the apolitical rhetoric of professional economists, those politicians and popular writers identified the new fortress hubs with poor service and jacked-up prices. "For the second time in less than two weeks," reported a writer for the *Business Journal* in late March 1988, "the major airlines that serve Milwaukee have sharply increased fares and eliminated several highly discounted rates." No longer content to celebrate the advantages of markets, a U.S. senator talked in frightening terms about passengers "looking down a gun barrel." Months earlier, a writer for the *Wall Street Journal* writer had warned ominously about "signs of a regulatory backlash against the industry." In February 1989, another *Wall Street Journal* writer asked rhetorically whether "it is not time for re-regulation."[58]

Proponents of that "regulatory backlash" failed to develop a common agenda and widespread support for reregulating airline prices and service. As early as 1986, a journalist reported that "a few calls for 're-regulation' can already be heard around the nation's capital." Late in 1986, concerned about delays at TWA's St. Louis hub, Senator John C. Danforth of Missouri sought legislation to require airlines to report late and cancelled flights. In April 1989, three additional senators joined Danforth in writing letters to Secretary of Transportation Skinner and Attorney General Richard "Dick" Thornburgh. Danforth and his colleagues asked for answers to questions about the workings of the airlines' fortress hubs and prices charged customers for tickets. One question was whether justice department officials had identified a pattern of "predatory" price cuts by executives of airlines that dominated a hub to the detriment of new entrants.[59] As historian Vietor points out, Robert Crandall had used precisely that technique in defending business at his Chicago hub against new competition from Donald Burr's People Express.

During the fall of 1989, senators turned from writing letters to preparation of specific proposals for reducing prices. For instance, Danforth and

Senator John S. McCain discussed the idea of requiring airline executives, including Robert Crandall, to sell their computerized reservation systems. They also discussed whether the federal government ought to limit the percentage of gates Crandall and his counterparts controlled at an airport. "Viscerally," McCain contended, "I'm not in favor of government intervention, but I see a clear need in this case." Yet another idea under consideration for promoting greater price competition was elimination of the airlines' frequent-flyer programs, which critics characterized as "legalized kickbacks." According to McCain, however, elimination of frequent-flyer programs "would be 'political dynamite.'" Unlike the years leading up to deregulation, moreover, airline executives now defended the absence of a federal regulatory agency and specific federal pricing guidelines. Writing in October 1988, a writer for the *Los Angeles Times* observed that the "airlines . . . will fight any proposed legislation."[60] Reminiscent of Eisenhower and Weeks's first efforts in 1955 and 1956 to bring about limited deregulation of rail and trucking firms, in the late 1980s Danforth and McCain found few in the Senate and House interested in refashioning the airline market once again.

At first glance, proponents of deregulation and often-celebrated markets had triumphed in the field of air transportation. In reality, the absence of overt federal action to limit the growth of fortress hubs had framed the postderegulation airline industry. Sounding like Senator McCain and his colleagues, Alfred Kahn found "a lamentable failure of the administration to . . . disallow a single merger or to press for divestiture of the computerized reservation systems." The decision by senior officials at the departments of transportation and justice not to intervene in the airlines' version of merger mania constituted a policy. By their cumulative decision to permit mergers to go forward, authors of that policy enabled Crandall and his counterparts to restructure their firms and eventually to reorganize the industry around a hub and spoke system dominated by a few large carriers.[61] During the 1980s, the nation's dominant transportation policy consisted of authorizing truck, air, and rail executives to merge operations, including a limited number of mergers between operators of different transportation "modes."

In a brilliant book, historian Vietor asks, "[W]hat causes governmental intervention in and withdrawal from markets?" In the transportation field, however, government did not intervene and withdraw from markets that in some organic fashion had sprung up of their own volition and independently of government. Instead, whether in 1920, 1935, 1938, or again in 1978 and 1980, legislators and administrators formed the transportation market. Put another way, for all the market talk that surrounded transportation politics before and after 1980, state officials had been and remained constitutive of those markets.

The barrier to understanding deregulation of transportation firms in 1978 and 1980 as more than a simple withdrawal of the federal government from markets rests upon the limits of language and with our ideologically driven conceptualization of a market as a counterpart to an imagined state of political nature—a place sacred in its origin and lacking institutional constraint. Rather than dichotomizing markets and regulation, it makes more sense to perceive them along a continuum shaped in both cases by the leaders of the American state—with regulation and deregulation representing different types of legal and administrative strategies for organizing the activities of transportation managers and workers.[62]

Nor had deregulation brought an end to direct subsidies for construction and maintenance of the transportation infrastructure. Starting in the nineteenth century and extending to the end of the twentieth, federal officials financed construction and maintenance of waterways and highways, and then airways. By any standard, those subsidies were lavish, especially for highway building. Between 1956 and 1990, federal officials paid 90 percent of the costs of constructing the National System of Interstate and Defense Highways, known popularly as the Interstate system. Although in 1956 leaders of the American Trucking Associations had agreed to higher gasoline and diesel taxes to cover part of the immense cost of constructing the Interstate system, once completed, that system, which by 2002 included forty-seven thousand miles of limited-access highways, made coast-to-coast trucking operations possible and then routine. In 1991, the federal government spent $19.5 billion for ground transportation facilities (mostly highways) and another $8.1 billion on airways and $3.1 billion on waterways. In fact, subsidies paid on a mode-by-mode basis added to the political construction of the transportation industries rather than to creation of transportation companies. Starting only in 1991, as part of the Intermodal Surface Transportation Efficiency Act, Congress and the president authorized expenditure during the next six years of a portion of $153 billion in federal transportation funds for local officials to build connections between airports, seaports, truck depots, and railyards.[63] Because local officials rather than state or federal officials directed construction of those connections, however, no one person or agency possessed the capacity or authority to coordinate those urban-intermodal connections from one city to the next.

Context had also mattered greatly in shaping the idea of three transportation industries rather than one. In the nineteenth century, railroads emerged as the nation's first "big" business, and rail executives suffered from a reputation for poor treatment of shippers and riders. In 1887, Congress created the Interstate Commerce Commission as a first step in regulating railroads. With the Hepburn Act of 1906 and the Mann-Elkins Act of

1910, Congress and two presidents established federal authority to determine railroad rates. Starting in 1920, Congress and President Woodrow Wilson authorized substantial regulation of railroad rates, service, and even profits by the Interstate Commerce Commission. A decade later, with the onset of harsh depression days, many believed that regulation comprised one of the paths to economic recovery. In 1935 Congress and President Franklin Roosevelt brought truckers under their own regulatory wing at the ICC. In 1938, those same federal officials placed airlines under the supportive supervision of a new agency, the Civil Aeronautics Administration (in 1942, the Civil Aeronautics Board). By the end of the 1930s, however, the incipient idea of transportation companies so favored by transportation experts such as Harold Moulton and at least rhetorically by President Roosevelt had been supplanted by the reality of three bodies of governing legislation, three administrative agencies, three areas of litigation, three distinct subsidy systems, and consequently by the appearance for administrative and legal purposes of three industries.

During the 1960s, presidents and their top aides asserted that another round of administrative coordination would foster a "fine-tuning" of the economy. Between 1966 and 1968, Alan Boyd, the first secretary of transportation, hoped to guide improved coordination among surface and air transportation. By the early 1970s, however, economists and journalists were reporting arrival of "stagflation," that unpredicted and hurtful mix of rising prices and falling levels of employment. Up to 1974, President Richard Nixon supported both enhanced administrative controls and deregulation. In his plan to create a number of "super" agencies, President Nixon sought to merge transportation and land use planning, creating more coherent cities and more coherent transportation. With the Penn Central bankruptcy, starting in 1970 Nixon also set in motion a search for a constituency that would support deregulation. Ultimately, Nixon's resignation tarnished the politics of enhanced transportation coordination. Starting with President Gerald Ford and concluding with President Jimmy Carter and his energetic aides, the politics of deregulation superseded the politics of administrative coordination. In the idiom of that day, deregulation was "the only show in town." During the period between 1920 and 1980, federal officials, including members of Congress, judges, administrators, and especially presidents of the United States, had constituted the nation's transportation systems and the nation's transportation markets.[64] History had set the frameworks within which those politicians, including their successors of the 1980s and 1990s, worked.

PREFACE

1. Mark H. Rose and Bruce E. Seely, "Building the Interstate Highway System: Road Engineers and the Implementation of Public Policy," *Journal of Policy History* 2 (January 1990): 23–55. See also Brian Balogh, "Reorganizing the Organizational Synthesis: Federal-Professional Relations in Modern America," *Studies in American Political Development* 5 (Spring 1991): 119–72, which historian William R. Childs brought to our attention several years after publication and which proved immensely helpful as we began to formulate key concepts.

2. David A. Kirsch, *The Electric Vehicle and the Burden of History* (New Brunswick, NJ: Rutgers University Press, 2000).

3. Books that influenced our understanding of experts and expertise in American politics include Robert S. Wiebe, *The Search for Order, 1877–1920* (New York: Hill & Wang, 1967); Samuel P. Hays, *Conservation and the Gospel of Efficiency: The Progressive Conservation Movement, 1890–1920* (Cambridge, MA: Harvard University Press, 1959); and Thomas L. Haskel, ed., *The Authority of Experts: Studies in History and Theory* (Bloomington: Indiana University Press, 1984). In his cogent and wide-ranging "Reorganizing the Organizational Synthesis," Balogh makes clear that scholars of expertise such as Wiebe developed greater sophistication over time, largely by jettisoning the progressive era's flawed image of experts as neutral decision makers working outside the political process. Our previous publications as well as results of research on this book confirm that insight.

4. K. Austin Kerr, *American Railroad Politics: Rates, Wages, and Efficiency* (Pittsburgh, PA: University of Pittsburgh Press, 1968).

CHAPTER 1

1. Harold G. Moulton, *The American Transportation Problem* (Washington, DC: Brookings Institution, 1933).

2. Albro Martin, *Railroads Triumphant: The Growth, Rejection, and Rebirth of a Vital American Force* (New York: Oxford University Press, 1992), 81.

3. Theda Skocpol and Kenneth Finegold, "State Capacity and Economic Intervention in the Early New Deal," *Political Science Quarterly* 97 (1982): 255-78; Stephen

Skowronek, *Building a New American State: The Expansion of National Administrative Capacities, 1877–1920* (New York: Cambridge University Press, 1982); Martin J. Sklar, *The Corporate Reconstruction of American Capitalism, 1890–1916: The Market, the Law, and Politics* (New York: Cambridge University Press, 1988); Morton Keller, *Regulating a New Economy: Public Policy and Economic Change in America, 1900–1933* (Cambridge, MA: Harvard University Press, 1990); and Olivier Zunz, *Making America Corporate, 1870–1920* (Chicago: University of Chicago Press, 1990), among others. See also Brian Balogh, "Reorganizing the Organizational Synthesis: Federal-Professional Relations in Modern America," *Studies in American Political Development* 5 (Spring 1991): 119–72; Mark H. Leff, "Revisioning U.S. Political History," *American Historical Review* 100 (June 1995): 829–53; and Larry G. Gerber, "Corporatism and State Theory: A Review Essay for Historians," *Social Science History* 19 (Fall 1995): 313–32.

4. This observation is not intended to suggest that the absence of a national transportation is necessarily bad, because many factors, some of them structural, conspire to prevent the development of such policies. Foremost among these is the federalist nature of American government, which imposes substantial burdens of cooperation upon officials working across different levels of government. This theme figures prominently, for example, in Bruce Seely's history of the Bureau of Public Roads: *Building the America Highway System: Engineers as Policy Makers* (Philadelphia: Temple University Press, 1987), and in William R. Childs, *The Texas Railroad Commission: Understanding Regulation in America to the Mid-Twentieth Century* (College Station, TX: Texas A&M University Press, 2005).

5. This description of the politics of transportation aligns well with the formulation offered by Keith D. Revell, *Building Gotham: Civic Culture and Public Policy in New York City, 1898–1938* (Baltimore: Johns Hopkins University Press, 2003), 275. "The conflicts of industrial society created winners and losers who competed for state assistance, each demanding that the work of the government advance their own special interest and each conceiving of the general interest as merely an extension of their own concerns."

6. Historians have found railroads a vital subject for understanding issues at the intersection of American society, politics, and economic reform at the turn of the century, such as regulation. Their work demonstrates the multitude of factors that prompted the emergence of railroad regulation, including the concerns of investors, merchants, shippers, consumers, farmers, and citizens in general. This constellation of factors was apparent by the last decades of the nineteenth century, as seen in Lee Benson, *Merchants, Farmers, & Railroads: Railroad Regulation and New York Politics, 1850–1887* (Cambridge, MA: Harvard University Press, 1955); and George H. Miller, *Railroads and the Granger Laws* (Madison: University of Wisconsin Press, 1971). A selective sample of the library of broader works on the origin and character of railroad regulation includes Robert Wiebe, *The Search for Order, 1877–1920* (New York: Hill and Wang, 1967); Gabriel Kolko, *Railroads and Regulation, 1877–1916* (Princeton, NJ: Princeton University Press, 1965); K. Austin Kerr, *American Railroad Politics, 1914–1920: Rates, Wages, and Efficiency* (Pittsburgh, PA: University of Pittsburgh Press, 1968); William Francis Deverell, *Railroad Crossing: Californians and the Railroad, 1850–1910* (Berkeley: University of California Press, 1994); Gerald Berk, *Alternative Tracks: The Constitution of American Industrial Order, 1865–1917* (Baltimore: Johns Hopkins University Press, 1994); and David Vogel, *Kindred Strangers: The Uneasy Relationship between Politics and Business in America* (Princeton, NJ: Princeton University Press, 1996). Steven W. Usselman, *Regulating Railroad Innovation: Business, Technology, and Politics in America, 1840–1920* (Cambridge,

New York: Cambridge University Press, 2002), offers the most recent view of the subject, emphasizing the combination of technological, economic, and structural concerns that railroads confronted at the turn of the century. Childs, *Texas Railroad Commission,* especially 11–141, examines a leading state-level actor in the history of regulation and counters the perception that regulation was strictly a national development. Perhaps the best short overview on regulation in general remains Thomas K. McGraw, "Regulation in America: A Review Article," *Business History Review* 49 (Summer 1975): 159–83, but his review is supplemented by the recent summary from Maury Klein, "Competition and Regulation: The Railroad Model," *Business History Review* 64, no. 2 (Summer 1990): 311–25, and by a review of the history and development of regulation in the nineteenth and early twentieth centuries, including attention to the various academic theories of regulation, in Roger B. Horowitz, *The Irony of Regulatory Reform: The Deregulation of American Telecommunications* (New York: Oxford University Press, 1989), 22–89. See also Richard H. K. Vietor, *Contrived Competition: Regulation and Deregulation in America* (Cambridge, MA: Belknap Press of Harvard University Press, 1994).

7. Much recent scholarly attention to government regulation by economists has focused on the efficiency (or lack thereof) and economic consequences of regulation. But regulatory programs also were driven by other visions, including the elusive concept of the "public interest," which often translated into demands to use the power of government to balance the potentially coercive powers of large corporations. That this attitude could foster demands for regulatory oversight is evident beyond the railroads. For example, during the 1920s concerns in Congress about the possible monopolization of political speech on the airwaves guided creation of radio regulations amidst antidemocratic rhetoric similar to that surrounding the railroads. See David A. Moss and Michael R. Fein, "Radio Regulation Revisited: Coase, the FCC, and the Public Interest," *Journal of Policy History* 15 (2003): 389–416; also McCraw, "Regulation in America."

8. Summaries of important regulatory legislation can be found in Keith L. Bryant Jr., *Railroads in the Twentieth Century; Encyclopedia of American Business History and Biography* (New York: Bruccoli Clark Layman/Facts on File, 1988), and Martin, *Enterprise Denied;* see also Emory R. Johnson and Thurman W. Van Metre, *Principles of Railroad Transportation* (New York: D. Appleton and Company, 1916), and H. G. Taylor, "Simplification of Railroad Regulation," *Annals of the American Academy of Political and Social Science* no. 187 (September 1936): 49–50. We thank Al Churella for drawing to our attention comments on the Panama Canal Act by James W. Ely Jr., *Railroads and American Law* (Lawrence,KS: University Press of Kansas, 2001), 236.

9. The role of state regulators in this process is treated by William R. Childs, "State Regulators and Pragmatic Federalism in the United States, 1889–1945," *Business History Review* 75, no. 4 (2001): 701–39, and Childs, *Texas Railroad Commission,* 11–141. Childs's study emphasizes the day-to-day workings of regulators, as well as the give-and-take between state and federal agencies. His concept of "pragmatic federalism" emphasizes the importance of this complex intergovernmental minuet, which in turn demonstrates that regulation was not strictly a national-level enterprise.

10. See Kerr, *American Railroad Politics;* also Walker Hines, *War History of American Railroads* (New Haven, CT: Yale University Press, 1929); William J. Cunningham, *American Railroads* (New York: McGraw-Hill Book Co., 1922); Sidney Miller, *Inland Transportation* (New York: McGraw-Hill Book Company, 1933), 156–69; John F. Stover, *American Railroads* (Chicago: University of Chicago Press, 1961), 190–91; Aaron A. Godfrey, *Government Operation of the Railroads: Its Necessity, Success and Consequences*

(Austin, TX: Jenkins Publishing Co., 1974); Ely, *Railroads and American Law,* 241–46; and "Walker D. Hines," in Bryant, *Railroads in the Twentieth Century,* 201–21.

11. Again, see Kerr, *American Railroad Politics;* and Miller, *Inland Transportation,* 170–83. The following section draws heavily upon these works.

12. Biographical information from http://bioguide.congress.gov/scripts/biodisplay. pl?index=C000988 and http://columbia.thefreedictionary.com/Esch,%20John%20Jacob.

13. See "Esch-Cummins Bill Passed by Senate and House," *Railway Age* 68 (February 27, 1920): 617–27; summary discussions of the bill are in Kerr, *American Railroad Politics,* 204–27; Miller, *Inland Transportation,* 170–83; Ely, *Railroads and American Law,* 246–50. Brian Balogh, in "Reorganizing the Organizational Synthesis," 157, observes that "The National Transportation Act (1920) completed the authority of the ICC."

14. Quotation from Ari Hoogenboom and Olive Hoogenboom, *A History of the ICC: From Panacea to Palliative* (New York: W. W. Norton & Company, 1976), 97. Herbert H. Harwood Jr., *Invisible Giants: The Empires of Cleveland's Van Sweringen Brothers* (Bloomington: Indiana University Press, 2003), 73, presented the problems that the act sought to address quite succinctly: overcompetition, overregulation, and underinvestment.

15. See I. Leo Sharfman, *History of the Interstate Commerce Commission: A Study in Administrative Law and Procedure,* 4 vols. (New York: Commonwealth Fund, 1931–1937), and Pendleton Herring, *Public Administration and the Public Interest* (New York: Russell & Russell, 1936), 179–225.

16. U.S. Interstate Commerce Commission, *Interstate Commerce Commission Activities, 1887–1937* (Washington, DC: Government Printing Office, 1937), 44.

17. Alfred P. Thom, "The Reconstruction of Railway Transportation," *Railway Age* 69 (December 10, 1920): 767.

18. See U.S. Interstate Commerce Commission (hereafter cited as ICC), *34th Annual Report* (1920), 6–11. The Railway Labor Board was a compromise element in the 1920 Transportation Act. Charged with overseeing labor relations in the industry, the Board actually possessed limited power. See Joshua Bernhardt, *The Railroad Labor Board: Its History, Activities, and Organization* (Baltimore: Johns Hopkins University Press, 1923); Harry D. Wolf, *The Railroad Labor Board* (Chicago: University of Chicago Press, 1927); Robert H. Zieger, *Republicans and Labor, 1919–1929* (Lexington: University of Kentucky Press, 1969); and Colin H. Davis, *Power at Odds: The 1922 National Railroad Shopmen's Strike* (Urbana: University of Illinois Press, 1997).

19. Such contests between state and federal officials figure prominently in Keller, *Regulating a New Economy.*

20. U.S. ICC, *35th Annual Report* (1921), 6–11.

21. ICC historian I. L. Sharfman considered the 1922 rate case the commission's "high-water mark in rate regulation." Quoted by Hoogenboom and Hoogenboom, *History of the ICC,* 102.

22. U.S. ICC, *34th Annual Report* (1920), 11–25; *36th Annual Report* (1922), 6–16.

23. See U.S. ICC, *ICC Activities,* 142–43; and Sharfman, *The Interstate Commerce Commission,* vol. 3A, 95–319; and Gerald Berk, "Whose Hubris? Brandeis, Scientific Management, and the Railroads," 131–32, 137, in Kenneth Lipartito and David B. Sicilia, *Constructing Corporate America: History, Politics, Culture* (Oxford : Oxford University Press, 2004). See also E. I. Lewis, "Railroad Valuation," *Annals of the American Academy of Political and Social Science* no. 171 (January 1934): 172–79; William Z. Ripley, *Railroads: Finance and Organization* (New York: Longmans, Green, & Co., 1915; repr., New York: Arno Press, 1981), 334–39; Harold G. Moulton, *American Transporta-*

tion Problem (Washington, DC: Brookings Institution, 1933), 366–76; Kent T. Healy, *The Economics of Transportation in America* (New York: Ronald Press Company, 1940), 540–41. The general question of watered stock is discussed in Jonathan Barron Baskin and Paul J. Miranti Jr., *A History of Corporate Finance* (New York: Cambridge University Press, 1997), 1242–44; 189–97.

24. U.S. ICC, *39th Annual Report* (1925), *41st Annual Report* 17; (1927), 61; *43rd Annual Report* (1929), 64.

25. The legal questions revolved around competing definitions of how to define and implement valuation. See U.S. ICC, *34th Annual Report* (1920), 69–70; *35th Annual Report* (1921), 13, 51, 55–56; *43rd Annual Report* (1929), 25; Sharfman, *Interstate Commerce Commission*, vol. 3A, 102–103, 206–95; Paul J. Miranti Jr., "The Mind's Eye of Reform: The ICC's Bureau of Statistics and a Vision of Regulation, 1887–1940," *Business History Review* 63 (Autumn 1989): 496–99; Keller, *Regulating a New Economy*, 54–55; and J. F. Christ, "The Supreme Court Decision in O'Fallon Case," *Journal of Business* 2 (July 1929): 233–47.

26. U.S. ICC, *37th Annual Report.* (1923), 16–17; *39th Annual Report* (1925), 17; *41st Annual Report* (1927), 61.

27. See, for example, "N.I.T. League Desires Repeal of Valuation Act," *Railway Age* 83 (December 3, 1927): 1123–24.

28. See Sharfman, *Interstate Commerce Commission*, vol. 3A, 39–42; Ripley, *Railroads: Finance and Organization*, 334–39; Moulton, *American Transportation Problem*, 366–76; Healy, *The Economics of Transportation*, 540–41.

29. Such naiveté led historian Albro Martin to scorn the entire proceeding. "Except to take up incredible amounts of space on library shelves, the reports of the valuation agency have never served any viable purpose." Sharfman offered a more charitable assessment, claiming valuation "met a real need in the 'trial and error' development of a method of control that after 1920 moved away from a restrictive toward a more affirmative approach." Martin, *Railroads Triumphant*, 357–58; Sharfman quoted from "Valuation Act of 1913," in Bryant, *Railroads in the Twentieth Century*, 449.

30. Recent articles by Miranti Jr., "The Mind's Eye of Reform"; Gregory L. Thompson, "Misused Product Costing in the American Railroad Industry," *Business History Review* 63 (Autumn): 510–54; idem, "How Cost Ignorance Derailed the Pennsylvania Railroad's Efforts to Save Its Passenger Service, 1929–1961," *Journal of Transport History*, 3rd ser., 16 (September 1995): 134–58; and Berk, "Whose Hubris?" deal with accounting, regulation, and the railroads. The section that follows rests heavily upon their work. The more general proposition that developments in accounting help expand our understanding of regulation and other changes in this time period can be seen in Robert Cuff, "Creating Control Systems: Edwin F. Gay and the Central Bureau of Planning and Statistics, 1917–1919," *Business History Review* 63 (Autumn 1989): 614–56; see also the work of Theodore M. Porter, *Trust in Numbers: The Pursuit of Objectivity in Science and Public Life* (Princeton, NJ: Princeton University Press, 1995). Judith McGaw notes the importance of accounting information for a very different industry (papermaking) in *Most Wonderful Machine: Mechanization and Social Change in Berkshire Paper Making, 1801–1885* (Princeton, NJ: Princeton University Press, 1987).

31. Significantly, the first technical division formed inside the ICC was the Bureau of Statistics, organized in 1887 to gather information that appeared annually after 1889 as *Statistics of Railways in the United States*. Henry Carter Adams, the ICC's first chief statistician, and his mentor, commissioner Thomas M. Cooley, saw accounting data as a

means of removing politics from the ICC's deliberations in the setting of rates. According to political scientist Gerald Berk, the strategy of ICC officials called for using accounting data to regulate the rate of return earned by rail corporations. See Miranti, "Mind's Eye of Reform," 478–79; Paul J. Miranti Jr., *Accountancy Comes of Age: The Development of an American Profession, 1886–1940* (Chapel Hill: University of North Carolina Press, 1990), 89–90; Berk, "Whose Hubris?" 122–25.

32. The ICC's efforts in terms of accounting are outlined in U.S. ICC, *Activities,* 73–75, 105–10, 112–14. Over the next twenty years, the ICC and railroads continuously updated railroad accounting practices, such as their attempt to cover depreciation during the 1920s. See every ICC *Annual Report* through the 1920s; and articles in the trade journals such as "I.C.C. to Prescribe Depreciation Charges," *Railway Age* 75 (September 1, 1923): 383–88; J. E. Slater, "I.C.C. Statistics and Operating Efficiency," *Railway Age* 75 (September 8, 1923): 427–30; and "Depreciation Accounting Prescribed by I.C.C.," *Railway Age* 91 (September 12, 1931): 401–402, 465.

33. Berk, "Whose Hubris?" 130–33; Miranti, *Age of Accountancy,* 90; Miller, *Railroads and the Granger Laws,* 17–23; T. W. Van Metre, *Transportation in the United States* (Chicago: Foundation Press, 1939), 184–85; and Sharfman, *History of the ICC,* vol. 3A, 316. See also John Bauer, "The Federal Valuation of Railroads in Relation to a Definite Policy of National Railway Control," *American Economic Association Review* 9 (March 1919): 124; "Professor Irving Fisher on Railroad Cost Accounting," *Railway Age* 87 (November 9, 1929): 1083–84; and "Cost Accounting Not Applicable to Railroads," *Railway Age* 84 (March 31, 1928): 738–42.

34. Historian Gregory L. Thompson, among others, has disputed the assertion about the high fixed costs of railroad operation and also argued that railroad executives simply failed to pursue the question of product costing. Thompson claims that railroad managers actually "feared the effects of accurate cost data on railroads' relations with shippers, regulatory agencies, and the general public." Thompson, "Misused Product Costing," 513. See also his "Misused Product Costing in the American Railroad Industry: Southern Pacific Passenger Service between the Wars," *Business History Review* 63 (Autumn): 510–54.

35. Martin, *Railroads Triumphant,* 200.

36. A number of economists have written about these competing philosophies of rate setting. See especially Owen Ely, *Railway Rates and Cost of Service* (Boston and New York: Houghton Mifflin Company, 1924), 40–73, but information is also found in Sharfman, *History of the ICC,* vol. 3A, 319, 425–63., and Childs, *Texas Railroad Commission,* 21–24.

37. Students of the ICC have long debated whether the commissioners should have done more to address this challenging dilemma of the basis for rate setting. All have noted that changing from value of service to cost of service would have been an enormously complicated exercise that would have affected railroads, shippers, manufacturers, farmers, and the economy as a whole. See John R. Meyer, Merton J. Peck, John Stenason, and Charles Zwick, *The Economics of Competition in the Transportation Industries* (Cambridge, MA: Harvard University Press, 1959, 1964), 171–88; Hoogenboom and Hoogenboom, *History of the ICC,* 55–56, 69–70; Van Metre, *Transportation in the United States,* 184; Ely, *Railway Rates and Cost of Service,* 6.

38. The Brandeis episode also has been examined by many historians. See, for example, Thomas K. McCraw, ed., *Prophets of Regulation* (Cambridge, MA: Harvard University Press, 1984), 80–142, and Berk, "Whose Hubris?"

39. Berk, "Whose Hubris?" 140, 142. In fact, in his examination of Brandeis's work on railroad rates, Berk indicts the entire regulatory approach adopted by the ICC, concluding that after 1910, "Regulation was paralyzed" (120).

40. In 1915, the ICC ordered the carriers to begin separating the operating expenses of freight and passenger service, and in 1926 the commission began issuing a separate publication devoted to revenues and costs of the difference services. U.S. ICC, *Activities,* 79. Economist Leo Sharfman noted that the ICC had always considered cost factors, but that as the industry reached maturity, cost had to become a more important factor in rate setting. Sharfman, *History of the ICC,* vol. 3A, 15, 72, 413–63; see also Ripley, *Railroads: Rates and Regulation,* 184.

41. Harold F. Lane, "General Railroad Developments during the Year," *Railway Age* 72 (January 7, 1922): 10.

42. The commission initially set the cut at 15 percent, but then accepted a railroad proposal to cut all agricultural rates in the country by 10 percent. Quotation from "Reductions on Rates in Agricultural Products," *Railway Age* 71 (November 26, 1921): 1022.

43. Lane, "General Railroad Developments," 10.

44. Theodore Roosevelt had been involved in railroad issues, but as an antitrust issue rather than as a transportation policy matter.

45. "President Finds Railroad Problem Difficult," *Railway Age* 70 (April 29, 1921): 1041.

46. The scholarship of historian Ellis W. Hawley is central in understanding Hoover's role in American society and politics at this time. See his *Herbert Hoover as Secretary of Commerce: Studies in New Era Thought and Practice* (Iowa City: University of Iowa Press, 1981); idem, *The Great War and the Search for a Modern Order: A History of the American People and Their Institutions, 1917–1933* (New York: St. Martin's Press, 1979); John M. Barry, *Rising Tide: The Great Mississippi Flood of 1927 and How It Changed America* (New York: Simon & Schuster, 1997); and "Railroad Executives Asked to Confer with the President," *Railway Age* 72 (May 13, 1922): 1110.

47. Herbert Hoover, "Real Program of Railroad Construction Needed," *Railway Age* 72 (February 11, 1922): 381, 382; Harold F. Lane, "President Urges Voluntary Rate Reduction," *Railway Age* 72 (May 27, 1922): 1227.

48. Ellis Hawley discusses the associative approach in "Herbert Hoover, the Commerce Secretariat, and the Vision of an Associative State, 1921–1928," *Journal of American History* 61 (June 1974): 116–40, and idem, "Three Facets of Hooverian Associationalism: Lumber, Aviation, and Movies, 1921–1930," in *Regulation in Perspective,* 95–123.

49. Lane, "President Urges Voluntary Rate Reduction."

50. Responses to the entire idea can be found in the cartoons and comments in "A Hint of Coolidge's Railway Policy," *Literary Digest* 79 (November 3, 1923): 15–16.

51. "A New Development in Rate Regulation," Railway Age 75 (October 27, 1923): 753.

52. "I.C.C. Sees No Need of General Rate Overhauling," *Railway Age* 76 (April 12, 1924): 943–47; "Proposed National Railroad Legislation," *Railway Age* 76 (January 19, 1924): 251.

53. See "Senate Hearings on Repeal of Section 15A," *Railway Age* 76 (May 3, 1924): 1089–93; "Railroad Legislation in Congress," *Railway Age* 76 (May 31, 1924): 1089.

54. Quoted in the ICC, *39th Annual Report* (1925), 38. See also Warren H. Wagner,

The Hoch-Smith Resolution: The Contentions as to Its Interpretation and Application (1929); "Proposed Railroad Legislation in Congress," *Railway Age* 76 (April 19, 1924): 1002; "Railroad Legislation," *Railway Age* 76 (May 17, 1924): 1200–1201; and "Rate Readjustment Resolution Fails," *Railway Age* 76 (June 14, 1924): 1517–18.

55. A massive literature exists on railroad rate-setting efforts and their implications. Useful historical summaries include Van Metre, *Transportation in the United States,* 206–23; see also William Z. Ripley, *Rates and Regulation* (New York: Longmans, Green, and Co., 1912; repr. Arno Press, 1973), 300–55; Ely, *Railway Rates and Cost of Service,* 22–39; and Sharfman, *History of the Interstate Commerce Commission,* vol. 3B. See also Meyer, Peck, Stenason, and Zwick, *The Economics of Competition in the Transportation Industries,* 171–88; and Hoogenboom and Hoogenboom, *A History of the ICC,* 56–70.

56. Sharfman, *History of the ICC,* vol. 3B, 735; ICC, *40th Annual Report* (1926), 37, 38. The Transportation Act of 1920 had placed the reasonable rate of return at 6.0, but directed the ICC commissioners to review this figure. They lowered the rate to 5.75 percent by the mid-1920s.

57. "Commissioner Meyer on the Hoch-Smith Resolution," *Railway Age* 86 (January 26, 1929): 230–31; see also "Hoch-Smith Resolution Nullified," *Railway Age* 88 (June 14, 1930): 1405.

58. "Senate Hearings on Repeal of Section 15A," *Railway Age* 76 (May 3, 1924): 1091.

59. ICC, *41st Annual Report* (1927), 67–68; *42nd* (1928), 66–67.

60. ICC, *41st Annual Report* (1927), 67.

61. "An Unjust and Unwise Act," *Railway Age* 84 (March 24, 1928): 662; see also "The Hoch-Smith Resolution," *Railway Age* 84 (January 28, 1928): 223–24; "Using Freight Rates to Equalize Prosperity," *Railway Age* 84 (March 10, 1928): 463–64; "An Indictment of Regulation," *Railway Age* 84 (May 26, 1928): 1187–88; "Hoch on Rate Regulation," *Railway Age* 84 (June 16, 1928): 1369–70.

62. ICC, *44th Annual Report* (1930), 61–63, quotation from 62; see also "Hoch-Smith Resolution Nullified."

63. "Senator Brookhart's Radical Railroad Bill," *Railway Age* 74 (March 3, 1923): 503; also "Senator Brookhart Attacks Railroads," *Railway Age* 73 (December 23, 1923): 1190–91.

64. "Proposed Railroad Legislation in Congress," *Railway Age* 76 (April 19, 1924): 1001.

65. "Proposed National Railroad Legislation," *Railway Age* 76 (January 19, 1924): 251; see also "Proposed Railroad Legislation Drags," *Railway Age* 76 (February 9, 1924): 373–74; and "Investigating Railroad Propaganda," *Railway Age* 76 (April 26, 1924): 1018.

66. "Progress on Railroad Legislation in Congress," *Railway Age* 76 (May 24, 1924): 1264.

67. Quotations from "Long and Short Haul Bill Reported," *Railway Age* 76 (March 29, 1924): 840; "The Gooding Bill," *Railway Age* 77 (December 27, 1924): 1152.

68. "Two Victories for Sound Regulation," *Railway Age* 80 (April 3, 1926): 947; and A. H. Elder, "Tendencies in Railway Legislation," *Railway Age* 81 (October 2, 1926): 637–38.

69. A. M. Schoyer, "The Reasons for the Unpopularity of Railroads," *Railway Age Gazette* 57, December 4, 1914, 1053. Historian William Deverell reached a similar conclusion, reporting "an astonishing degree of antagonism at the railroad and the railroad

corporation." See his *Railroad Crossing: Californians and the Railroad, 1850–1910* (Berkeley: University of California Press, 1994).

70. Herbert Hoover, "Real Program of Railroad Construction Needed," *Railway Age* 72 (February 11, 1922): 380.

71. "Appointments to the Commission," *Railway Age* 83 (December 3, 1927): 1095–96. One notable exception was Winthrop M. Daniels, appointed to the ICC in 1914 by Woodrow Wilson despite the complaints of western progressives who thought Daniels too favorable to business. And Daniels did reject Louis Brandeis's arguments during the rate advance cases of the 1910s. See "Winthrop M. Daniels," *Dictionary of American Biography*, John A. Garraty and Kenneth T. Jackson, eds., supp. 3 (New York: Scribner, 1973), 211–13. General information on the commissioners can be found in C. A. Miller, *The Lives of the Interstate Commerce Commissioners and the Commission Secretaries* (Washington, DC: Association of ICC Practitioners, 1946).

72. "Political Interference with Regulation," *Railway Age* 80 (January 23, 1926): 261; "Appointments to the Commission," 1045.

73. See Sharfman, *History of the ICC*, vol. 3B, 651–56, 661–67; coverage of the *New York Times*, especially February 18, 1928, 2; March 20, 1928, 42; April 18, 1928, 12; April 19, 1928, 37; June 13, 1928, 29; June 14, 1928, 39; August 16, 1928, 37, and December 12, 1928, II: 16; "Lake Cargo Rate Order Enjoined; Special Court Finds that Commission Exceeded its Powers," *Railway Age* 84 (April 21, 1928): 910–12; "Esch Defends Shift in Lake Cargo Case," *New York Times*, February 19, 1928, 17; and Miller, *Lives of the ICC Commissioners*, 105–108.

74. "Esch Fights Back on Lake Cargo Vote," *New York Times*, February 22, 1928, 43.

75. See "Glass Strikes Back on Lake Cargo Case," *New York Times*, February 29, 1928, 44; "Esch Confirmation Loses in Committee," *New York Times*, March 7, 1928, 18; and "Senate Refuses to Confirm Esch," *New York Times*, March 17, 1928, 1; also "Minority of Committee Defends Mr. Esch," *Railway Age* 84 (March 17, 1928): 641–42; "U.S. Senate Rejects Renomination of John J. Esch as Member of Interstate Commerce Commission," *Commercial and Financial Chronicle* 126 (March 24, 1928): 1755–56; and "Senate Committee Queries I.C.C. Rate Policies," *Railway Age* 84 (March 3, 1928): 531.

76. Quotations from "The Election and the Railways," *Railway Age* 85 (November 17, 1928): 954; see also "The Presidential Candidates and the Railroad Problem," *Railway Age* 85 (September 15, 1928): 480.

77. The only instance of government action even remotely similar to the railroad consolidation plans was the decision of the federal government during World War I to merge the nation's express agencies, several of which were owned by railroads and others of which were in private hands, into a single enterprise known as American Railway Express Co. When the government returned the railroads to private control in 1920, it was determined to be too difficult to split up the express operation. Thus American Railway Express remained in business, a product of the government's wartime intervention into the economy. See Alvin F. Harlow, *Old Waybills: The Romance of the Express* Companies (New York: D. Appleton-Century Co., 1934), 480–83; V. S. Roseman, *Railway Express Agency: An Overview* (Denver: Rocky Mountain Publishing, 1992). We are indebted to historian Richard R. John for drawing the Railway Express case to our attention.

78. William Zebina Ripley, *Trusts, Pools and Corporations* (Boston: Ginn & Co., 1905); idem, *Railroads; Rates and Regulation* (New York: Longmans, Green, 1912); idem, *Railway Problems*, rev. ed. (Boston: Ginn & Company, 1913); and idem, *Railroads:*

Finance and Organization (New York: Longmans, Green, and Co., 1915); Emory R. Johnson (with Grover G. Huebner), *Railroad Traffic and Rates* (New York: D. Appleton, 1911); see also Kerr, *American Railroad Politics,* 132–33. Both men had extensive experience as advisers and consultants to the government on a range of transportation issues.

79. F. J. Lisman, "The Future of the Railroads of the United States," *Railway Age Gazette* 65, July 12, 1918, 91.

80. Johnson, *Railroad Traffic and Rates;* William Norris Leonard, *Railroad Consolidation under the Transportation Act of 1920* (New York: Columbia University Press, 1946), 39; quotation from 34. See also Ralph L. Dewey, "Transport Coordination," in U.S. National Resources Planning Board, *Transportation and National Policy* (Washington, DC: Government Printing Office, 1942), 140–45; Van Metre, *Transportation in the United States,* 72–80; Charles L. Dearing and Wilfred Owen, *National Transportation Policy* (Washington, DC: Brookings Institution, 1949), 316–50. A very solid overview of the consolidation effort, albeit from the viewpoint of the Van Sweringen brothers, is also found in Harwood, *Invisible Giants.*

81. Leonard, *Railroad Consolidation,* 41. Leonard offers the best single overview of the effort to implement this consolidation plan.

82. See "Esch-Cummins Bill Passed by Senate and House," *Railway Age* 68 (February 27, 1920): 617–27; summary discussions of the bill are in Kerr, *American Railroad Politics,* 204–27; and Miller *Inland Transportation,* 170–83. Quotation from Leonard, *Railroad Consolidation,* 53.

83. Information on Ripley from "Ripley, William Zebina," *Dictionary of American Biography,* supp. 3 (1973), 632–33; correspondence in the Papers of William Z. Ripley, 1895–1940, Harvard University Archives, Cambridge, MA; "Obituary," *New York Times,* August 17, 1941, 39; "When Ripley Speaks, Wall Street Heeds," *New York Times Magazine,* September 26, 1926, 7; and Albro Martin, "The Troubled Subject of Railroad Regulation in the Gilded Age—A Reappraisal," in *The Rise of Big Business and the Beginning of Antitrust and Railroad Regulation, 1870–1900,* ed. Richard Himmelberg (New York: Garland Publishing, 1994), 340. His books included Ripley, *Trusts, Pools and Corporations;* idem, *Railroads: Rates and Regulation;* idem, *Railway Problems;* idem, *Railroads: Finance and Organization;* idem, *Main Street and Wall Street* (Boston: Little, Brown, and Company, 1927).

84. Ripley advised the U.S. Industrial Commission on railways and anthracite coal in 1901 and served on President Wilson's Eight-Hour Commission. He was Administrator of Labor Standards for the War Department in 1917–18 and in 1919–20 chaired the National Adjustment Committee of the U.S. Shipping Board. For general background on the role of academics in reform movements, including information on Ely and Taussig, see Benjamin G. Rader, *The Academic Mind and Reform: The Influence of Richard T. Ely in American Life* (Lexington: University of Kentucky Press, 1966); *The Wisconsin Progressives: The Papers of Richard T. Ely, Edward A. Ross, Charles McCarthy, Charles R. Van Hise and John R. Commons* (Teaneck, NJ: Chadwyck-Healey, 1985); *Explorations in Economics; Notes and Essays Contributed in Honor of F. W. Taussig* (New York: McGraw-Hill Company, 1936); The Papers of F. W. Taussig, 1859–1940, Harvard University Archives, Cambridge, MA; and Berk, "Whose Hubris?" 12–25, 130–31.

85. Ripley, *Railroads: Finance and Organization,* ix.

86. "Twenty Systems in I.C.C. Consolidation Plan," *Railway Age* 71 (September 3, 1921): 455–56; "Consolidation of Railroads," *Railway Review* 69 (October 1, 1921): 423–27; "Commission Presents Tentative Consolidation Plan," *Railway Age* 71 (October

1, 1921): 609–16.

87. Mark W. Potter to William Ripley, May 2, 1923, File 1923, Correspondence-Box 2, Papers of William Z. Ripley, Harvard University Archives, Cambridge, MA. Some railroad industry figures also favored giving the plan a fair hearing, although they wanted to assemble their own consolidations. See "Railroad Consolidations," *Railway Age* 71 (October 25, 1921): 701–702.

88. See "Hearings on Tentative Consolidation Plan," *Railway Age* 72 (June 24, 1922): 1731; "Hill Roads Oppose I.C.C. Consolidation Plan," *Railway Age* 73 (November 25, 1922): 1009; "Western Roads Heard on Consolidation Plan," *Railway Age* 73 (November 25, 1922): 1009; "Judge Lovett Disapproves of the Holden Plan," *Railway Age* 74 (April 1923): 918; "Hearing on Consolidation of Eastern Railroads," *Railway Age* 74 (May 19, 1923): 1225–27; "Hearings on I.C.C. Consolidation Plan," *Railway Age* 74 (May 26, 1923): 1272–73. See also Leonard, *Railroad Consolidation*, 87–88; and "House Committee Considers Consolidation Bill," *Railway Age* 80 (June 5, 1926): 1474.

89. John W. Owens, "The Rail Leaders Think," *New Republic* 35 (July 4, 1923): 142. Another commentator added, "Many of the parties offering testimony appeared to be interested not so much in assisting the Commission in arriving at a decision as in proving that it was impossible to arrive at any decision at all." See Leonard, *Railroad Consolidation*, 89.

90. "Hill Roads Oppose I.C.C. Consolidation Plan," *Railway Age* 73 (November 25, 1922): 1010.

91. National Industrial Conference Board, *The Consolidation of Railroads in the United States*, National Industrial Conference Board Report No. 56 (New York, 1923); John S. Worley, "A Modified Plan for Consolidation of Railroads," *Railway Age* 75 (July 21, 1923): 108–109.

92. "Final Hearings on I.C.C. Consolidation Plan," *Railway Age* 75 (November 24, 1923): 971; see also "Holds Final Hearings on Railway Consolidations before I.C.C.," *Railway Review* 73 (November 24, 1923): 774–75.

93. Leonard, *Railroad Consolidation*, 119–20.

94. See "President Harding on Railroad Consolidations," *Railway Age* 75 (June 30, 1923): 1676–77; "President's Address on Transportation," *Railway Review* 72 (June 30, 1923): 1164–67; "Washington Correspondence," *Railway Review* 73 (December 8, 1923): 840–41; "President Coolidge Urges Expedition of Consolidation," *Railway Age* 77 (December 6, 1924): 1027–28; and comments by Hoover in "The National Transportation Conference," *Railway Age* 76 (January 12, 1924): 202–203. See also Leonard, *Railroad Consolidations*, 121–24.

95. "Senator Cummins Proposes Consolidation Law," *Railway Age* 76 (February 2, 1924): 331–35. Cummins added his bill "would take the railroads out of politics for a long time to come." See "Cummins Hopes for Compromise on Legislation," *Railway Age* 77 (November 22, 1924): 929–30.

96. "Hearings on Consolidation Bill," *Railway Age* 78 (January 10, 1925): 190–91; (January 17, 1925): 220–23; "Railroad Legislation in Congress," *Railway Age* 78 (February 7, 1925): 383; "The Cummins Consolidation Bill," *Railway Age* 80 (January 9, 1926): 164–65; "Hearing on Consolidation Bill," *Railway Age* 76 (May 24, 1924): 1259; "Cummins' New Consolidation Bill," *Railway Age* 79 (December 26, 1925): 1197–98; "Hearings on Consolidation Bills," *Railway Age* 80 (January 30, 1926): 333–37; "Senator Cummins' New Consolidation Bill," *Railway Age* 80 (April 24, 1926): 1128–29; "Winslow Bill Provides Voluntary Consolidation," *Railway Age* 77 (December 13,

1924): 1091–92; "Parker Consolidation Plan Approved by I.C.C.," *Railway Age* 80 (May 29, 1926): 1445–46; "Senator Cummins' Death May Affect Consolidation Legislation," *Railway Age* 81 (August 14, 1926): 268. On later legislation see "New Consolidation Bill Introduced in Senate," *Railway Age* 81 (December 25, 1926): 1278; "Little Interest Shown in Consolidation Bill," *Railway Age* 82 (January 22, 1927): 290; "Hearings on Consolidation Bill," *Railway Age* 82 (January 22, 1927): 371–72; and Joseph Eastman to President Calvin Coolidge, November 21, 1924, Box 26, Letterbooks, Papers of Joseph Eastman, University Archives, Amherst College, Amherst, MA, hereafter cited as Eastman Papers.

97. See "Four Great Eastern Systems Proposed to I.C.C.," *Railway Age* 77 (October 18, 1924): 683–84; "Pennsylvania Objects to Four-System Plan," *Railway Age* 77 (November 1, 1924): 807–809; "The Four-System Consolidation Plan," *Railway Age* 78 (January 31, 1925): 315–19. Executives from the Pennsylvania disagreed about the allocation of several smaller companies. See Pennsylvania Railroad, *78th Annual Report* (1924), 11–12. For a superbly detailed view of the Van Sweringens and the consolidation process among eastern railroads, see Herbert H. Harwood Jr., *Invisible Giants: The Empires of Cleveland's Van Sweringen Brothers* (Bloomington: Indiana University Press, 2003). Among his many insights into the consolidation program, Harwood emphasizes the close relationship between the Van Sweringens and the president of the New York Central (A. H. Smith), and the intense rivalry between the New York Central and the Pennsylvania Railroads.

98. These events are summarized in Leonard, *Railroad Consolidations*, 128–142, 152–54; see also articles in *Railway Age*, including "History of the Van Sweringen System," 77 (August 30, 1924): 381–84; "Van Sweringen Merger," 77 (September 6, 1924): 398–99; "Hearings on Nickel Plate," 78 (April 18, 1925): 983–84; "Van Sweringens Propose New Plan," 82 (February 19, 1927): 512–14; also Ripley, *Main Street and Wall Street*, 229–75. Harwood, *Invisible Giants*, offers the most detailed account of the Cleveland brothers' activities in this area, and the responses of other Eastern railroads. The brothers' financial practices also figure prominently in histories of the stock market crash of 1929. See, for example, Maury Klein, *Rainbow's End: The Crash of 1929* (New York: Oxford University Press, 2001); and Robert Sobel, *The Great Bull Market: Wall Street in the 1920s* (New York: Norton, 1968).

99. See Harwood, *Invisible Giants*; Leonard, *Railroad Consolidations*, 142–43; also Ralph Budd, "The New Northern Railway System," *Railway Age* 82 (February 26, 1927): 585–89; "K.C.S. Merger Plan Rejected," *Railway Age* 82 (May 28, 1927): 1572–74; and Harold F. Lane, "Progress toward Consolidation," *Railway Age* 82 (January 1, 1927): 62–63.

100. Leonard, *Railroad Consolidations*, 183–92; "Recent Developments in the Consolidation Situation," *Railway Age* 86 (March 2, 1929): 515; "I.C.C. Consolidation Plan," *Railway Age* 87 (December 28, 1929): 1469–72; and F. J. Lisman, "The Feasibility of the I.C.C. Consolidation Plan," *Railway Age* 88 (January 25, 1930): 231–36; (February 1, 1930): 337–41.

101. "Hearings on Couzens Resolution," *Railway Age* 88 (April 26, 1930): 972–77; "Couzens Resolution in House Committee," *Railway Age* 88 (May 31, 1930): 1336; "Couzens Resolution Fails of Passage," *Railway Age* 89 (July 12, 1930): 79; "Couzens Resolution Adversely Reported," *Railway Age* 88 (July 19, 1930): 1198. Couzens exhibited a similar attitude of concern about large radio corporations during this same time period. See Moss and Fein, "Radio Regulation."

102. "Northern Lines May Merge without C.B.& Q.," *Railway Age* 88 (March 1, 1930): 556–58. Wheeler's comments can be found in U.S. Congress, Senate, Committee on Interstate Commerce, *To Suspend Railroad Consolidation. Hearings before the Committee on Interstate Commerce, United States Senate, Seventy-first Congress, Second Session, on S. J. Res. 161, a Joint Resolution to Suspend the Authority of the Interstate Commerce Commission to Approve Consolidations or Unifications of Railway Properties* (April 15, 16, 17, 18, 21, 23, and 24, 1930), 47–49. On the earlier episode, see Balthasar Henry Meyer, *A History of the Northern Securities Case*. Bulletin of the University of Wisconsin, no. 142: Economics and Political Science Series, vol. 1, no. 3, 215–30 (Madison, WI, 1906). Wheeler reflected a deep-rooted antipathy toward the railroads, as seen in his lengthy investigation of the Van Sweringens and railroad holding companies. See Harwood, *Invisible Giants*, 286–87.

103. See "When Ripley Speaks, Wall Street Heeds," *New York Times Magazine*, September 26, 1926, 7, 19; also *New York Evening Post*, March 3, 1926; both in File: Clippings about W. Z. Ripley and the Interstate Commerce Commission, Box: Clippings, Ripley Papers, Harvard University Archives, Cambridge, MA; and Ripley, *Main Street and Wall Street*, esp. 229–54.

104. Sharfman, *History of the ICC*, vol. 3, 488–99; also correspondence in File 1930, Ripley Papers; and Ripley to J. B. Eastman, January 21, 1930, File: Trunkline Consolidation, Box 40, Eastman Papers; and a number of articles in *Business Week*: "Eastern Lines Work toward 4-Trunk Consolidation Plan" (December 31, 1930): 8; (January 7, 1931): 5–6; and "Eastern Rail Chiefs Clear Line to Rush Their Merger Through" (March 25, 1931): 16, as well as heavy coverage in *Railway Age*. See also Van Metre, *Transportation in the United States*, 84–89. Congress did not repeal the consolidation section until 1940.

105. See, for example, Sharfman, *History of the ICC*, vol. 3, 482; Van Metre, *Transportation in the United States*, 335, 380–81; Hoogenboom and Hoogenboom, *History of the ICC*, ix–x; 105–12; Harwood, *Invisible Giants*, 182–87. A defense of the ICC is found in Walter C. Splawn, *Consolidation of Railroads* (New York: Macmillan Company, 1925).

106. Ely, *Railroads and American Law*, 250.

CHAPTER 2

1. Statistics drawn from U.S. Interstate Commerce Commission, Bureau of Statistics, *Statistics of Railways in the United States* (Washington, DC: Government Printing Office, 1920), xxxii; and U.S. Department of Commerce, Bureau of the Census, *Historical Abstract of the United States: Colonial Times to 1970* (Washington, DC: Government Printing Office, 1975), 711, 765.

2. Statistics from Margaret Walsh, *Making Connections: The Long-Distance Bus Industry in the USA* (Burlington, VT: Ashgate Publishing Company, 2000), 27.

3. U.S. Bureau of the Census, *Historical Statistics of the United States* (Washington, DC: Government Printing Office, 1976), II:707. The ICC did not keep statistics on freight and passenger traffic carried by modes other than railroads until the end of the 1920s, making comparisons difficult. These numbers, however, clearly indicate the basic trends.

4. See Brice Edwards, *Motor-truck Transportation of Fruits and Vegetables: Southern Indiana and Southern Illinois 1928 Crop* (Washington, DC: U.S. Department of Agricul-

ture, Bureau of Agricultural Economics, 1930); Sidney L. Miller, *Inland Transportation; Principles and Policies* (New York: McGraw-Hill Book Company, 1933), 588; and C. S. Duncan, "What the Motor Transport Investigation Has Shown," *Railway Age* 81 (October 23, 1926): 814.

5. See Paul Barrett, *The Automobile and Urban Transit: The Formation of Public Policy in Chicago, 1900–1930* (Philadelphia: Temple University Press, 1983).

6. See Michael A. Bernstein, *A Perilous Progress: Economists and Public Purpose in Twentieth Century America* (Princeton, NJ: Princeton University Press, 2001), 173. On apolitical expertise in another context, see Bruce E. Seely, *Building the American Highway System: Engineers as Policy Makers* (Philadelphia: Temple University Press, 1987); also Thomas L. Haskell, *The Authority of Experts: Studies in History and Theory* (Bloomington: Indiana University Press, 1984).

7. Summaries of inland waterway development can be found in Miller, *Inland Transportation;* Charles Whiting Baker, "What Is the Future of Inland Water Transportation?" *Engineering News-Record* 84 (January 1, 1920): 19–29; (January 8, 1920): 85–89; (January 15, 1920): 137–44; (January 22, 1920): 184–91; (January 29, 1920): 234–42; Dearing and Owen, *National Transportation Policy,* 81–104; also George Rogers Taylor, *The Transportation Revolution, 1815–1860* (New York: Holt, Rinehart and Winston, 1951). On development of the Mississippi River, see Arthur Frank De Wit, *The Development of the Federal Program of Flood Control on the Mississippi River* (New York: Columbia University Press, 1930); Michael C. Robinson, *The Mississippi River Commission: An American Epic* (Vicksburg, MS: Mississippi River Commission, U.S. Army Corps of Engineers, 1989); and Martin Reuss, "Andrew A. Humphreys and the Development of Hydraulic Engineering: Politics and Technology in the Army Corps of Engineers, 1850–1950," *Technology and Culture* 26 (January 1985): 1–33.

8. This section draws upon the analysis of Miller, *Inland Transportation,* 429–53, 641; Harold G. Moulton, *The American Transportation Problem* (Washington, DC: Brookings Institution, 1933); and U.S. National Resources Planning Board, Committee for the Transportation Study, *Transportation and National Policy* (Washington, DC: Government Printing Office, 1942), 359–83, 427–55. See also William J. Hull and Robert W. Hull, *The Origin and Development of the Waterways Policy of the United States* (Washington, DC: National Waterways Conference, 1967), 36. On the St. Lawrence project, Harold G. Moulton, Charles S. Morgan, and Adah L. Lee, *The St. Lawrence Navigation and Power Project* (Washington, DC: Brookings Institution, 1929); Theo L. Hills, *The St. Lawrence Seaway* (New York: Praeger, 1959); and John B. Lansing, *Transportation and Economic Policy* (New York: Free Press, 1966), 356–59.

9. Miller, *Inland Transportation,* 645. Every president of the 1920s supported inland waterways as an aid to farmers, but Hoover was the most "ardent proponent of improving the inland waterways system," seeing them as capital investments that were not local in their benefits, and thus compatible with his vision of the federal role. Hull and Hull, *Origin and Development of the Waterways Policy,* 33.

10. Information is drawn from Baker, "Future of Inland Waterway Transportation?" (January 8, 1920): 85–89; "What the Barge Lines Are Doing," *Railway Age* 85 (October 24, 1928): 801–804; (November 13, 1928): 865–69; Harold A. Van Dorn, *Government Owned Corporations* (New York: Alfred A. Knopf, 1926), 206–26; and Dearing and Owens, *National Transportation Policy,* 89–90; Marshall Edward Dimock, *Developing America's Waterways; Administration of the Inland Waterways Corporation* (Chicago: University of Chicago Press, 1935); Samuel Thomas Bledsoe, *Government Operation of Fed-*

eral Barge Line in Competition with Rail and Other Transportation (n.p., 1932); U.S. Congress, House Committee on Interstate and Foreign Commerce, *Repealing the Inland Waterways Corporation Act; Report to Accompany H. R. 2876* (Washington, DC: Government Printing Office, 1963); Kenneth Hall McCartney, "Government Enterprise: A Study of the Inland Waterways Corporation" (Ph.D. diss., University of Minnesota, 1958); and "Administrative History," Records of the Inland Waterways Corporation, Record Group 91, National Archives and Records Administration (http://www.nara.gov /guide/rg91.html). For rather different reasons, the federal government also operated the Alaska Railroad, beginning in 1914. See Edwin M. Fitch, *The Alaska Railroad* (New York: Praeger, 1967).

11. For typical railroad reaction, see Daniel Willard, "Taxpayers as Well as Railways Are Victimized," *Railway Age* 89 (November 8, 1930): 971–72, 994; "Competition of Inland Waterways," *Railway Age* 90 (January 3, 1931): 14–16; "Inland Waterways: An Unfair Form of Competition," *Railway Age* 93 (December 3, 1932): 815–18. Baker, "Future of Inland Water Transportation?" 20–21, quotation on 23. Compare this to "A River in the Red," *Washington Post,* January 9, 2000, A1, A16–A17.

12. Harold G. Moulton, *Waterways versus Railways* (Boston: Houghton Mifflin Company, 1912); idem, *The St. Lawrence Navigation and Power Project* (Washington, DC: Brookings Institution, 1929). Statistics from Lansing, *Transportation and Economic Policy,* 356–59, who reported that by 1963, waterways moved 16 percent of all intercity freight.

13. On Lindberg and the early development of flying, see John William Ward, "Charles A. Lindberg: His Flight and the American Ideal," in Caroll W. Pursell Jr., *Technology in America: A History of Individuals and Ideas,* 2nd ed. (Cambridge, MA: MIT Press, 1990). On popular enthusiasm for aviation, see Tom D. Crouch, *A Dream of Wings: Americans and the Airplane, 1875–1905* (New York: Norton, 1981); Joseph J. Corn, *The Winged Gospel: America's Romance with Aviation, 1900–1950* (New York: Oxford University Press, 1983); and Roger E. Bilstein, *Flight in America: From the Wrights to the Astronauts,* rev. ed. (Baltimore: Johns Hopkins University Press, 1994, 2001).

14. Nick A. Komons, *Bonfires to Beacons: Federal Civil Aviation Policy under the Air Commerce Act, 1926–1938* (Washington, DC: U.S. Department of Transportation, 1978), 16; Bilstein, *Flight in America;* David D. Lee, "Herbert Hoover and the Development of Commercial Aviation," *Business History Review* 58 (Spring 1984): 78–102, esp. 83.

15. Komons, *Bonfires to Beacons,* 3. On the role of the government in aviation, see F. Robert van der Linden, *Airlines and the Mail: The Post Office and the Birth of the Commercial Aviation Industry* (Lexington: University of Kentucky Press, 2002), and W. David Lewis, *Airline Executives and Federal Regulation: Case Studies in American Enterprise from the Airmail Era to the Dawn of the Jet Age* (Columbus: Ohio State University Press, 2000). On Trippe, see Robert Daley, *An American Saga: Juan Trippe and his Pan Am Empire* (New York: Random House, 1980); Marylin Bender, *The Chosen Instrument: Pan Am, Juan Trippe, The Rise and Fall of an American Entrepreneur* (New York: Simon and Schuster, 1982); Matthew Josephson, *Empire of the Air: Juan Trippe and the Struggle for World Airways* (New York: Harcourt, Brace & Co., 1944).

16. See Alex Roland, *Model Research: The National Advisory Committee for Aeronautics, 1915–1958* (Washington, DC: National Aeronautics and Space Administration, 1985); James R. Hansen, *Engineer in Charge: A History of The Langley Aeronautical Laboratory, 1917–1958* (Washington, DC: National Aeronautics and Space Administration,

1987); and Komons, *Bonfires to Beacons,* 18–19, 126–32.

17. Hoover is quoted in Komons, *Bonfires to Beacons,* 22, 27. Historian Richard John (private communication with the authors) noted that Hoover was wrong on this point, as the telegraph and telephone industries as well as segments of agriculture had welcomed government oversight.

18. Quotation from Komons, *Bonfires to Beacons,* 32. This section is drawn from several surveys of commercial aviation policy in the United States. See Komons, *Bonfires to Beacons,* 32–35; Moulton, *American Transportation Problem,* 717–55; Miller, *Inland Transportation,* 693–716; National Resources Panning Board, *Transportation and National Policy,* 329–58; Henry Ladd Smith, *Airways: The History of Commercial Aviation in the United States* (New York: Russell & Russell, 1965); Lee, "Hoover and the Development of Commercial Aviation," 78–102; and Ellis W. Hawley, *Herbert Hoover as Secretary of Commerce: Studies in New Era Thought and Practice* (Iowa City: University of Iowa Press, 1981); and on the role of the Post Office, van der Linden, *Airlines and the Mail.*

19. Smith, *Airways,* 108–13, 123–29; Komons, *Bonfires to Beacons,* 191–96; "Air Transport Development in 1929," *Aviation* 28 (February 15, 1930): 318–22; "The Subsidized Air Lines," *Railway Age* 93 (December 3, 1932): 822–33.

20. Komons, *Bonfires to Beacons,* 96–104, 124–45, 163–75, quotation from 160; Paul Barrett, "Cities and Their Airports: Policy Formation, 1926–1952," *Journal of Urban History* 14 (November 1987): 112–37.

21. Komons, *Bonfires to Beacons,* 121–22. The bureau also paid a little more attention to safety beginning about this time. This subject is at the center of the study by Donald R. Whitnah, *Safer Skyway: Federal Control of Aviation, 1926–1966* (Ames: Iowa State University Press, 1966).

22. Komons, *Bonfires to Beacons,* 198–216; Smith, *Airways,* 157–213; and van der Linden, *Airlines and Airmail,* 62–186; see also John Thomas McClintock Jr., "Air Transportation: Its Growth under Government Subsidy and Its Future," *Annalist* 43 (March 9, 1934): 403–404

23. Komons, *Bonfires to Beacons,* 209–11; see also Bilstein, *Flight in America,* 85–96, and Roland, *Model Research.*

24. The air carriers caught in Brown's manipulation underwent hasty cosmetic reorganizations so they could submit new bids. This episode is dealt with by Komons, *Bonfires to Beacons,* 249–75; Smith, *Airways,* 249–301; and in the greatest level of detail by van der Linden, *Airlines and Airmail,* 187–291.

25. See "The Effect of the Automobile on Railway Traffic," *Scientific American Supplement* 74 (November 16, 1912): 311; "Motor-Car Travel Greater than Railroad Travel," *Literary Digest* 54 (January 20, 1917): 164, 166–67. On highway policy, see Moulton, *American Transportation Problem,* 530–46; Miller, *Inland Transportation,* 571–601; Charles L. Dearing, *American Highway Policy* (Washington, DC: Brookings Institution, 1941); and Seely, *Building the America Highway System.*

26. The nation's road-building program may be the largest and most successful example of federalism. See Austin F. MacDonald, *Federal Aid: A Study of the American Subsidy System* (New York: T. Y. Crowell, 1928).

27. This is the primary point made in Seely, *Building the America Highway System.*

28. Statistics from U.S. Department of Agriculture, Bureau of Public Roads, *Annual Reports* (1921–1930), and U.S. Bureau of the Census, *Historical Statistics.*

29. Statistics from U.S. Department of Agriculture, Bureau of Public Roads, *Annual*

Report (1921–1930). On highway finance, see Thomas H. MacDonald, "How Highway Financing Has Evolved," *Engineering News-Record* 104 (January 2, 1930): 4–7; U.S. Department of Transportation, Federal Highway Administration, *America's Highways, 1776–1976: A History of the Federal-Aid Highway Program* (Washington, DC: Government Printing Office, 1976), 239–48; and John Chynoweth Burnham, "The Gasoline Tax and the Automobile Revolution," *Mississippi Valley Historical Review* (December 1961): 435–59. Quotation from Harold Ickes, *Back to Work: The Story of PWA* (New York: MacMillan Co., 1935), 82.

30. Historians who have presented highway policy as an extension of the desires of the automobile industry include David J. St. Clair, *The Motorization of American Cities* (New York: Praeger, 1986), and Stephen B. Goodard, *Getting There: The Epic Struggle between Road and Rail in the American Century* (New York: Basic Books, 1994). Matthew W. Roth, "Mulholland Highway and the Engineering Culture of Los Angeles in the 1920s," *Technology and Culture* 40, no. 3 (July 1999): 545–75, discusses one instance of public concern about road-building activities. See also Raymond H. Mohl, "Stop the Road: Freeway Revolts in American Cities," *Journal of Urban History* 30, no. 5 (2004): 674–706; also Mohl, "Ike and the Interstates: Creeping toward Comprehensive Planning," *Journal of Planning History* 2 (Summer 2003): 237–62.

31. See Donald F. Davis, *Conspicuous Consumption: Automobiles and Elites in Detroit, 1899–1933* (Philadelphia: Temple University Press, 1988); Barrett, *Public Policy and Urban Transit;* Howard L. Preston, *Automobile Age Atlanta: The Making of a Southern Metropolis, 1900–1935* (Athens: University of Georgia Press, 1979); and Mark S. Foster, *From Street Car to Superhighway: American City Planners and Urban Transit, 1900–1940* (Philadelphia: Temple University Press, 1981).

32. Statistics from "Bus and Rail Men Testify before I.C.C.," *Bus Transportation* 9 (December 1930): 661; Miller, *Inland Transportation,* 582, 598–99; Moulton, *American Transportation Problem,* 517–46.

33. See H. R. Trumbower, "Railroad Abandonments and Their Relationship to Highway Transportation," *Public Roads* 6 (October 1925): 169–73; "What about the Patrons on Abandoned Roads?" *Railway Age* 76 (May 3, 1924): 1077–79.

34. Harwood, *Invisible Giants,* 163.

35. William R. Childs, *Trucking and the Public Interest: The Emergence of Federal Regulation, 1914–1940* (Knoxville: University of Tennessee Press, 1985), 1–12, 16–18.

36. C. S. Duncan, "What the Motor Transport Investigation Has Shown," *Railway Age* 81 (October 23, 1926): 813–14; Miller, *Inland Transportation,* 586–90; Childs, *Trucking and the Public Interest,* is the best source on the early trucking industry. Less-than-carload freight involved, just as it sounds, shipments that did not require a full freight car.

37. General information from Walsh, *Making Connections,* 18–19, 75–77; Miller, *Inland Transportation,* 583–86, 622–35; and B. B. Crandell, "The Growth of the Intercity Bus Industry" (Ph.D. diss., Syracuse University, 1954).

38. "Bus Industry Climbs to New Heights during 1923," *Bus Transportation* 3 (January 1924): 6–7; "News of the Road Reviewed," *Bus Transportation* 4 (February 1925): 64.

39. Walsh, *Making Connections,* 81–82, 92–95; John C. Emery, "Railways Adopting Motor Transport," *Railway Age* 82 (January 1, 1927): 59–61; idem, "Motor Transport Looms Larger in Railway Picture," *Railway Age* 88 (January 4, 1930): 106–8; idem, "Motor Transport by Railways," *Railway Age* 90 (January 3, 1931): 107–10; and Bruce

E. Seely, "Railroads, Good Roads, and Motor Vehicles: Managing Technological Change," *Railroad History*, no. 155 (Autumn 1986): 35–63.

40. On regional services, see "California Thoroughly Covered by Motor Stage Network," *Bus Transportation* 1 (June 1922): 336–43; "Transcontinental Bus Service Now a Reality!" *Bus Transportation* 7 (May 1928): 251–52; "Happenings during 1930," *Bus Transportation* 10 (February 1931): 52; Walsh, *Making Connections*, 77–81, 89–125, 108–15. On bus technology, see Gregory L. Thompson, *California's Rail and Bus Industries, 1910–1941* (Columbus: Ohio State University Press, 1993), 98–99; Walsh, *Making Connections*, 20, 24, 164–65; "Unleashing the Super Greyhound," *Bus Transportation* 14 (June 1935): 224–25; "And Now . . . the Sleeper Bus," *Bus Transportation* 7 (1928): 480–81; "Eleven Months of Nite Coach Operation," *Bus Transportation* 9 (June 1930): 322–23; "The Nite Coach Rolls On!" *Bus Transportation* 11 (July 1932):303–304.

41. Walsh, *Making Connections*, 144–46; "Greyhound Lines Merger," *Railway Age* 101 (November 28, 1936): 801; "Make-Up of the Greyhound Lines," *Railway Age* 103 (December 25, 1937): 917–19; Thompson, *California's Rail and Bus Industries*, 91–112; "National Trailways Begins Operations," *Railway Age* 100 (April 25, 1936): 692–96; 100 (May 23, 1936): 837–38, 844–45.

42. Walsh, *Making Connections*, 95, 97–99, 139; see also "Motor Bus Laws Abstracted," *Bus Transportation* 1 (September 1922): 485–86; Henry Meixell, "Six States Make Bus a Common Carrier," *Bus Transportation* 3 (January 1924): 4–6; Hall Johnson, "Trend of Regulatory Practice," *Bus Transportation* 4 (February 1925): 67–68; Russell Huffman, "Buses Declared Common Carriers in Seven More States," *Bus Transportation* 4 (December 1925): 609–12; "Happenings during 1930," *Bus Transportation* 10 (February 1931): 55; R. E. Plimpton, "Why 49 Varieties of State Regulations?" *Bus Transportation* 9 (February 1930): 89–93.

43. "How the Motor Bus Serves Pennsylvania," *Bus Transportation* 1 (April 1922): 229; Plimpton, "49 Varieties," 89. For information on other states, see "Commission Opposed to Parallel Service," *Bus Transportation* 1 (April 1922): 251; and "Wildcat Operation Gone for Good in Providence, R.I.," *Bus Transportation* 1 (November 1922): 573–75. Walsh, *Making Connections*, 95–98, 138–40, explores regulation; see also "State Commissioner Comment on Highway Transport," *Railway Age* 80 (June 26, 1926): 1977–78.

44. Childs, *Trucking and the Public Interest*, 93–94.

45. See "States Cannot Prohibit Interstate Competition," *Bus Transportation* 4 (April 1925): 179–81; "Regulation of Interstate Motor Carriers Endorsed," *Bus Transportation* 4 (June 1925): 282–84; S. A. Markel, "Why I Favor Federal Interstate Regulation," *Bus Transportation* 6 (October 1927): 545–46; and "Review of Interstate Regulation," *Bus Transportation* 5 (February 1926): 89–92.

46. Debates about motor vehicle regulation are summarized in Walsh, *Making Connections*, 140–43; Childs, *Trucking and the Public Interest*, 93–95; see also "Hearings on Bill to Regulate Motor Bus Traffic Started," *Bus Transportation* 5 (April 1926): 195–201; "Motor Transportation Hearings End," *Railway Age* 81 (October 20, 1926): 839–40; "Examiner's Report on Motor Transport," *Railway Age* 84 (January 28, 1928): 269–77; "Two Interstate Regulation Bills," *Railway Age* 84 (January 28, 1928): 281–82; "Parker Bill Attacked," *Bus Transportation* 7 (May 1928): 245–47; "News of the Road," *Bus Transportation* 9 (March 1930): 170–71; and "News of the Road," ibid., 9 (April 1930): 228–29. The idea of delegating significant regulatory authority to the state public utility commissions was evidence of the cooperation between the ICC and state officials dis-

cussed in William R. Childs, "State Regulators and Pragmatic Federalism in the United States, 1889–1945," *Business History Review* 75, no. 4 (2001): 701–39, and idem, *Texas Railroad Commission*, 15–40.

47. William D. Middleton, *When the Steam Railroads Electrified* (Milwaukee: Kalmbach Books, 1974); Mark Reutter, ed., *Railroad History: The Diesel Revolution* (Westford, MA: Railway & Locomotive Historical Society, 2000); and John F. Kirkland, *Dawn of the Diesel Age: The History of the Diesel Locomotive in America* (Glendale, CA: Interurbans Publications, 1983).

48. On transport cooperation, see John R. Hall, "Co-ordination of All Transportation Facilities," *Railway Age* 64 (April 5, 1918): 943–46; Frederic Howe, "Wanted—A National Railroad Program," *Nation* 110 (May 29, 1920): 716–17; "Giving Force to a Hackneyed Word," *Railway Age* 72 (June 20, 1922): 1321–22. On a department of transportation, see "Proposal for a Commissioner General of Transportation," *Railway Age* 72 (January 28, 1922): 273; "Washington Correspondence," *Railway Review* 70 (February 11, 1922): 198–99; and "Plan for Commissioner General of Transportation Not Approved," *Railway Age* 72 (February 18, 1922): 424; "Current Topics," *Railway Review* 71 (December 30, 1922): 946–48. Carl Condit, *The Port of New York*, vol. 2, *A History of the Rail and Terminal System of the Grand Central Electrification to the Present* (Chicago: University of Chicago Press, 1981), 122–31.

49. Condit, *Port of New York*, 131–36; Robert Fishman, "The Regional Plan and the Transformation of the Industrial Metropolis," 106–25, in *The Landscape of Modernity: Essays on New York City*, ed. David Ward and Olivier Zunz (New York: Russell Sage Foundation, 1992); "Report of the New York Regional Plan Committee," *Railway Age* 86 (June 1, 1929): 1285–86.

50. See Harwood, *Invisible Giants*, 66–67, and Foster, *From Streetcars to Superhighways.*

51. See especially Steven W. Usselman, *Regulating Railroad Innovation: Business, Technology, and Politics in America, 1840–1920* (New York: Cambridge University Press, 2002), 177–326

52. Meyer, Peck, Stenason, and Zwick, *The Economics of Competition in the Transportation Industries*, 208–11, and James C. Nelson, "The Role of Regulation Re-Examined: New Concepts in Transportation Regulation," in U.S. National Resources Planning Board, *Transportation and National Policy* (Washington, DC: United States Government Printing Office, 1942), 219–224.

53. This pragmatic tendency to plan cooperatively is in line with the patterns identified by Ellis W. Hawley, *The Great War and the Search for a Modern Order: A History of the American People and Their Institutions, 1917–1933* (Prospect Heights, IL: Waveland Press, 1992, 1997).

54. George D. Ogden, "Co-ordinated Transportation," *Railway Age* 88 (April 26, 1930): 1026–38; G. Lloyd Wilson, *Coördinated Motor-Rail-Steamship Transportation* (New York: Appleton & Company, 1930), 5; and *Relation of Highways and Motor Transport to Other Transportation Agencies* (Washington, DC: U.S. Chamber of Commerce, 1923).

55. Examples of early railroad discussions about motor vehicles include "The Co-ordination of All Transportation," *Railway Age* 74 (March 24, 1923): 801–802; "Markham Discusses Co-ordination of Various Agencies of Transportation," *Railway Age* 74 (May 23, 1923): 1154 (Markham was president of the Illinois Central Railroad); "Competition of Motor Buses," *Railway Age* 77 (August 30, 1924): 356–57. See also Seely, "Good Roads, Motor Vehicles, and Railroads."

56. Emory R. Johnson, "The Railroad Situation," *Engineers and Engineering* 49 (March 1932): 33–36; Seely, "Good Roads, Motor Vehicles, and Railroads," 48–52; "Oldest Rail-Highway Co-ordination Is Still Successful," *Railway Age* 98 (June 22, 1935): 985–86; Walsh, *Making Connections,* 21; Pennsylvania Railroad Company, *80th Annual Report* (1926), 7; "Pennsylvania Bus Charters Disapproved by Governor," *Railway Age* 81 (October 16, 1926): 714; "Pinchot Raps Commission," *Electric Railway Journal* (October 23, 1926): 783; George D. Ogden, "Co-ordinated Transportation," *Railway Age* 88 (April 26, 1930): 1026–38.

57. "A Problem That Must Be Met," *Railway Age* 78 (June 6, 1925): 1374–75; "Both Trucks and Railways Needed," *Railway Age* 78 (June 6, 1925): 1407–10; "Motor Transport Association Formed," *Railway Review* 79 (September 18, 1926): 435–37; "Motor Transport Conference Meets," *Railway Age* 81 (September 25, 1926): 588–91; "The Motor Transport Section," *Railway Age* 81 (September 25, 1926): 585. Statistics from John C. Emery, "Railways Adopting Motor Transport," *Railway Age* 82 (January 1, 1927): 59–61; idem, "Motor Transport Looms Larger in Railway Picture," *Railway Age* 88 (January 4, 1930): 106–8; idem, "Motor Transport by Railways," *Railway Age* 90 (January 3, 1931): 107–10. Quotation from "A Question Vitally Affecting Railway Bus Operation," *Railway Age* 80 (March 27, 1926): 888.

58. Quotation from "The T.A.T. Air Rail Service," *Railway Age* 87 (July 6, 1929): 12–16; see also "Should Railroads Engage in All Forms of Transportation?" *Railway Age* 86 (April 6, 1929): 769, and "Railroads Take to the Air," *Literary Digest* 102 (July 20, 1929): 8.

59. "Giving Force to a Hackneyed Word," *Railway Age* 72 (June 20, 1922): 1321–22.

60. Wilson, *Coördinated Motor-Rail-Steamship Transportation,* 2–3.

61. Samuel O. Dunn, "Our National Transportation Problem," *Railway Age* 90 (May 30, 1931): 1067–70.

62. Silas H. Strawn, "Interests of Carriers and Shippers Are Inseparable," *Railway Age* 91 (August 1, 1931): 177–79; Miller, *Inland Transportation,* 787–88.

63. "Reforms in Railway Regulation Recommended," *Railway Age* 93 (October 1, 1932): 461–64. Johnson wrote consistently about "the need to establish coöperative relations between the several agencies of transportation . . . each agency performing the service it can render most economically and efficiently." He added, "There must be a national transportation policy." Emory R. Johnson, *Government Regulation of Transportation* (New York: D. Appleton-Century Company, 1938), 645.

64. Miller, *Inland Transportation,* 752–53; see also "Joint Rail-Highway Conference Committee," *Railway Age* 93 (October 29, 1933): 619, and "No Rail-Highway Body Moratorium Agreement," *Railway Age* 93 (November 5, 1932): 655. See also William J. Cunningham, "The Correlation of Rail and Highway Transportation," *American Economic Review* 24 (March 1934): 48.

65. Moulton became the first president of the Brookings Institution in 1927, a post he held until 1952. Harold Glenn Moulton, *Waterways versus Railroads* (Boston: Houghton Mifflin, 1912); Charles B. Saunders, *The Brookings Institution: A Fifty Year History* (Washington, DC: Brookings Institution, 1966); and Donald T. Critchlow, *The Brookings Institution, 1916–1952: Expertise and the Public Interest in a Democratic Society* (DeKalb: Northern Illinois University Press, 1985).

66. Critchlow, *The Brookings Institution,* 113; "Coolidge Committee Holds First Meeting," *Railway Age* 93 (October 15, 1932): 549; "Coolidge Committee Hearings," *Railway Age* 93 (December 17, 1932): 904–908; "Railways Propose Legislative Pro-

gram," *Railway Age* 93 (December 10, 1932): 859–64; "National Transportation Committee Makes Comprehensive Report," *Railway Age* 94 (February 18, 1933): 247–50, 255; Miller, *Inland Transportation*, 754–55; and "Transport Problem Analyzed By N.T.C. Staff," *Railway Age* 94 (March 18, 1933): 399–401. Quotation from Moulton, *American Transportation Policy*, 881. Former governor Alfred Smith's minority report was harder on the railroads and employed traditional rhetoric about the need to protect railroad workers.

67. "I.C.C. Examiners Begin Series of Hearings on Co-ordination of Motor Transportation," *Automotive Industries* 63 (November 22, 1930): 776. The hearings can be followed in detail during 1930 and 1931 in *Railway Age*, beginning with "Motor Transport Hearings Begin," 89 (December 27, 1930): 1393–98, 1415. Similar coverage was found in *Bus Transportation*, vols. 10 and 11.

68. "Co-ordination of Transportation Agencies Recommended," *Railway Age* 92 (January 9, 1932): 74–78.

69. In his detailed account of the Van Sweringen brothers, the most notorious speculators in railroad finance during the 1920s, Herbert Harwood identifieds a practice he labeled "creative complexity" in the industry. Even so, Harwood finds that the brothers from Cleveland were in business not only to turn large profits, but also because of a commitment to railroads. See Harwood, *Invisible Giants*, quotation from page 127; also vii–xii, 263–75.

70. "Efforts to Avert Receiverships," *Railway Age* 91 (December 26, 1931): 980–83; "Government Railroad Loans," *Railway Age* 92 (June 4, 1932): 948; "Hoover Seeks Way to Induce Railway Spending," *Railway Age* 93 (August 6, 1932): 187–88; Pierce H. Fulton, "Will Government Aid Help Rails?" *Magazine of Wall Street* 50 (August 20, 1932): 510–11, 524; and "Regulation of Competing Carriers Favored by Hoover," *Railway Age* 91 (December 12, 1931): 907; U.S. Congress, Senate Committee on Banking and Currency, *Loans to Railroads by Reconstruction Finance Corporation* (Washington, DC: Government Printing Office, 1938). For a general account, see James Stuart Olson, *Herbert Hoover and the Reconstruction Finance Corporation, 1931–1933* (Ames: Iowa State University Press, 1977), and Hoogenboom and Hoogenboom, *History of the ICC*, 122–23.

71. This view of Hoover conforms to the main currents of recent historiography. See Joan Hoff-Wilson, *Herbert Hoover, Forgotten Progressive* (Boston: Little, Brown, 1975); Ellis W. Hawley et al., *Herbert Hoover and the Crisis of American Capitalism* (Cambridge, MA: Schenkman Publishing Co., 1973); Ellis W. Hawley et al., *Herbert Hoover and the Historians* (West Branch, IA: Herbert Hoover Presidential Library Association, 1989); and Jordan A. Schwarz, *The Interregnum of Despair: Hoover, Congress, and the Depression* (Urbana: University of Illinois Press, 1970), and idem, *The New Dealers: Power Politics in the Age of Roosevelt* (New York: Knopf, 1993), 32–56.

72. "Governor Roosevelt on Railroads," *Railway Age* 94 (September 24, 1932): 425–27.

73. "Unified Regulatory Plan Considered by Roosevelt," *Railway Age* 94 (February 4, 1933): 191. See Claude Moore Fuess, *Joseph Eastman: Servant of the People* (Westport, CT: Greenwood Press, 1952), 180–210; Hoogenboom and Hoogenboom, *A History of the ICC*, 125–217; "New Transport Policy Planned by President," *Railway Age* 94 (March 25, 1933): 445–46; "Railroad Plans Near Completion," *Railway Age* 94 (April 8, 1933): 509–14.

74. "New Transport Policy," *Railway Age* 94 (April 1, 1933): 479–80; "Federal Railroad Co-ordinator Planned," *Railway Age* 94 (April 1, 1933): 479; "Railroad Plans Near

Completion," *Railway Age* 94 (April 8, 1933): 509–14; "President Roosevelt Approves Transportation Bill," *Railway Age* 94 (May 6, 1933): 668–70; "Commissioner Eastman Appointed Federal Co-ordinator," *Railway Age* 94 (June 24, 1933): 899–900; Ellis W. Hawley, *The New Deal and the Problem of Monopoly* (Princeton, NJ: Princeton University Press, 1969), 227–31. Others had called for a "railroad umpire" as early as 1931. See F. J. Lisman, "A Railroad Umpire Would Remedy Many Major Ills," *Railway Age* 90 (April 4, 1931): 665–68, 670. Historian Ellis Hawley, on the other hand, interpreted the bill as an example of "declining, overly competitive, or particularly depressed industries" seeking to claim the status of public utility as "a means of economic salvation, a way to use . . . the power of the state to stabilize prices, reduce competition, and insure profitable returns on overcapitalized investments." Hawley, *The New Deal and the Problem of Monopoly*, 226–28.

75. "Joseph B. Eastman-Public Servant," *Public Administration Review* 5 (Winter 1945): 34–54; C. A. Miller, *The Lives of the Interstate Commerce Commissioners and the Commission Secretaries* (Washington, DC: Association of ICC Practitioners, 1946), 87–95; Fuess, *Joseph Eastman*, 180–210; Earl Latham, *The Politics of Railroad Co-ordination, 1933–1936* (Cambridge, MA: Harvard University Press, 1959); idem, *Joseph Eastman.*

76. "Co-ordinator Organizes for Work," *Railway Age* 95 (July 15, 1933): 117–19; Eastman to James A. Farley, October 5, 1933, Letterbooks, Box 28, Papers); "Eastman's Views on Motor Transport Regulation," *Railway Age* 95 (October 28, 1933): 636–37; Fuess, *Joseph Eastman;* Latham, *The Politics of Railroad Co-ordination.*

77. Joseph B. Eastman, "The Work of the Federal Co-ordinator," *Railway Age* 95 (September 30, 1933): 468–71; "Railroads Must Co-operate," *Railway Age* 90 (May 23, 1931): 1022–24.

78. "Eastman's Views on Motor Transport Regulation," *Railway Age* 95 (October 28, 1933): 636–37. See letters between Eastman and Moulton, October 9, 1926, September 20, 1929; and Eastman to Mark M. Jones, July 6, 1933, Letterbooks, Box 26, Eastman Papers.

79. "Eastman Asks Views on Transportation Legislation," *Railway Age* 95 (November 11, 1933): 697–98; "Transportation Service Surveyed by Co-ordinator," *Railway Age* 95 (August 19, 1933): 278–79, 287–88; "Co-ordinator Studies Pooling, Standards Research," *Railway Age* 95 (August 26, 1933): 308–309; "Eastman Studies Control of Water, Motor Transport," *Railway Age* 95 (September 23, 1933): 437–38; Joseph B. Eastman, "The Work of the Federal Co-ordinator," *Railway Age* 95 (September 30, 1933): 468–71; Latham, *The Politics of Railroad Co-ordination.*

80. U. S. Office of the Federal Co-ordinator of Transportation, *Summary of the Work of the Federal Coordinator of Transportation, under the Emergency Railroad Transportation Act, 1933, June, 1933 to June, 1935* (Washington, DC: Government Printing Office, 1935); "Eastman's Views on Motor Transport Regulation," *Railway Age* 95 (October 28, 1933): 636–37; "Eastman Asks Co-operation to Increase Employment," *Railway Age* 95 (September 9, 1933): 369–70; "Eastman Warns Roads on Labor Relations," *Railway Age* 95 (December 16, 1933): 849–50; "Blue Eagle Code Not Needed for Railroads," *Railway Age* 95 (September 9, 1933): 367–69; "Railroad Labor to Press Its Legislative Program," *Railway Age* 96 (February 3, 1934): 208; "Railroad Labor Asks for Six-Hour Day," *Railway Age* 96 (March 10, 1934): 353–56; "Eastman Again Urges National Adjustment Board," *Railway Age* 96 (April 28, 1934): 611–12, 616. Quotations from "Not One of the 'Brain Trust,'" *Railway Age* 96 (June 9, 1934): 839–41; and Fuess, *Joseph Eastman*, 203.

81. "Regulation of Water and Motor Carriers Recommended," *Railway Age* 96 (March 17, 1934): 377–85; "The Future of the Railroads," *Railway Age* 96 (May 19, 1934): 731–33, 738. See also U.S. Office of Federal Coordinator of Transportation, *Regulation of Transportation Agencies. Letter from the Chairman of the Interstate Commerce Commission transmitting pursuant to law, a report of the Federal Coordinator of Transportation on the regulation of transportation agencies other than railroads and on proposed changes in the railroad regulation* . . . (Washington, DC: Government Printing Office, 1934); and "Co-ordinated Service and Regulation," *Bus Transportation* 13 (March 1934): 82–84.

82. Childs, *Trucking and the Public Interest,* 128; "New Bill Would Regulate Bus and Truck Service," *Railway Age* 96 (January 20, 1934): 80–81; "Railroads Support Motor Carrier Regulation Bill," *Railway Age* 96 (February 3, 1934): 210–11; "Shippers, Farmers, and Truckers Flay Rayburn Bill at Congressional Hearing," *Automotive Industries* 70 (February 3, 1934): 148; "'More Perfect Union' Urged by Eastman," *Railway Age* 96 (January 27, 1934): 113–18; "President Wants Railroad Reorganization," *Railway Age* 96 (April 28, 1934): 610, 624; "Federal Co-ordinator Continued for Another Year," *Railway Age* 96 (May 5, 1934): 668; "President Roosevelt and the Railroads," *Railway Age* 96 (May 5, 1934): 643–45; "President Giving Attention to Railroad Situation," *Railway Age* 97 (September 8, 1934): 291.

83. "Co-ordinated Transportation Regulation," *Railway Age* 97 (November 17, 1934): 612–14; "Eastman Discusses Railroad Future," *Railway Age* 97 (October 13, 1934): 444–46, 448; Joseph B. Eastman, "The Motor Carrier and the Transportation Problem," *Bus Transportation* 13 (October 1934): 359–62; "Eastman Urges Regulation of Water Carriers,"*Railway Age* 97 (December 1, 1934): 749–50; "Enemy or Ally? Is the Bus Inimical to the Railroads?" *Bus Transportation* 13 (September 1934): 341–42; "Will the Motor Carriers Get Federal Regulation? The Bus Men Urge It; the Truckmen Want It, Too," *Bus Transportation* 13 (December 1934): 455–456. Quotation from H. F. Lane, "Activities of the Co-ordinator in 1934," *Railway Age* 98 (January 26, 1935): 114–19, 120–22.

84. H. F. Lane, "The Outlook for Transportation Legislation," *Railway Age* 98 (January 26, 1935): 120–22; "Legislative Program Recommended by Eastman," *Railway Age* 98 (February 2, 1935): 198–206; see also "Eastman's Labor Protection Plans," *Railway Age* 98 (February 9, 1935): 23–24.

85. Childs, *Trucking and the Public Interest,* 130–39; "Motor Carrier Bill Passed," *Railway Age* 99 (August 10, 1935): 187–88; "Fifteen-Year Campaign Wins Motor Carrier Regulation," *Railway Age* 99 (August 10, 1935): 214, 217–18; "Federal Regulation at Last," *Bus Transportation* 14 (August 1935): 317; "What Congress Did to and for the Bus Industry," *Bus Transportation* 14 (September 1935): 359–60; "Final Hearings on Motor Carrier Regulatory Bill," *Railway Age* 98 (March 9, 1935): 368, 371–72; "Hearings Begun on Motor Carrier Regulation Bill," *Railway Age* 98 (February 23, 1935): 313–15; "Hearings on Eastman Bills," *Railway Age* 98 (March 2, 1935): 334–37; Fuess, *Joseph Eastman,* 230–31.

86. The president's message reached Congress on June 7. "President Asks Transportation Legislation," *Railway Age* 98 (June 15, 1935): 938–39; "Legislation Lags," *Bus Transportation* 14 (March 1935): 99–101; "Railroad Reorganization Bill Passed," *Railway Age* 99 (August 24, 1935): 248–49; "Revised Waterway Bill Reported to Senate," *Railway Age* 98 (June 29, 1935): 1005; "Hearings on Water Carrier Bill," *Railway Age* 98 (March 23, 1935): 451–53, 466; "Water Carrier Regulation Urged by Co-ordinator," *Railway Age* 98 (May 4, 1935): 699; "Much Opposition to Long-and-Short-Haul

Repeal," *Railway Age* 98 (June 29, 1935): 1014–15; "Investigation of Railroad Financing Proposed in Senate," *Railway Age* 98 (March 30, 1935): 507–9; "Senator Wheeler's Government Ownership Bill," *Railway Age* 98 (April 20, 1935): 603–4, 614; "Labor Leaders Favor Government Operation," *Railway Age* 98 (June 29, 1935): 1017.

87. See "Pelley Finds Co-ordinator No Longer Needed," *Railway Age* 98 (March 9, 1935): 366–67; Fuess, *Joseph Eastman,* 236–38.

88. "President Urges Centralized Transportation Regulation," *Railway Age* 98 (February 9, 1935): 231–32, 242; "President Plans One Agency to Regulate All Transport," *Railway Age* 98 (January 12, 1935): 42, 51, 54.

89. The following discussion of aviation policy draws from Erik Dunton Carlson, "The Origins and Development of the Civil Aeronautics Board and the Economic Regulation of Domestic Airlines, 1934–1953" (Ph.D. diss., Texas Tech University, 1996), 61–73; Komons, *Bonfires to Beacons,* 347–54; and Smith, *Airways,* 285–89.

90. "President Urges Centralized Transportation," 242

91. Hawley, *New Deal and the Problem of Monopoly,* 230–31; "Continuation of Co-ordinator Office Doubtful," *Railway Age* 100 (June 13, 1936): 960–51; Fuess, *Joseph Eastman,* 239–43; "Eastman Urges Labor-Saving Economies," *Railway Age* 99 (November 16, 1935): 631–34; "Protecting Labor in Co-ordination Projects," *Railway Age* 99 (December 21, 1935): 824; "Eastman Favors Unemployment Compensation," *Railway Age* 100 (April 11, 1936): 623–24.

92. Komons, *From Bonfires to Beacons,* 362–63; Fuess, *Joseph Eastman,* 253–54.

93. Komons, *From Beacons to Bonfires,* 357; Carlson, "Origins and Development of the Civil Aeronautics Board," 78–79.

94. As throughout this section, information from Kommons, *From Bonfires to Beacons;* Smith, *Airways;* and Carlson, "Origins and Development of the Civil Aeronautics Board," especially pages 82–83; see also "Air Transport Board; Roosevelt Wants to Lodge Control with a New Commission," *Business Week* (January 15, 1938): 42; "Civil Aviation Act Passes as Congress Adjourns," *Aero Digest* 33 (July 1938): 18; and O. Ryan, "Civil Aeronautics Act," *Public Utilities* 23 (April 27/May 11, 1939): 515–25, 597–605.

95. Charles S. Rhyne, *The Civil Aeronautics Act Annotated,* foreword by Senator Pat McCarran (Washington, DC: National Law Book Co., 1939), vi.

96. "Roosevelt Wants Private Ownership," *Railway Age* 103 (December 18, 1937): 887.

97. Members included Carl Gray of Union Pacific, the only railroad executive and FDR's frequent contact within the industry; Senators Burton K. Wheeler and Harry S. Truman, Representative Charles F. Lea (all involved in congressional interstate commerce committees); Secretary of the Treasury Henry Morgenthau; Henry Bruere of the Bowery Savings Bank; SEC chairman William O. Douglas; George M. Harrison, chair of the Railway Labor Executive Association; W. H. Alexander from the Farm Security Administration; and Assistant Secretary of Commerce Ernest G. Draper.

98. "President Roosevelt Names Special Committee to Formulate Legislation for Aid to Railroads," *Commercial and Financial Chronicle* 146 (March 19, 1938): 1805–1806; "White House Action on Railway Situation Next Week," *Railway Age* 104 (March 26, 1938): 570–71; Fuess, *Joseph Eastman,* 258–62; "President's Railroad Message," *Railway Age* 104 (April 16, 1938): 699–704; and James C. Nelson, "The Splawn Committee Report on Relief for the Railroads," *Journal of Land and Public Utility Economics* 14 (May 1938): 227–30.

99. Fuess, *Joseph Eastman,* 262; "President's Railroad Message," *Railway Age* 104

(April 16, 1938): 699–704.

100. "I.C.C. Legislative Proposals," *Railway Age* 106 (March 25, 1939): 522–27; Fuess, *Joseph Eastman,* 262–63; "Report of the Committee-of-Six," *Railway Age* 105 (December 31, 1938): 944–46; "Summary of the Recommendations of the President's Committee on Railroad Legislation," *Commercial and Financial Chronicle* 147 (December 31, 1938): 3989–90; "Centralized Control of Transport Urged by President's Committee," *Engineering News-Record* 121 (December 29, 1938): 803; and D. P. Locklin, "Report of the President's Committee on the Transportation Situation," *Journal of Land and Public Utility Economics* 15 (February 1939): 117–19. One of the railroad members was M. W. Clement of the Pennsylvania Railroad. See Files on the Committee of Six, Box 1134, Legal Department—General Correspondence, Accession 1810, Records of the Pennsylvania Railroad, Hagley Library, Wilmington, DE.

101. S. Chesterfield Oppenheim, *The National Transportation Policy and Inter-Carrier Competitive Rates* (Harrisburg, PA: The Evangelical Press, 1945), 5; see also "Committee of Six Bill Introduced," *Railway Age* 106 (March 11, 1939): 421–23. The following section rests on "Transportation Act of 1939," *Railway Age* 106 (January 21, 1939): 154–56; "Hearing on Senate Transport Bills," *Railway Age* 106 (April 18, 1939): 614–18; and regular and extensive reports on the progress of the bills in *Railway Age* (vols. 107–108) and *Bus Transportation* (vol. 18) during the spring and summer of 1939.

102. Fuess, *Joseph Eastman,* 263. The key question about freight forwarders during the 1940 debates was whether the ICC could regulate their activities, a step that the ICC commissioners wanted to take after an investigation indicated that the three largest forwarders were tightly connected to the New York Central, the Erie/Chesapeake & Ohio system, and the Baltimore & Ohio. The issue became even more important after the war. See "Would Regulate Forwarders," *Railway Age* 103 (August 7, 1937): 165–66; "Roads Should Perform Freight Forwarding Services," *Railway Age* 105 (November 19, 1938): 745–47; and detailed coverage of Senate hearings on the subject in *Railway Age* 108 (June 8, 15, 22, 29, 1940): 1006–1007; 1057–62, 1064; 114–18; 1181–84.

103. "Conferees Agree on a New Wheeler-Lea Bill," *Railway Age* 109 (August 10, 1940): 220–21; "House Passes S. 2009," *Railway Age* 109 (August 17, 1940): 257–58.

104. Charles Layng, "Motor Transport Operations Continue to Grow," *Railway Age* 104 (January 1, 1938): 95–99; "Northern Pacific Builds Truck-Bus System," *Railway Age* 103 (December 25, 1937): 917–18; Harold G. Moulton, "The Need for Companies Providing All Forms of Transportation," *Railway Age* 99 (September 7, 1935): 303–306; C. D. Cass, "Congress Considers Bill to Regulate Interstate Highway Transportation," *American Electric Railway Association Journal* (February 1932): 836–38.

105. Despite the experiments of some rail carriers, it was not until 1925 or so that most railroads seriously explored motor vehicle usage. By then, independent owners had already established operations and secured the all-important certificates of convenience and necessity that were enshrined in common law and allow the holder exclusive rights to provide a service to the public. Lacking such certificates, railroads often could not develop motor vehicle operations. Seely, "Railroads, Good Roads, and Motor Vehicles."

106. The ICC's views on railroad use of motor vehicles had started to take shape even before 1940. See "Extension of Rail-Motor Co-ordination Vetoed," *Railway Age* 105 (October 8, 1938): 525–26; "No Rail-Truck Tie-up; ICC Refuses Union Pacific, Burlington, and North Western Railroads," *Business Week* (October 8, 1938): 37–38. Quotation from Emory R. Johnson, *Transport Facilities, Services and Policies* (New York: D. Appleton-Century Company, 1947), 125–26.

107. U.S. Office of Federal Coordinator of Transportation, *Public Aids to Transportation*, 4 vols. (Washington, DC: Government Printing Office, 1938–40).

108. Examples of support for reexamining consolidation during the depression include "Regional Railroad Consolidations," *Railway Age* 94 (April 1, 1933): 465–67; "General Atterbury Urges Nation-wide Consolidation," *Railway Age* 94 (May 13, 1933): 702, 706; Ralph Budd, "Merge Railways into 20 Systems," *Railway Age* 99 (November 23, 1935): 665–68; "Chamber of Commerce Urges Voluntary Consolidations," *Railway Age* 100 (February 15, 1936): 290, 294; "Miller Favors One Big Railroad," *Railway Age* 103 (September 4, 1937): 308–10; "Do Shippers Want a Unified Rail System?" *Railway Age* 103 (October 16, 1937): 525–27; "Wants Six Region Merger for Roads," *Railway Age* 105 (November 19, 1938): 753–54; and Carroll Miller, "Commissioner Miller Again Urges Merger," *Railway Age* 107 (July 1, 1939): 41–43.

109. James C. Nelson, "Politics and Economics in Transport Regulation and Deregulation—A Century Perspective of the ICC's Role," *Logistics and Transportation Review* 23, no. 1 (1987): 5–32, quotation from page 14.

110. Ibid.

111. Claude Moore Fuess, *Joseph B. Eastman—A Study in Public Service*, http://books.yanco.com/jbeastman/. Also Fuess, *Joseph Eastman;* Joseph B. Eastman and George Lloyd Wilson, *Selected Papers and Addresses of Joseph B. Eastman, Director, Office of Defense Transportation, 1942–1944* (New York: Simmons-Boardman Pub. Corp., 1948).

CHAPTER 3

1. U.S. Congress, Senate Committee on Interstate and Foreign Commerce, *Air-Line Industry Investigation: Hearings before the Committee on Interstate and Foreign Commerce Eighty—First Congress First Session Pursuant to S. Res. 50* (Washington, DC: U.S. Government Printing Office, 1949).

2. Richard H. K. Vietor, *Contrived Competition: Regulation and Deregulation in America* (Cambridge, MA: Belknap Press of Harvard University Press, 1994), 29–30; Charles S. Rhyne, *The Civil Aeronautics Act Annotated, with the Congressional History Which Produced It, and the Precedents upon Which It Is Based* (Washington, DC: National Law Book Company, 1939), 96–104; U.S. Civil Aeronautics Authority, *Aeronautical Statutes and Related Material: The Civil Aeronautics Act of 1938 and Other Statutory Provisions Relating to Civil Aeronautics, Together with Reorganization Plans No. III and No. IV and Certain Other Non-Statutory Material Affecting Civil Aeronautics, October 15, 1940* (Washington, DC: U.S. Government Printing Office, 1940), 9.

3. For features of the Boeing-377, see Robert J. Serling, *Legend and Legacy: The Story of Boeing and Its People* (New York: St. Martin's Press, 1992), 75–76; and Kenneth Hudson, *Air Travel: A Social History* (Totowa, NJ: Rowman and Littlefield, 1972), 128, 165; for accounts of the flying experience in the early 1950s, see Roger E. Bilstein, "Air Travel and the Traveling Public: The American Experience, 1920–1970," in *From Airships to Airbus: A History of Civil and Commercial Aviation,* vol. 2, *Pioneers and Operations,* ed. William F. Trimble (Washington, DC: Smithsonian Institution Press, 1995), 102–105; David T. Courtwright, "The Routine Stuff: How Flying Became a Form of Mass Transportation," in *Reconsidering a Century of Flight*, ed. Roger D. Launius and Janet R. Daly-Bednarek (Chapel Hill: University of North Carolina Press, 2003), 218–19.

4. Frank A. Smith, *Transportation in America: A Statistical Analysis of Transportation*

in the United States: 1939–1985 (Washington, DC: Eno Foundation for Transportation, 1989), 10, 14; Air Transport Association of America, *Annual Traffic and Capacity, 1926–2001;* Lucile Sheppard Keyes, *Federal Control of Entry into Air Transportation* (Cambridge, MA: Harvard University Press, 1951), 51–105, 311–13. Through 1954, airlines carried fewer than 5 percent of all intercity passengers.

5. *Aviation Week* (hereafter cited as *AW*) 48, no. 18 (November 18, 1947), 51–52; U.S. Congress, House Committee on the Judiciary, Antitrust Subcommittee (Subcommittee No. 5), 84th Congress, 2nd session, *Monopoly Problems in Regulated Industries: Hearings Before the Antitrust Subcommittee Volumes 1, 2, 3: Airlines* (Washington, DC: U.S. Government Printing Office, 1957), 3:1705, 1709.

6. On the nonsked's trade association, see U.S. Congress, Senate, Select Committee on Small Business, Subcommittee on Irregular Airlines, *Role of Irregular Airlines in United States Air Transportation Industry: Hearings Before the United States Senate Select Committee on Small Business, Subcommittee on Irregular Airlines, Eighty-Second Congress, First Session, on April 23–25, 27, 30, May 1, 5, 1951* (Washington, DC: U.S. Government Printing Office, 1951); Roger D. Launius, "Right Man, Right Place, Right Time? Orvis M. Nelson and the Politics of Supplemental Air Carriers," in *Airline Executives and Federal Regulation: Case Studies from the Airmail Era to the Dawn of the Jet Age,* ed. W. David Lewis (Columbus: Ohio State University Press, 2000), 322–55, quotation on page 322.

7. U.S. Civil Aeronautics Board, *The Role of Competition in Commercial Air Transportation: Report of the Civil Aeronautics Board Submitted to the Subcommittee on Monopoly of the Select Committee on Small Business, Unites States Senate,* Subcommittee Print No. 9, 82nd Congress, 2nd Session (Washington, DC: U.S. Government Printing Office, 1952), 31; *Air Transportation—Air Commerce* 3, no. 4 (October, 1943): 35–42, and 5, no. 2 (August, 1944), hereafter cited as *ATAC;* James C. Nelson comments on William N. Leonard, "Some Problems of Postwar Air Transportation," *American Economic Review* 37, no. 1 (May 1947): 492–97; Launius, "Right Man, Right Place, Right Time?" 331; and Donna M. Corbett, "Donald W. Nyrop: Airline Regulator, Airline Executive," both in Lewis, *Airline Executives and Federal Regulation,* 131.

8. U.S. Civil Aeronautics Board, *Economic Decisions of the Civil Aeronautics Board* (Washington, DC: U.S. Government Printing Office, c. 1946–1947), 1052; idem, "Page Airways Investigation," 1061–70; "Trans-Marine Airline, Inc. Investigation," 1071–82; Launius, "Right Man, Right Place, Right Time?" in Lewis, *Airline Executives and Federal Regulation,* 343.

9. *Wall Street Journal,* July 9, 1947 (Editorial); *Washington Post,* August 11, 1947. *AW* 47, no. 4 (July 28, 1947), 11; 49, no.14 (October 4, 1948), 7; U.S. House Committee on the Judiciary, Antitrust Subcommittee (Subcommittee No. 5), *Monopoly Problems in Regulated Industries,* pt. 1, vol. 2: 639–743, and pt. 1, vol. 3: 1678–83, 1702–19, 1746–50, 1766–69.

10. *ATAC* 8, no. 44 (April 1946): 46–47, 52; 10, no. 1: 32; *Aviation* 45, no. 9 (September 1946): 111; 45, no.11 (November 1946):107.

11. House Committee on the Judiciary, Antitrust Subcommittee (Subcommittee No. 5), *Monopoly Problems in Regulated Industries,* especially pt. 1, vol. 2: 639–743; Thomas K. McCraw, *Prophets of Regulation: Charles Francis Adams, Louis D. Brandeis, James M. Landis, Alfred E. Kahn* (Cambridge, MA: Belknap Press of Harvard University, 1984), 205–206; Smith, *Transportation in America,* 10, 14.

12. *ATAC* 9, no.11 (November, 1946): 43–44; 10, no. 5 (May, 1947): 29–30; *AW* 47, no. 14 (October 6, 1947): 59–60; *AW* 47, no.15 (October 13, 1947); Donald M. Ritchie,

James M. Landis, Dean of the Regulators (Cambridge, MA: Harvard University Press, 1980), 143–54; John R. M. Wilson, *Turbulence Aloft: The Civil Aeronautics Administration amid Wars and Rumors of Wars, 1938–1953* (Washington, DC: U.S. Federal Aviation Administration, 1979), 159–63; Karen Miller, "'Air Power is Peace Power,' The Aircraft Industry's Campaign for Public and Political Support, 1943–1949," *Business History Review* 70, no. 3 (Autumn 1996): 297–325.

13. U.S. Civil Aeronautics Board, "Airfreight Case," in *Economic Decisions of the Civil Aeronautics Board* (May 1951–December 1951) (Washington, DC: Government Printing Office, 1956), 590, 614, 616.

14. CAB, Docket 3945 et al., in U.S. Civil Aeronautics Board, *Economic Decisions of the Civil Aeronautics Board* (December, 1949–August, 1950) (Washington, DC: U.S. Government Printing Office, 1953), 609–50, CAB Docket 3397 et al., in idem, *Economic Decisions of the Civil Aeronautics Board* (May 1951–December 1951) (Washington, DC: U.S. Government Printing Office, 1956), 720–90; U.S. Civil Aeronautics Board, *Economic Regulations in Force July 1, 1949, As Amended,* paragraph 291 as revised June 1950; Harry S. Truman, Presidential Papers, Official File, 3–1 Box 36, file 1949–1950, Harry S. Truman Library, Independence, MO, hereafter HSTL; Donna M. Corbett, "Donald W. Nyrop: Airline Regulator, Airline Executives," in Lewis, *Airline Executives and Federal Regulation,* 131; Nick A. Komons, *Bonfires to Beacons: Federal Civil Aviation Policy under the Air Commerce Act, 1926–1938* (Washington, DC: U.S. Department of Transportation, 1978), 254–59; Vietor, *Contrived Competition,* 34–37.

15. *AW* 48, no.16 (April 19, 1948): 13–14; *American Aviation* 14, no.11 (October 2, 1950): 1.

16. Paul Tillett and Myron Weiner, *The Closing of Newark Airport* (University, AL: Published for the ICP by University of Alabama Press, ICP Case Series No. 27, 1955); President's Airport Commission, *Proceedings . . . Institute of Aeronautical Sciences,* March 24–26, 1952, 1–2, 5, 34–39; Truman Presidential Papers, President's Airport Commission, Stenographic Report, HSTL.

17. See "Proceedings of Meetings with Various Aviation Organizations, Tuesday, March 18, 20, 1952," typescript, President's Airport Commission Series, Box 2, file ATA, in Truman, Presidential Papers, President's Airport Commission Series, Box 7, National Advisory Committee on Aeronautics, HSTL.

18. Nelson A. Rockefeller to Sherman Adams, April 10, 1953, in Dwight D. Eisenhower, Presidential Papers, Official File 460, Box 103-A, File April, 1053 (1), Dwight D. Eisenhower Presidential Library, Abilene, KS; *Transport Topics* 962 (January 18, 1954): 16. On the PACGO in 1953, see Peri E. Arnold, *Making the Managerial Presidency: Comprehensive Reorganization Planning, 1905–1980* (Princeton, NJ: Princeton University Press, 1986), 162–67; The President's Air Coordinating Committee, *Civil Air Policy, May 1954* (Washington, DC: United States Government Printing Office, 1954), 2.

19. *AW* 63, no. 16 (October 17, 1955): 7; no. 17 (October 24, 1955): 12–14, 122; no. 18 (October 31, 1955): 83–84; no. 19 (November 7, 1955): 107–109

20. *Aviation Week & Space Technology* (hereafter cited as *AW&ST*) 90, no. 2 (January 13, 1969): 26; U.S. Civil Aeronautics Board, *Domestic Passenger—Fare Investigation, January 1970 to December 1974* (Washington, DC: U.S. Government Printing Office, 1976).

21. Paul W. Cherington, *Airline Equipment Investment Program: Communication from the President of the United States Transmitting a Report Concerning the Status and Economic Significance of the Airline Equipment Investment Program, Dated June 30, 1958* (Washington, DC: U.S. Government Printing Office, August 5, 1958), 5–7, 11–12, 18; U.S. Con-

gress, Senate Committee on Foreign and Interstate Commerce, 85th Congress, 2nd Session, *Operating the Jet: A Symposium Presented to the Subcommittee on Aviation of the Committee on Interstate and Foreign Commerce Together with a Report of Progress and Developments on Jet Age Planning by the Civil Aeronautics Administration of the Department of Commerce* (Washington, DC: U.S. Government Printing Office, 1958), 61.

22. Jesse J. Friedman and Murray N. Friedman, "The New Economics of the Air-Line Industry," *Public Utilities Fortnightly* 68, no. 4 (August 17, 1961): 230–35; 231, 233; *AW&ST* 90, no. 2 (January 13, 1969): 26; Courtwright, "The Routine Stuff," 219.

23. Paul Howell Associates, *A Report on Fair and Reasonable Rate of Return for Domestic Air Carriers, for [the] Bureau of Operations, Civil Aeronautics Board in the General Passenger Fare Investigation* (New York: Paul Howell Associates [typescript], October 15, 1957), 4.25, 4.42; Emmette S. Redford, *The General Passenger Fare Investigation* (University, AL: Published for the ICP by University of Alabama Press, ICP Case Series No. 56, 1962), 9, 11–17, 47; U.S. Civil Aeronautics Board, *General Passenger Fare Investigation: Docket 8008 et al.* (Washington, DC: Civil Aeronautics Board [mimeograph], 1960), 10, 32.

24. James M. Landis, *Report on Regulatory Agencies to the President Elect, December 21, 1960* (New York: AD Press, 1961), 41–45.

25. *AW* 74, no. 10 (March 13, 1961): 144; 75, no. 14 (October 16, 1961): 40; *AW&ST* 77, no. 19 (November 19, 1962): 42; 78, no. 14 (April 8, 1963): 45; *AW&ST* 91, no. 21 (December 8, 1969): 31–32; 92, no. 2 (January 12, 1970): 28–29; 92 no. 5 (February 2, 1970): 29–31; *New York Times,* January 1, 1970, 1, 62.

26. U.S. Bureau of Labor Statistics Consumer Price Index Calculator, http://146.142.4.24/cgi—bin/surveymost; fares calculated from U.S. Civil Aeronautics Board, Bureau of Economics, Rates Division, *A Study of the Domestic Passenger Air Fare Structure* (Washington, DC: mimeograph, January 1968), 4; William E. Fruhan Jr., *The Fight for Competitive Advantage: A Study of United States Domestic Trunk Air Carriers* (Boston: Division of Research, Graduate School of Business Administration, Harvard University, 1972), 79. Productivity figures calculated from data in ibid., 24.

27. U.S. Task Force on National Aviation Goals, *Selected Characteristics of U.S. Air Carrier, General Aviation, and Military Flying Activity—Historical and as Projected through 1970* (Washington, DC: U.S. Federal Aviation Agency, 1961), 4–9.

28. Warren Rose, "The Air Coach Policies of the Civil Aeronautics Board" (pamphlet, dated 1961, Northwestern University Transportation Library), 30–32; *AW* 72, no. 10 (March 14, 1960): 38–39; *AW&ST* 75, no. 15 (October 16, 1961): 40; *New York Times,* November 17, 1961, 69; (June 30, 1961), 54; (July 18, 1961), 58; (July 24, 1961), 40; (July 24, 1961), 54; (August 1, 1961), 60; (August 5, 1961), 38; (August 29, 1961), 62; *AW&ST* 75, no. 14 (October 9, 1961): 37–38.

29. Michael H. Gorn, "Robert F. Six: Continental Giant," in Lewis, *Airline Executives and Federal Regulation,* 174, 176–79; *AW&ST* 75, no. 18 (November 6, 1961): 37; *New York Times,* October 31, 1961, 61; November 8, 1961, 70; November 18, 1961, 24; (January 3, 1992), 66; *AW&ST* 75, no. 21 (November 27, 1961): 36; 78, no. 4 (January 28, 1963): 36–37; *Business Week* 1693 (September 23, 1961): 90–91, 93.

30. Opinion Research Corporation, *The Domestic Travel Market with Emphasis on Prospect for Diversion from Auto to Air: A Nationwide Study /Opinion Research Corporation; Sponsored by American Airlines, Inc., Eastern Airlines, Inc., United Airlines, Inc., Trans World Airlines, Inc., Boeing Commercial Airplane Company, Inc., Douglas Aircraft Corporation* (Princeton, NJ: Opinion Research Corporation, 1962); *New York Times,* December 29,

1961, 2; *AW&ST* 78, no. 21 (December 4, 1961): 38; 76, no. 1 (January 1,1 962): 27.

31. U.S. Civil Aeronautics Board, *Domestic Passenger Fare Investigation, January, 1970 to December, 1974,* Appendix C and text, p. 232; *New York Times,* January 27, 1964, 42.

32. *New York Times,* July 29, 1965, 1, 56; *AW&ST* 83, no. 4 (July 26, 1965): 29–30.

33. *Business Week* no. 1825 (August 7, 1965): 34; *AW&ST* 82, no. 10 (March 15, 1965): 160; 83, no. 5 (August 2, 1965): 36; and 84, no. 4 (January 24, 1966): 41; *Time* 88, no. 4, July 7, 1966, 80–85.

34. *Business Week* 1825 (August 7, 1965): 34; *AW&ST* 83, no. 6 (August 9, 1965): 35–36; U.S. Civil Aeronautics Board, *Forecasts of Passenger Traffic of the Domestic Trunk Air Carriers, Domestic Operations, Scheduled Service, 1965—1975* (Washington, DC: U.S. Government Printing Office, September, 1965), 8, 28–30.

35. *New York Times,* June 4, 1966, 58; June 5, 1966, 88; August 20, 1966, 13; December 29, 1966, 1.

36. *Jane's All The World's Aircraft* (New York: McGraw-Hill, 1974), 274, 276, 375; *AW&ST* 84, no. 12 (March 28, 1966): 38.

37. James C. Miller, "An Aircraft Routing Model for the Airline Firm," *American Economist* 12, no. 1 (Spring 1969): 24–32; Nawal K. Teneja, *The Commercial Airline Industry* (Lexington, MA: D. C. Heath, 1976), 97–101, 312.

38. U.S. Congress, Senate Committee on Commerce, Aviation Subcommittee, *Economic Condition of the Air Transportation Industry: Hearings before the Subcommittee on Aviation of the Committee on Commerce,* 92nd Congress, 1st Session, February 2, 3 , 4 , 8, 9, 10, 11, 18, May 19, 20, 1971 (Washington, DC: U.S. Government Printing Office, 1972), 15, 144.

39. U.S. Congress, House Committee on Interstate and Foreign Commerce, 89th Congress, 2nd Session, *Airline Labor Dispute: Hearings on Senate Joint Resolution 186 to provide for the Settlement of the Labor Dispute Currently Existing Between Certain Air Carriers and Certain of Their Employees, and for Other Purposes, August 5, 6, 8, 9, 10, 1966* (Washington, DC: U.S. Government Printing Office, 1966), 5–7.

40. *New York Times,* August 16, 1966, 1; August 21, 1966, 1, 62; *Business Week* no. 1829 (August 20, 1966): 3.

41. *New York Times,* October 6, 1966, x, 9; November 14, 1967, 93; *AW&ST* 86, no. 4 (January 30, 1967): 45; 86, no. 13 (April 3, 1967): 38; 86, no. 14 (April 10, 1967): 37–38; Vietor, *Contrived Competition,* 45–48; and for the emerging political strength of the consumer movement during this period, see Lizabeth Cohen, *A Consumer's Republic: The Politics of Mass Consumption in Postwar America* (New York: Alfred A. Knopf, 2003), 359–63, 383–87.

42. *New York Times,* February 3, 1969, 71; July 22, 1969, 78; January 25, 1970, 181; June 3, 1970, 62–63; December 20, 1970, 66; *AW&ST* 91, no. 17 (November 3, 1969): 28.

43. *AW&ST* 92, no. 10 (March 8, 1971): 130–31; Vietor, *Contrived Competition,* 41–47.

44. *AW&ST* 96, no. 13 (April 3, 1972): 21; 88, no. 12 (March 25, 1968): 26; *New York Times,* August 22, 1971, v–24; February 13, 1972, xxi, F5; Fruhan, *The Fight for Competitive Advantage,* 79–110.

45. U.S. Senate, Committee on Commerce, Aviation Subcommittee, 92nd Congress, 1st Session, *Economic Condition of the Air Transportation Industry,* 7–11; U.S. Civil Aeronautics Board, Bureau of Economics, Rates Division, *A Study of the Domestic Passenger Air Fare Structure* (Washington, DC: U.S. Government Printing Office, 1968), 56, 62.

46. U.S. Senate, *Economic Condition of the Air Transportation Industry,* 70.

47. *AW&ST* 91, no. 18 (November 11, 1969): 24–25; *New York Times,* September 12, 1969, 1, 85.

48. *New York Times,* September 8, 1970, 81.

49. *AW&ST* 92, no. 24 (June 29, 1970): 28–29; 94, no. 12 (March 29, 1971): 32–33; U.S. Civil Aeronautics Board, Bureau of Enforcement, *Consumer Complaint Survey Reports* (Washington, DC: U.S. Government Printing Office, September 1967 *et sequentia*); *AW&ST* 92, no. 18 (May 18, 1970): 34; 93, no. 1 (July 6, 1970): 29; 93, no. 6 (August 17, 1970): 24; 94, no. 15 (May 17, 1971): 25; *New York Times,* November 17, 1969, 89; November 20, 1969, 70; December 19, 1972, 1.

50. U.S. Civil Aeronautics Board, *Domestic Passenger Fare Investigation, January, 1970 to December, 1974* (Washington, DC: U.S. Government Printing Office, 1976), 216 and throughout; *AW&ST* 94, no. 10 (March 8, 1971): 108; *New York Times,* March 21, 1971, 66.

51. *AW&ST* 92, no. 21 (June 8, 1970): 25–30; 93, no. 14 (October 12, 1970): 29, 33–34. U.S. Senate, Committee on Commerce, Subcommittee on Aviation, 92nd Congress, 1st Session, *Economic Condition of the Air Transportation Industry,* 13; U.S. Civil Aeronautics Board, *Productivity and Employment Costs in System Operations of the Trunk Airlines and Pan American from 1957 through 1970, with Additional Data for the First Quarter of 1971* (typescript, July 1971), 9–10; *New York Times,* January 6, 1971, 51; *AW&ST* 94, no. 1 (January 4, 1971): 25–26.

52. *New York Times,* January 6, 1971, 51; U.S. Senate, Committee on Commerce, Aviation Subcommittee, *Economic Condition of the Air Transportation Industry,* 7.

53. Ibid., 11, 13–15, 17–19, 363, 694–95, 853–58, 791–93.

54. Ibid., 374, 377, 379–80, 383–88, 390–92, 396; on Six's views, see Gorn, "Robert F. Six," 199–201; and also Robert J. Serling, *Maverick: The Story of Robert Six and Continental Airlines* (Garden City, NY: Doubleday, 1974), 303.

55. *New York Times,* February 3, 1971, 47.

56. U.S. Civil Aeronautics Board, *Domestic Passenger Fare Investigation,* 461–66, 469, 475; *New York Times,* April 13, 1971, 1.

57. U.S. Civil Aeronautics Board, *Domestic Passenger Fare Investigation,* 525, 528, 550–59, 564, 669–72.

58. *New York Times,* April 15, 1971, 85; George W. Douglas and James C. Miller III, *Economic Regulation of Domestic Air Transport: Theory and Practice* (Washington, DC: Brookings Institution, 1974), 39–44, 163–69.

59. Professor Richard R. John helped bring this point into a precise focus.

CHAPTER 4

1. Urban Land Institute, *Technical Bulletin No. 23—Space for Industry: An Analysis of Site and Location Requirements for Modern Manufacture* (Washington, DC: Urban Land Institute, 1954), 6, 12, 21, 23; Association of American Railroads, Railroad Committee for the Study of Transportation, *Report on Merchandise Traffic,* vol. 2 (Washington, DC: Author, 1946), 87, 161, 162, 171, 173; *ICC Practioners's Journal* 132 (June 9, 1952): 17. For the failure of a serious rail drive to retain passengers, see U.S. Congress, Senate, Subcommittee on Domestic Land and Water Transportation, *Study of Domestic Land and Water Transportation: Hearings Before the United States Senate Committee on Interstate and*

Foreign Commerce, Subcommittee on Domestic Land and Water Transportation, Eighty-First Congress, Second Session, on April 4, 6, 11, 18, 20, 25, 27, May 4, 9, 11, 16, 18, 23, 25, June 1, 6, 9, 13, 15, 20, 27, 29, July 6, 11, 13, 18, 20, 25, 27, 28, 1950 (Washington, DC: U.S. Government Printing Office, 1950), 52–54.

2. Henry F. McCarthy, "Railway Transport," *ICC Practioners' Journal* 17 (November 1949): 112–14; U.S. Senate Committee on Interstate and Foreign Commerce, Subcommittee on Domestic Land and Water Transportation, *Study of Domestic Land and Water Transportation,* 318–19. During the period 1949–1957, the words deregulate or deregulation appeared only twice in the business-oriented *Wall Street Journal*—once in a short article dated May 3, 1949, and again in a letter to the editor dated May 14, 1956. See *Proquest Historical Wall Street Journal.* For that same period of seven years, the words "deregulate" or "deregulation" never appeared in the titles of articles covered by the electronic Readers' Guide Retrospective produced by H. W. Wilson.

3. Cross-reference sheet dated April 5, 1949, in Box 36, File 3–5-I 1949–1950 (CAB); Harry S. Truman to Charles A. Sawyer, August 30, 1949, Box 652, File 173 (1949), both in Harry S. Truman Papers, Truman Presidential Library, Independence, MO.

4. Sinclair Weeks to the Hon. A. S. Monroney, January 31, 1956; Milton Eisenhower to Arthur Kimball, March 1, 1954, in Series PACGO, Box 21, File 175, "Transportation Policy and Coordination, 1954–1956," all at Dwight D. Eisenhower Presidential Library, Abilene, KS.

5. William M. Blair, "Transport Panel Urges Freer Rein for Competition," *New York Times,* April 19, 1955, 1.

6. Ironically, Eisenhower had reinvigorated the effort to secure funding for the Interstate highway program during the summer of 1954, announcing his support for a massive spending increase and appointing a blue-ribbon study committee chaired by war-time compatriot Lucius D. Clay. The Clay Committee's report brought road funding front and center after a political stalemate had held from the late 1940s through 1954. Many of Clay's specific ideas—and the president's—were not enacted by Congress in 1956. See Dwight D. Eisenhower, *Mandate for Change, 1953–1956* (Garden City, NY: Doubleday & Company, 1963), 501; and Stephen E. Ambrose, *Eisenhower,* vol. 2, *The President* (New York: Simon & Shuster, 1984), 250–55. For detailed discussions of the Interstate programs, see Mark H. Rose, *Interstate: Express Highway Politics, 1941–1989,* rev. ed. (Knoxville: University of Tennessee Press, 1990); Bruce E. Seely, *Building the American Highway System: Engineers as Policymakers* (Philadelphia: Temple University Press, 1987); Gary T. Schwartz, "Urban Freeways and the Interstate System," *Southern California Law Review* 49 (1975–76): 406–13; and archival information in the Records of the President's Advisory Committee on a National Highway Program, Eisenhower Presidential Library, Abilene, KS; and correspondence in the Box 1233, GF 158–a-1, General File, Central Files, Dwight D. Eisenhower Papers, Eisenhower Presidential Library, Abilene, KS, cited hereafter as DDEL.

7. "Congress Gets Bill to Carry Out Plan of Cabinet Committee," *Transport Topics* (May 9, 1955): 1. For Eisenhower, the cold war, and consumers, see Lizabeth Cohen, *A Consumer's Republic: The Politics of Mass Consumption in Postwar America* (New York: Charles A. Knopf, 2003), 125, 127; and also see Meg Jacobs, *Pocketbook Politics: Economic Citizenship in Twentieth-Century America* (Princeton, NJ: Princeton University Press, 2005), 253.

8. Eisenhower's interest in the relationship between transportation and the econ-

omy shows clearly in his 1954 proposal to devote $25 billion to construction of the Interstate highway system. The impetus for action came from Arthur F. Burns, chair of Council of Economic Advisers, who wanted to use "self-liquidating highway projects in a counter-cyclical program." Burns was not the first presidential adviser to think in these terms; Truman's staff attempted, unsuccessfully, to adjust road expenditures to meet economic conditions. Congress generally resisted this approach to highway expenditures, especially in the case of the 1956 Interstate legislation. See Charles L. Dearing to Arthur L. Burns, August 18, 1953; and Robert B. Murray to Maj. Gen. William Persons, December 1, 1953, Folder 141-B (2), Box 728, Highways and Thoroughfares, Central File OF 141-B, Official File, DDEl; and Seely, *Building the American Highway System,* 195. See also Jason Scott Smith, *Building New Deal Liberalism: The Political Economy of Public Works, 1933–1956* (New York: Cambridge University Press, 2006), who examines the Interstate system as a public works project with its origins in the New Deal. We are grateful to Professor Smith for kindly sharing a portion of his book in typescript form.

9. Impressions gained from a systematic reading of *Transport Topics* between the mid-1950s and 1980. The specific phrase was used repeatedly in the pages of this journal over the years.

10. William S. Odlin Jr., "ATA Opposes all Points of Cabinet Report" (May 2, 1955), 1; "ATA Executives Outline Stand on Cabinet Committee Report" (May 9, 1955), 6; "Cabinet Plan Seen as Wedge for Rail Entry into Trucking" (May 16, 1955), 29, all in *Transport Topics.*

11. "Unending Mission" (May 16, 1955), 46; "Cabinet Report Aims at Killing Control of Rates, Curry Says" (May 16, 1955), 60, both in *Transport Topics.*

12. "ICC Attacks Key Proposals of Cabinet Report Measure" (April 30, 1956), 13; "Rails Fight to Grab Rate-Juggling Power" (May 14, 1956), 2; "Weeks Contends Fervently for Rail-Tinted Regulation" (June 25, 1956), 1; "Arpaia and Rothschild Clash over Railroad Rate-Cutting Scheme" (October 1, 1956), 1, all in *Transport Topics.*

13. "Williams Foresees No Let-up in Effort to Create Barriers," *Transport Topics* (October 29, 1956), 10.

14. Ibid. Ironically, given the heated response of truckers to Weeks's recommendation for rate competition, during this same time period members of the Eisenhower administration worked with leaders in Congress to finance construction of the National System of Interstate and Defense Highways, known popularly as the Interstate Highway System. Approved in 1956, federal officials funded 90 percent of the cost of building a national freeway system that by the year 2002 ran more than forty-seven thousand miles in length. President Eisenhower and his key aides perceived construction of the Interstate system not only as a way of relieving traffic congestion, but also as a vast public works program aimed at fostering national economic growth. As part of the legislative package assembled by leaders in Congress, directors of the American Trucking Associations who had so energetically opposed Weeks's deregulation plan accepted higher taxes on gasoline, tires, and trucks. Curiously, the Eisenhower administration's official records betray no discussion among the president's aides regarding connections between this vast, highway-development program and their simultaneous effort to address the failing health of the nation's railroads. Weeks was one of several cabinet-level officials who had formulated both initiatives. Not including beleaguered railroad executives, apparently no one in the Eisenhower administration recognized that a national system of high-speed, coast-to-coast expressways would further energize long-haul trucking and further complicate the financial situation facing the railroads. By the mid-1950s, identification of rail-

road and trucking industries as independent modes legally operating only in their own markets was firmly entrenched indeed. As for those beleaguered railroad leaders, they had been complaining about federal subsidies to trucking for so long that by 1956, no one was listening, not even those such as Secretary Weeks who were disposed to acknowledge their plight. For development of the Interstate Highway System extending back to the 1930s, see Rose, *Interstate*, and Seely, *Building the American Highway System*.

15. Charles A. Taff, *Commercial Motor Transportation* (Chicago: Richard D. Irwin, 1951), 77–79.

16. Vee H. Kennedy, "Contract Carrier Conference Fills Need over 20-Year Period" (October 20, 1958), 135; "R. J. McBride—'Mr. Common Carrier'" (October 20, 1958), 67, both in *Transport Topics*.

17. Dudley F. Pegrum, *Transportation Economics and Public Policy* (Homewood, IL: Richard D. Irwin, 1963), 344; Paul J. Wilson, "Trucks Gird to Fight Rail Invasion," *Transport Topics* (January 31, 1955), 1, 9.

18. Taff, *Commercial Motor Transportation*, 80–82; "Regular Common Carriers Report on Pending Cases," *Transport Topics* (July 18, 1955), 71.

19. "McBride, Rosenbaum Are Promoted by Common Carriers," *Transport Topics* (February 6, 1956), 3.

20. Pegrum, *Transportation Economics and Public Policy*, 344; "R. J. McBride—'Mr. Common Carrier,'" *Transport Topics* (October 20, 1958), 67.

21. "More than a Score of Years Closed Out by 'Vee' Kennedy," *Transport Topics* (February 14, 1966), 37; Kennedy, "Contract Carrier Conference Fills Need over 20-Year Period," 135.

22. Kennedy, "Contract Carrier Conference Fills Need over 20-Year Period," 138.

23. "Trend to Mergers Unsupported by ICC Trucking Data," *Transport Topics* (July 23, 1956), 1.

24. "Six Bonacci Brothers Built AAA Trucking from One Reo in 1931," *Transport Topics* (October 28, 1958), 65.

25. Ibid.

26. Ibid.; James C. Johnson, *Trucking Mergers: A Regulatory Viewpoint* (Lexington, MA: Lexington Books, 1973), 98; "AAA Trucking Is . . . Really Growing" [advertisement], *Transport Topics* (October 28, 1958), 65.

27. For PIE as one of the largest, we relied on "Revenue Data of Top Carriers for Second Quarter of 1956," *Transport Topics* (September 17, 1956), 1.

28. Harry D. Wohl, "Vital and Dramatic Role Played by PIE in U.S. Distribution," *Transport Topics* (January 13, 1958), 8.

29. Ibid.

30. Ibid.

31. Johnson, *Trucking Mergers*, 82.

32. ICC findings as cited in Johnson, *Trucking Mergers*, 83; see also Pegrum, *Transportation Economics and Public Policy*, 345, who finds that ICC commissioners rejected the PIE-Keeshin merger based on concern for "other lines with whom Pacific Intermountain Express had interchange arrangements."

33. Wohl, "Vital and Dramatic Role Played by PIE in U.S. Distribution," 8; "Revenue Data of Top Carriers for Second Quarter of 1956," *Transport Topics* (September 17, 1956), 1.

34. Richard Hagood, *Ryder Truck Lines—The First Half-Century* (Lake City, FL: Columbia Publications, 1982), 4, 56. Writing in 1989, economists Dale G. Anderson and

Ray C. Huttsell Jr., "Trucking Regulation, 1935–1980," in *Regulation and Deregulation of the Motor Carrier Industry,* ed. John Richard Felton and Dale G. Anderson (Ames: Iowa State University Press, 1989), 88, find that truck-rate bureaus "operate[d] as price-fixing cartels to maximize industry joint profits."

35. Ibid., 35, 44; "Lewis A. Raulerson Dies at 85; Operator Helped Organize ATA," *Transport Topics* (March 6, 1967), 2. Asking why the "myth" of the lone American and limited government had survived during an age of big business and big government, historian David A. Moss, *When All Else Fails: Government as the Ultimate Risk Manager* (Cambridge, MA: Harvard University Press, 2002), 318, observes that "perhaps . . . the myth survived because there is at least some truth to it."

36. Taff, *Commercial Motor Transportation,* 234–36, 241.

37. Charles A. Taff, *Commercial Motor Transportation,* 236; "Central States Motor Freight Tariff Bureau Docket" (January 3, 1955), 12; Harry D. Wohl, "Huge Tariff-Publishing Task of Middle Atlantic Conference Is Endless" (June 20, 1955), 82, both in *Transport Topics.*

38. Ibid.

39. "ATA's Traffic Department Is Invaluable Arm of Industry" (September 19, 1955), 82; Wohl, "Huge Tariff-Publishing Task of Middle Atlantic Conference Is Endless," 82, both in *Transport Topics.*

40. Harry M. Baker to Brock Adams, August 11, 1971, Papers of Brock Adams, Acc. No. 1096–2, 3, 4, Box 128, Folder: General correspondence-Legislation-Freight Forwarders, 1971–72, University of Washington Libraries, Seattle, WA, cited hereafter as Adams Papers, UWL.

41. Untitled text, n.d., c. 1960 in Adams Papers, Box 139, Folder: Legislation-Freight Forwarders, 1968–70, UWL; William S. Odlin Jr., "Freight Forwarders Oppose Change in Rate Making," *Transport Topics* (June 11, 1956), 1; Paul J. Tierney to Samuel N. Friedel, January 23, 1968, in U.S. Congress, House Committee on Interstate and Foreign Commerce, Subcommittee on Transportation and Aeronautics, *Freight Forwarder-TOFC Contracts* (Washington, DC: U.S. Government Printing Office, 1968), 4.

42. John L. Sweeney to Harley O. Staggers, October 27, 1968, in ibid., 2.

43. Testimony of Milton Strickland Jr., January 24, 1968; Statement of J. Robert Evans, January 16, 1968, both typescripts in Adams Papers, Box 139, Folder: Legislation-Freight Forwarders (HR 10831), 1967–68, UWL.

44. Testimony of Milton Strickland Jr., in ibid.

45. Statement of Peter T. Beardsley, January 24, 1968, typescript in Adams Papers, Box 139, Folder: Legislation-Freight Forwarders (HR 10831), 1967–68, UWL.

46. Statement of Peter Beardsley; M. T. Richmond to Brock Adams, March 27, 1968, Adams Papers, Box 139, Folder: Legislation-Freight Forwarders (HR 10831), 1967–68, UWL.

47. Statement of Sam Hall Flint, n.d., c. late January 1968, typescript in Adams Papers, Box 139, Folder: Legislation-Freight Forwarders (HR 10831), 1967–68, UWL.

48. Typescript Statement of Charles L. Smith, n.d., c. January 1968; Notes of Brock Adams, undated, c. January–March 1968, both in Adams Papers, Box 139, Folder: Legislation-Freight Forwarders, 1968–1970, UWL.

49. Fred H. Tolan to Ralph Hall et al., January 17, 1968, Adams Papers, Box 139, Folder: Legislation-Freight Forwarders (HR 10831), 1967–68, UWL.

50. "Mrs. Kennedy's Five Pounds of Sugar," a leaflet prepared by the Association of American Railroads, n.p., c. mid-1955; and see also William T. Faricy (president of the

AAR), "The Right to Compete: Cornerstone of Modern Transportation Regulation" [advertisement], *Dun's Review and Modern Industry* (April 1956), 64–66, which made a similar argument to the one advanced in the leaflet, but which leaders of the AAR aimed at business executives rather than consumers. Both items in Papers of Hubert H. Humphrey, Box 150, D.13.1B, Folder: Transportation. Railroads. General, 1950, 1954–1956, Minnesota Historical Society, St. Paul, MN. For the efforts of railroad executives during the 1950s to "injure other modes by the advocacy of restrictive [highway] legislation and attempts at influencing public opinion," see Carl H. Fulda, *Competition in the Regulated Industries: Transportation* (Boston: Little, Brown and Company, 1961), 375–77, including quotation on page 375. Finally, authors of the leaflet, "Mrs. Kennedy's Five Pounds of Sugar" relied on the image of one ordinary person explaining to another the desirability of stable prices, an approach taken by candidate Eisenhower during the election campaign of 1952. See Jacobs, *Pocketbook Politics*, 253, for Eisenhower's citation to his wife, Mamie, "who gets after me for the high cost of living."

51. Robert E. Bedingfield, "Railroads to Analyze Promotion," *New York Times*, June 27, 1956, 41.

52. Albert J. Churella, *From Steam to Diesel: Managerial Customs and Organizational Capabilities in the Twentieth-Century American Locomotive Industry* (Princeton, NJ: Princeton University Press, 1998), 75, 95.

53. Ibid., 95; Burton N. Behling, "1964: Review of Railway Operations," *Railway Age* 158 (January 18, 1965): 87; John F. Stover, *American Railroads*, 2nd ed. (Chicago: University of Chicago Press, 1997), 212.

54. Churella, *From Steam to Diesel*, 98; Stover, *American Railroads*, 212–13.

55. Stover, *American Railroads*, 209.

56. Ibid.; "Piggyback: How It Started and Where It's Going," *Railway Age* 153 (November 26, 1962), 25; Richard C. Overton, *Burlington Route: A History of the Burlington Lines* (New York: Knopf, 1965), 416–17; "Piggyback on Trial," *Railway Age* 153 (November 26, 1962): 13.

57. "Piggyback: How it Started and Where It's Going," 25.

58. Stover, *American Railroads*, 209; Taff, *Commercial Motor Transportation Service*, 135; John R. Meyer et al., *The Economics of Competition in the Transportation Industries* (Cambridge, MA: Harvard University Press, 1960), 110; Gus Welty, "TOFC/COFC: Why the Future Looks So Good," *Railway Age* 162 (May 29, 1967): 29, 32, including quotations on page 29.

59. "Growth of Auto Traffic Shows What Rails Can Do," *Railway Age* 161 (August 22, 1966): 14, 17; "They're Piggybacking at Full Throttle Now," *Louisville* 13 (September 20, 1962): 13–14, including title on page 13 and description of auto racks on page 14.

60. Stover, *American Railroads*, 209; Welty, "TOFC/COFC: Why the Future Looks So Good," 33; Daniel P. Loomis, "The Competition's Challenge," *Commercial Car Journal* 108 (January 1965): 96–97. Whether reduced rates led to increases in business sufficient to cover costs remains unclear. Historian H. Roger Grant, *Erie Lackawanna: Death of an American Railroad, 1938–1992* (Stanford, CA: Stanford University Press, 1994), 72, determines that reductions in rates for piggyback service often "conferr[ed] unintended windfalls on customers."

61. William H. Tucker and John H. O'Brien, "The Public Interest in Railroad Mergers," *Boston University Law Review* 42 (September 1962): 168–70; George R. Horton and L.A. Drewry Jr., "Railway Mergers: Recent ICC Policy," *Traffic Quarterly* 21 (1967): 124–25; and Gregory S. Prince, "Railroads and Government Policy: A Legally Oriented

Study of an Economic Crisis," *Virginia Law Review* 48 (1962): 269.

62. Richard L. Saunders Jr., *The Railroad Mergers and the Coming of Conrail* (Westport, CT: Greenwood Press, 1978), 85, 107, 130; Grant, *Erie Lackawanna,* 84–94; John F. Stover, *History of the Baltimore and Ohio Railroad* (West Lafayette, IN: Purdue University Press, 1987), 363–64; Lou Dombrowski, "Merger Madness," *Modern Cities via Transportation* 1 (July–August 1966): 34, 38–39, including quotation on page 34.

63. "Seaboard Coast Line: Anatomy of a Merger,"163 (July 24, 1967): 18; John D. Mitros, "'Have-Nots' Cloud the Merger Picture," 162 (January 16, 1967): 79, both in *Railway Age.*

64. William H. Orrick Jr. et al., "Exceptions of the United States Department of Justice to the Examiner's Recommended Report and Order," January 15, 1965, Warren G. Magnuson Papers, Accession Number 3181–4, Box 253, Folder: 4, University of Washington Libraries, Seattle, WA., cited hereafter as Magnuson Papers, UWL.

65. Association of American Railroads, "Background on Transportation" (February 1965), in Magnuson Papers, Box 253, Folder: 4, UWL; Stover, *American Railroads,* 239.

66. Saunders, *The Railroad Mergers and the Coming of Conrail,* 89–90, 185, and quotation on page 186.

67. Richard L. Saunders Jr., *Merging Lines: American Railroads, 1900–1970* (DeKalb: Northern Illinois University Press, 2001), 354; idem, *The Railroad Mergers and the Coming of Conrail,* 188.

68. Stephen M. Aug, "Mergers Point to One Great Railroad System," *Washington Star,* February 5, 1967, D-10, in Adams Papers, Folder: General Correspondence-Railroads, 1967–68, UWL; Saunders, *The Railroad Mergers and the Coming of Conrail,* 189.

69. Saunders, *The Railroad Mergers and the Coming of Conrail,* 191, 197; Aug, "Mergers Point to One Great Railroad System."

70. Saunders, *The Railroad Mergers and the Coming of Conrail,* 92, 195–96, including quotation on page 196.

71. Ibid., 192, 197; "Pennsy-Central Leaders See 'Evolution' for Merged Line," *New York Times,* January 31, 1968, 58.

72. Richard Witkin, "States Rush Talks on Commuter Line," *New York Times,* January 1, 1968, 54; Saunders, *The Railroad Mergers and the Coming of Conrail,* 182; Frederic B. Whitman, "Report of the Railroad Professional Survey Group on Various Aspects of the New York, New Haven & Hartford Railroad Company's Problems Along with Conclusions and Recommendations as to Suggested Policies to Be Followed or Action to Be Taken" (Washington, DC: U.S. Department of Commerce, June 1962), typescript; Statement of Senator John O. Pastore at the Commencement of Hearings on the Northeast Passenger Railroad Crisis, March 2, 1965, before the Senate Committee on Commerce, both in Magnuson Papers, Box 253, Folder: 5, UWL.

73. Saunders, *The Railroad Mergers and the Coming of Conrail,* 199; idem, *Merging Lines,* 274; Robert E. Bedingfield, "Pennsy, Central Allowed to Join; New Haven Aided," *New York Times,* January 16, 1968, 1, 54.

74. "Railroading's New Era," *New York Times,* January 20, 1968, 28; Merrill Folsom, "Westchester 'Delighted,'" *New York Times,* January 20, 1968, 54; "Pennsy-Central Leaders See 'Evolution' for Merged Line," 58; Saunders, *The Railroad Mergers and the Coming of Conrail,* 188.

75. Saunders, *The Railroad Mergers and the Coming of Conrail,* 268–71; "How Decaying Service, Bickering Officials Led to Penn Central Crisis," *Wall Street Journal,* June 12, 1970, in Adams Papers, Box 9, Folder: Railroad Merger-General-1969, UWL.

76. Saunders, *The Railroad Mergers and the Coming of Conrail,* 273.

77. Ibid., 279.

78. "How Decaying Service, Bickering Officials Led to Penn Central Crisis"; "Penn Central's Announcement," *New York Times,* June 22, 1970, 59; Robert B. Semple Jr., "Rejection of Pennsy Loan Is Laid to Political Risks," *New York Times,* June 23, 1970, 20.

CHAPTER 5

1. Robert Dallek, *Flawed Giant: Lyndon Johnson and His Times, 1961–1973* (New York: Oxford University Press, 1998), 184, 190.

2. Robert M. Collins, *More: The Politics of Economic Growth in Postwar America* (New York: Oxford University Press, 2000), 59–60.

3. Joseph A. Califano, *A Presidential Nation* (New York: W. W. Norton and Company, 1975); and also see Sidney M. Milkis, "Remaking Government Institutions in the 1970s: Participatory Democracy and the Triumph of Administrative Politics," *Journal of Policy History* 10, no. 1 (1998): 52, for the observation that like Roosevelt, "Johnson was a presidentialist." For the accompanying idea that Johnson sought to use federal spending and federal policies as components of an inflation-fighting strategy, see David Shreve, "Lyndon Johnson and the Keynesian Revolution: The Struggle for Full Employment and Price Stability," in *Looking Back at LBJ: White House Politics in a New Light,* ed. Mitchell B. Lerner (Lawrence: University Press of Kansas, 2005), which Professors Shreve and Lerner were kind enough to share with us prior to publication.

4. James M. Landis, *Report on Regulatory Agencies to the President-Elect,* U.S. Senate, Committee on the Judiciary, 86th Cong., 2nd Sess. (Washington, DC: Government Printing Office, 1960), 37, 41. For the centrality of Landis in the process of building the regulatory regime and the earliest stages of urging its dismantling, we relied upon Thomas K. McCraw's magisterial *Prophets of Regulation: Charles Francis Adams, Louis D. Brandeis, James M. Landis, and Alfred E. Kahn* (Cambridge, MA: Belknap Press of Harvard University Press, 1984), including quotation on page 206.

5. Landis, *Report on Regulatory Agencies to the President-Elect,* 4, 77–78; McCraw, *Prophets of Regulation,* 206–207.

6. McCraw, *Prophets of Regulation,* 207, 357n11; "Special Message to the Congress on Transportation," April 5, 1962, in United States President, *Public Papers of the President of the United States: John F. Kennedy: 1962, Containing the Public Messages, Speeches, and Statements of the President* (Washington, DC: Government Printing Office, 1963), 293–94. See also Ellis W. Hawley, "Challenges to the Mixed Economy: The State and Private Enterprise," in *American Choices: Social Dilemmas and Public Policy since 1960,* ed. Robert H. Bremner, Gary W. Reichard, and Richard J. Hopkins (Columbus: Ohio State University Press, 1986), 161, for the observation that during the early 1960s, "there was talk also of regulatory reform as an alternative route to better economic performance." Brian Balogh, "Introduction," *Journal of Policy History* 8, no. 1 (1996): 30n24, brought this aspect of Hawley's article to our attention.

7. McCraw, *Prophets of Regulation,* 220.

8. Political scientist David M. Welborn describes deregulation as "part of Johnson's inheritance" from Kennedy. See his *Regulation in the White House: The Johnson Presidency* (Austin: University of Texas Press, 1993), 224, which Professor Welborn was kind enough to bring to our attention.

9. Johnson quotation as cited in Emmette S. Redford and Richard T. McCulley, *White House Operations: The Johnson Presidency* (Austin: University of Texas Press, 1986), 79, and other quotations in ibid., 80, 84.

10. Economist and historian Michael A. Bernstein was kind enough to bring to our attention the contemporary conviction that economists really could convert abstruse ideas about tax policy and especially tax reductions into solid economic growth. Also see his *A Perilous Progress: Economists and Public Purpose in Twentieth-Century America* (Princeton, NJ: Princeton University Press, 2001), 138; Kermit Gordon to Mr. Cater, June 22, 1964, Folder: FG600/Task Force on Transportation, Lyndon B. Johnson Library, Austin, TX, cited hereafter as LBJL.

11. Ibid.

12. 'National Transportation Policy: Report of a Task Force to the President of the United States, November 1964, 14, 43, "The 1964 Task forces," Legislative Background: Transportation Department, Box 1, LBJL.

13. National Transportation Policy," including quotation on page 8.

14. Califano Jr., *A Presidential Nation,* 15, 17; idem, *The Triumph & Tragedy of Lyndon Johnson: The White House Years* (New York: Simon & Schuster, 1991), 123.

15. Joseph A. Califano Jr. to Alan Boyd, August 12, 1965, Folder: FG600/Task Force on Transportation, LBJL.

16. Joseph A. Califano Jr. to Alan Boyd, August 27, 1965, in ibid.

17. Alan S. Boyd to Joseph A. Califano Jr., September 2, 1965, Legislative Background Transportation Department, Folder: Foundation for Action—1965 Task Forces (1 of 2), LBJL.

18. Arthur Okun to Gardner Ackley, September 11, 1965; William M. Capron to The Director, September 13, 1965, both in ibid.

19. Joe Califano to the President, September 22, 1965, Legislative Background, Transportation Department, Folder: Legislative Struggle-Vol. II, LBJL.

20. Joe Califano for the President, October 12, 1965, Legislative Background Transportation Department Box 1, Folder: Foundation for Action—1965 Task Forces (2 of 2), LBJL; Dallek, *Flawed Giant,* 313.

21. Joe Califano for the President, December 13, 1965, Legislative Background, Transportation Department, Box 1, Folder: Decision on Transportation, LBJL.

22. Lee C. White, Memorandum for the Files, December 14, 1965 (truckers), in Legislative Background, Transportation Department, Box 1, Folder: Decision on Transportation, LBJL; Johnson as quoted in Dallek, *Flawed Giant,* 314.

23. Lee C. White to the President, January 10, 1966 and January 25, 1966, Legislative Background, Transportation Department, Box 1, Folder: Decision on Transportation, LBJL; Emmette S. Redford and Marlan Blissett, *Organizing the Executive Branch: The Johnson Presidency* (Chicago: University of Chicago Press, 1981), 57.

24. "Transportation Message," Legislative Background, Transportation Department, Box 1, Folder: The Message-Vol. 1 (1 of 2), LBJL.

25. Telegram, Mark O. Hatfield to The President, March 22, 1966; "ATA Executive Committee Announces Position on Creation of Department of Transportation," press release, March 23, 1966; W. A. Bresnahan to Joseph A. Califano Jr., March 30, 1966, all in Legislative Background, Transportation Department, Box 2, Folder: Legislative Struggle-Vol. 1 (1 of 3), LBJL.

26. Statement of Senator Warren G. Magnuson on S. 3010, To Establish a Department of Transportation, Before the Committee on Government Operations, March 29,

1966, 14, in Magnuson Papers, Box 182, Folder: Legislation-WGM Bills-S.3010-Department of Transportation-1966, UWL; Mike Manatos for the President, April 29, 1966, Legislative Background, Transportation Department, Box 2, Folder: Legislative Struggle-Vol. 1 (1 of 3), LBJL.

27. Alan S. Boyd to John T. Connor, May 11, 1966, Legislative Background, Transportation Department, Box 2, Folder: Legislative Struggle-Vol. 1 (1 of 3), LBJL.

28. Section-By-Section Summary Department of Transportation, c. early 1966; Michael P. Semer for the President, May 12, 1966, both in Legislative Background, Transportation Department, Box 2, Folder: Legislative Struggle-Vol. 1 (1 of 3), LBJL; Redford and Blissett, *Organizing the Executive Branch*, 71–72.

29. Monroney, *Hearings before the Committee on Government Operations*, U.S. Senate, 89th Cong., 2nd Sess., on S. 3010, part 1, 293–301, as cited in Redford and Blissett, *Organizing the Executive Branch*, 66.

30. "Transport Dept. Plan Stirs Diverse Views," *Transport Topics* (March 21, 1966): 1, 34; "The Week in Transportation," *Traffic World* 125 (March 19, 1966): 17, 19.

31. Joe Califano for the President, May 24, 1966; Charles J. Zwick for Mr. Califano, June 1, 1966, both in Legislative Background, Transportation Department, Box 2, Folder: Legislative Struggle-Vol. I (2 of 3), LBJL.

32. Undated memo noting participants in weekend meeting, c. early August 1966; Department of Transportation: Explanation; The National Transportation Safety Board, August 8, 1966; and Alan S. Boyd to the Secretary, August 9, 1966, all in Legislative Background, Transportation Department, Box 2, Folder: Legislative Struggle-Vol. I (2 of 3); Legislative Background, Transportation Department, Box 3, Folder: Legislative Struggle-Vol. II (1 of 2), all in LBJL. See also John L. Hazard, *Managing National Transportation Policy* (Westport, CT: Eno Foundation for Transportation, 1988), 47, for the observation that "to be certain of no other central control, Congress lowered the ranks of Assistant Secretaries below those of modal administrators." Richard R. John Sr. was kind enough to send a copy to us.

33. Earl W. Clark and Hoyt S. Haddock to Russell B. Long, September 14, 1966, EXFG 175, Folder: FG 175 Department of Transportation 11/23/63–11/7/66; Larry Levinson, The Transportation Department and the Maritime Administration: Chronology of Negotiations at the White House, c. August 30, 1966, Legislative Background, Transportation Department, Box 3, Folder: Legislative Struggle-Vol. II (1 of 2), both in LBJL.

34. Redford and Blissett, *Organizing the Executive Branch*, 73; Dallek, *Flawed Giant*, 316.

35. Dallek, *Flawed Giant*, 316; "Remarks of the President upon signing a bill creating a department of transportation," October 15, 1966, Legislative Background, Transportation Department, Box 3, Folder: Passage and Signature, LBJL, a document originally brought to our attention in Redford and Blissett, *Organizing the Executive Branch*, 75.

36. Wilfred H. Rommel for the President, c. October 14, 1966, Legislative Background, Transportation Department, Box 3, Folder: Passage and Signature, LBJL. Compare with Brian Balogh's perceptive "Reorganizing the Organizational Synthesis: Federal-Professional Relations in Modern America," *Studies in American Political Development* 5 (Spring 1991): 119–72, quotation on page 121, who finds that federal officials "not only responded to well-organized interest groups, it now had the capacity to create them." Not until the mid-1970s did Presidents Gerald R. Ford and Jimmy Carter

begin the long-term process of mobilizing opposition to the regulatory regime. We are pleased to thank William Childs for bringing the Balogh essay to our attention.

37. Joseph A. Califano Jr. to John T. Connor, October 25, 1966; Attachment 8, n.d., both in files of Joseph A. Califano Jr., Box 64, Folder: Transportation, LBJL.

38. Califano, *A Presidential Nation*, 51.

39. "This week in Transportation," *Traffic World* 128 (November 12, 1966): 24; David G. McComb, "Interview with A. Scheffer Lang," November 1, 1968; David G. McComb, "Interview with Alan S. Boyd," November 20 and December 18, 1968, all in LBJL; Dan Fenn, "Regulatory Agencies Panel," oral history interview with Alan S. Boyd, William L. Cary, Newton N. Minow, Joseph C. Swidler, and William Tucker, August 18, 1964, John F. Kennedy Presidential Library, Boston, MA. See also John Burby, *The Great American Motion Sickness: Why You Can't Get There from Here* (Boston: Little, Brown and Company, 1971), 268–94, for the lament of a journalist and early employee at the new Department of Transportation about Boyd's inability to coordinate transportation networks. Richard R. John Sr. also brought this book to our attention.

40. "Coordinated Transportation Concept Seen as Likely to Force Legislative Actions," *Traffic World* 133 (February 3, 1968): 17.

CHAPTER 6

1. Richard M. Nixon was elected president, reports historian Joan Hoff, during a "period of disorientation in American foreign and domestic policies." On the domestic scene, Nixon confronted "a structural as well as cyclical downturn in the U.S. economy." In turn, argues Hoff, a president such as Nixon who was willing to "take risks" enjoyed what she characterizes as "a unique opportunity for domestic . . . innovations." Deregulation was among those risks Nixon judged worth taking in order to foster economic growth and in order to bolster his own hand as director of a presidential nation. See also Hoff's observation that during his first term in office, transportation remained a low-visibility item for President Nixon. According to Hoff, Nixon delegated responsibility for transportation and other low-profile matters to his senior aides, especially John D. Ehrlichman. In reality, Nixon took an active role in efforts to bring about deregulation. Joan Hoff, *Nixon Reconsidered* (New York: Basic Books, 1994), 7, 8, 20. Also see Richard H. K. Vietor, *Contrived Competition: Regulation and Deregulation in America* (Cambridge, MA.: Belknap Press of Harvard University Press, 1994), 14, who finds that leaders in the Nixon administration were "not concerned with the economic effects of regulation or interested in pursuing major legislation." In this matter, Vietor follows the lead established in 1985 by political scientists Martha Derthick and Paul J. Quirk, *The Politics of Deregulation* (Washington, DC: Brookings Institution, 1985), 45–47. Historians such as Allen J. Matusow have also determined that Nixon perceived himself as the chief executive of a political nation. According to Matusow, *Nixon's Economy: Booms, Busts, Dollars, and Votes* (Lawrence: University Press of Kansas, 1998), 1, 3, "politics provided whatever consistency there was" in Nixon's "conduct of domestic policy and management of the U.S. economy." See as well David Greenberg, "Richard the Bleeding Hearted" [review essay], *Reviews in American History* 30 (March 2002): 159, who repeats the argument that "Nixon never cared all that much about domestic policy, except . . . if it directly affected domestic politics." As we shall see, Nixon's work on transportation deregulation and executive reorganization amounted to more than "politics."

2. "How Decaying Service, Bickering Officials Led to Penn Central Crisis," *Wall Street Journal,* June 12, 1970, 1, in Adams Papers, Acc. No. 1096–2, 3, 4, Box 9, Folder: Railroad Merger-general-1969, UWL; Richard L. Saunders Jr., *The Railroad Mergers and the Coming of Conrail* (Westport, CT: Greenwood Press, 1978), 294; U.S. Congress, Senate, Committee on Commerce, *Failing Railroads,* Hearings, 91st Congress, 2nd Session, on S. 4011, S. 4014, and S. 4016 (Washington, DC: U.S. Government Printing Office, 1970), 299.

3. Matusow, *Nixon's Economy,* 73; John F. Stover, *American Railroads,* 2nd ed. (Chicago: University of Chicago Press, 1997), 238; Notes dated June 4, 1970, White House Special Files, Staff Member and Office Files: John D. Ehrlichman Notes of Meetings with the President, 1969–1973, Box 3, Folder: JDE Notes of Meetings with the President, 1/1/70–6/30/70 [5 of 5], in Richard M. Nixon Presidential Files, Nixon Presidential Materials Staff, National Archives and Records Administration, College Park, MD, cited hereafter as Ehrlichman Notes of Meetings, NPMS, NA2.

4. Ehrlichman Notes of Meetings with the President, 3/5/70 [3 of 5], NPMS, NA2. As an example of economists advocating deregulation, see the influential George J. Stigler, "The Theory of Economic Regulation" (1971), in his edited volume, *Chicago Studies in Political Economy* (Chicago: University of Chicago Press, 1988), including 211–12 for the observations that "the Civil Aeronautics Board has not allowed a single new trunk line to be launched [1970] since it was created in 1938" and that in the case of trucking, "no even ostensibly respectable case for restriction on entry can be developed."

5. Peter Flanigan to John A. Volpe, Paul McCracken, Robert Mayo, Henry Cashen, and Clay T. Whitehead, May 4, 1970, White House Central Files, Subject Files, TN-Transportation Box 1, Folder: [EX] TN Transportation Beginning 10/1/70, NPMS, NA2, White House Central Files, cited hereafter as WHCF.

6. Improving the Performance of the Transportation Industries: Executive Summary, c. September 22, 1970; Subcommittee on Transportation to Cabinet Committee on Economic Policy, September 24, 1970, both in WHCF, Subject Files, TN-Transportation Box 1, Folder: [EX] TN Transportation Beginning 10/1/70, NPMS, NA2. For membership on the Cabinet Committee on Economic Policy, see Melvin Small, *The Presidency of Richard Nixon* (Lawrence: University Press of Kansas, 1999), 49.

7. Ehrlichman Notes of Meetings with the President, 1/1/70–6/30/70 [1 of 5]; Jim Loken to Peter Flanigan, December 23, 1970, White House Central File, Subject Files, TN Transportation, Box 1, Folder: [EX] TN 10/3/70–12/31/70, both in NPMS, NA2. During the twentieth century, determines historian Lawrence I. Glickman, political and business leaders periodically rediscovered the consumer and a consumer movement. See his "The Strike in the Temple of Consumption: Consumer Activism and Twentieth-Century American Political Culture," *Journal of American History* 88 (June 2001): 99. In particular, historian Lizabeth Cohen, *A Consumer's Republic: The Politics of Mass Consumption in Postwar America* (New York: Knopf, 2003), 346, 362, finds Nixon interested in consumers but unwilling to support creation of a federal consumer agency. Finally, see Albert R. Karr, "A Broad Transportation Program of Nixon's Would Aid Rails, Trucks, Perhaps Consumers," *Wall Street Journal,* April 2, 1971, 26, *Proquest Historical Newspapers,* April 5, 2005, for a report that Nixon's aides viewed deregulation as helpful to consumers.

8. Charles L. Clapp, Memorandum for the Records, June 10, 1971, White House Special Files, Staff Member and Office Files, Charles W. Colson, Box 23, Folder: RR Labor Leaders Mtg/President, Monday 6/14/71, 4:30, NPMS, NA2, cited hereafter as Colson files.

9. Ibid.

10. George T. Bell, Memorandum for the President's File, June 14, 1971, White House Special Files, Staff Member and Office Files, Colson Files, Box 23, Folder: RR Labor Leaders Mtg/President, Monday 6/14/71, 4:30; "Deregulation Is Backed by Rail Union Officials," *Journal of Commerce,* February 2, 1971, White House Central File, Subject Files, TN Transportation, Box 1, Folder: [EX] TN Transportation, 1/1/71 [1 of 3], both in NPMS, NA2.

11. James V. Springrose to Peter M. Flanigan, July 6, 1971; Frank L. Merwin to Peter Flanigan, July 27, 1971, both in WHCF, Subject Files, TN Transportation, Box 1, Folder: [EX] TN Transportation, 1/1/71 [1 of 3], NPMS, NA2.

12. John Glancy to Peter Flanigan, July 9, 1971; J. Phil Campbell to Peter M. Flanigan, July 9, 1971, both in WHCF Subject Files, TN Transportation, Box 1, Folder: [EX] TN Transportation 1/1/71 [1 of 3], NPMS, NA2.

13. John Glancy through Peter Flanigan to Charles Colson, August 6, 1971, WHCF Subject Files, TN Transportation, Box 1, Folder: [EX] TN Transportation 1/1/71 [1 of 3], NPMS, NA2.

14. Peter M. Flanigan to The Attorney General, Paul A. McCracken, and Charles D. Baker, August 24, 1971, WHCF Subject Files, TN Transportation, Box 2, Folder: [EX] TN 1 1/1/71, NPMS, NA2.

15. Peter M. Flanigan to Frank E. Fitzsimmons, October 22, 1971, WHCF Subject Files, TN Transportation, Box 1, Folder: [EX] TN Transportation 1/1/71 [2 of 3], NPMS, NA2.

16. Harry Dent to Peter Flanigan, September 22, 1971; Memorandum for the Transportation File, October 26, 1971; Peter M. Flanigan to The Attorney General, et al., October 28, 1971, all in WHCF Subject Files, TN Transportation, Box 1, Folder: [EX] TN Transportation 1/1/71 [2 of 3], NPMS, NA2. Hoff, *Nixon Reconsidered,* 53, finds that Nixon "began to centralize most decision-making power within his White House staff."

17. Flanigan as quoted in Vera Hirschberg, "Transportation Report: Congress Plods through Complex Arguments over Transport Regulation," *National Journal* 4 (May 6, 1972): 772; John Glancy to Peter M. Flanigan, October 29 and November 24, 1971; Dave Gunning to Peter M. Flanigan, May 11, 1972, last three in WHCF Subject Files, TN Transportation, Box 1, Folder: [EX] TN Transportation 1/1/71 [2 of 3], NPMS, NA2.

18. James M. Beggs to Peter M. Flanigan, June 30, 1972, WHCF Subject Files, TN Transportation, Box 1, Folder: [EX] TN Transportation 1/1/71 [3 of 3], NPMS, NA2.

19. Dave Gunning to Peter M. Flanigan, July 11, 1972, Box 1, Folder: [EX] TN Transportation 1/1/71 [3 of 3]; details of the two bills in American Enterprise Institute for Policy Research, "Legislative Analysis No. 22: Transportation Legislation," June 21, 1972, Box 2, Folder [Gen] TN Transportation 1/1/72–9/30/72, all in WHCF Subject Files, TN Transportation, NPMS, NA2.

20. Harold F. Hammond to Peter Flanigan, July 26, 1972; William I. Spencer to Peter Flanigan, July 26, 1972; and A.G. Anderson to Peter Flanigan, July 28, 1972, all in WHCF Subject Files, TN Transportation, Box 2, Folder: [Gen] TN Transportation 1/1/72–9/30/72 (CTD), NPMS, NA2.

21. John A. Volpe to John Ehrlichman, August 8, 1972, WHCF Subject Files, TN Transportation, Box 1, Folder: [EX] TN Transportation 1/1/71 [3 of 3], NPMS, NA2. See also "4 Rails Plead for U.S. Disaster Aid," *New York Times,* August 3, 1972, 43, *Pro-*

quest Historical Newspapers New York Times. Technically speaking, in August 1972, seven railroads were in bankruptcy. Perhaps Volpe did not judge one of those railroads "major." We are immensely pleased to acknowledge historian Albert J. Churella's guidance in identifying the bankrupt railroads.

22. Hirschberg, "Transportation Report," 772–73; Dave Gunning to Ken Dam, February 7, 1973; Miscellaneous materials prepared as part of meetings among transportation advisory panels on January 3, January 9, February 12, filed March 20, 1973 all including Gunning letter in WHCF Subject Files, TN Transportation, Box 1, Folder: [EX] TN Transportation 1/1/73 [1 of 2], NPMS, NA2.

23. Mark H. Rose, *Interstate: Express Highway Politcs, 1939–1989,* 2nd ed., rev. (Lawrence: University Press of Kansas, 1990), 110–11; B . . . ? [indecipherable on letterhead of the Undersecretary of Transportation] to Ken Cole, March 19, 1973, WHCF Subject Files, TN Transportation, Box 2, Folder: [EX] TN 1 Highways 1/1/71–, NPMS, NA2.

24. Michael Raoul-Duval to Melvin Laird through Dana G. Mead, July 30, 1973, WHCF Subject Files, TN Transportation, Box 1, Folder: [EX] TN Transportation, 1/1/73 [1 of 2], NPMS, NA2; Stigler, "The Theory of Economic Regulation."

25. Hoff, *Nixon Reconsidered,* 58.

26. Peri Arnold, *Making the Managerial Presidency: Comprehensive Reorganization Planning, 1905–1966,* 2nd ed. (Lawrence: University Press of Kansas, 1986, 1998), 278.

27. U.S. Congress, House Committee on Government Operations, Executive and Legislative Reorganization Subcommittee, *Reorganization Plan No. 1 of 1969: Interstate Commerce Commission* (Washington, DC: U.S. Government Printing Office, 1969), 2, 4. See also Hoff, *Nixon Reconsidered,* 59, for her focus on senior federal and corporate officials in shaping corporate forms of organization for the government's executive branch. Finally, compare with Greenberg, "Richard the Bleeding Hearted," 158, who argues in 2002 that "many of Nixon's programs that now pass for liberal actually represented the dominant conservative if not hard-right positions of the time." By conceptualizing along a liberal-conservative continuum, however, Greenberg overlooks the emphasis on organization that was common among postwar political and business leaders.

28. U.S. Congress, House Committee on Government Operations, Executive and Legislative Reorganization Subcommittee, *Reorganization Plan No. 1 of 1969: Interstate Commerce Commission* (Washington, DC: U.S. Government Printing Office, 1969), 38, 43, and quotes on 26, 39, and 55.

29. Hoff, *Nixon Reconsidered,* 66–67; see also Otis L. Graham Jr., *Toward a Planned Society: From Roosevelt to Nixon* (New York: Oxford University Press, 1976), 206–207, where the emphasis is on government reorganization as part of Nixon's desire to plan economic development in detail.

CHAPTER 7

1. Gerald R. Ford, "Address to a Joint Session of the Congress on the Economy," October 8, 1974, in United States, President, *Public Papers of the Presidents of the United States: Gerald R. Ford, 1974* (Washington, DC: U.S. Government Printing Office, 1975), 232, 238. Compare with Richard H. K. Vietor, *Contrived Competition: Regulation and Deregulation in America* (Cambridge, MA: Belknap Press of Harvard University Press,

1994), 14, who finds that "after a few months [in office], President Ford began speaking of regulatory reform as an end in itself, drawing a favorable parallel between competition in business and competition in sports. Vietor follows Martha Derthick and Paul J. Quirk, *The Politics of Deregulation* (Washington, DC: Brookings Institution, 1985), 45–47. See also Michael A. Bernstein, *A Perilous Progress: Economists and Public Purpose in Twentieth-Century America* (Princeton, NJ: Princeton University Press, 2001), 162, who locates the sources of high unemployment and high inflation in military spending during the Vietnam War, a drought in the early 1970s that brought high prices to food, and rising oil prices starting in 1973 that had been induced by members of the international oil cartel. In turn, Bernstein determines that critics of government programs "nonetheless frame[d] the economic turmoil of the times as a direct outgrowth of a muscle-bound and irresponsible public sector," including the agencies that regulated many of the nation's industries such as transportation and communications. During the 1970s, however, even proponents of government programs and agencies such as Ralph Nader and Senator Edward M. Kennedy often linked high prices to government, or at least to specific government agencies such as the Interstate Commerce Commission and the Civil Aeronautics Board. Historian David Shreve also identifies "the maturation and veiled growth of U.S. managerial bureaucracies and perquisites" as another factor contributing to rising prices. See his "Lyndon Johnson and the Keynesian Revolution: The Struggle for Full Employment and Price Stability," in *Looking Back at LBJ: White House Politics in a New Light,* ed. Mitchell B. Lerner (Lawrence: University Press of Kansas, 2005).

2. Gerald R. Ford, "Remarks to the Annual Convention of the Future Farmers of America," October 15, 1974, in United States, President, *Public Papers of the Presidents of the United States: Gerald R. Ford, 1974,* 309.

3. Gerald R. Ford, "Address before a Conference of the National Federation of Independent Business," June 17, 1975, in United States, President, *Public Papers of the Presidents of the United States: Gerald R. Ford, 1975,* Book I (Washington, DC: U.S. Government Printing Office, 1977), 519, 827, 831, 1339. For fifty regulatory agencies employing 100,000 persons, see "Federal Regulators: Impact on Every American," *U.S. News & World Report* 82 (May 9, 1977): 61–62.

4. Vietor, *Contrived Competition,* 52; Gerald R. Ford, "Remarks at the White House Conference on Domestic and Economic Affairs in Concord, New Hampshire," April 18, 1975, in United States, President, *Public Papers of the Presidents of the United States: Gerald R. Ford, 1975,* Book I, 520, 522–23; Louis M. Kohlmeier, "The Politics of Deregulation," *National Journal* (May 10, 1975): 703, in James M. Cannon Files, Box 28, Folder: Regulatory Reform May 1975, Gerald R. Ford Library, Ann Arbor, MI, cited hereafter as Cannon Files, GRFL.

5. *New York Times Index,* 1970–1975; Thomas K. McCraw, *Prophets of Regulation: Charles Francis Adams, Louis D. Brandeis, James M. Landis, Alfred E. Kahn* (Cambridge, MA: Belknap Press of Harvard University Press), 290. During the period 1970–1977, the electronic Readers' Guide Retrospective produced by H. W. Wilson shows forty-three stories with the words deregulate or deregulation in the title, but only four of those stories appeared between 1970 and 1974.

6. "Federal Regulators: Impact on Every American," *U.S. News & World Report* 82 (May 9, 1977): 61.

7. James Cannon, meeting with American Railroads Association Board of Directors, April 12, 1975; William T. Coleman Jr., Memorandum for the President, April 12, 1975, both in Cannon Files, Folder: Railroads, March–October, 1975, both in GRFL;

"Regional Rail Reorganization Act Cases," 419 U.S.102 (1974), at www.laws.findlaw.com/us/419/102 html (February 8, 2005); Warren Weaver Jr., "Rescue of 8 Bankrupt Railroads Is Upheld by Supreme Court, 7–2," *New York Times,* December 17, 1974, 77, *Proquest Historical Newspapers New York Times.* For slow orders, see John W. Barnum to L. William Seidman and James T. Lynn, March 8, 1975, Domestic Council Administrative File, Folder: Domestic Needs, also in GRFL. Again, we are pleased to acknowledge historian Albert Churella's guidance in identifying the precise number of bankrupt railroads, as well as the U.S. Supreme Court case cited above.

8. William H. Jones, "3-System Rail Reorganization Approved," *Wall Street Journal,* May 30, 1975, in Cannon Files, Box 46, Folder: Northeast and Midwest Governors, June 7, 1975 (Railroads)(1), GRFL; Richard Saunders Jr., *The Railroad Mergers and the Coming of Conrail* (Westport, CT: Greenwood Press, 1978), 182.

9. Richard L. Saunders Jr., *Main Lines: Rebirth of the North American Railroads, 1970–2002* (De Kalb: Northern Illinois University Press, 2001), 63; Richard O. Davies, *Main Street Blues: The Decline of Small-Town America* (Columbus: Ohio State University Press, 1998), 168–70; Joseph P. Schwieterman, *When the Railroad Leaves Town: American Communities in the Age of Rail Line Abandonment,* vol. 1 (Kirksville, MO: Truman State University Press, 2001), 261; Buckley as quoted in Richard Blumenthal, "U.S. Would Drop Losing Rail Lines," *New York Times,* February 25, 1975, 73, *Proquest Historical New York Times;* meeting with Northeast and Midwest Governors, June 6, 1975, Cannon Files, Box 46, Folder: Northeast and Midwest Governors, June 7, 1975 (Railroads)(1), GRFL. In the "Introduction" to a collection of essays, *America during the 1970s* (Lawrence: University Press of Kansas, 2004), 4, historians Beth Bailey and David Farber report that Americans "described their world and their future in a language of loss, limits, and failure."

10. Stephen M. Aug, "He Tackles Rail Woe," *Washington Star,* June 1, 1975; "N&W Head Says Sale of Northeast Lines to Profitable Roads Won't Solve Crisis," *Wall Street Journal,* June 2, 1975, both in Box 46, Folder: Northeast and Midwest Governors, June 7, 1975 (Railroads)(1), GRFL; "The Rail Booby Trap, *Wall Street Journal,* February 17, 1976, Folder: Railroads, November 1975–December 1976, all three in Cannon files, GRFL; George W. Hilton, *The Northeast Railroad Problem* (Washington, DC: American Enterprise Institute for Public Policy Research, 1975), 48.

11. Meeting with Northeast and Midwest Governors, June 6, 1975; "N&W Head Says Sale of Northeast Lines to Profitable Roads Won't Solve Crisis," *Wall Street Journal,* June 2, 1975, both in Cannon Files, Box 46, Folder: Northeast and Midwest Governors, June 7, 1975 (Railroads)(1), GRFL.

12. Office of the White House Press Secretary, Fact Sheet: The Railroad Revitalization Act, May 19, 1975, Box 31, Folder: Railroads-Revitalization Act, May–June 1975; "Draft Presidential Message on the Railroad Revitalization Act," c. May 1975, Folder: President and Secretary Coleman, May 19, 1975 Railroad Revitalization, both in Cannon Files, GRFL. We are pleased to acknowledge historian Richard R. John's keen insight regarding the essence of government in the recent period.

13. William H. Jones, "3-System Rail Reorganization Approved," *Wall Street Journal,* May 30, 1975, Cannon Files, Box 46, Folder: Northeast and Midwest Governors, June 7, 1975 (Railroads)(1), GRFL). Somehow, members of Congress needed to prepare a formula for the omnibus bill that required little sacrifice by rail employees or shippers, that kept Conrail's expenses low, and that led to deregulation. The president, as the lender of last resort, planned to exercise the clout available to him.

14. Paul A. London to New England Congressional Caucus, September 6, 1973, Acc. No. 1096–2, 3, 4, Box 154, Folder: Regional Rail Services Act of 1973, Adams-Shoup Amendments, Brock Adams Papers, University of Washington Libraries, cited hereafter as Adams Papers, UWL.

15. Quotations in: Brock Adams, "Regulation—Strawman or Reality?" speech to the Air Transport Association, Williamsburg, VA, November 6, 1975; idem, "The Sense and Nonsense of Congress and Transportation," speech to the Mitre Corporation Symposium on Transportation, September 17, 1975, McLean Virginia, both in Folder: Speeches 1975; Woody M. Price to Brock Adams, c. mid-August 1975, Folder: Omnibus Railroad Bill (HR 9802) 1975, all in Adams Papers, UWL.

16. Saunders, *The Railroad Mergers and the Coming of Conrail,* 308–309; Woody M. Price to Brock Adams, October 23, 1975, Folder: Omnibus Railroad Bill (HR 9802) 1975, Adams Papers, UWL

17. William T. Coleman Jr. to Director of the Office of Management and Budget, November 24, 1975, Cannon Files, Box 53, Folder: Economic Policy Board, November 26, 1975, GRFL; Untitled, December 19, 1975, Box 153, Folder: Railroad Revitalization and Regulatory Reform Act of 1975, Adams Papers, UWL; as quoted in *Congressional Quarterly Almanac,* 94th Congress, 1st Session: 1975 XXXI (1976), 763.

18. William H. Jones, "Hill Votes Rail Bill as Ford Vows Veto," *Washington Post,* December 20, 1975, Fred H. Tolan to Joel Pritchard, December 19, 1975; J. Paul Malloy to J. Paul Marshall, December 23, 1975, all three in Box 153, Folder: Railroad Revitalization and Regulatory Reform Act of 1975; John M. Kinnaird to Brock Adams, October 23, 1975; Joe Skibbutz to Dear Colleague, December 15, 1975, both in Box 152, Folder: Omnibus Railroad Bill (HR 9802) 1975, all in Adams Papers, UWL; James T. Lynn and William T. Coleman to the President, c. late December 1975, Cannon Files, Box 55, Folder: Economic Policy Board, January 15, 1976, GRFL

19. *Congressional Quarterly Almanac,* 94th Congress, 1st Session: 1975 XXXI (1976), 757; William T. Coleman Jr., Memorandum for the Economic Policy Board, January 14, 1976, Cannon Files, Box 55, Folder: Economic Policy Board, January 15, 1976, GRFL.

20. William T. Coleman Jr. to the President, February 23, 1976; "Blocked Track" [editorial], *New York Times,* February 24, 1976; "The Rail Booby Trap," *Wall Street Journal,* February 17, 1976, all in Cannon Files, Folder: Railroads, November 1975–December 1976, GRFL. Historian Richard Saunders, *The Railroad Mergers and the Coming of Conrail,* 332, concludes that labor officials were only responding to "two decades of merger graspiness by the other side."

21. Russell D. Jones, "Controlled Transfer: A History of Ford Administration Railroad Policy" (MA thesis, Eastern Michigan University, 1996), 152–63.

22. As cited in *Congressional Quarterly Weekly Report* (November 22, 1975): 2550. See also Ralph Blumenthal, "Those Truckers Love Their Chains," *New York Times,* June 13, 1976, 115, *Proquest Historical New York Times.*

23. George Eads to Roderick Hills, June 19, 1975, Edward C. Schmults Files, Box 28, Folder: Airlines, January 1975–June 1975, GRFL.

24. Paul H. O'Neill to the President, September 29, 1975, Presidential Handwriting File, Box 6, Folder: Civil Aviation-Regulatory Reform, GRFL.

25. Edward M. Kennedy to Gerald R. Ford, February 13, 1976; Gerald R. Ford to Edward M. Kennedy, February 19, 1976; Ed Schmults to the President, February 18, 1976, all in Edward C. Schmults Files, Box 29, Folder: Airlines, February 25–29, 1976, GRFL.

26. John W. Snow to the Secretary, December 1, 1975, Judith R. Hope Files, Folder: Aviation Act of 1975 Legislative Strategy, GRFL; McCraw, *Prophets of Regulation*, 290.

27. John W. Snow to Edward C. Schmults, Paul MacAvoy, and Stan Morris, March 9, 1976, Schmults Files, Box 29, Folder: Airlines, March 1976, GRFL.

28. John W. Snow to Edward C. Schmults, Paul MacAvoy, and Stan Morris, March 9, 1976, Schmults Files, Box 29, Folder: Airlines, March 1976, GRFL.

29. Andrew de Voursney to John H. Harper, January 23, 1976, Schmults Files, Box 29, Folder: Airlines, February 25–29, 1976, GRFL; John W. Snow, "The Problems of Airline Regulation and the Ford Administration Proposal for Reform," in *Regulation of Passenger Fares and Competition among the Airlines*, ed. Paul W. MacAvoy and John W. Snow (Washington, DC: American Enterprise Institute for Public Policy Research, 1977), 6, 7, 20, 24, 25. This essay was edited from testimony presented to the U.S. Congress, House, Subcommittee on Aviation of the Committee on Public Works and Transportation, May 11, 1976.

30. "Coleman Seeks Commuter-Airline Aid," *New York Times*, March 30, 1976, 53, *Proquest Historical New York Times*.

31. Richard E. Cohen, "Up, Up and Away with Airline Reform," *National Journal* 38 (July 24, 1976): 1045; idem, "The Regulatory Reform Void," *National Journal* 38 (September 18, 1976); Jim Cavanaugh to the President, September 17, 1976, Presidential Handwriting File, Box 47, Folder: Transportation Trucking Industry Deregulation, GRFL. Despite their public opposition to deregulation proposals, airline executives provided members of the Council of Economic Advisers with confidential statements regarding plans for new routes in the event President Ford succeeded in easing entry requirements. See Mike Roach and Jim Miller, "Effects of Discretionary Entry Provision," draft of August 13, 1975, marked "Incomplete," in Schmults Files, Box 29, Folder: Airlines-Background of Regulation and Rationale for Change, GRFL.

32. U.S. Domestic Council, Review Group on Regulatory Reform, *The Challenge of Regulatory Reform: A Report to the President* (Washington, DC: U.S. Government Printing Office, 1977), 30, 32.

33. "The Problems Are Desperate," *Railway Age* 176 (July 14, 1975): 24.

34. United States Railway Association, *Final System Plan for Restructuring Railroads in the Northeast and Midwest Region Pursuant to the Regional Rail Reorganization Act of 1973*, vol. 1 (Washington, DC: The Association, 1975), 208. Mike Duval to Jim Cannon, March 19, 1975, Cannon Files, Folder: President and Frank Fitzsimmons, March 19, 1975, GRFL.

CHAPTER 8

1. Stu Eizenstat and David Rubenstein, *President Carter's Campaign Promises* (Chicago: Commercial Clearing House, 1977), 47, 48. Compare with Otis L. Graham Jr., *Losing Time: The Industrial Policy Debate* (Cambridge, MA: Harvard University Press, 1992), 36, for the contention that "the Carter administration did not see . . . [deregulation of airlines, banks, and trucking] at first as a promising part of its general economic strategy." Also see Lizabeth Cohen, *A Consumer's Republic: The Politics of Mass Consumption in Postwar America* (New York: Knopf, 2003), 390, who finds that in an age of stagflation, Ford and Carter (and later President Ronald Reagan) had concluded that "regulation, once a prime consumerist strategy for coercing private companies into

upholding the public interest, became viewed as stifling growth and penalizing consumers through its tendency to create expensive bureaucracy and suppress healthy competition. Consumers would see lower prices and more product choice, it was argued, if firms had greater flexibility in a freer marketplace." Also see W. Carl Biven, *Jimmy Carter's Economy: Policy in an Age of Limits* (Chapel Hill: University of North Carolina Press, 2002), x, for the contention that "by the time President Carter took office, the increasing abundance that characterized the golden age of growth of the 1950s and 1960s was over." Finally, see Naomi Lamoreaux, Daniel M. G. Raff, and Peter Temin, "Beyond Markets and Hierarchies: Toward a New Synthesis of American Business History," *American Historical Review* 108 (April 2003): 404–33, for a superbly crafted reconceptualization of main developments in American business history that also overlooks the specific role played by federal officials in fostering regulation and deregulation of transportation firms.

2. Stuart Eizenstat to the President, February 22, 1977, Files of Stuart Eizenstat, Folder: Aviation—Airline Regulatory Reform(1)[1], Jimmy Carter Presidential Library, Atlanta, GA, cited hereafter as Eizenstat Files, JCL.

3. Thomas K. McCraw, *Prophets of Regulation: Charles Francis Adams, Louis D. Brandeis, James M. Landis, Alfred E. Kahn* (Cambridge, MA: Belknap Press of Harvard University Press, 1984), 268.

4. Ibid., 276–77.

5. As cited in ibid., 282.

6. As cited in ibid., 290.

7. "Congress Is Urged by Carter to Ease Airline Regulation," *New York Times*, March 5, 1977, 26, *Proquest Historical Newspapers New York Times*, April 5, 2005.

8. John Crown, "The Success of Airline Regulatory Reform Depends on Executives' Abilities," *Atlanta Journal and Constitution*, August 20, 1977, in Eizenstat Files, Box 148, Folder: Aviation—Airline Regulatory Reform (2)[2], JCL; "A Commanding Voice in Airline Reform," *Business Week*, November 14, 1977, 170, 174; Dorothy Robyn, *Braking the Special Interests: Trucking Deregulation and the Politics of Policy Reform* (Chicago: University of Chicago Press, 1987), 208. In March 2003, Stuart Eizenstat described Schuman as "my key staff person and more than any other person, was responsible for the development of the bill and its eventual passage." E-mail from Stuart E. Eizenstat to Mark Rose, March 27, 2003, in authors' possession.

9. W. T. Beebe to the President, August 8, 1977, Folder: Aviation—Airline Regulatory Reform (2)[2]; for Delta's objection to easing entry, see R. S. Maurer to Rep. Elliott H. Levitas, March 7, 1977; and W. T. Beebe to Bert Lance, March 8, 1977, Folder: Aviation—Airline Regulatory Reform (2)[o/a 6232] [3], all in Eizenstat Files, Box 148, JCL.

10. Stu Eizenstat to the President, February 22, 1977; Stu Eizenstat to the President, no date, both in Folder: Aviation—Airline Regulatory Reform (1)[2]; Carole Shifrin, "Adams Voices Doubts on Airline Industry Deregulation," *Washington Post*, March 3, 1977, D-13, in Folder: Aviation—Airline Regulatory Reform (2)[O/A 6232] [3], all Eizenstat Files, Box 148, JCL.

11. Mary Schuman to Stu Eizenstat, March 18, 1977, Eizenstat Files, Box 148, Folder: Aviation—Airline Regulatory Reform (2), JCL.

12. Stu Eizenstat to the President, March 23, 1977, and Carter's handwritten response in corner of Eizenstat's memo, c. March 24, 1977, Eizenstat Files, Box 148, Folder: Aviation—Airline Regulatory Reform (1)[1], JCL; Richard E. Cohen, "Carter

Shows Who's the Boss When It Comes to Airline Deregulation," *National Journal* 9 (March 5, 1977): 352.

13. Schuman to Eizenstat, March 31, 1977, Eizenstat Files, Box 148, Folder: Aviation—Airline Regulatory Reform (1)[1], JCL.

14. Mary Schuman to Stu Eizenstat, March 31, 1977; Statement of Brock Adams . . . , April 1, 1977, both in Folder: Aviation—Airline Regulatory Reform (1)[1]; Stu Eizenstat to the President, March 25, 1977, Folder: Aviation—Airline Regulatory Reform (2), all in Eizenstat Files, Box 148, JCL. Albert Nason and Martin Elzy at the Jimmy Carter Library were kind enough to confirm Carter's handwriting for us. See also Paul W. MacAvoy and John W. Snow's three edited volumes devoted to showing the advantages of transportation deregulation. Members of the Ford administration had prepared most of the essays in these volumes for publication and presentation during the period 1975 and 1976. Paul W. MacAvoy and John W. Snow, eds., *Regulation of Passenger Fares and Competition among the Airlines* (Washington, DC: American Enterprise Institute for Public Policy Research, 1977); idem, eds., *Railroad Revitalization and Regulatory Reform* (Washington, DC: American Enterprise Institute for Public Policy Research, 1977); and idem, eds., *Regulation of Entry and Pricing in Truck Transportation* (Washington, DC: American Enterprise Institute for Public Policy Research, 1977). Perhaps because economists had written many of these essays in their own esoteric language, MacAvoy included concise introductory sections that linked abstract findings about matters such as small-town service and predatory pricing to clear policy recommendations. MacAvoy never intended publication of these volumes as an excursion in economic analysis that would find an audience only among academics. The purpose of these papers, he noted in an introduction, was to "address particular questions on the effects from deregulation." Members of Congress, MacAvoy added, wanted answers regarding "deregulation effects." A member of Congress whose constituents feared a loss of service, MacAvoy pointed out, "was rarely satisfied with a reference to the [academic] literature." MacAvoy and Snow, *Regulation of Passenger Fares and Competition among the Airlines*, Preface.

15. Stu Eizenstat and Mary Schuman, memo titled Meetings on Airline Reform Monday, June 20, 1977, June 18, 1977, Eizenstat Files, Box 148, Folder: Aviation—Airline Regulatory Reform (2)[2], JCL (emphasis in original).

16. Stu Eizenstat and Mary Schuman, memo titled Meetings on Airline Reform Monday, June 20, 1977, June 18, 1977, Eizenstat Files, Box 148, Folder: Aviation—Airline Regulatory Reform (2)[2], JCL.

17. Mary to Stu, July 26, 1977, Eizenstat Files, Box 148, Folder: Aviation—Airline Regulatory Reform (2)[2], JCL (emphasis in original).

18. Mary Schuman to Stu Eizenstat, Wayne Granquist, Frank Moore, and Charlie Schultze, September 22, 1977, Eizenstat Files, Box 148, Folder: Aviation—Airline Regulatory Reform (2)[2], JCL. See also McCraw, *Prophets of Regulation*, 278.

19. Schuman to Eizenstat, Granquist, Moore, and Schultze, September 22, 1977; Frank Moore and Stu Eizenstat to the President, October 24, 1977; Talking Points, c. October 25, 1977, all in Eizenstat Files, Box 148, Folder: Aviation—Airline Regulatory Reform (2)[2], JCL.

20. W. Bowman Cutter to Stu Eizenstat and Frank Moore, May 26, 1978; Frank Moore and Stu Eizenstat to the President, September 27, 1978; Office of Management and Budget, Memorandum for the President, October 23, 1978, 6, all in Eizenstat Files, Box 148, Folder: Aviation—Airline Regulatory Reform (2)[1], JCL.

21. Martha Derthick and Paul J. Quirk, *The Politics of Deregulation* (Washington, DC: Brookings Institution, 1985), 148, 150–51, 152; Remarks for Signing of Airline Deregulation Legislation, Eizenstat Files, Box 148, Folder: Aviation—Airline Regulatory Reform (2)[1], JCL. ' t owed the lead of Derthick and Quirk in quoting President Carter that by late 19, , deregulation had "few enemies."

22. Jimmy Carter handwritten notes on James T. McIntyre to the President, April 17, 1978; and on Stu Eizenstat and Mary Schuman to the President, May 12, 1978, both in Eizenstat Files, Box 148, Folder: Aviation—Airline Regulatory Reform (2)[2], JCL.

23. James M. Frey, Memorandum for the President, October 23, 1978, files of Stuart Eizenstat, Box 148, Folder: Aviation—Airline Regulatory Reform (2)[1]; Richard H. K. Vietor, *Contrived Competition: Regulation and Deregulation in America* (Cambridge, MA: Belknap Press of Harvard University Press, 1994), 54; Kahn quotation is in Albert R. Karr, "Carter Signs Airline-Deregulation Law; CAB Will Grant Routes More Generously," *Wall Street Journal,* October 25, 1978, 2, *Proquest Historical Newspapers Wall Street Journal;* Anthony E. Brown, *The Politics of Airline Deregulation* (Knoxville: University of Tennessee Press, 1987), 128–59, 176, including quotations on page 176; and see also Alan A. Altshuler and Roger F. Teal, "The Political Economy of Airline Deregulation," in *Current Issues in Transportation Policy,* ed. Alan A. Altshuler (Lexington, MA: D.C. Heath and Company, 1979), 49. For the centrality of the Carter administration in fostering deregulation of rail, air, and trucking firms, see Biven, *Jimmy Carter's Economy,* 222.

24. Larry Kramer, "Consumer Bill Goals Revealed by Eizenstat," *Washington Post,* February 8, 1979, at http://infoweb.newsbank.com, June 9, 2003; Albert R. Karr, "Truck Firms Gear Up Major Lobbying Effort to Fight Deregulation," *Wall Street Journal,* July 5, 1979, in Files of Rick Neustadt, Folder: [Trucking Deregulation]—Clippings file, cited hereafter as Neustadt Files, JCL.

25. Attendees: Consultations on Motor Carrier Regulatory Reform, November 22, 1977; Minutes of Meeting with Representatives of Minority Truckers, November 18, 1977, both in Neustadt Files, Folder: [Trucking Deregulation]—Consultations, JCL.

26. Robyn, *Braking the Special Interests,* 140–41.

27. Minutes of Meetings of November 17, 1977, with Representatives of Various Conferences of the Motor Carrier Industry, Neustadt Files, Folder: [Trucking Deregulation]—Consultations, JCL.

28. Minutes of Meetings of November 17, 1977, with Representatives of Various Conferences of the Motor Carrier Industry, Neustadt Files, Folder: [Trucking Deregulation]—Consultations, JCL.

29. Summary of Meeting with Freight Forwarders' Institute, December 18, 1978, Neustadt Files, Folder: [Trucking Deregulation]—Consultations, JCL. See also Robyn, *Braking the Special Interests,* 136–42.

30. See also Derthick and Quick, *The Politics of Deregulation,* 23.

31. Robyn, *Braking the Special Interests,* 138; Options for Trucking Bill, undated c. October 1979, Neustadt Files, Box 89, Folder: Trucking [Deregulation]—General, [10/70–1/80], JCL.

32. Interview with Dorothy Robyn, as cited in her *Braking the Special Interests,* 139.

33. Ibid., 139–40, including quotation on page 139.

34. Handwritten reply on memo: The Vice President et al. to the President, May 15, 1979, Eizenstat Files, Box 297, Folder: Trucking [3], JCL.

35. Kennedy in "Remarks of the President upon Announcing Trucking Deregulation," June 21, 1979, 4; Frank Moore et al., Announcement Ceremony for Trucking

Deregulation, c. June 20, 1979, Eizenstat Files, Box 297, Folder: Trucking [2], both in JCL.

36. Sue Grabowski to the "New" White House Task Force on Trucking Deregulation, October 18, 1979, Neustadt Files, JCL; Robyn, *Braking the Special Interests,* 208.

37. Alan Butchman to Inter-Agency Task Force on Trucking Legislation, June 25, 1979; and also see Susan Williams to White House Trucking Task Force, June 29, 1979, both in Neustadt Files, Folder: [Trucking Deregulation]—DOT General [June 21, 1979–June 29, 1979], JCL.

38. The Vice President et al. to the President, May 15, 1979, Eizenstat Files, Folder: Trucking [3], JCL.

39. *Washington Star,* July 27, 1979, as cited in Robyn, *Braking the Special Interests,* 39.

40. Ibid., 39–41; Remarks of Darius W. Gaskins Jr. before Regular Common Carrier Conference, Board of Governors, Tarpon Springs, FL, February 4, 1980, in Neustadt Files, Box 89, Folder: Trucking [Deregulation]—General [2/80–6/80], JCL. Even before Carter appointed those three new members, ICC officials had begun the process of eliminating truck regulation. In mid-1977, an ICC task force had recommended a number of steps aimed at reducing regulation of truckers; and in November 1978, ICC officials permitted private truckers such as Safeway to carry merchandise for other shippers. Robyn, *Braking the Special Interests,* 33.

41. Robyn, *Braking the Special Interests,* 138–40; on calculation of elements of the legislation to win the contract and private carriers, see Agenda for Trucking Deregulation Meeting, Monday, April 30, 1979, Neustadt Files, Folder: [Trucking Deregulation]-DOT General, [April 20, 1979–June 14, 1979], JCL. See also, Richard D. Stone, "Administrative Deregulation of the Railroads: the ICC's Change of Philosophy," *Transportation Practitioners Journal* 61, no. 3 (1994): 287–88, who also finds that President Carter supervised a process of administrative deregulation of railroads, airlines, and trucking that preceded legislative deregulation.

42. Bennett C. Whitlock Jr., "To All Persons Interested in the Survival of the Motor Carrier Industry," March 1, 1980, March 21, 1980, both in Neustadt Files, Box 89, Folder: Trucking [Deregulation]—General, [2/80–6-80], JCL; Derthick and Quirk, *The Politics of Deregulation,* 172.

43. *Ohio Teamster* 18 (April 1980); handbill titled "Teamsters! The Kennedy-Carter Deregulation Bill Is a Union Bustin' Tactic!!!" both in Neustadt Files, Box 89, Folder: Trucking [Deregulation]—General, [2/80–6/80], JCL.

44. Derthick and Quirk, *The Politics of Deregulation,* 169; *Ohio Teamster* 18 (April 1980); handbill titled "Teamsters! The Kennedy-Carter Deregulation Bill Is a Union Bustin' Tactic!!!"

45. As cited in Robyn, *Braking the Special Interests,* 175.

46. "Congress Clears Major Bill Cutting Trucking Regulation," *Congressional Quarterly Weekly Report* (June 28, 1980), 1807; "Truck Decontrol Bill Is Signed into Law," *Wall Street Journal,* July 2, 1980, 20, in *Proquest Historical Newspapers Wall Street Journal,* March 21, 2006.

47. Robyn, *Braking the Special Interests,* 175–79, including quotation on page 179.

48. "Congress Clears Major Bill Cutting Trucking Regulation," *Congressional Quarterly Weekly Report* (June 28, 1980), 1807. Again, Richard John was especially helpful in bringing this concept to an exact point.

49. Impressions gained from a review of *Transport Topics* published between the early 1950s and 1980.

50. Ibid.; Derthick and Quirk, *The Politics of Deregulation,* 169; Robyn, *Braking the Special Interests,* 142.

51. Brock Adams to the President, January 6, 1978, Adams Papers, Folder: Cabinet Meeting January 9, 1978, accession 1096–5, UWL.

52. Executive Summary, c. December 1978 (attached to Rick Hutcheson, Memorandum for the President), Eizenstat Files, Folder: Trucking [1], JCL.

53. Hutcheson, Memorandum for the President, December 15, 1978; Brock Adams to the President, January 5, 1979, Folder: Monday January 15, 1979, accession 1096–5, UWL.

54. Stu Eizenstat and Bill Johnston to the President, March 2, 1979; Jimmy Carter to Jim [McIntyre and Stu(art) Eizenstat], March 6, 1979, both in Eizenstat Files, Folder: Rail Deregulation [3], JCL.

55. Bill Johnston to Stu Eizenstat, January 24, 1979; Steve Simmons to Stu Eizenstat, November 21, 1979; Steve Simmons to Stu Eizenstat et al., November 21, 1979, all three in Eizenstat Files, Box 265, Folder: Rail Deregulation [3], JCL; Robert J. Samuelson, "Congress Stops, Looks and Listens to Railroad Deregulation Complaints," *National Journal* 11 (November 3, 1979): 1844–45, 1847.

56. Simmons to Eizenstat, November 21, 1979; Simmons to Eizenstat et al., November 21, 1979; Steve Simmons to Stu Eizenstat, March 6, 19, and 25, 1980, all three in Eizenstat Files, Box 265, Folder: Rail Deregulation [3], JCL.

57. Steve Simmons to Stu Eizenstat, April 7, 1980, Eizenstat Files, Folder: Rail Deregulation [2], JCL.

58. Steve Simmons to Stu Eizenstat, August 21, 1980, Eizenstat Files, Box 265, Folder: Rail Deregulation [1], JCL.

59. Ibid.

60. Ibid.; Steve Simmons to Fred Kahn et al., September 2, 1980, Eizenstat Files, Box 265, Folder: Rail Deregulation [1], JCL; "Rail Deregulation Passes House," *New York Times,* September 10, 1980, D7, in *Proquest Historical Newspapers New York Times,* January 24, 2005.

61. "Rail Decontrol Bill Is Signed by Carter," *New York Times,* October 14, 1980, in Files of Kitty Bernick, Box 13, Folder: Rail Deregulation [clippings], JCL; "Bill Deregulating Railroads Sent to President," *Congressional Quarterly Weekly Report* 38 (October 4, 1980): 2902–2903.

62. David L. Sparkman, "'1935 All Over Again'" (July 28, 1980): 1, 27; idem, "Commissioner Stafford Retires from ICC" (September 1, 1980): 1, 18, both in *Transport Topics.*

CHAPTER 9

1. Edward H. Kolcum, "Airline Mainstay Eastern Stops Flying After 62 Years," *Aviation Week & Space Technology* 134 (January 28, 1991): 64; Kathie O'Donnell, "Bankrupt Pan Am Corp. Sues Delta in Action Seeking Over $2.5 Billion," Bond Buyer 299 (January 31, 1992); "IU to Spin Off Trucking Unit, Reduce Debt—Dividend Will Be Halved; Changes Are Part of Plan to Restructure Concern," *Wall Street Journal,* Eastern edition, July 12, 1985, 1, all at www.fau.edu (August 27, 2003) and cited hereafter as www.fau.edu plus the date on which we located that document. Note: page numbers for electronically retrieved materials sometimes vary from the print version.

2. "For Truck Bureaus, Breaking Up Is So Very Hard to Do," *Purchasing* 111

(November 21, 1991): 47–49; John D. Schulz, "Shrinking RCCC Reviews Stance," *Traffic World* 230 (April 13, 1992): 10. For a valuable discussion of the evolving scholarly literature of historical institutionalism, see Amy Louise Nelson Dyble, "Paying the Toll: A Political History of the Golden Gate Bridge and Highway District, 1923–1971" (PhD diss., University of California-Berkeley, 2003), 19–43, which Dr. Dyble was kind enough to share with us.

3. John S. Ying and Theodore E. Keeler, "Pricing in a Deregulated Environment: The Motor Carrier Experience," *RAND Journal of Economics* 22 (Summer 1991): 272; Jill Cosper, "Deregulation Sends Ripples through Lehigh Valley Trucking Industry," *Lehigh Valley Business Digest* 3, no. 8 (1985): 1, both at www.fau.edu (August 27, 2003); Charles R. Perry with the assistance of Craig M. Waring and Peter N. Glick, "Deregulation and the Decline of the Unionized Trucking Industry," *Major Industrial Research Unit* 64 (Wharton School, c. 1986): 87.

4. Gary Ewing, "Letters to the Editor: the Ravages of Truck Deregulation," *Wall Street Journal,* Eastern edition, July 22, 1985, 1, at www.fau.edu (August 28, 2003); Perry, "Deregulation and the Decline of the Unionized Trucking Industry," 87–90; "Competition Drives the Trucking Industry," *Monthly Labor Review* 121, no. 4 (April 1998): 34–41. See also Barry T. Hirsch, "Trucking Regulation: Unionization, and Labor Earnings: 1973–85," *Journal of Human Resources* 23 (Summer 1988): 316, at www.fau.edu (August 27, 2003); and for the finding by two economists that the effects of deregulation brought about approximately one-third of the decline in drivers' wages during the period 1980–1995, see Dale L. Belman and Kristen A. Monaco, "The Effects of Deregulation, De-Unionization, Technology, and Human Capital on the Work and Work Lives of Truck Drivers," *Industrial and Labor Relations Review* 54, no. 28 (Extra Issue #1) (March 2001): 521.

5. U.S. Bureau of the Census, *Statistical Abstract of the United States: 1997* (Washington, DC: U.S. Government Printing Office, 1997), 642; "Darius Gaskins on Deregulation" [Interview], *Traffic Management* 30 (May 1991): 69–71; James P. Rakowski, "The Continuing Structural Transformation of the U.S. Less-Than-Truckload Motor Carrier Industry," *Transportation Journal* 34 (Fall 1994): 1, at www.fau.edu (August 28, 2003).

6. Kenneth G. Elzinga, "The Relevant Market for Less-Than-Truckload Freight: Deregulation's Consequences," *Transportation Journal* 34 (Winter 1994): 1, at www.fau.edu (January 27, 2004); "Truckers: Continual Change From 'Dereg,'" *Indiana Business* 31, no. 10 (1987): 1; and also Randy Brown, "Kansas Trucking Industry: Finding the Road to Profitability," *Kansas Business News* 10, no. 1 (January 1989): 1, last two at www.fau.edu (August 27, 2003); "Deregulation a 'Disaster,' Tank Truck Leader Says," *Traffic World* 221 (January 1990): 12.

7. Nicholas A. Glaskowsky, *Effects of Deregulation on Motor Carriers* (Westport, CT: Eno Foundation for Transportation, 1986), 8; James P. Rakowski, "The Continuing Structural Transformation of the U.S. Less-Than-Truckload Motor Carrier Industry," *Transportation Journal* 34 (Fall 1994): 1, at www.fau.edu (August 28, 2003).

8. Jim Ostroff, "White House Appears to Favor an End to Trucking Regs," *Supermarket News* 33 (September 26, 1983): 1; idem, "White House Targets Trucking Regs," *Daily News Record* 15 (September 16, 1985): 1, both at www.fau.edu (August 28, 2003). See also political scientist Hugh Heclo, "Ronald Reagan and the American Public Philosophy," in *The Reagan Presidency: Pragmatic Conservatism and Its Legacies,* ed. W. Elliot Brownlee and Hugh Davis Graham (Lawrence: University Press of Kansas, 2003), 34, for Heclo's observation that President Reagan "undervalued the importance of government

regulation for the creation and maintenance of orderly markets." Heclo's fine essay reached us after we had completed research and writing for this chapter.

9. Lloyd Schwartz, "Government Truckers Disagree over Outcome of Partial Deregulation," *American Metal Market* 95 (October 12, 1987): 5, at www.fau.edu (August 28, 2003).

10. Statement by Secretary of Transportation Samuel K. Skinner, February 13, 1991; The White House, Office of the Press Secretary, "Fact Sheet: The Surface Transportation Assistance Act of 1991"; J. Dennis Hastert to C. Boyden Gray, January 19, 1992, Americans for Safe and Competitive Trucking, "News" (August 1991): 3, all four in White House Office of Records Management, Transportation Files, George Bush Presidential Library, College Station, TX; Kevin G. Hall, "House Passes Radical Highway Bill, Waters Down Trucking Reforms," *Traffic World* 228 (October 28, 1991): 9; and for the interest of presidents starting with Carter in fostering the private interests of consumers, see Lizabeth Cohen, *A Consumer's Republic: The Politics of Mass Consumption in Postwar America* (New York: Knopf, 2003), 390–97.

11. "Man on a Mission" [Interview with Andrew H. Card Jr.], *Traffic Management* 31 (October 1992): 3, at www.fau.edu (August 27, 2003); John D. Schulz, "ATA, Key Members Go Separate Ways in Newest Deregulation Posturing," *Traffic World* 230 (April 13, 1992): 9.

12. "For Truck Bureaus, Breaking Up Is So Very Hard to Do," 47–49; Schulz, "Shrinking RCCC Reviews Stance," 10.

13. John D. Schulz, "Strange Forces Coalesce to Support Broad Intrastate Trucking Deregulation," *Traffic World* 239 (August 1, 1994): 8–9; Robert P. James, "Controversies over Airline Fees, Truck Regulation Cloud Consideration of Airport Improvement Bill," *Traffic World* 238 (April 18, 1994): 16–17; Edward M. Emmett, "The Shippers' Legacy of 1994," *Distribution* 93 (November 1994): 2, at www.fau.edu (December 17, 2003); Saunders, *Main Lines: Rebirth of the North American Railroads, 1970–2002,* 310. Between the late 1970s and mid-1990s, editors of *Chilton's Distribution* changed the magazine's name several times. We used *Chilton's Distribution* in the text, and the contemporary title in the footnotes.

14. Tom Moore, "Fading into the Sunset," *Fleet Owner* 91 (January 1996): 1; "Last Days of the ICC Wind Down," *Worcester Telegram & Gazette* (December 27, 1995): 1; and David E. Singer, "A U.S. Agency, Once Powerful, Is Dead at 108," *New York Times,* January 1, 1996, 1, all at www.fau.edu (January 7, 2004); and for a critical view of journalistic celebration of triumphant markets, see Thomas Frank, *One Market under God* (New York: Doubleday, 2000), 68–73, which Richard R. John was kind enough to bring to our attention; "Truckers Gain Leeway," *Purchasing* 118 (March 16, 1995): 1; Andrew F. Popper, "In Defense of Antitrust Immunity for Collective Ratemaking: Life after the ICC Termination Act of 1995," *Transportation Journal* 35 (Summer 1996): 1–5, both at www.fau.edu (December 17, 2003). And also see Daniel T. Rodgers, "Vanishing Actions: Power and Society in American Social Thought in the 1980s," Fellows Conference Paper, Program in American Political Development, University of Virginia, October 15, 2004, posted for the Fall 2004 series at www.americanpoliticaldevelopment.org for his observation on page 9 that by the late 1980s, "markets began to be touted as continuous, choice-sensitive, referendum machines, paradigms of direct democracy." Our thanks to Professor Rodgers for permission to cite this paper.

15. Jay Gordon, "A Record Year for Railroads," *Distribution* 90 (July 1991): 52; "Truckers Gain Leeway," *Purchasing* 118 (March 16, 1995): 1; Andrew F. Popper, "In

Defense of Antitrust Immunity for Collective Ratemaking: Life after the ICC Termination Act of 1995," *Transportation Journal* 35 (Summer 1996): 1–5, last two at www.fau.edu (December 17, 2003); "Expect Higher Rail Rates," *Transportation and Distribution* 36 (February 1995): 1, at www.fau.edu (February 11, 2004); and also see Gus Welty, "It's Time for Up-Sizing: Rebuilding America's Railroads," *Railway Age* 194 (December 1993): 32, at www.fau.edu (August 27, 2003); U.S. Census Bureau, *Statistical Abstract of the United States: 1997* (Washington, DC: U.S. Government Printing Office, 1997), 643; and Saunders, *Main Lines*, 26.

16. Stan Kulp, "The Golden Spike: Mergers Are Putting Railroads on a Fast Track," *Barron's National Business and Financial Weekly* 62 (April 19, 1982): 8, at www.fau.edu (March 1, 2004); and Saunders, *Main Lines*, 198–200.

17. Stephen Wermiel, "Supreme Court Backs Railroads' Leeway on Rates—Justices Turn Down Appeal by Shippers on Way ICC Sets Market Dominance," *Wall Street Journal*, Eastern edition, April 24, 1984, 1, at www.fau.edu (August 28, 2003).

18. See also political-economist Karl Polanyi's observation in *The Great Transformation* (New York: Rinehard & Company, 1944), 139, that "free markets could never have come into being merely by allowing things to take their course." Professor Mark V. Frezzo was kind enough to bring Polanyi's writings to our attention.

19. Stan Chapman, "Time to Tear Up Staggers?" *Chilton's Distribution for Traffic & Transportation Decision Makers* 84 (April 1985): 7, at www.fau.edu (August 27, 2003; Henry Boyd Hall and Daniel Machalaba, "CSX's Purchase of a Barge Line Is Cleared by ICC—First Such Merger Expected to Bring Spate of Others as Firms Act to Compete," *Wall Street Journal*, Eastern edition, July 25, 1984, 1, at www.fau.edu (September 9, 2003); Brian S. Moskal, "Are Rails Headed for Re-Regulation?" *Industry Week* 222 (May 13, 1985): 57, at www.fau.edu (February 16, 2004).

20. "Time to Tear Up Staggers?" 7–10, including quotes on pages 5, 9.

21. "The Captive Shipper Issue Seven Years after Staggers Enactment," *Public Utilities Fortnightly* 121 (January 7, 1988): 25, at www.fau.edu (February 16, 2004).

22. U.S. Bureau of the Census, *Statistical Abstract of the United States: 1997*, 644; Daniel Machalaba, "Rail Executives Lobby Congress in Bid to Defeat Bill Restoring Regulations," *Wall Street Journal*, Eastern edition, October 29, 1987, 1, at www.fau.edu (February 15, 2004).

23. Martha M. Hamilton, "Commission Acts to Cap Railroad Rates," *Washington Post*, November 18, 1989, D-01, at www.fau.edu (February 16, 2004); for changes in ICC policy regarding achievement of revenue adequacy, see Richard D. Stone, *The Interstate Commerce Commission and the Railroad Industry: A History of Regulatory Policy* (New York: Praeger, 1991), 123–25; "US Rail Shippers Call for Reform," *Materials Management and Distribution* 40 (June 1995): 38, at www.fau.edu (February 16, 2004).

24. Stone, *The Interstate Commerce Commission and the Railroad Industry*, 95; Allan Dodds Frank, "Railroads," *Forbes* 129 (January 4, 1982): 1, at www.fau.edu (March 1, 2004); U.S. Bureau of the Census, *Statistical Abstract of the United States: 1997*, 643; James A. Cooke, "Will Congress Fix the Rails," *Logistics Management Distribution Report* 38 (August 31, 1999): 87, at Infotrac, Duke University Library (May 9, 2000).

25. Harlan S. Byrne, "Santa Fe Southern Is Flush with Cash, Eager to Diversify through Acquisition," *Wall Street Journal*, Eastern edition, September 27, 1984, 1; Robert E. Dallos, "Southern Pacific-Santa Fe Merger Prohibited by ICC," *Los Angeles Times*, July 25, 1986: 1, both at www.fau.edu (February 20, 2004).

26. "Justice Dept. Had Urged Rejection of Deal on Tuesday DOT Endorses Merger

of Santa Fe, SP," *Los Angeles Times,* October 24, 1985, 7, at www.fau.edu (February 20, 2004); Dallos, "Southern Pacific-Santa Fe Merger Prohibited by ICC."

27. Ibid.; Laurie McGinley et al., "ICC Rejects Merger of Santa Fe and Southern Pacific Railroads—Decision Stuns the Industry; Panel Orders Divestiture of One or Both Carriers," *Wall Street Journal,* Eastern edition, July 25, 1986, 1, at www.fau.edu (February 20, 2004).

28. Ibid.; Robert F. Dallos, "ICC Refuses to Reverse Ban on SP-Santa Fe Rail Merger; Selloff Ordered Agency Gives Holding Company 90 Days to Submit Plan to Divest One or Both Lines Within 2 Years," *Los Angeles Times,* July 1, 1987, 1 at www.fau. edu (February 20, 2004).

29. Robert E. Dallos, "SFSP Receives 7 Offers to Buy Its SP Railroad," *Los Angeles Times,* October 17, 1987, 3; Robert A. Rosenblatt, "SP Is Allowed to Merge With Denver Rail Line Decision by ICC Ends Battle Over Ownership of Carrier and Creates 5th-Biggest System in U.S.," *Los Angeles Times,* August 10, 1988, 1, both at www.fau.edu (March 4, 2004); Chris Kraul, "Proposed Deal Would Create Rail Monolith Mergers: Burlington Northern and Santa Fe Pacific Hope to Persuade ICC and Stockholders to OK $2.7-Billion Union," *Los Angeles Times,* July 1, 1994, 1, at www.fau.edu (February 20, 2004).

30. James F. Peltz and Jube Shiver Jr., "U.S. Approves $5.4-Billion Rail Merger," *Los Angeles Times,* July 4, 1996, 1, at www.fau.edu (February 20, 2004); chapter 1 above.

31. Tom Foster, "Rail Shippers Seek Major Change," *Distribution* 96 (September 1997): 54, at www.fau.edu (February 11, 2004); Daniel W. Gottlieb, "Uncle Stays Involved," *Purchasing* 121 (August 15, 1996): 26, at www.fau.edu (February 20, 2004).

32. Stone, *The Interstate Commerce Commission and the Railroad Industry,* 157; Paul Stephen Dempsey, "The Law of Intermodal Transportation: What It Was, What It Is, What It Should Be," at www.ie.msstate.edu/ncit/ NCIT_WEB_UPDATE/Final%20 Report.INTERMODAL ARTICLE29AUG00version2.htm (which Professor Albert J. Churella was kind enough to call to our attention); Paul Stephen Dempsey, *The Social and Economic Consequences of Deregulation: The Transportation Industry in Transition* (New York: Quorum Books, 1989), 86.

33. Brian S. Moskal, "Transportation Shifts into Superdrive," *Industry Week* 215 (November 1, 1982): 31, at www.fau.edu (March 11, 2004).

34. Richard Koenig, "AT CSX, Snow Gets His Show on the Road," *Wall Street Journal* (Eastern edition: April 8, 1987), 1, at www.fau.edu (March 5, 2004).

35. Theresa Engstrom, "ICC to Rule on CSX Ownership of Unit, Decision May Spur Rail-Barge Mergers," *Wall Street Journal,* Eastern edition, June 19, 1984, 1, at www.fau.edu (September 9, 2003); "Court Upholds Approval by ICC of CSX Purchase," *Wall Street Journal,* Eastern edition (January 24, 1986), 1, at www.fau.edu (March 5, 2004).

36. Daniel Machalaba, "Railroads Seek to Become Megacarriers—Expansion Beyond Rails Grows; Obstacles Remain," *Wall Street Journal,* Eastern edition (September 25, 1986), 1, at www.fau.edu (March 5, 2004); M.B. Regan, "John Snow Named Head of CSX Transportation Group," *Wall Street Journal,* Final edition (January 19, 1987), F16, at www.fau.edu (February 20, 2004); Laurie McGinley, "CSX's Purchase of Sea-Land Gets Go-Ahead—Firms Aren't Competitors, Don't Require Clearance for Merger, ICC Rules," *Wall Street Journal,* Eastern edition (February 12, 1987), 1, at www.fau.edu (March 5, 2004).

37. Jay Gordon, "Intermodal Continues to Make Inroads," *Distribution* 90 (May

1991): 63; Peter Bradley, "Intermodal Service Stacks Up," *Purchasing* 110 (May 16, 1991): 87; "CSX to Buy Assets of Sequa Barge Unit," *Wall Street Journal* (Eastern edition: November 14, 1991), C17; "CSX Services Opens Two New Facilities," *Railway Age* 193 (August 1992): 22; "CSX Intermodal to Expand Rail Line," *Wall Street Journal* (December 9, 1991): F32; Alex Friend, "CSX Eyes Truck Market Share," *The* [Baltimore] *Daily Record* (December 28, 1992): 1; "Masters of the Game," *Business Week* (October 12, 1992): 110, and all at www.fau.edu (March 5, 2004; and for an historically-grounded account of the increasingly common use of "master of the game" and other such romantic metaphors to describe business leaders in a period of economic growth and a diminished number of direct federal regulations, see Eric Guthey, "New Economy Romanticism, Narratives of Corporate Personhood, and the Antimanagerial Impulse," in Kenneth Lipartito and David B. Sicilia, eds., *Constructing Corporate America: History, Politics, Culture* (New York: Oxford University Press, 2004), 321–42.

38. Albro Martin, *Railroads Triumphant: The Growth, Rejection, and Rebirth of a Vital American Force* (New York: Oxford University Press, 1992), 383–98; John F. Stover, *American Railroads*, 2nd ed. (Chicago: University of Chicago Press, 1997), 245–62; and Saunders, *Main Lines.*

39. Richard H. K. Vietor, *Contrived Competition: Regulation and Deregulation in America* (Cambridge, MA.: Belknap Press of Harvard University Press, 1994), 66–77, including quotations on pages 69, 77. For examples of the large corpus of literature regarding airline deregulation and its consequences, see books by distinguished economists John R. Meyer and Clinton V. Oster Jr., eds., *Airline Deregulation: The Early Experience* (Boston: Auburn House Publishing Company, 1981); and also John R. Meyer and Clinton V. Oster Jr., with Marni Clippinger et al., *Deregulation and the New Airline Entrepreneurs* (Cambridge, MA: The MIT Press, 1984), and attorney Paul Stephen Dempsey and geographer Andrew R. Goetz, *Airline Deregulation and Laissez-Faire Mythology* (Westport, CT: Quorum Books, 1992); and by journalists including John J. Nash, *Splash of Colors: The Self-Destruction of Braniff International* (New York: William Morrow and Company, 1984); and Thomas Petzinger Jr., *Hard Landing: The Epic Contest for Power and Profits That Plunged the Airlines into Chaos* (New York: Times Books, 1995).

40. See also Thomas K. McCraw, *Prophets of Regulation: Charles Francis Adams, Louis D. Brandeis, James M. Landis, Alfred E. Kahn* (Cambridge, MA: Belknap Press of Harvard University Press, 1984), 296–99, who finds that up to 1982, only small cities, business travelers, and poorly managed Braniff Airlines suffered in the early days of deregulation. For a depiction of nineteenth-century "associations [corporations] as legal and political constructions rather than [as] spontaneous private collaborations," see William J. Novak, "The American Law of Association: The Legal-Political Construction of Civil Society," *Studies in American Political Development* 15 (Fall 2001): 163.

41. William M. Carley, "Rapid Ascent: People Express Flies Into Airlines' Big Time in Just 3 Years Aloft—Its Newark, N.J., Hub Hums With 150 Takeoffs a Day, Tops in New York Area—Will Growing Pains Set In?" *Wall Street Journal,* March 30, 1984, 1, at www.fau.edu (May 4, 2004); Petzinger, *Hard Landing,* 115–16, 265–66; Toni Taylor, "The Rise and Fall of People Express," *Los Angeles Times,* November 30, 1986, 2, at www.fau.edu (April 20, 2004).

42. Carley, "Rapid Ascent"; Petzinger, *Hard Landing,* 265.

43. Carley, "Rapid Ascent."

44. Taylor, "The Rise and Fall of People Express"; Petzinger, *Hard Landing,* 267, 276.

45. Ibid., 268, 270–71.

46. Ibid., 268, and Carty quotation on page 272.

47. Ibid., 312, 321–22.

48. Taylor, "The Rise and Fall of People Express."

49. Kolcum, "Airline Mainstay Eastern Stops Flying After 62 Years"; Dempsey and Goetz, *Airline Deregulation and Laissez-Faire Mythology*, 227–28.

50. Ibid., 229, table 1; John H. Huston and Richard V. Butler, "The Effects of Fortress Hubs on Airline Fares and Service: The Early Returns," *Logistics and Transportation Review* 24 (September 1988): 203, at www.fau.edu (April 22, 2004); Vietor, *Contrived Competition*, 88.

51. Scott Kilman, "Growing Giants: An Unexpected Result of Airline Decontrol Is Return to Monopolies—Big Carriers Are Dominating Nation's Hub Airports; Legislators Are Concerned—Higher Fares and Less Service," *Wall Street Journal*, Eastern edition, July 20, 1987, 1, at www.fau.edu (April 20, 2004).

52. For Secretary of Commerce Herbert Hoover as an architect of that administrative state and his inclusion of economists among his co-builders, see Michael A. Bernstein, *A Perilous Progress: Economists and Public Purpose in Twentieth-Century America* (Princeton, NJ: Princeton University Press, 2001), 53–59.

53. Ibid., 173–74, 176.

54. Meyer and Oster, eds., *Airline Deregulation*, 259; Elizabeth E. Bailey, David R. Graham, and Daniel P. Kaplan, *Deregulating the Airlines* (Cambridge, MA: MIT Press, 1985), 153. During 1964, John Meyer was a member of President Johnson's deregulation-minded Task Force on Transportation Policy.

55. Ibid., 167, and quotations on page 171.

56. Paul W. Bauer and Thomas J. Zlatoper, "The Determinants of Air Fares to Cleveland: How Competitive?" *Economic Review—Federal Reserve Bank of Cleveland* (First Quarter 1989): 7, at www.fau.edu (May 5, 2004); Severin Borenstein, "Hubs and High Fares: Dominance and Market Power in the U.S. Airline Industry," *RAND Journal of Economics* 20 (August 1989): 362, at www.fau.edu (May 5, 2004).

57. Alfred E. Kahn, "Surprises of Airline Deregulation," *American Economic Review* 78 (May 1988): 318, at www.fau.edu (May 5, 2004).

58. Jennifer Lieffers, "Airline Fares Climb Even Higher: Discounts Disappear," [Milwaukee] *Business Journal* 5 (March 28, 1988): 8, at www.fau.edu (April 13, 2005); Kilman, "Growing Giants," 1, at www.fau.edu (April 20, 2004); George W. James, "Airline Deregulation Still Flies," *Wall Street Journal*, Eastern edition, February 1, 1989, 1, at www.fau.edu (April 9, 2004).

59. Robert E. Dallos and Lee May, "Airlines, Buses, Trains Debate Still Rages over Deregulation," *Los Angeles Times*, November 2, 1986, 1, at www.fau.edu (March 6, 2004); Albert R. Karr, "Four Senate Panel Members Campaign to Reverse Effects of Airline Mergers," *Wall Street Journal*, Eastern edition, April 21, 1989, 1, at www.fau.edu (April 9, 2004).

60. Laurie McGinley, "Republicans Grit Their Teeth and Lead a Call for Partial Reregulation of Airline Industry," *Wall Street Journal*, Eastern edition, September 21, 1989, 1, at www.fau.edu (April 20, 2004); Peter S. Greenberg, "Ups and Downs of Deregulation," *Los Angeles Times*, October 16, 1988, 2, at www.fau.edu (April 9, 2004).

61. Alfred E. Kahn, "Surprises of Airline Deregulation," *American Economic Review* 78 (May 1988): 318; Bernstein, *A Perilous Progress*, 177.

62. Vietor, *Contrived Competition*, 24. See also Fred Block, "The Roles of the State

in the Economy," in *The Handbook of Economic Sociology,* ed. Neil J. Smelser and Richard Swedberg (Princeton, NJ: Princeton University Press; New York: Russell Sage Foundation, 1994), 696–98, including Block's contention on page 696 that "state action *always* plays a major role in constituting economies, so that it is not useful to posit states as lying outside of economic activity" (emphasis in original). Professor Frezzo brought this valuable article to our attention. See also Ted V. McAllister, "Reagan and the Transformation of American Conservatism," in Brownlee and Graham, *The Reagan Presidency,* 41, for the observation, similar to our own, that "confusion" among scholars regarding President Reagan's policies rests on "the limitations of our political vocabulary." Also, see economist John McMillan, *Reinventing the Bazaar: A Natural History of Markets* (New York: W. W. Norton & Company, 2002), x, for his contention that "markets need help from the government," a process he characterizes as market design; as well, see Kathryn Ibata-Arens, Julian Dierkes, and Dirk Zorn, "Guest Editors' Introduction: Theoretical Introduction to the Special Issue on the Embedded Enterprise," *Enterprise & Society* 7 (March 2006): 7, for their contention that "dichotomous formulations" such as "market versus nonmarket" reduce "the ability to measure complexity"; and finally, for a study of meatpacking and distribution, but similar to our own study in terms of their attention to "shifting boundaries between state regulation and individual economic activity," see Roger Horowitz, Jeffrey M. Pilcher, and Sydney Watts, "Meat for the Multitudes: Market Culture in Paris, New York City, and Mexico City over the Long Nineteenth Century," *American Historical Review* 109 (October 2004): 1056. We turned to McMillan's book and to the essays by McAllister, Ibata-Arens, and Horowitz et al. after completing research and writing for this chapter.

63. U.S. Census Bureau, Statistical Abstract of the United States: 1995, 338, at www.census.gov/prod/1/gen/95statab/fedgov.pdf, 338 (June 3, 2004); Mark H. Rose, "Reframing American Highway Politics, 1956–1995," *Journal of Planning History* 2 (August 2003): 225–32.

64. See also Richard R. John, "Farewell to the 'Party Period': Political Economy in Nineteenth-Century America," *Journal of Policy History* 16, no. 2 (2004): 120, who finds that during the nineteenth century, the American political economy was "open to radical refashioning by legislators, judges, and government administrators." John's fine essay reached us as we concluded work on this manuscript.

INDEX

AAA Trucking Corporation. *See* Bonacci
   brothers
AAdvantage. *See* American Airlines;
   Crandall, Robert L.
accounting: and railroad rate setting,
   8–11; railroad valuation project, 6–8
Adams, Brock, 173–75, 179, 182, 183,
   184, 189–90, 191, 193, 195, 206, 209,
   217
Adams, Henry Carter, 246n31
Air Cal. *See* American Airlines
Air Florida, 229, 230
Air Freight Motor Carrier Associa-
   tion. *See* U.S. Interstate Commerce
   Commission, and chair, presidential
   appointment of
Air Transport Association of America,
   79, 80, 93
Air West, 180
Airline Deregulation Act (1978), 194. *See
   also* Carter, Jimmy; deregulation
airmail. *See* aviation, airmail program
airport hubs, creation of, 233–237. *See
   also* deregulation
Ambrose, Stephen E., 272n6
American Airlines, 38, 39, 75, 78, 84, 88,
   90, 91, 94, 187, 188, 228–33, 235, 236
American Automobile Association, 108
American Commercial Lines. *See* CSX
American Enterprise Institute, 226
American Farm Bureau Federation, 199,
   207
American Trucking Associations, 61,

74, 97, 98, 102–4, 105, 112, 113,
   114–15, 117–18, 122, 143, 195,
   196, 198, 199, 201–2, 203, 204, 216,
   217, 218, 273n14. *See also* trucking
   industry
Americans for Safe and Competitive
   Trucking, 217
Amster, Barbara R., 231
antitrust, xii–xiii, 52
Armstrong, Christopher, xxii
Arnold, Peri, 268n16
Arpaia, Anthony F., 103. *See also* U. S.
   Interstate Commerce Commission
Association of American Railroads, 64,
   119, 123, 126, 219, 222
Atchison, Topeka, and Santa Fe Railway,
   223–24
Atlanta-Florida Motor Lines, 112. *See
   also* Raulerson, Lewis A.
Atlantic Airlines, 82
Atterbury, W.W., 25, 26, 30, 53, 226;
   during the Depression, 57, 58–70, 74
aviation, 28–29; air navigation system,
   37–38, 39; airmail program, 37–40,
   79; combined air-rail transcontinental
   service, 53; deregulation of, 176–83,
   186–95; development of, 35–40; during the cold war, 76–96; jets and their
   impact, 83–85; labor relations, 89–90;
   map of early routes, 41; nonscheduled
   cargo operators, 81; nonscheduled
   passenger carriers, 79–83; oligopoly,
   77, 95; overcapacity of, 84, 86, 87,